THE COMPLETE HANDBOOK OF PRO FOOTBALL
1975

SIGNET Books You'll Enjoy Reading

☐ **NORTH DALLAS FORTY by Peter Gent.** Eight days in the life of a football player. Eight days that take you into the heart of a man, a team, a sport, a game, and the raw power and violence that is America itself. "The only novel ever written from this deep inside pro football. I strongly recommend it."—Edwin Shrake, **Sports Illustrated** (#J6057—$1.95)

☐ **PAPER LION by George Plimpton.** When a first-string writer suits-up to take his lumps as a last-string quarterback for the Detroit Lions, the result is the best book ever about pro football. "A great book that makes football absolutely fascinating to fan and non-fan alike . . . a tale to gladden the envious heart of every weekend athlete."—The New York Times (#W6029—$1.50)

☐ **PLAYING PRO-FOOTBALL TO WIN (Revised) by John Unitas with Harold Rosenthal.** Foreword by Carroll Rosenbloom. Johnny Unitas, the highest-paid professional football star ever, tells his story and others in a fascinating book that no football fan can lose with.
(#Y5686—$1.25)

☐ **SEMI-TOUGH by Dan Jenkins.** This super bestseller is "funny . . . marvelous . . . outrageous . . . Dan Jenkins has written a book about sports, but not about sports . . . it mocks contemporary American mores; it mocks Madison Avenue; it mocks racial attitudes; it mocks writers like me . . . Women abound . . . I loved it." David Halberstam, **New York Times Book Review**
(#E5598—$1.75)

THE NEW AMERICAN LIBRARY, INC.,
P.O. Box 999, Bergenfield, New Jersey 07621

Please send me the SIGNET BOOKS I have checked above. I am enclosing $_____(check or money order—no currency or C.O.D.'s). Please include the list price plus 25¢ a copy to cover handling and mailing costs. (Prices and numbers are subject to change without notice.)

Name_____

Address_____

City_____State_____Zip Code_____
Allow at least 3 weeks for delivery

THE COMPLETE HANDBOOK OF PRO FOOTBALL
1975

A ZANDER HOLLANDER BOOK

SIGNET BOOKS
NEW AMERICAN LIBRARY
TIMES MIRROR

SIGNET AND MENTOR BOOKS ARE ALSO AVAILABLE AT DISCOUNTS IN BULK QUANTITY FOR INDUSTRIAL OR SALES-PROMOTIONAL USE. FOR DETAILS, WRITE TO PREMIUM MARKETING DIVISION, NEW AMERICAN LIBRARY, INC. 1301 AVENUE OF THE AMERICAS, NEW YORK, NEW YORK 10019.

Copyright © 1975 by Associated Features Inc. All rights reserved.

SIGNET TRADEMARK REG. U.S. PAT. OFF. AND FOREIGN COUNTRIES
REGISTERED TRADEMARK—MARCA REGISTRADA
HECHO EN CHICAGO, U.S.A.

SIGNET, SIGNET CLASSICS, MENTOR and PLUME BOOKS are published by
The New American Library, Inc.
1301 Avenue of the Americas, New York, New York 10019

First Printing, August, 1975

1 2 3 4 5 6 7 8 9

PRINTED IN THE UNITED STATES OF AMERICA

THE COMPLETE HANDBOOK OF PRO FOOTBALL
1975 EDITION

CONTENTS

Curt Gowdy's All-Time Pro Team .... by Curt Gowdy 6
The Rating Game .... by Larry Felser 10
Who Will Be the Next 2000-yard Man? .... by Joe Pollack 12
Super Bowl: The First Decade .... by Reid Grosky 14
Inside the AFC .... by Phil Musick 18

Pittsburgh Steelers 20	New England Patriots 74
Cincinnati Bengals 29	New York Jets 83
Houston Oilers 38	Baltimore Colts 92
Cleveland Browns 47	Oakland Raiders 101
Miami Dolphins 56	Denver Broncos 110
Buffalo Bills 65	San Diego Chargers 119

Kansas City Chiefs 128

Winning Plays 138
Inside the NFC .... by Ray Didinger 140

Los Angeles Rams 142	Philadelphia Eagles 196
San Francisco 49ers 151	St. Louis Cardinals 205
New Orleans Saints 160	New York Giants 214
Atlanta Falcons 169	Minnesota Vikings 223
Dallas Cowboys 178	Green Bay Packers 232
Washington Redskins 187	Detroit Lions 241

Chicago Bears 250

NFL TV Games 259
WFL Schedule 260
Inside the WFL 262
NFL Schedule 279
NFL Statistics 282

ACKNOWLEDGMENTS

If football in 1975 can match the pre-season cliff-hanger—entertainer Joe Namath's turning down the lead role in "Hello Chicago"—we're in for quite a year. One can't guarantee the predictions herein, but we'll vouch for the way all hands went about producing this mammoth first edition of THE COMPLETE HANDBOOK OF PRO FOOTBALL. We acknowledge the behind-the-scenes contributions of Roger Director, Reid Grosky, 20th Century and Libra Graphics. And for their cooperation we thank the NFL publicity directors and the underdog WFL.—*Zander Hollander*

The material herein includes trades up to the final printing deadline. Cover photo credit: Walter Iooss, Jr. Other photos: George Gojkovich, Carl Skalak, Cliff Boutelle, Malcolm Emmons, Jerry Wachter, Ken Regan, Vernon Biever, John Biever, UPI, the NFL and WFL teams.

Curt Gowdy's All-Time Pro Team

By CURT GOWDY

What better way to precipitate a barroom argument than by picking an "all-time" sports team? And an all-pro football team is certainly no exception.

"What about Bronko Nagurski?" an old-timer will ask. "How could you leave him off? Or Sammy Baugh ... now there was one fine quarterback." By the same token, a fan of more recent vintage would cast his vote for players like Cleveland Brown running back Jimmy Brown or Baltimore Colt defensive end Gino Marchetti, both of whom belong on any all-time football team.

During my career as a broadcaster I've been fortunate to see the best of both the National and American Football Leagues, the latter growing from infancy to adulthood during an association with NBC-TV that began in 1965 and reached fruition in the New York Jets' 16-7 triumph over Baltimore in Super Bowl III in 1969.

But whereas I go back to 1949 with Major League Baseball, I'm a relative newcomer to the professional football scene. My football broadcasting career got its start during the years of Bud Wilkinson's great Oklahoma teams of the late 1940s and early '50s. In 1953 I became the play-by-play reporter on NBC Radio's "College Football Game-of-the-Week," then later worked for five years on NBC's NCAA college football telecasts.

In 1962 the late Paul Christman and I started broadcasting the American Football League, which had come into existance two years before, for ABC. When NBC acquired the telecast rights in 1965, Paul and I moved over to provide the commentary, marking the continuation of my association with the AFL (and American Football Conference) that starts its 14th season in 1975.

Joe Namath gets Curt Gowdy's call at QB.

It's this very AFL-AFC association that prompts me to restrict my football selections to those players who have appeared in games that I've actually broadcast. By taking this approach I realize I'm leaving off some great names, players of the past whom I never broadcast or more recent athletes who, until the merger, I saw only rarely. But I don't feel I can arbitrarily pick players I'm not familiar with, just because they have a great reputation. Since this is to be *my* all-time, all-pro football team, I'm going to be partial in these selections—these are the men I broadcast and who impressed me over the years.

Chicago's Dick Butkus makes it as the man in the middle.

So, even through seeing him in films and on television I consider Gino Marchetti the greatest defensive end in the history of football, I have to leave him off the team.

Jim Brown, whose accomplishments (12,312 yards rushing, eight ground-gaining titles in nine years, seven 1,000-yard seasons, never missing a starting call) speak for themselves, decided after the 1965 season—before the first Super Bowl and subsequent merger between the two leagues—that he wanted to be an actor. Consequently, I never did broadcast a game in which he played. And the Baughs and Nagurskis were all before my time.

My knowledge of the players and their abilities comes from 13 years of play-by-play, the commentary on five Super Bowls, and innumerable interviews and discussions with the athletes themselves and their coaches.

Here, then, is my all-time, all-pro football team. I've named alternates at many positions because, as the fact is brought home to NFL coaches week after week, a modern club needs 40 players.

OFFENSE

- **QB** —Joe Namath, New York Jets
- **RB** —O.J. Simpson, Buffalo Bills
  Larry Csonka, Miami Dolphins
- **WR** —Paul Warfield, Cleveland Browns, Miami Dolphins
  Lance Alworth, San Diego Chargers, Dallas Cowboys
- **C** —Jim Otto, Oakland Raiders
- **G** —Jerry Kramer, green Bay Packers
  Billy Shaw, Buffalo Bills
- **T** —Rayfield Wright, Dallas Cowboys
  Ron Yary, Minnesota Vikings
- **TE** —John Mackey, Baltimore Colts, San Diego Chargers
- **K** —Jan Stenerud, Kansas City Chiefs
  George Blanda, Chicago Bears, Houston Oilers, Oakland Raiders

DEFENSE

- **E** —Rich "Tombstone" Jackson, Oakland Raiders, Denver Broncos, Cleveland Browns
  David "Deacon" Jones, Los Angeles Rams, San Diego Chargers
- **T** —Bob Lilly, Dallas Cowboys
  "Mean" Joe Green, Pittsburgh Steelers
- **LB** —Dick Butkus, Chicago Bears
  Dave Robinson, Green Bay Packers, Washington Redskins
  Bobby Bell, Kansas City Chiefs
- **CB** —Willie Brown, Denver Broncos, Oakland Raiders
  Herb Adderley, Green Bay Packers, Dallas Cowboys
- **S** —Dick Anderson, Miami Dolphins
  Johnny Robinson, Dallas Texas/Kansas City Chiefs
- **P** —Ray Guy, Oakland Raiders

COACH—Don Shula, Baltimore Colts, Miami Dolphins

My basic yardstick in picking the members of this team—aside from having broadcast them—had to be longevity, coupled

continued on page 292

THE RATING GAME

By LARRY FELSER
Buffalo Evening News

Obviously not everyone can be named to the Pro Bowl, or can be all-pro this or all-pro that, or make it high in the statistics column.

Bob Kuechenberg, the chatty Miami guard, swears he'll jump off the top of the Eden Rock if Reggie McKenzie is named to the Pro Bowl ahead of him. Mack Herron's heart is broken when Greg Pruitt is knighted by the coaches' poll as the AFC kick returner. Clearly there are wounded egos down the line—and in the backfield.

So in an effort to relieve the pain, spread the laurels and fill a void, THE COMPLETE HANDBOOK OF PRO FOOTBALL presents its player rankings for 1975:

MOST POLITICAL

Long before he was elected to the U.S. Congress, Jack Kemp was cultivating a speaking delivery like Pete McCloskey. He had three or four Kennedy poses down pat. The clincher was his threat to voters of his Western New York district: "If you don't elect me, I'll come back to play quarterback for the Buffalo Bills." He wins by a landslide every two years.

Although Francis Tarkenton can shovel it faster than most politicians, the top ranking goes to Bill Currey, who has been telling people what Ed Garvey "really meant" for the last two years.

1. Bill Curry, 2. Francis Tarkenton, 3. John Schmitt, 4. O.J. Simpson, 5. Mercury Morris

Is Fran Tarkenton ready for public office?

MEANEST

Joe Greene was a victim of his nickname all of Super Bowl week. Joe, who is actually an affable man, kept saying, "I'm not mean. You take Jack Lambert. Now there is a mean football player."

Any list of mean football players must be heavy with linebackers and Dick Butkus should get some mention in retrospect. John Reaves asked Bill Bergey's two-year-old son

continued on page 304

O.J. Simpson did it once. Again? Wow!

Who Will Be The Next 2,000-Yard Man?

By JOE POLLACK
St. Louis Post-Dispatch

Perhaps he is playing in Pop Warner League ball now. Or he may be a rookie in the National Football League. Or that other league. After all, they said, nobody would break Babe Ruth's record of 714 home runs. And that's the same sort of posture

Fabulous Jim Brown had the record before O.J.

taken in support of O.J. Simpson's one-season NFL rushing record of 2,003 yards. Yes, you say, records are made to be broken and somebody out there is going to do it. Okay.

But isn't the Simpson mark so special that it is inconceivable that it will be surpassed? It was made in a special season, under a special set of circumstances. It was, in some respects, a record that was set as a team project.

This is not to denigrate the performance. Carrying a football 332 times from scrimmage in one season is a real task. Gaining 2,003 yards is an amazing feat.

But around that magic season, Simpson's 1972 and 1974 totals were 1,251 yards and 1,125 yards, certainly highly respectable totals, but no threat to any one-season record.

So it is going to take another set of special circumstances for anyone—including Simpson himself—to get past that 2,000-yard barrier. Those circumstances include items like a good offensive line, a coach whose preference is for the running game, a defense that will not only keep the team in contention but will

continued on page 298

SUPER BOWL
The First Decade

By REID GROSKY
The New York Times

The 10th anniversary of the Super Bowl, which will take place in Miami on Jan. 18, 1976, coincides roughly with the start of the Bicentennial, or 200th anniversary of the United States. And why not? The Super Bowl became a slice of Americana right from that January afternoon in 1967 when the streets emptied in Green Bay, the water pressure dropped abruptly in Kansas City, and 60 million people watched on television as the Packers and Chiefs played for the championship of pro football.

On the field, the game appeared to be bitter warfare between the established National Football League and the seven-year-old upstart, the American Football League. In effect, however, it represented peaceful coexistence.

The Super Bowl had grown out of the merger plans of both leagues, a move that received approval from Congress. But amid business and politics, it also grew out of the mouths of babes. The young daughter of Lamar Hunt, the multimillionaire founder of the AFL, came up one day with a name for her lively, toy rubber ball. "It's my 'super ball,' daddy," she said. Hunt's eyes lit up. "Super Bowl," he would later blurt out during a league meeting to discuss prospects for the game. And so, Super Sunday was born, and it would soon develop into the biggest buildup in pro sports history.

A one-minute television commercial during the last Super Bowl cost the sponsor $214,000, a price exceeded only by "The Godfather." The winning players got $15,000 apiece, the losers $7,500, and, as per custom, the winning team received the Super Bowl trophy designed by Tiffany's.

On Jan. 18 in Miami, it will be big business as usual. About

SUPER BOWL 15

80,000 spectators and 75 million television viewers will watch Super Bowl X, which likely will be won by the team with the best defense. AFC teams lead the series, 6 games to 3, an indication of how far things have come since 1967. Vince Lombardi said then of the AFL champions, the Kansas City Chiefs, "Their team doesn't compare with the top National Football League teams."

But a decade of Super Sundays has changed all that. And it would seem only appropriate now to touch on some of the hereos and zeroes of Super Bowls past, on some of the 32 touchdowns, 17 field goals, 32 fumbles and 24 interceptions—and on the one "Presidential play" of the first nine years.

SUPER BOWL I

LOS ANGELES, Jan. 15, 1967—Amid the pomp of the first Super Bowl, a curious circumstance arose: At halftime, the

Max McGee scores his second TD in first Super Bowl.

Bart Starr won another car in second Super Bowl.

Green Bay Packers led the Kansas City Chiefs by only four points, 14-10. The Packers, heavy favorites, had been matched almost score for score. A Bart Starr touchdown pass to Max McGee was answered by a Len Dawson pass to Curtis McClinton. Jim Taylor ran 14 yards for a second Packer TD, but Mike Mercer kicked a 31-yard field goal for Kansas City before halftime.

Coach Vince Lombardi, his Packers an NFL dynasty, was not happy. Earlier, he had growled to his players, "There is no way the Green Bay Packers are going to lose this football game." He told them they were carrying the banner of their league, and he read them letters and telegrams of encouragement from George Halas, Wellington Mara and other major-domos of the NFL.

Now, at halftime, he exhorted his defense to be more aggressive and rush Dawson, the Kansas City quarterback who put the Chiefs on the warpath in the first half.

Said Willie Wood, Packer safety, "We got the message." When Dawson was pressured into a bad pass in the third quarter, Wood intercepted. He returned the ball 50 yards to the Kansas City 5-yard line, a play that broke the game open. Green Bay scored on a run by Elijah Pitts and went on to a 35-10 victory. "The Packers beat us in the first half," said Kansas City's Jerry Mays. "The Packers and the Packer mystique beat us in the second half."

SUPERSTAR—Starr won an automobile as the game's MVP, but the day really belonged to the aging McGee, a 34-year-old substitute end who had caught only four passes all season. "I wonder if I'll get to play in this thing," he had said before the game. The answer came on the first series of downs when Boyd Dowler, the starting flanker, was injured. McGee played the rest of the way and became the first player to score a touchdown in a Super Bowl. He caught seven of Starr's passes for 138 yards and two TDs.

GOAT—Fred Williamson, Chiefs' cornerback and karate buff, boasted he would stop the Packers by using the clothesline tackles that had earned him his nickname, The Hammer. Instead, Williamson was knocked cold making a tackle in the fourth quarter and was carried off the field.

```
Kansas City Chiefs (AFL) ........ 0  10   0   0—10
Green Bay Packers (NFL) ........ 7   7  14   7—35
```

GB—McGee, pass from Starr 37 (Chandler kick)

KC—McClinton, pass from Dawson 7 (Mercer kick)

GB—Taylor, run 14 (Chandler kick)

KC—Mercer (FG) 31

GB—Pitts, run 5 (Chandler kick)

GB—McGee, pass from Starr 13 (Chandler kick)

GB—Pitts, run 1 (Chandler kick)

A—63,036

SUPER BOWL II

MIAMI, Jan. 14, 1968—It would be Vince Lombardi's last game as coach of the Green Bay Packers, and as Jerry Kramer, the Packer guard, said, "We didn't want to let him down." Under such circumstances, the Oakland Raiders were figured to stay in the game right down to the opening minutes. "A lot of people say we're going to the slaughterhouse," said Raider quarterback Darryl Lamonica. "I hope not."

continued on page 310

INSIDE THE AFC

By PHIL MUSICK
Pittsburgh Press

PREDICTED ORDER OF FINISH

EAST	CENTRAL	WEST
Miami	Pittsburgh	Oakland
Buffalo	Cincinnati	Denver
New England	Houston	San Diego
New York Jets	Cleveland	Kansas City
Baltimore		

AFC Champion: Pittsburgh

Stamped right there on the Oakland Raiders' stationery and, some say, on owner Al Davis' scivvies as well, is the motto: Pride and Poise. Maybe, as they have not, lo, these six winters of discontent, the Raiders will get to exercise both in 1975. For six years, they've won the AFC West title and then failed to win what is known as "the big one."

This, then, would be the AFC's burningest question: Are the Raiders determined to establish themselves as history's most successful failure since Napoleon?

A year ago, the Raider poise crumbled against Pittsburgh in the conference championship game, rendering pride rather unseemly. Still, they are the class of the conference, if not the league, according to most observers. If the Raiders are not, certainly either Pittsburgh or Miami is.

So it will be a three-horse race for the right to represent the AFC in Peter Rozelle's annual burnt offering to the gods of football.

Oakland should easily mop up the West. Denver is coming on, San Diego clinging to the status quo, and Kansas City plummeting, and none of the three has the talent to challenge Davis' crew.

Cincinnati could give the Steelers some heat in the Central division, but not enough. Houston is still undermanned and in

Pittsburgh's Franco Harris grinds it out in the Super Bowl.

Cleveland one can almost hear the scream of Brown fans subjected to mediocrity at long last.

Weakened by the defections of Larry Csonka and Paul Warfield to the WFL, Miami will pit coach Don Shula's legendary smarts against O.J. Simpson's feet. Buffalo could overhaul Miami; New England, Baltimore and New York are chopped meat.

PITTSBURGH STEELERS

TEAM DIRECTORY: Pres.: Art Rooney; Pub. Rel. Dir.: Ed Kiely; Dir. Player Pers.: Dick Haley; Head Coach: Chuck Noll; Trainer: Ralph Berlin. Home: Three Rivers Stadium, Pittsburgh, Pa. (50,350).

Terry Bradshaw rolls out protected by Jim Clack.

SCOUTING REPORT

OFFENSE: The Steelers' poor cousin. After 10 games last year, coach Chuck Noll, normally a placid man, would get a tad huffy when people asked, "What's a matter with your offense?" The answer was three-fold: a line that was having trouble sustaining blocks; quarterback Terry Bradshaw's tendency to kill one team and give artificial respiration to the next; and power back Franco Harris' habit of dancing at the line instead of doing his usual cha-cha on linebackers. Ah, but come the last six weeks and the only thing heard regarding the offense was, "Wow!"

Line coach Dan Radakovich's strict insistence on fundamentals resulted in, among other things, bigger holes for Harris and the finest pass protection in the AFC. Bradshaw, who'd lost his job to Joe Gilliam, used the pass cautiously but found the strike zone and, given daylight, Harris simply flashed through it without one swivel.

Whether or not the playoff offense was for real remains to be proven. But there is depth and talent everyplace but at tight end, where Larry Brown came on last year, and the world has ceased questioning Bradshaw's I.Q., hottest subject of Super Bowl week. And one must remember this—the Steelers don't need a whole lot of offense.

DEFENSE: Oh, yeah! But in Pittsburgh they spell it deeefense. As in Joe Greene and L.C. Greenwood, heart and soul of the best front four in the league. And as in Jack Ham and Andy Russell, two of the four best outside linebackers in the game. First off, nobody runs against the Steelers. Not O.J. or Zonk or the 82nd Airborne. In three playoff games, the Steelers permitted a total of 90 yards rushing. They led the AFC in 13 defensive categories, including the most important one, points allowed (189).

And, sports fans, it's going to improve. Middle linebacker Jack Lambert was the defensive rookie of the year, but one season's experience will make him better. If it doesn't, old reliable Henry Davis, out last season with a neck injury, will take the job.

No. 1 draft pick Dave Brown, a safetyman whom one club scout says "could come in here and move someone out," will help the secondary. And No. 2 choice Robert Barber is a defensive lineman who could have trouble making the club, such is the Steeler depth up front. No one has quite enough temerity to come right out and say the Steelers have the best defense to be seen in the NFL in years—but a whole lot of football people think it.

KICKING GAME: Ageless Bobby Walden snapped back from a poor '73 season and punted well enough that the defense always enjoyed good fielding position. Placekicker Roy Gerela led the AFC in scoring-via-the-toe, or in this instance, instep. The coverage wasn't much early in the season, but was more than

STEELERS VETERANS ROSTER

HEAD COACH—Chuck Noll. Assistant Coaches—Leon "Bud" Carson, Richard Hoak, George Perles, Daniel Radakovich, Louis Riecke, Lionel Taylor, Paul Uram, Robert "Woody" Widenhofer

No.	Name	Pos.	Ht.	Wt.	NFL Exp.	College
45	Allen, Jim	CB	6-2	194	2	UCLA
20	Bleier, Rocky	RB	5-11	210	7	Notre Dame
47	Blount, Mel	CB	6-3	205	7	Southern University
38	Bradley, Ed	LB	6-2	239	3	Wake Forest
12	Bradshaw, Terry	QB	6-3	218	6	Louisiana Tech
87	Brown, Larry	TE	6-4	229	5	Kansas
50	Clack, Jim	G-C	6-3	250	5	Wake Forest
22	Conn, Dick	S	6-0	185	2	Georgia
77	Davis, Charlie	DT	6-1	265	2	Texas Christian
53	Davis, Henry	LB	6-3	235	7	Grambling
57	Davis, Sam	G	6-1	255	9	Allen University
35	Davis, Steve	RB	6-1	218	4	Delaware State
73	Druschel, Rick	OT-G	6-2	248	2	North Carolina State
27	Edwards, Glen	S	6-0	185	5	Florida A&M
33	Fuqua, John	RB	5-11	195	7	Morgan State
64	Furness, Steve	DT-DE	6-4	255	4	Rhode Island
86	Garrett, Reggie	WR	6-1	172	2	Eastern Michigan
10	Gerela, Roy	K	5-10	185	7	New Mexico State
17	Gilliam, Joe	QB	6-2	187	4	Tennessee State
71	Gravelle, Gordon	OT	6-5	250	4	Brigham Young
75	Greene, Joe	DT	6-4	275	7	North Texas State
68	Greenwood, L.C.	DE	6-6	245	7	Arkansas AM&N
84	Grossman, Randy	TE	6-1	215	2	Temple
59	Ham, Jack	LB	6-1	225	5	Penn State
5	Hanratty, Terry	QB	6-1	210	7	Notre Dame
32	Harris, Franco	RB	6-2	230	4	Penn State
46	Harrison, Reggie	RB	5-11	215	2	Cincinnati
63	Holmes, Ernie	DT	6-3	260	4	Texas Southern
54	Kellum, Marv	LB	6-2	225	2	Wichita State
55	Kolb, Jon	OT	6-3	262	7	Oklahoma State
58	Lambert, Jack	LB	6-4	215	2	Kent State
43	Lewis, Frank	WR	6-1	196	5	Grambling
56	Mansfield, Ray	C	6-3	260	13	Washington
89	McMakin, John	TE	6-3	232	4	Clemson
72	Mullins, Gerry	G-OT	6-3	244	5	Southern California
26	Pearson, Preston	RB	6-1	205	9	Illinois
—	Pettus, Larry	OT	6-5	244	1	Tennessee State
74	Reavis, Dave	OT	6-5	250	2	Arkansas
34	Russell, Andy	LB	6-2	225	11	Missouri
25	Shanklin, Ron	WR	6-1	190	6	North Texas State
31	Shell, Donnie	S	5-11	190	2	South Carolina State
82	Stallworth, John	WR	6-2	183	2	Alabama A&M
88	Swann, Lynn	WR	5-10	178	2	Southern California
24	Thomas, J.T.	CB	6-2	196	3	Florida State
51	Toews, Loren	LB	6-3	212	3	California
23	Wagner, Mike	S	6-1	210	5	Western Illinois
39	Walden, Bobby	P	6-0	190	12	Georgia
52	Webster, Mike	C-G	6-1	232	2	Wisconsin
78	White, Dwight	DE	6-4	255	5	East Texas State
62	Wolf, Jim	DE	6-2	230	2	Prairie View

TOP FIVE DRAFT CHOICES

Rd.	Name	Pos.	Ht.	Wt.	Age	College
1	Dave Brown	CB	6-1	190	22	Michigan
2	Bob Barber	DE	6-3	231	23	Grambling
3	Walter White	TE	6-3	208	23	Maryland
4	Harold Evans	LB	6-3	208	23	Houston
5	Brent Sexton	CB	5-11	178	22	Elon

PITTSBURGH STEELERS 23

adequate in the second half of the year. Lynn Swann set an NFL record for punt return yardage.

OUTLOOK: On to Miami in January if two things occur. One, the offense will have to retain its newly-found confidence. "No sweat, we believe now," claims Bradshaw. Two, Noll's ability to shake any feeling of contentment. "We're not going to get fat," insists Joe Greene, "because we were hungry too long."

STEELER PROFILES

ROCKY BLEIER 29 5-11 210   Running Back

Given name is Robert but father nicknamed him "Rocky" in cradle. Steelers call him boulder... Dependable runner (4.2 average) but forte is blocking in fullback-oriented defense... Only NFL player to see combat in Viet Nam. Wounded and decorated... Won job from Preston Pearson at mid-year and will probably keep it this season... Immensely popular in Pittsburgh... Had big year on banquet circuit... Born March 5, 1946, in Appleton, Wisc.... Ex-Notre Dame captain but never big name... Rehabilitated foot, which was badly shot-up, through gutty, two-year effort... Credits Steelers "with keeping me on the payroll until I could contribute"... Co-player rep... Active worker with retarded kids.

TERRY BRADSHAW 27 6-3 215   Quarterback

Came of age during 1974 playoffs and cooly guided Steelers to Super Bowl win... Bum-rapped as dumb when problem was lack of poise, since acquired... Classic example of five-year theory... Probably outstanding tools in game... Lost job to Joe Gilliam first six games last year, but won it back and finished strong although posting poorest quarterback rating among AFC regulars... "He was superb in the second half of the season," says Steeler coach Chuck Noll... Born Sept. 12, 1948, in Shreveport, La.... Devout and credited "getting back to my religion" for success... Holds all passing records at Louisiana Tech and was first player chosen in 1970 draft... Rancher in off-season... Divorced from former Miss Teenage America... Fine runner with 6.6 average on 34 pops last year.

24 THE COMPLETE HANDBOOK OF PRO FOOTBALL

JOE GREENE 29 6-4 275   Defensive Tackle

Mean Joe a gentle man, except on field ... Says, "I am a nice person, but I am capable of being mean. Very capable" ... Nickname comes from college team, North Texas State, where defensive unit was called The Mean Green ... Club's resident all-pro and NFL Defensive Player of Year ... "I've been in the game a while and I never saw anyone play the defensive line the way Joe did in the playoffs," says Noll, who hoards superlatives ... Born Sept. 24, 1946, in Temple, Tex. ... Quickest defensive lineman alive ... In every sense, the Steeler Main Man ... Has had parts in two movies ... Nucleus for league's dominant front four ... First draft pick in 1969 and became cornerstone for Noll's reconstruction ... Real name not Joseph, but Charles ... Mean Charlie? ... All-everything in 1974.

JACK HAM 26 6-1 225   Linebacker

Hammer (ball-peen, not sledge) ... Middle name Raphael ... Game is quickness but strong enough to handle run ... Has led league LBs in interceptions twice in four years ... Best of Penn State linebackers although went to college without scholarship ... Generally considered one of four best outside LBs in league ... Great paddleball player ... Married in off-season ... Born Dec. 23, 1948, in Johnstown, Pa. ... One of best, and best-liked, players on club ... Would make excellent tight end ... Extraordinarily droll wit ... All-American boy image (once took reporter $18 throwing a frisbee into a laundry hamper) ... Very likeable but genuine disinterest in publicity causes him to get little ink ... Three-time all-pro ... Five interceptions in '74.

FRANCO HARRIS 25 6-2 230   Running Back

Key to Steeler offense built around him ... Rebounded from off-year caused partly by "dancing" at the hole to gain more than 1,000 yards (1,006) for second time in three years ... Finished fifth in NFL rushing ... Most private Steeler, but well-liked in locker-room ... Black-Italian ancestry ... NFL Offensive Rookie of Year in 1972; all-pro all three seasons... Born March 17, 1950, in Ft. Dix, N.J.... Lousy practice player and Steelers thought they'd drafted a stiff in the first round of 1972 lottery until fourth game of exhibition season... "We were sick until we saw him get serious in a game," says a Steeler assistant... Reliable blocker and receiver... 5.3 average at Penn State. Once missed starting assignment in bowl game because he was late to practice... One of NFL's tough interviews.

ERNIE HOLMES 27 6-3 260   Defensive Tackle

Fats because he was large baby... Next to OT Jon Kolb, strongest Steeler... Given name best description of way he plays, practice or game: Earnest Lee... Shot a policeman in off-season incident two years ago and put on probation... Super competitor but gets little attention because he plays next to Greene... Wore Arrowhead haircut most of 1974... Born July 11, 1948, in Jamestown, Tex.... One of most underrated players in league. "Watch the guard he's playing over come off the field and you get an idea how good Fats is," says Noll... Pressures passer as well as any Steeler lineman... Low draft pick out of Texas Southern but won job in second season (1973).

L.C. GREENWOOD 29 6-6½ 240   Defensive End

Hollywood Bags... Carries shoulder bag and has interest in movie or TV career... Also, Birmingham Bags because jumped to WFL club and played out option in 1974... Will probably return to Steelers as WFL contract no longer valid... Didn't get awards but was really MVP in Super Bowl and Pro Bowl... His harassment of Minnesota QB Fran Tarkenton was key to Super Bowl win... Actual given name is L.C. Henderson Greenwood. Tells people L.C. stands for "Lover Cool"... Gregarious and likeable... Dude dresser... Very independent but no locker-room lawyer... Two-year Pro Bowl pick... Born Sept. 8, 1946, in Canton, Miss... Does it all but main virtue is pass rush... Most adept NFL end at not being picked by OTs... Fifth-round choice in 1969 out of Arkansas AM&N... Has had contractual hassles during career... One of most popular Steelers.

ANDY RUSSELL 33 6-2 225   Linebacker

Thinking man's LB and probably smartest defensive player in NFL ... Prominent businessman; sells tax shelters ... Warmly respected ... Steelers' playing-hurt champ ... Coming off excellent season after being hampered by injuries in 1973 ... Hasn't missed a game in 10 seasons ... Whizzer White Humanitarian Award in 1973 for contributions to team, community and country ... Not particularly strong or quick but plays the sweep like scythe ... Only weakness an occasional tendency to gamble ... Born Oct. 29, 1941, in Detroit ... In Pro Bowl five years ... Coach-on-the-field type ... Two-year MVP at Missouri, where he played fullback and linebacker ... Was Steeler player rep for several seasons ... Defensive captain.

LYNN SWANN 23 5-10 178   Wide Receiver

Should become one of fine receivers in AFC this year after a rookie season that showed deceptive statistics ... Caught only 16 balls but had fine 18.9 average and missed almost half season with compound dislocated fingers ... Excellent tools. Runs 40 in 4.5, is smart and durable. Has grace of, well, swan ... "We drafted him No. 1 because he is a winner, has always been a winger," says Chuck Noll ... Fifth in NFL punt returns (14.1 average) and his 41 were an all-time record ... Consensus All-American at Southern Cal. ... First receiver to go in '74 draft ... Could keep excellent receiver, Ron Shanklin, on bench a lot of the time this winter.

RAY MANSFIELD 34 6-3 260   Center

What they mean by the term unsung hero ... Guy who's always there (played in 171 straight games) and displays the enthusiasm that belies his 13 years in league ... Hugely underrated center ... Called The Old Ranger after TV character ... A tough, seasoned pro who had excellent year as bulwark of an offensive line that showed great improvement ... Born Jan. 21, 1941, in Bakersfield, Calif ... Two-way center-tackle at Washington and drafted No. 2 by Philadelphia

PITTSBURGH STEELERS 27

... In one of decade's dumber deals, Eagles sold him to Steelers in 1964 and he's been a regular ever since ... Staved off innumerable challenges to retain job ... "It seemed like every year there was some kid who was going to put me on the bench," he chuckles ... Insurance salesman.

TOP ROOKIES

DAVE BROWN 22 6-1 190   **Safety**
Three-year regular at Michigan as free safety but projected as pro cornerback ... Consensus All-American and scouts say could beat out regular as rookie ... Runs 40 in consistent 4.6 ... Team lost twice in his three years ... Interested in TV career ... Outstanding high school quarterback in Akron, Ohio ... All-Big Ten three times.

COACH CHUCK NOLL ... Called "The Pope" when he was a player and deserves it after resurrecting Steelers from 40 years of decay and guiding them to Super Bowl win ... Strongly disciplined man who has complete control of football-end of club ... Coined phrase "whatever it takes" ... For the Steelers it took five years during which Noll steadfastly stuck to draft to build ... Says "there are three ways to get talent, and trades are the worst" ... Quiet, contained ... When club won first title ever in 1973, a veteran said "that's the first time I ever saw him smile" ... Messenger-guard and linebacker for Browns ... Quit prematurely to go into coaching and was assistant under Sid Gillman at San Diego and Don Shula at Baltimore.

CLUB HISTORY

For four decades, kindly old Art Rooney wore the Pittsburgh Steelers around his neck like a millstone. They were, having known only 10 winnings seasons in 40 years, the NFL's sick joke.

Then came 1972 and, at long last, their very first championship of any kind. Fate had finally smiled. "We never won, but we always beat up people a lot," observed veteran Andy Russell on the occasion.

The man behind the reformation, and subsequently last year's Super Bowl win, was Chuck Noll. His secret is hard work, attention to the minutest detail and an abiding belief in doing "whatever it takes."

Before him there was nothing of serious import. A halfback named Whizzer White who eventually wound up playing for the United States Supreme Court. A coach named Johnny Blood who occasionally didn't show up for games. Bobby Layne in his salad days. And carrying the single-wing into the 1950s. Right, a gag team. Until Chuck Noll came along.

INDIVIDUAL STEELER RECORDS

Rushing

Most Yards Game:	218	John Fuqua, vs Philadelphia, 1970
Season:	1,141	John Henry Johnson, 1962
Career:	4,383	John Henry Johnson, 1960-65

Passing

Most TD Passes Game:	4	Dick Shiner, vs San Francisco, 1968
	4	Ed Brown, vs Dallas, 1963
	4	Jim Finks, vs Cleveland, 1952 and 1954
	4	Jim Finks, vs N.Y. Giants, 1952
Season:	21	Ed Brown, 1963
Career:	67	Bobby Layne, 1958-62

Receiving

Most TD Passes Game:	4	Roy Jefferson, vs Atlanta, 1968
Season:	12	Buddy Dial, 1961
Career:	42	Buddy Dial, 1959-63

Scoring

Most Points Game:	24	Roy Jefferson, vs Atlanta, 1968
	24	Ray Mathews, vs Cleveland, 1954
Season:	123	Roy Gerela, 1973 (36 PATS-29 FG)
Career:	413	Roy Gerela, 1971-74 (131 PATS-94 FG)
Most TDs Game:	4	Roy Jefferson, vs Atlanta, 1968
	4	Ray Mathews, vs Cleveland, 1954
Season:	12	Roy Jefferson, 1968
	12	Buddy Dial, 1961
Career:	43	Ray Mathews, 1951-59

CINCINNATI BENGALS 29

CINCINNATI BENGALS

TEAM DIRECTORY: Pres: John Sawyer; GM-Head Coach: Paul Brown; Asst. GM: Michael Brown; Dir. Player Pers.: Pete Brown; Dir. Pub. Rel.: Allan Heim; Bus. Mgr.: John Murdough; Trainer: Marvin Pollins. Home: Riverfront Stadium, Cincinnati, Ohio (56,200).

Ken Anderson was NFL's leading passer.

SCOUTING REPORT

OFFENSE: There's nothing wrong with the Bengal offense that Michael DeBakey, the surgical staff of the Mayo Clinic and Kathryn Kuhlmann couldn't handle. Injuries cost the Bengals backs Boobie Clark, Essex Johnson, Doug Dressler and Ed Williams and tackle Vern Holland. Two guys named Lenvil Elliott and Charlie Davis wound up staggering under the running load. Davis proved quick but small; Elliott large but slow. Even Ken Anderson's brilliant short passing game couldn't compensate and the Bengals fell to 7-7.

Given the miracles of modern medicine, the Bengals should bounce back. Healthy, their offense is diversified and powerful. Anderson, who led the league in completions and percentage (64.9), throws an accurate, soft pass. On swings, flares and screens, he is peerless; at medium range, almost as good. He has a tendency to lay it up on the deep stuff, but who among us is perfect?

The running game is explosive behind a mature, cohesive offensive line headed by Holland and center Bob Johnson. They specialize in drive blocking. Clark runs the tackle flawlessly, getting as much second-effort yardage as anyone, while Johnson gives the Bengals what most clubs don't have, a quick outside runner smart enough to read his blocking. In Issac Curtis, the Bengals have a guy who makes it rain on people. Charlie Joiner holds forth on the other side, but the passing game seems most productive with Curtis going from the slot and Chip Myers coming in as a third wide receiver, a tactic coach Paul Brown has gone to increasingly the past two years. Bob Trumpy is, when healthy, an all-pro tight end.

DEFENSE: Not the sort of unit they had in the Phnom Penh suburbs, but capable of providing the crack through which the Bengal playoff hopes could slide away. Brown may have outsmarted himself in the season finale last year in Pittsburgh when he obviously made no effort to win. This let the defense play most of the game and take a humiliating pounding. Two days later, DE Royce Berry asked to be traded and there were reports several other defenders were equally bitter. The Bengal defense can't handle a loss of morale.

The line will be hampered by the retirement of Mike Reid, who has decided to withdraw his battered knees to the peace of the piano stool. When Bill Bergey slipped off to Philadelphia, he left a huge hole at middle linebacker and the Bengals haven't filled it. As a result, Cincinnati has been susceptible to the run inside. The secondary doesn't tackle as well as most and that hurts, too. Of course, there are some strengths. Tackle Ron Carpenter is badly underrated; cornerman Lemar Parrish is an all-pro; and Tommy Casanova hasn't let a lack of tools keep him from becoming a dependable safetyman.

KICKING GAME: If grass wasn't allowed in the NFL, everything would be fine here. But placekicker Horst Muhlmann doesn't like the real stuff and most of his seven misses in 18 tries came on natural turf. Rookie Dave Green gave the Bengals more than adequate punting and Parrish led the league in

CINCINNATI BENGALS

BENGALS VETERANS ROSTER

HEAD COACH—Paul Brown. Assistant Coaches—Bill Johnson, Bill Walsh, Jack Donaldson, Chuck Studley, Chuck Weber, Howard Brinker, Kim Wood

No.	Name	Pos.	Ht.	Wt.	NFL Exp.	College
52	Adams, Doug	LB	6-1	222	5	Ohio State
14	Anderson, Ken	QB	6-2	211	5	Augustana, Ill.
58	Beauchamp, Al	LB	6-2	237	8	Southern U.
82	Berry, Royce	DE	6-4	250	7	Houston
29	Blackwood, Lyle	S	6-0	189	3	Texas Christian
70	Carpenter, Ron	DE	6-4	261	6	North Carolina State
37	Casanova, Tom	S	6-2	202	4	Louisiana State
81	Chandler, Al	TE	6-3	229	3	Oklahoma
42	Clark, Charles	RB	6-2	240	3	Bethune-Cookman
11	Clark, Wayne	QB	6-3	203	5	U.S. International
88	Coslet, Bruce	TE	6-3	227	7	Pacific, Ore.
85	Curtis, Isaac	WR	6-1	193	3	San Diego State
26	Davis, Charlie	RB	5-11	200	2	Colorado
44	Dressler, Doug	RB	6-3	228	5	Chico State
36	Elliott, Lenvil	RB	6-0	200	3	Northeast Mo. State
72	Fest, Howard	T	6-6	262	8	Texas
41	Green, Dave	P	5-11	200	3	Ohio U.
59	Hicks, Richard	C	6-4	245	1	Humboldt State
76	Holland, Vernon	T	6-6	268	5	Tennessee State
23	Jackson, Bernard	S-CB	6-0	173	4	Washington State
54	Johnson, Bob	C	6-5	262	8	Tennessee
19	Johnson, Essex	RB	5-9	201	8	Grambling
80	Johnson, Ken	DT	6-6	265	5	Indiana
18	Joiner, Charlie	WR	5-11	188	7	Grambling
57	Jolitz, Evan	LB	6-2	225	2	Cincinnati
32	Jones, Bob	S	6-3	194	3	Virginia Union
56	Kearney, Tim	LB	6-2	227	4	Northern Michigan
68	Kollar, Bill	DT	6-3	255	2	Montana
62	Lapham, Dave	T	6-3	255	2	Syracuse
55	Leclair, Jim	LB	6-2	226	4	North Dakota
77	Maddox, Bob	DE	6-5	232	2	Frostburg State
73	Matson, Pat	G	6-1	245	10	Oregon
71	Mayes, Rufus	T	6-5	260	7	Ohio State
86	McDaniel, John	WR	6-1	193	2	Lincoln, Mo.
16	Muhlmann, Horst	K	6-1	219	7	None
25	Myers, Chip	WR	6-5	210	8	N.W. Oklahoma
20	Parrish, Lemar	CB	5-11	185	6	Lincoln, Mo.
60	Pritchard, Ron	LB	6-1	235	7	Arizona State
13	Riley, Ken	CB	5-11	181	7	Florida A&M
22	Sawyer, Ken	S	6-0	192	2	Syracuse
64	Shinners, John	G	6-3	255	7	Xavier
84	Trumpy, Bob	TE	6-6	228	8	Utah
75	Walters, Stan	T	6-6	270	4	Syracuse
83	White, Sherman	DE	6-5	255	4	California
43	Williams, Ed	RB	6-2	245	2	Langston

TOP FIVE DRAFT CHOICES

Rd.	Name	Pos.	Ht.	Wt.	Age	College
1	Glenn Cameron	LB	6-2	229	22	Florida
2	Al Krevis	T-G	6-5	265	23	Boston College
3	Gary Burley	DE	6-3	255	22	Pittsburgh
3	Gary Sheide	QB	6-2	195	22	Brigham Young
3	Bo Harris	LB	6-3	230	22	Louisiana State

returns. But the Bengal coverage on punts gave a lot of yardage back.

OUTLOOK: A playoff team if the veterans forgive Brown's unbelievable gaffe in Pittsburgh. If they do not, it and a general feeling among the troops that the front office still have the first dollar taken in at the box-office, could ruin a potentially strong club.

BENGAL PROFILES

KEN ANDERSON 26 6-2½ 210   Quarterback

Paul Brown with an arm ... Fine dissector of defenses and learned early the patience to chip away until the other side crumbles ... Statistically, the finest passer in NFL last year with a fine 95.9 rating ... In fact, not the league's best thrower, merely one of the top five ... Has few peers at short-range consistency and is excellent on medium routes, but there are better bomb-throwers (Namath and Charley Johnson and Ken Stabler, that's who) ... Born Feb. 15, 1949, in Batavia, Ill. ... Epitome of the big, bright young quarterbacks now infesting game ... A third-round pick out of tiny Augustana (Ill.) College ... Highest completion rate in NFL last year (64.9) ... Rewrote Bengal passing records ... Owns sporting goods store ... Strong runner (314 yards on 43 attempts) but Brown doesn't like it and is curtailing him ... Amiable, modest ... Eagle Scout of NFL quarterbacks.

RON CARPENTER 27 6-5 250   Defensive Tackle

Bengals' best defensive lineman, and that included Mike Reid, but always overlooked by writers, fans, etc. ... Led team in sacks and tackles for second straight year ... "He doesn't play like Reid, he's not flamboyant, but he's always around," says club official ... Born June 24, 1948, in Thomasville, N.C. Can play both DT and DE, but lacks quickness to work the outside ... A rock against the run and better-than-average pass rusher ... Two-year All-American at North Carolina State ... Stock broker and chemical products salesman in off-season ... A stay-at-home DT who may have to move more with the retirement of Reid.

CINCINNATI BENGALS 33

TOMMY CASANOVA 25 6-2 195 — Safety

The Honest Workman type, made Pro Bowl for first time in 1974... Lacks speed, but has more than first thought. As rookie, it was generally felt that a lack of quickness and durability would keep him out of league... Coming off fine season, although interceptions dropped from four to two... Born July 29, 1950, in Crowley, La.... Ranked ninth in AFC in punt returns with respectable 11.0 average... Better hands than teammate Lemar Parrish, whose 18.8 average led league in punt returns... Has returned two kickoffs in career, one for 34 yards, other for 48... Medical student at Cincinnati U... One of better free safetys in AFC... Calls defensive signals... One of best athletes in LSU history.

ISAAC CURTIS 24 6-1 195 — Wide Receiver

Thought too good to be true after rookie season (1973) and sure enough... Receptions dropped 33 percent, from 45 to 30, but remains one of most dangerous, if not the most dangerous, receiver in game... Led AFC in average yardage, 21.1, but was not helped by rule change that restricted cutting receivers... Ten TD catches... Super moves and power after catch... Could be fastest man in pro football... Target for a barrage of elbows and fists as DBs try to discourage him from going over the middle, sometimes successfully... Born Oct. 20, 1950, in Santa Ana, Calif.... Top draft pick two years ago... Draws double coverage as surely as decolletage draws eyeballs... One of few receivers who force teams to make special defensive preparations for him.

VERN HOLLAND 27 6-6 270 — Offensive Tackle

One of four or five best OTs in game until he was sidelined for season in second game with a badly broken leg... "His leg was shattered, and so were we," sighs club official of injury that forced Bengals to reshuffle offensive line... Excellent size and good quickness... Great drive blocker and handles the pass rush well... Born June 27, 1948, in Sherman, Tex.... Club says leg is 100 percent, but rumor has it that his mobility has been affected... Until injury, played every game since 1971, when he was a first-round pick out of Tennessee State... A starter as rookie and had shown consistent improvement... Has overall speed to pull.

BOB JOHNSON 29 6-5 260   Center

The guy Paul Brown calls "the core of our football team"... One of top centers in game... Also suffered a broken leg and missed last five games, four of which Bengals lost to fall from playoff picture... Team leader... Probably best center in NFL in 1973... Heavily involved in civic affairs in Cincinnati... First player ever drafted by Bengals and captain from rookie season... Born Aug. 19, 1946, in Cleveland, Tenn.... All-American at Tennessee... Leader in Fellowship of Christian Athletes... Honorary chairman of American Cancer Society crusade... Strong pass blocker... Excellent at cutting middle linebacker... Very intelligent... One of most popular players on club.

ESSEX JOHNSON 29 5-10 197   Running Back

Another of the walking wounded who made the 1974 Bengals look like the victims of a mid-air collision... Knee surgery forced him out of most '74 games and he is the club's No. 1 question mark this year... After missing thousand-yard club in 1973 by three yards, gained just 44 yards last season... Called The Express... Leans in for extra yardage despite lack of bulk... "He has the finest balance of any player I ever coached," says Paul Brown... Pass receiving skills also missed ... Not a particularly strong blocker... Born Oct. 14, 1946, in Shreveport, La.... Sixth-round choice in 1969 after fine career at Grambling.

JIM LECLAIR 24 6-2½ 225   Linebacker

Another big question mark on a team which has a bunch of them... Moved into middle last year to replace traded Bill Bergey, but after two excellent exhibition games, tendonitis in foot kept him on bench whole regular campaign... Owns hunting lodge... Will be challenged for job by No. 1 draft pick, Glenn Cameron... Headhunter... Has fine

CINCINNATI BENGALS 35

quickness, strength for middle is questionable ... Could play outside ... Top college wrestler who pinned a bear in off-season bout ... Born Oct. 30, 1950, in South St. Paul, Minn. ... At North Dakota, was one of better LBs in 1972 draft ... Has potential, but could wind up hurting club at MLB through lack of experience ... Sells insurance in off-season (when not wrestling bears, that is) ... Fine all-around athlete.

LEMAR PARRISH 27 5-11 185   **Cornerback**

Didn't make an interception in 1974 after averaging four a year, but still had excellent season ... One of best cornerbacks in AFC for the third straight year ... Has penchant for head-hunting and receivers are wary of him ... Led NFL in punt return average (18.8) ... Scored twice in nationally-televised game against Washington on fumble recovery and punt return ... Exciting player ... Key to game is acceleration ... Strength in a rather weak secondary that had fewest interceptions (9) in league ... Born Dec. 13, 1947, in Riviera Beach, Fla. ... Too valuable to use as kickoff return man, although has career average of 24.9 ... Low draft pick from Lincoln (Nebr.).

TOP ROOKIES

GLENN CAMERON 22 6-2 230   **Linebacker**
Could fill hole in the middle left by Bill Bergey, although probably better suited as outside LB ... One of two fastest LBs in draft ... Excellent covering pass ... Florida trainer says "his tolerance of pain is exceptional" ... Anchored SEC's finest defense ... Consensus All-American ... Prep school running back sensation ... One of best college boxers in South.

AL KREVIS 23 6-3 255   **Guard**
Surprise not taken in first round ... "He was the best player on the board in second round," says Paul Brown ... Has everything but height, which will cause him some problems ... Could start due to unsettled OL scene ... One of better heavyweight wrestlers in East ... Excellent student at Boston College.

COACH PAUL BROWN ... A coaching genius ... Says so in Bengal press guide ... May have outsmarted self in final game of 1974 at Pittsburgh when made no serious attempt to win game ... Bengal players were enraged and a couple asked to be traded ... Reports say move cost Brown a lot of player loyalty ... Still, at 67, he is football's all-time winningest coach ... Career record of 340-130-16 ... Part owner, GM and head coach ... Has won 13 division or conference titles and seven league championships, four in defunct All-American Conference with Cleveland Browns ... Great innovator who introduced, among other things, a year-round staff, classroom techniques, grading of players from film, intelligence tests for players, calling plays from sideline, the messenger system and face masks ... Dour man, somewhat embittered by experiences ... Enemy of Cleveland owner Art Modell, who fired him after players threatened to rebel following 1962 season.

CLUB HISTORY

A deity in Cleveland for more than a decade, Paul Brown has been forced nose-to-nose with intimations of his mortality down river in Cincinnati. But there is still magic in football's mightiest wand ever.

As a result, the Cincy franchise, under Brown's demanding tutelage, has struggled into prominence. Struggle, as the Bengals did last year when they were ruined by injuries, is the operative word.

The Cincinnati Bengals are Paul Brown, who owns some of them and runs all of them with the result the club has thrived or thrashed according to the judgments of a single man.

Like the little girl with the curl, Brown has won two AFC Central titles in seven years, and known four non-winning seasons.

En route he has drafted and developed such luminaries as **Ken Anderson, Mike Reid, Isaac Curtis and Boobie Clark.** And with his coolness and harsh grip on the club purse-strings, has embittered many others. Whatever they have been or will become, the Bengals are Brown.

CINCINNATI BENGALS 37

INDIVIDUAL BENGAL RECORDS

Rushing

Most Yards Game:	159	Paul Robinson, vs Oakland, 1968
Season:	1,023	Paul Robinson, 1968
Career:	2,893	Essex Johnson, 1968-74

Passing

Most TD Passes Game:	4	Greg Cook, vs Houston, 1969
Season:	18	Ken Anderson, 1973 and 1974
Career:	48	Ken Anderson, 1971-74

Receiving

Most TD Passes Game:	3	Bob Trumpy, vs Houston, 1969
	3	Issac Curtis, vs Cleveland, 1973
Season:	9	Bob Trumpy, 1969
	9	Issac Curtis, 1973
Career:	26	Bob Trumpy, 1968-74

Scoring

Most Points Game:	19	Horst Muhlmann, vs Buffalo, 1970
	19	Horst Muhlmann, vs Houston, 1972
Season:	111	Horst Muhlmann, 1972
Career:	549	Horst Muhlmann, 1969-74
Most TDs Game:	3	Bob Trumpy, vs Houston, 1969
	3	Issac Curtis, vs Cleveland, 1973
	3	Paul Robinson, vs Miami, 1968
	3	Doug Dressler, vs Houston, 1972
Season:	9	Bob Trumpy, 1969
	9	Issac Curtis, 1973
Career:	26	Bob Trumpy, 1968-74

Bob Trumpy's 26 career TDs are a Bengals team record.

HOUSTON OILERS

TEAM DIRECTORY: Pres.: K.S. (Bud) Adams; VP-Treas.: L. Wayne Fisher; GM-Head Coach: O.A. Phillips; Asst. GM: Tom Williams; Dir. Scouting: Joe Madro; Dir. Pub. Rel.: Jim McLemore; Trainer: Charlie Henry. Home: Astrodome, Houston, Texas (50,000).

Dan Pastorini threw 10 TD passes, best of his career.

SCOUTING REPORT

OFFENSE: The unit that will determine how many jokes are made involving the name of the Oilers' new coach. O.A. (Bum)

Phillips. In his legacy from Sid Gillman, Phillips will find the seeds of either his fruition or destruction. While the Oilers called their 1974 highlight film, "Turnaround," their mid-year about-face and dramatic march to the .500 level (7-7) was primarily the product of the defense. Flaws in the offense weren't entirely corrected by what Gillman called "the best draft we've had in years."

Don Hardeman brings more muscle to a running attack that primarily needs quickness. But there were some offensive line prospects culled from the field and the Oilers could get guard Booker Brown, now free of his WFL obligations.

Still, the upgrading must come at the so-called skill positions. Quarterback Dan Pastorini, for all of his talent, has yet to become a respected NFL quarterback because he lacks consistency. There are a slew of journeyman backs, but no standout. Which could be said of the pass receivers were it not for little Billy Johnson. If his stamina improves (he's 5-8 and 165), Johnson has the speed to be a game-breaker.

The offensive line is comprised of people named Elbert Drungo, but in the second half it became a cohesive unit on the ground and started protecting the passer on odd occasions. If the turnaround is to continue, however, the Oilers will need another good draft.

DEFENSE: Who'd have thunk it? The Oilers playing good D? Yup. Good enough to give up 146 fewer points than they had the previous year. Much of the credit is given to Curly Culp. He came from Kansas City and moved into the middle of a three-man line that played the run particularly tough. And, lo, there came a pass rush that produced 40 sacks, second to Pittsburgh in the AFC.

When teams went outside, the Oiler linebackers, all four, were harsh tacklers. The key was Gregg Bingham finally learning to play the middle, but Steve Kiner, Al Cowlings and Dave Washington proved able against the run. A secondary sharply criticized for its inability to handle the medium-range pass suddenly could, and for a change, owner Bud Adams didn't fire the coach when the season ended (Gillman quit).

In 1975, the Oiler defense should keep coming on. Rookie linebacker Bob Brazile is a quick, strong talent who will start and Jess O'Neal is a typical Grambling defensive tackle. Which means he'll start, too. He wasn't drafted in the first two rounds because a knee injury cost him his last six games as a senior, but at Grambling not even All-American DT Gary Johnson was more respected.

OILERS VETERANS ROSTER

HEAD COACH—O.A. "Bum" Phillips. Assistant Coaches—King Hill, Andy Bourgeois, Sam Boghosian, Fran Polsfoot, Glen Ray Hines, Ed Biles, Richie Petitbon, George Rice, Larry Peccatiello, Joe Madro

No.	Name	Pos.	Ht.	Wt.	NFL Exp.	College
19	Alexander, Willie	CB	6-3	190	5	Alcorn A&M
82	Alston, Mack	TE	6-3	230	6	Maryland State
12	Amundson, George	RB	6-3	215	3	Iowa State
48	Atkins, Bob	S	6-3	210	8	Grambling
50	Babinecz, John	LB	6-1	222	4	Villanova
52	Benson, Duane	LB	6-2	218	9	Hamline
65	Bethea, Elvin	DE	6-2	255	8	North Carolina A&T
4	Beverly, David	P	6-2	180	2	Auburn
54	Bingham, Gregg	LB	6-1	230	3	Purdue
00	Burrough, Ken	WR	6-3	210	6	Texas Southern
2	Butler, Skip	K	6-0	200	5	Texas-Arlington
63	Carroll, Ronnie	G	6-2	265	2	Sam Houston State
47	Coleman, Ronnie	RB	5-10	195	2	Alabama A&M
76	Cowlings, Al	LB	6-5	245	6	South California
78	Culp, Curley	G	6-1	265	8	Arizona State
58	Davis, Marvin	LB	6-4	235	2	Southern
10	Dickey, Lynn	QB	6-4	210	5	Kansas State
75	Drungo, Elbert	T	6-4	265	7	Tennessee State
70	Fisher, Ed	C	6-3	245	2	Arizona State
11	Foote, James	QB	6-2	210	2	Delaware Valley
—	Ford, Charley	CB	6-3	195	5	Houston
69	Freelon, Solomon	G	6-2	249	4	Grambling
68	Goodman, Brian	G	6-2	250	3	UCLA
36	Gresham, Bobby	RB	5-11	195	5	West Virginia
53	Hoaglin, Fred	C	6-4	250	10	Pittsburgh
72	Hunt, Kevin	T	6-5	260	4	Doane
15	Johnson, Al	S	6-0	200	4	Cincinnati
84	Johnson, Billy	WR	5-9	170	2	Widener
61	Jones, Harris	G	6-4	245	4	Johnson C. Smith
57	Kiner, Steve	LB	6-1	220	5	Tennessee
51	Lou, Ron	C	6-2	235	3	Arizona State
32	Lumpkin, Ron	DB	6-2	197	2	Arizona State
42	Maxwell, Tommy	S	6-2	195	7	Texas A&M
71	McCollum, Bubba	G	6-0	250	2	Kentucky
24	Montgomery, Mike	WR	6-3	210	5	Kansas State
22	Moore, Zeke	CB	6-3	196	9	Lincoln
20	Parks, Billy	WR	6-1	190	5	Cal State-Long Beach
7	Pastorini, Dan	QB	6-3	205	5	Santa Clara
46	Queen, Jeff	TE	6-1	217	7	Morgan State
56	Roberts, Guy	LB	6-1	217	4	Maryland
34	Rodgers, Willie	RB	6-1	210	4	Kentucky State
73	Sampson, Greg	T	6-6	260	4	Stanford
64	Saul, Ron	G	6-2	255	6	Michigan State
45	Severson, Jeff	S	6-0	185	4	Cal State-Long Beach
31	Simpson, Mike	DB	5-9	170	6	Houston
77	Smith, Sid	C	6-4	260	6	USC
85	Smith, Tody	DE	6-5	250	5	USC
88	Stroud, Morris	TE	6-10	285	7	Clark College
77	Thomas, Lee	DE	6-6	245	5	Jackson State
59	Washington, Ted	LB	6-1	240	2	Mississippi Valley
23	Washington, Vic	RB	5-10	196	5	Wyoming
41	Wells, Terence	RB	5-11	195	2	Southern Mississippi
79	White, Jim	DE	6-4	255	3	Colorado State
38	Whittington, C.L.	S	6-1	200	2	Prairie View A&M
44	Willis, Fred	RB	6-0	205	5	Boston College

TOP FIVE DRAFT CHOICES

Rd.	Name	Pos.	Ht.	Wt.	Age	College
1	Robert Brazile	LB	6-4	230	22	Jackson State
1	Don Hardeman	RB	6-2	230	23	Texas A&I
2	Emmett Edwards	WR	6-1	187	23	Kansas
6	Jesse O'Neal	DE	6-3	240	23	Grambling
7	Mike Biehle	T	6-4	255	22	Miami

HOUSTON OILERS 41

KICKING GAME: Might be described as mediocre were it not for Johnson, probably the finest all-around return man in the game. Punter Dave Beverly, a rookie, hits them short but high. Skip Butler, who did the placekicking, doesn't hit them enough (9 of 19 field goal tries). Pastorini is a fine punter, but has a tendency to pull leg muscles and the Oilers won't use him.

OUTLOOK: If Adams keeps his nose out of the coach's office, and Phillips helps instead of hinders, the improvement should maintain a steady pace. This is a club fraught with no-names, but last year many of them played as though trying to acquire a reputation. There isn't enough offensive talent, but the defense now knows it can play and that could make all the difference. Another good shot at .500.

OILER PROFILES

DAN PASTORINI 26 6-2½ 205   **Quarterback**

Outstanding credential may be wife, June Wilkinson, busty onetime Playboy centerfold ... In danger of becoming perennial rose-that-never-blooms ... Emotional. Cried so often after Oiler defeats that someone said "he almost drowns himself" ... Brilliant pure skills, still needs to mature as play-caller ... Ranked fifth in AFC quarterback ratings ... Threw less in 1974, completed more, fewer interceptions ... Real name is Dante; called Pasta by teammates ... Born May 26, 1949, in Sonora, Calif. ... Outstanding high school baseball player, drafted by New York Mets ... Had weight problems but was still small-college All-America at Santa Clara ... Stubborness often brought clashes last year with departed Oiler GM Sid Gillman.

BILLY PARKS 27 6-1 190   **Wide Receiver**

Team recluse and paradox nonpareil ... Cordial, but won't sign autographs; pleasant to reporters, won't be interviewed. Perfectionist, but never catches with two hands unless absolutely necessary ... Had mediocre year in 1975 when 20 receptions placed him fifth on club after he caught 43 balls the previous season ... Born Jan. 1, 1948, in Long

Beach, Calif.... Outspoken anti-NFL man... Avid back-packer and boating enthusiast in off-season... Committed environmentalist who shuns motor vehicles whenever possible and rides bike to practice... Called a "truly fascinating guy" by one Houston writer... 79 catches as a junior at Cal State Long Beach ... Paradox as receiver, too. Marginal speed and moves, unmuscular, slightly paunchy, but has Hall of Fame hands that are probably best in the game... Statistically, always has 40-plus year following poor season.

LYNN DICKEY 26 6-3½ 210   Quarterback

Now healthy after one of guttier comebacks in game's history... Out 15 months after suffering dislocated hip during 1972 exhibition game, which reportedly would've crippled him permanently had Oiler doctor not put it in place on field... Rep for throwing percentage pass to keep average up, but still considered outstanding prospect... Labors under dual handicaps of injury and playing behind Dan Pastorini... Says "I'm fine technically," but slower in setting up ... Doesn't force pass, as Pastorini does... Had one of poorer quarterback ratings in AFC for a backup man... Born Oct. 19, 1949, in Paola, Kan.... High school stadium named for him... Greatest passer in Big Eight history while at Kansas State... Excellent quarterback mechanic.

STEVE KINER 28 6-1 220   Linebacker

NFL's answer to Marco Polo after revealing he had bad drug problem... Been with four different clubs (New England twice)... Called "The Original Flake" by Oilers, but not popular with teammates... Excellent against run, sieve against pass because of poor mobility... Strong side inside LB in four-man Houston setup... Wild man right before and after games... Born June 12, 1947, in Sandstone, Minn.... Says he's "leading the redemptive life" and evidence supports claim... One of last of the high-top shoe men... Wears tennis shoes and jeans on road trips; disdains coat in any weather... One of league's most quotable players... Two-time consensus All-American at Tennessee and once called by Albama's Bear Bryant "the finest linebacker in the SEC since LeRoy Jordan."

HOUSTON OILERS 43

KEN BURROUGH 27 6-3 210   **Wide Receiver**

Generally considered Oilers' chief hot dog (00 uniform number; taped wrists; Continental with "Ken—00" plates, etc.) ... Oilers' top receiver with 36 receptions which placed him 14th in AFC ... Lives in penthouse suite ... Deceptive stride and 4.4 speed make him excellent deep threat, but doesn't like that role ... More comfortable with hooks, I-cuts and other short stuff ... Courage is questioned by league's defensive backs and doesn't catch well over the middle ... Rep has it that teams try to belt him early in game, after which he can safely be forgotten ... Born June 14, 1948, in Jacksonville, Fla. ... Caught 138 passes at Texas Southern ... No. 1 draft pick of New Orleans in 1970; traded to Oilers for draft choice and three stiffs.

RONNIE COLEMAN 24 5-10 195   **Running Back**

One of few bright spots in a Houston offense that wouldn't have been threatening in the Lone Star Conference, and totaled less yards rushing (1,361) than individual leader Otis Armstrong ... Respectable 3.7 average noteworthy considering Oiler offensive line ... Houston's flashiest dresser ... Hampered by failure to remember assignments ... May have led league in blown plays ... Won't wear regulation NFL socks—orders his from alma mater, Florida A&M ... Free agent rookie in 1974; given new contract when he surprisingly made team.

BILLY JOHNSON 23 5-8 165   **Wide Receiver**

Along with Curly Culp, man most responsible for Oilers' turnabout in 1974 ... Caught 39 passes to rank second on club to Burrough and 25th in AFC ... "He might be the most dangerous player in the league," says Steeler coach Chuck Noll ... Fifth in NFL in kickoff returns (27.1), seventh in punt returns (13.6) ... A 15th-round draft pick in 1974, he scored a touchdown every 7.7 times he touched ball at Widener (Pa.) College ... Lack of stamina slows him down in fourth quarter ... Down to 160 at times last year ... Most popular Oiler with teammates, who made him club MVP, and fans ... A 9.5

44 THE COMPLETE HANDBOOK OF PRO FOOTBALL

sprinter but had usual rookie problems getting off line ... Says "my size isn't a handicap," but it is ... Does rubber-knee dance in end-zone ... Fearless receiver over the middle.

CURLY CULP 29 6-1 265 — Defensive Tackle

Called Mystery Man by Oilers, who acquired him in a summer trade with Kansas City, where he'd been warring with the departed Hank Stram ... Signed with Southern California of WFL, but isn't going ... Averted a disaster for Oilers, who had committed to a three-man defensive line and were getting nothing from two rookies in the middle until he appeared and performed brilliantly all year ... Big help to end Tody Smith, and his play noticeably subdued and made better player of the other end and noted malcontent, Elvin Bethea ... Born March 10, 1946, in Yuma, Ariz. ... One of game's most underrated stars ... Denver's No. 2 pick in 1970 ... NCAA heavyweight wrestling champion at Arizona State and named to 1968 Olympic team ... Drives $16,000 Mercedes.

ELVIN BETHEA 29 6-3 255 — Defensive End

Big E ... Makes $88,000 and thinks he's underpaid ... Probably right, as he is one of game's premier DEs ... Had 17 of Oilers' 27 sacks in 1973 ... Proverbial griper, but always performs. Played in 112 straight Oiler games and never missed one with injury ... Called Animal by Oilers ... Has passion for recognition and fought unceasingly with Gillman: "We don't even talk; we avoid each other" ... Avid motorcyclist and tries to hide it from coaches ... Born March 1, 1946, in Trenton, N.J. ... Started as guard with Oilers after being drafter third in 1968 out of North Carolina A&T ... Pro Bowler for fourth straight year ... One of game's fine pass rushers.

GREGG BINGHAM 24 6-1 230 — Linebacker

One of league's larger egos ... Wanted to play in Houston, where father owns auto dealership, and was outright steal in fourth round of 1973 draft ... Reputed swinger who owns pieces of several Houston nightspots ... Says "my philosophy of life is to get eight hours sleep a night, or day" ... Born March 13, 1951, in Chicago, and been living it up ever since ... Middle guard in five-man line at Purdue—128 unassisted tackles as junior—which hurt him as pro ... Poor on the pass as rookie—"you got to the Oilers through him," says an AFC quarterback—but greatly improved in 1974 ... Super quick and will absorb block and then make tackle ... Pass-coverage ability makes up for Steve Kiner's inability.

TOP ROOKIES

ROBERT BRAZILE 22 6-4 230　　　　　　　　**Linebacker**
First team on most All-American squads ... Described as "Mr. Versatile" at Jackson State, where he started three years as LB ... Runs 40 in 4.6 ... Averaged more than 20 tackles a game ... Had super senior year—leading conference with nine interceptions and 208 tackles.

DON HARDEMAN 22 6-2 230　　　　　　　　**Running Back**
Could be sleeper of 1975 draft ... Only question is lack of experience at position ... Played fullback for first time as senior and led Texas A&I to NAIA team rushing title with 1,547 yards on 216 carries ... Linebacker first two years and led team in tackles ... Could play there as pro.

COACH BUM PHILLIPS ... Poorly-named since he was responsible in large part for Houston turn-around last year ... Sid Gillman protege and with him entire pro career ... Faces problems of all Houston head men after replacing Gillman, which is to say owner Bud Adams, who has changed coaches eight times in 14 years ... Highly-successful Texas schoolboy coach before moving into college ranks as an assistant at Texas A&M, Houston, SMU and Oklahoma State ... Defensive coordinator of Oilers last year and unit made fine breakthrough last half of season to propel Houston to 7-7 record ... Quiet, oldtime disciplinarian ... Comes into job at ideal moment since Oilers seem on verge of becoming contender if offense can catch defense.

CLUB HISTORY

The question here is: How could anything that started out so right end up so wrong? Well, about anything can happen to a club owned by K.S. (Bud) Adams, an oil tycoon who uses the Houston Oilers as a toy.

Adams has made nine coaching changes in the Oilers' 15 seasons, highlighted by firing Lou Rymkus in 1961 and then watching team win its second straight AFL title.

The Oilers were tough in the early 1960s, playing in the first three AFL championship games. Only Bud couldn't keep his hands off the operation and it sank lower than one of his oil wells.

There followed eight losing seasons in 11 years, culminated when Oilers managed to lose 18 straight. Left were only memories of George Blanda and Billy Cannon and Charlie Hennigan. And futuristic glimpses of Elvin Bethea and Dan Pastorini.

Uncle Sid Gillman got it turned around last year, 7-7, but how long can Bud Adams tolerate success?

INDIVIDUAL OILER RECORDS

Rushing
Most Yards Game:	216	Billy Cannon, vs New York, 1961
Season:	1,194	Hoyle Granger, 1967
Career:	3,339	Hoyle Granger, 1966-70

Passing
Most TD Passes Game:	7	George Blanda, vs New York, 1961
Season:	36	George Blanda, 1961
Career:	189	George Blanda, 1960-66

Receiving
Most TD Passes Game:	3	Bill Groman, vs New York, 1960 and 1961
	3	Billy Cannon, vs New York, 1961
	3	Charlie Hennigan, vs San Diego, 1961
	3	Charlie Hennigan, vs Buffalo, 1963
	3	Willie Frazier, vs New York, 1965
	3	Charles Frazier, vs Denver, 1966 (twice)
Season:	17	Bill Groman, 1961
Career:	51	Charles Hennigan, 1960-66

Scoring
Most Points Game:	30	Billy Cannon, vs New York, 1961
Season:	115	George Blanda, 1960 (4 TD-46PATS-15 FG)
Career:	596	George Blanda, 1960 (4 TD-299 PATS-91 FG)
Most TDs Game:	5	Billy Cannon, vs New York, 1961
Season:	18	Bill Groman, 1961
Career:	51	Charles Hennigan, 1960-66

CLEVELAND BROWNS

TEAM DIRECTORY: Pres.: Art Modell; VP Player Pers.: Robert Nussbaumer; VP Dir. Pub. Rel.: Nathan Wallack; Pub. Mgr. & Asst. to Pres.: Ed Uhas; Dir. Pro Scouting: Dick Evans; Dir. College Scouting: Mike Nixon; Head Coach: Forrest Gregg; Trainer: Leo Murphy. Home: Cleveland Stadium, Cleveland, Ohio (80,228).

Greg Pruitt led Browns in rushing and receiving.

SCOUTING REPORT

OFFENSE: The Browns without an offense? Jack Benny without his violin? Raquel Welch without her decolletage? Sure

48 THE COMPLETE HANDBOOK OF PRO FOOTBALL

'nuff. The Browns had, and probably will have, two major problems—throwing the football, stopping the other guys from running with it. Quarterback Mike Phipps lost his job last year to somebody named Brian Sipe because he couldn't rid himself of enchantment with the bomb.

"He looks deep first and that's not the way to do it," says a Brown assistant. Phipps and Sipe produced the next-to-lousiest pass offense in the AFC and the Browns couldn't find a power back to offset that handicap. Now, in the tradition of Jim Brown and Leroy Kelly comes, well, Billy Pritchett. A 240-pounder, Pritchett missed his rookie season because of a calcium deposit on his thigh. Phipps' passing should improve if for no other reason than the Browns traded for a wide receiver to help Steve Holden. Reggie Rucker, late of New England, gives the Browns two.

Write off the tight end spot. Milt Morin is slowing. A more mobile offensive line, which will be shaken up with the return from an injury of Pete Adams, could open up the outside for Greg Pruitt. But he still hasn't proven he can take the pounding over a long haul.

DEFENSE: Long live rookie end Mack Mitchell. The search is over and the Browns finally have a pass-rusher to go along with superb tackle Jerry Sherk. What they don't have is a tackle to replace Walter Johnson, who had a bad year and was one reason why Cleveland had fewer sacks than all but one AFC club. Mitchell, a 6-8 demon rusher, will take over a position in which the Browns have used 13 players in the last two seasons. He will also take some heat off the linebackers. Bob Babich is set in the middle and John Garlington is strong and quick on one side. Opposite him, Charlie Hall gets hurt by the pass and is usually worked over by opposing teams.

The secondary is strong at safety and at one corner. At the other is Van Green, a hitter who plays it recklessly and gets beaten like a drum. One of new coach Forrest Gregg's first jobs will be to shore up the defense, which probably cost Nick Skorich his job.

KICKING GAME: Don Cockroft is the league's only punter-placekicker and does both jobs admirably, missing only two FGs last year. Pruitt led the league in kickoff returns and is solid on punts. Not so solid is the Browns' coverage.

OUTLOOK: Key to the season will be Gregg, who must motivate a team that lost its confidence last year and hung up a 4-10

BROWNS VETERANS ROSTER

HEAD COACH—Forrest Gregg. Assistant Coaches—Blanton Collier, George Sefcik, Doug Gerhart, Rod Humenuik, Richie McCabe, Dick Modzelewski, Walt Carey, Al Tabor

No.	Name	Pos.	Ht.	Wt.	NFL Exp.	College
69	Adams, Pete	G	6-4	260	2	Southern California
40	Anderson, Preston	S	6-1	183	2	Rice
60	Babich, Bob	LB	6-2	231	6	Miami, Ohio
74	Barisich, Carl	DT	6-4	255	3	Princeton
64	Beams, Jeff	G	6-2	245	1	Ohio U.
23	Brooks, Clifford	CB	6-1	182	4	Tennessee State
28	Brown, Eddie	S	5-11	185	2	Tennessee
30	Brown, Ken	RB	5-10	203	6	None
12	Cockroft, Don	K	6-1	195	8	Adams State
16	Cureton, Will	QB	6-3	200	1	E. Texas State
27	Darden, Thom	S	6-2	193	4	Michigan
63	Darrow, Barry	T	6-7	260	2	Montana
54	DeLeone, Tom	C	6-2	248	4	Ohio State
61	DeMarco, Bob	C	6-2	248	15	Dayton
65	Demarie, John	G	6-3	248	9	Louisiana State
73	Dieken, Doug	T	6-5	252	5	Illinois
50	Garlington, John	LB	6-1	221	8	Louisiana State
10	Gartner, Chris	K	6-0	168	2	Indiana
82	George, Tim	WR	6-5	210	3	Carson-Newman
21	Green, Van	S	6-1	192	3	Shaw U.
59	Hall, Charlie	LB	6-3	230	5	Houston
42	Hepburn, Lonnie	CB	5-11	180	4	Texas Southern
88	Holden, Steve	WR	6-0	194	3	Arizona State
62	Holloway, Glen	G	6-3	250	6	N. Texas State
67	Hutchison, Chuck	G	6-3	250	5	Ohio State
77	Ilgenfritz, Mark	DT	6-4	254	2	Vanderbilt
71	Johnson, Walter	DT	6-4	265	11	California State (L.A.)
26	Lefear, Billy	WR	5-11	197	4	Henderson State
53	Long, Mel	LB	6-1	228	4	Toledo
57	McClowry, Bob	C	6-3	245	1	Michigan State
99	McDaniel, Mike	C	6-2	235	1	Kansas
78	McKay, Bob	T-G	6-5	265	6	Texas
37	McKinnis, Hugh	RB	6-1	219	3	Arizona State
89	Morin, Milt	TE	6-4	240	10	Massachusetts
15	Phipps, Mike	QB	6-3	205	6	Purdue
13	Polke, Ken	QB	6-0	190	1	Dayton
39	Pritchett, Billy	RB	6-3	230	1	W. Texas State
34	Pruitt, Greg	RB	5-10	190	3	Oklahoma
56	Romaniszyn, Jim	LB	6-2	224	3	Edinboro State
80	Rucker, Reggie	WR	6-2	190	6	Boston, U.
22	Scott, Clarence	CB	6-0	180	5	Kansas State
35	Scott, Robert (Bo)	RB	6-3	215	7	Ohio State
66	Seifert, Mike	DE	6-3	250	2	Wisconsin
72	Sherk, Jerry	DT	6-4	250	6	Oklahoma State
17	Sipe, Brian	QB	6-1	190	2	San Diego State
85	Smith, Ken	TE	6-4	225	2	New Mexico
48	Sullivan, Dave	WR	5-11	185	2	Virginia
79	Sullivan, Gerry	T	6-4	250	2	Illinois
29	Sumner, Walt	S	6-1	190	7	Florida State
31	Williams, Eddie	RB	5-11	215	1	West Virginia

TOP FIVE DRAFT CHOICES

Rd.	Name	Pos.	Ht.	Wt.	Age	College
1	Mack Mitchell	DE	6-7	240	22	Houston
3	Oscar Roan	WR	6-5	215	24	Southern Methodist
4	Tony Peters	CB	6-1	185	22	Oklahoma
5	John Zimba	DE	6-4	246	22	Villanova
5	Jim Cope	LB	6-1	234	22	Ohio State

50 THE COMPLETE HANDBOOK OF PRO FOOTBALL

record, poorest in club's proud history. He was slow organizing a staff and that will hurt. Ex-head coach Blanton Collier was dragged back from retirement to work with Phipps and that should help. Overall, though, the club lacks talent in the wrong places, faces a hard schedule and is playing in the best division in the league.

BROWN PROFILES

MILT MORIN 33 6-4 235   Tight End

World's toughest antique dealer... Alas, probably not swiftest and that cost him his job on and off during 1974 season to Jim Thaxton... Still, his 27 catches put him in the AFC's top 35 receivers and there were only six tight ends ahead of him... Has among "softest" hands in business... Called "Peaches" because of ability to pull down pass... Tough, durable ... Says "I know on certain pass routes over the middle that I'm going to get killed," but specializes in that catch... Born Oct. 15, 1942, in Leominster, Mass.... First-round pick in 1966 after fine career at UMass.... Very tough on strong safeties. "I try to make it a physical thing," he says... Injury problems his first few years (foot, knee, back) but now is able to play with hurts ... Owns Cape Cod gift shop.

BOB BABICH 28 6-2 230   Middle Linebacker

One of few strong performers on a defense that resembled the Siegfried Line... Plugged hole in the middle that Cleveland had been trying to fill for a decade when Browns got him from San Diego for first and second round draft picks... "He's our big answer against the run," coach Nick Skorich said at the time, a bit optimistically as it turned out ... Skorich was canned last January after Browns finished next-to-last in NFL against run, but it was no fault of Babich's... Quick and strongest Brown with 450-pound bench press... "He's fantastic," said teammate Bob Briggs. "Backs don't drive him; he bends them over on their backs"... Born May 5, 1947, in Youngstown, O.... Used outside by San Diego, which drafted him out of Miami (O.) in 1970... "I wasted my time playing the outside; I'm better suited for the middle and the outside is dull," says Babich.

CLEVELAND BROWNS 51

DON COCKROFT 30 6-1 195   Kicker

One of few pro kickers not regarded as flaky ... Key to an offense that ranked 20th in the NFL ... Led league in field goal percentage for second straight season (14 of 16) ... Only specialist in pros to handle both punting and placekicking ... "There's a lot of satisfaction in knowing I'm doing something no one else is," he says ... Writing a book called "Second Chance." Title comes from getting another opportunity to beat Steelers in 1973 after blowing chip shot in last three minutes ... Deep involvement in Fellowship of Christian Athletes caused him to quit as club player rep ... Turned career around after horrible 1971 season when "I learned to relax, not get as tied up in what I was doing" ... Streaky punter, but hangs ball well.

THOM DARDEN 25 6-2 195   Cornerback

No real speed or size; can't do anything but play ... "When I was in high school, they said I was too slow and too small to play in the Big Ten; in college, they said I was too slow and too small for the pros," he sighs. "If you know the game, you can play" ... Darden knows the game and at free safety is the steadiest man in a weak secondary ... Third in NFL with eight interceptions ... Club player rep ... Born Aug. 28, 1950, in Sandusky, O. ... Consensus All-American in 1971 at Michigan and Browns' top pick ... Starter ever since ... Tough against run ... "Thom's a real hitter and he has all the equipment," said Browns' assistant Richie McCabe ... Real estate broker.

STEVE HOLDEN 24 6-½ 200   Wide Receiver

Nightmare turned bedtime story ... Horrible rookie year in 1973 when he caught only three passes—in last game—after being a No. 1 draft choice. Caught 30 last year despite missing six games with a bum knee and only 12 AFC wide receivers caught more ... "Sitting on the bench as a rookie didn't make me mad, but it did make me think," he says ... What he has to think about this year is pass patterns, which he runs with the deftness of a spastic giraffe ... Browns almost gave up on him; now regard him as their only deep threat ... Born Aug.

2, 1951, in Los Angeles... Two-time All-American at Arizona State... Extrovert... Aspiring actor.

JOHN DEMARIE 30 6-3 245   Guard

Called one of league's more competent guards by no less an authority than Pittsburgh's Joe Greene... Hampered last three years by chronic shoulder injury and blocked most of 1974 with left shoulder... Playing hurt champ... May shift to center this year, with Bob McKay moving to his guard... Very versatile; in 1972 played three different positions... Lacked strength until got on weight program two years ago... Born Aug. 28, 1945, in Oxnard, Calif.... Defensive lineman at LSU... One of steadiest pass protectors on an offensive line so porous that Browns were sacked more often than all but two other teams in league.

GREG PRUITT 24 5-10 190   Running Back

The one they call The Franchise—with excellent reason... Led club in rushing (540 yards, 4.3 average) and receiving (21 receptions and 13.0 average)... Fourth in league in kickoff returns with 27.6 average... Sixth in AFC in punt returns... Oh, yeah, and he threw two passes for 119 yards and (what else?) two touchdowns... Says center Bob DeMarco, "He makes blocking fun. All he needs is a shield and he's gone"... Fine 4.5 speed; a stripper's moves... Will be used more this year as a receiver... Born Aug. 18, 1951, in Houston... Heisman runnerup in 1972 at Oklahoma, where he drove a car that had "Super Sport" lettered in gold-leaf across trunk... Journalism major... Was 4-3½ going into junior high school... Has gold tooth in omnipresent smile.

MIKE PHIPPS 27 6-3 205   Quarterback

Tarnished golden boy... Regressed last year and lost job at end of season to somebody named Brian Sipe... Has had two quarterback coaches in two years and word is he won't take advice... Overly preoccupied with the bomb with result has one of poorest completion averages (45.7) in league... Will be tutored by ex-Browns' head coach Blanton

CLEVELAND BROWNS 53

Collier, who developed Otto Graham and Frank Ryan, among others... "If that doesn't work, nothing will," says insider... Born Nov. 19, 1951, in Shelbyville, Ind.... Second in Heisman voting as Purdue All-American.. Will be pressed by Sipe and doesn't have Browns' confidence... "You earn loyalty by showing them you can win," he says... Hasn't done it yet... Throws to backs too much... Doesn't have much help anywhere on offense... Club president Art Modell still in his corner: "Nothing that's happened has convinced me he won't be a premier quarterback."

JERRY SHERK 27 6-4½ 255 — Defensive Tackle

Described as "our defensive line" by Cleveland football writer... Terribly underrated... "You hear all that talk about Joe Greene of Pittsburgh, but the attention should be going to Jerry," said ex-Brown coach Nick Skorich... Under constant pressure last three years because Browns haven't had decent end play (they've tried 14 different ends in three seasons)... Great lateral movement... Born July 7, 1948, in Grants Pass, Ore.... Excellent pass rusher... "You like to see the quarterbacks get up slow and sort of shake their head as they go back to the huddle," he says... Pro Bowl choice last two seasons... Big Eight heavyweight wrestling champion at Oklahoma State in 1970... Quiet, likeable... Always double-teamed last three years.

CLARENCE SCOTT 26 6-0 180 — Cornerback

Like AT&T stock, one of league's more dependable cornermen... "The most consistent member of our secondary," said Skorich... Starter since second quarter of first exhibition game his rookie season... Born April 9, 1949, in Atlanta... First round pick out of Kansas State in 1971 and a pro bowler in second pro season... Seals the corner particularly well against run... Says "tackling those backs isn't as bad as the average person thinks. Actually, I inflict more damage on them than they do on me"... Rather frail, but ever the hitter... Quiet but popular among Browns... Voted outstanding player of 1973 by Brown fans... Opposing teams discovered weakness on other side and quit throwing at him early last season.

54 THE COMPLETE HANDBOOK OF PRO FOOTBALL

TOP ROOKIES

MACK MITCHELL 23 6-8 250 Defensive End
Sure-pop starter for a team with big need at DE... Biggest virtue is pass rush and that's why Browns drafted him first... Had 13 sacks as a junior... Has super leverage... Played varsity basketball at Houston as sophomore... Played almost every minute during junior and senior football seasons... Rated one of three best DEs in draft.

OSCAR ROAN 22 6-6 215 Tight End
Skinnier than a test tube and because of it will probably wind up as a receiver... 4.6 speed, extra-special hands... Good college blocker but it's a question in pros... Played basketball at SMU... Was a transfer student from UCLA... A good third-round choice who may succeed aging Milt Morin... Had 3.2 average in school.

COACH FORREST GREGG... Replaces the canned Nick Skorich, who succumbed when quarterback Mike Phipps went sour... A 42-year-old all-time Packer great... Made all-pro eight times during Lombardi era and regarded as inspirational player... An assistant his last two seasons with Pack and in 1973 and '74 with San Diego... Faces handful of problems with Browns, not the least of which will be that he never was a Brown on a club that is very provincial... Will have to solve QB headache and rebuild old, tired offense... Along with keeping owner Art Modell in the front office... Will probably be given time to accomplish task.

CLUB HISTORY

He was small and smart and ill-tempered and demanding, but Paul Brown made the Browns and, if you are over 30, they somehow remain his. Which must gall present owner Art Modell, who fired Brown in 1962. But before he left, victim of a player rebellion, Paul Brown had led Cleveland to four consecutive All-America Conference championships, three NFL titles and a 10-year dominance of whatever conference the Browns happened to be in.

Further, he had found and driven to greatness such as Otto Graham, Marion Motley, Mac Speedie (has a receiver ever been better named?), Lou Groza, Jim Brown, Leroy Kelly and dozens of lesser lights.

Modell, too, has known achievement. Since he bought control of the club, Browns have won one NFL crown and three conference titles.

Now, though, he presides over mediocrity. Which must warm Paul Brown's heart.

INDIVIDUAL BROWN RECORDS

Rushing

Most Yards Game:	237	Jim Brown, vs Los Angeles, 1957
	237	Jim Brown, vs Philadelphia, 1961
Season:	1,863	Jim Brown, 1963
Career:	12,312	Jim Brown, 1957-65

Passing

Most TD Passes Game:	5	Frank Ryan, vs N.Y. Giants, 1964
	5	Bill Nelsen, vs Dallas, 1969
Season:	29	Frank Ryan, 1966
Career:	134	Frank Ryan, 1962-68

Receiving

Most TD Passes Game:	3	Mac Speedie, vs Chicago, 1951
	3	Darrell Brewster, vs N.Y. Giants, 1953
	3	Ray Renfro, vs Pittsburgh, 1959
	3	Gary Collins, vs Philadelphia, 1963
Season:	13	Gary Collins, 1963
Career:	70	Gary Collins, 1962-71

Scoring

Most Points Game:	36	Dub Jones, vs Chicago, 1951
Season:	126	Jim Brown, 1965
Career:	1,349	Lou Groza, 1950-59, 1961-67
Most TDs Game:	6	Dub Jones, vs Chicago, 1951
Season:	21	Jim Brown, 1965
Career:	126	Jim Brown, 1957-65

MIAMI DOLPHINS

TEAM DIRECTORY: Pres.-GM: Joseph Robbie; VP-Head Coach: Don Shula; VP: Philip Butler; Sec.-Treas.: Elizabeth Robbie; Dir. Player Pers.: Robert Beathard; Pub. Dir: Charles Callahan; P.R. Dir.: Beano Cook; Dir. Pro. Scouting: Pat Peppler; Trainer: Bob Lundy. Home: Orange Bowl, Miami, Fla. (80,047).

Bob Griese leads Miami offense minus Csonka and Warfield.

SCOUTING REPORT

OFFENSE: No more battering defenders to death with that human bludgeon, Larry Csonka; no more of those cute, little, long-gone slant-ins to Paul Warfield; no more 40-yard gains on those screen flips to Jimmy Kiick. A lot of the Dolphin offense deserted to Memphis of the WFL, and it won't be replaced by an armload of Benny Malones or Marlin Briscoes or Freddie Solomons. But they're what's left, and coach Don Shula will probably make do with them and produce a horrid 9-5 season.

The defectors will alter the Dolphin offense and it will have to depend less on ball-control and more on Merc Morris' sweeps and Bob Griese's arm. And therein lies the rub. Griese is a good passer; not a great one that can carry the club. Morris is a game-breaking, tackle-busting, whiz-bang of a runner, but he ain't Zonk and he gets hurt too badly, too often.

However, the line is still The Line, and without the sort of injuries that reduced its effectiveness a year ago, it means good offense. Malone had the best average on the club a year ago and if Solomon doesn't replace Kiick as a back, he'll be the new Warfield. Shula still has an abundance of talent and out of the ashes will come another playoff contender.

DEFENSE: Due to the above obituary, the No-Names are going to have to crank it up this time around. There will be none of this letting them have the short-pass stuff all day and then yanking them up short inside the 25. Now the Miami defense, that maze of impenetrable zones, must score some points and provide the sort of field position which emanated in the past from Csonka's ramming the tackles. That may be a bit of a problem. The fabled 5-3 defense didn't work as well last year with nose man Manny Fernandez injured and on the bench. People took liberties inside on the Dolphins.

And in the playoffs, Oakland's Ken Stabler found a way to whip the Miami zone, although that sort of accuracy won't often be matched. There is a small problem at linebacker, where middleman Nick Buoniconti is 34 and Doug Swift is on Shula's list and coming off a so-so year. The major problem will remain Shula's. More will be asked of the Dolphin defense this year and adjustments will have to be made. How well they are made will determine how badly Csonka & Co. are missed.

KICKING GAME: Anyone got a necktie Garo Ypremian can hang himself with? Ypremian probably considered it last year, when he went 8-for-15 on field goals and caused Shula to gamble

DOLPHINS VETERANS ROSTER

HEAD COACH—Don Shula. Assistant Coaches—Monte Clark, Howard Schnellenberger, Don Doll, Thomas Keane, Michael Scarry, Carl Taseff

No.	Name	Pos.	Ht.	Wt.	NFL Exp.	College
40	Anderson, Dick	S	6-2	196	8	Colorado
—	Anderson, Donny	RB	6-2	215	10	Texas Tech
49	Babb, Charlie	S	6-0	190	4	Memphis State
82	Baker, Melvin	WR	6-0	192	2	Texas Southern
51	Ball, Larry	LB	6-6	235	4	Louisville
58	Bannon, Bruce	LB	6-3	225	3	Penn State
85	Buoniconti, Nick	LB	5-11	220	14	Notre Dame
74	Crowder, Randy	DT	6-2	236	2	Penn State
77	Crusan, Doug	T	6-4	250	7	Indiana
83	Den Herder, Vern	DE	6-6	252	5	Central Iowa
73	Evans, Norm	T	6-5	250	11	Texas Christian
75	Fernandez, Manny	DT	6-2	250	8	Utah
80	Fleming, Marv	TE	6-4	230	13	Utah
25	Foley, Tim	CB	6-0	194	6	Purdue
70	Funchess, Tom	T	6-5	270	8	Jackson State
55	Goode, Irv	C-G	6-5	262	13	Kentucky
12	Griese, Bob	QB	6-1	190	9	Purdue
72	Heinz, Bob	DT	6-6	265	7	Pacific
45	Johnson, Curtis	CB	6-1	196	6	Toledo
57	Kolen, Mike	LB	6-2	222	6	Auburn
67	Kuechenberg, Bob	T-G	6-2	252	6	Notre Dame
62	Langer, Jim	C	6-2	253	6	South Dakota State
66	Little, Larry	G	6-1	265	9	Bethune-Cookman
32	Malone, Ben	RB	5-10	193	2	Arizona State
88	Mandich, Jim	TE	6-2	224	6	Michigan
53	Matheson, Bob	LB	6-4	235	9	Duke
—	McFarland, Jim	TE	6-5	225	6	Nebraska
65	Moore, Maulty	DT	6-5	265	4	Bethune-Cookman
89	Moore, Nat	WR	5-9	180	2	Florida
79	Moore, Wayne	T	6-6	265	6	Lamar Tech
15	Morrall, Earl	QB	6-2	210	20	Michigan State
22	Morris, Mercury	RB	5-10	192	7	West Texas State
26	Mumphord, Lloyd	CB	5-10	176	7	Texas Southern
64	Newman, Ed	G	6-2	245	3	Duke
36	Nottingham, Don	RB	5-10	210	5	Kent State
76	Reese, Don	DE-DT	6-6	255	2	Jackson State
13	Scott, Jake	S	6-0	188	6	Georgia
20	Seiple, Larry	P-TE	6-0	214	9	Kentucky
84	Stanfill, Bill	DE	6-5	252	7	Georgia
10	Strock, Don	QB	6-5	203	2	Virginia Tech
59	Swift, Doug	LB	6-3	226	6	Amherst
87	Tillman, Andy	TE	6-5	230	1	Texas Tech
81	Twilley, Howard	WR	5-10	185	10	Tulsa
41	White, Jeris	DB	5-11	180	2	Hawaii
60	Wickert, Tom	T	6-3	246	2	Washington State
1	Yepremian, Garo	K	5-8	175	9	None

TOP FIVE DRAFT CHOICES

Rd.	Name	Pos.	Ht.	Wt.	Age	College
1	Darryl Carlton	T	6-5	270	22	Tampa
2	Fred Solomon	RB	5-11	186	22	Tampa
2	Steve Winfrey	RB	5-11	223	22	Arkansas State
3	Gerald Hill	LB	6-0	223	22	Houston
4	Bruce Elia	LB	6-1	222	22	Ohio State

MIAMI DOLPHINS 59

more often on fourth down. Punter Larry Seiple isn't as long as most, but he's higher and straighter than all but a couple and nobody in the AFC covered kicks as well as Miami.

OUTLOOK: It would be foolish to bet against Shula's track record. Twice, he's built championship clubs quickly from zilch, and no one works harder. The Dolphins won't be the same, but they'll be tougher than a cob. Not less; just different.

DOLPHIN PROFILES

NICK BUONICONTI 34 5-11 220   Linebacker

Like the old gray mare and the rest of us, not what he used to be. But still good enough despite fact that age and injuries have slowed him some ... Dolphin defensive alignments allow him to roam and hit; still hits, roams less ... All-league or conference eight of 13 seasons ... Picked on all-time AFL squad ... Dolphin MVP in 1973 when led club in tackles for fifth straight year ... Born Dec. 15, 1940, in Springfield, Mass. ... Practicing attorney in Miami ... Some teams now try to wear him down, throwing into his zone and running up the pipe ... All-American at Notre Dame, where he was a two-way player ... Dolphin defensive captain ... Bright, well-spoken ... Rumor he plans to play only one more year.

MANNY FERNANDEZ 29 6-2 250   Defensive Tackle

Looks like the Frito Bandido, plays like Ghengis Khan ... Injuries benched or restricted him most of year ... Middle guard in Miami's 53 defense takes toll on him ... "There's a tremendous amount of pressure on Fernandez most of the time," says coach Don Shula, "but there wouldn't be if we didn't think he could handle it". . . Offsets lack of size with quickness and good strength ... Fights block as well as any DL in league ... Irreverent type ... Says "I play as well as anyone; I just don't get the ink" ... Born July 3, 1946, in San Lorenzo, Calif. ... Free agent from Utah, where he had rep as hard to handle ... Free spirit ... Usually second to Buoniconti in tackles and assists ... Should have been MVP of Super Bowl VII when he destroyed Redskins ... Pro Bowl in 1974.

BOB GRIESE 30 6-1 190　　　　　　　　　　　Quarterback

Still looks boyish in Sears TV ads but now a polished veteran ... Coming off average season in which he finished eighth in league in passing because of high interception rate (5.9 per cent) ... One of the best play-callers, although occasionally criticized by league people for being overly conservative ... Excellent reader ... Has patience to work with what defense gives ... Good short passer but not the strongest arm around ... One of only five NFL passers with better than a 60 percent completion average ... Born Feb. 3, 1945, in Evansville, Ind. ... Austere personality; "a wise ass," according to one NFL quarterback ... Dolphins' No. 1 draft pick in 1967 after brilliant passing career at Purdue ... Dive-and-survive type as scrambler ... Active civic leader in Miami area.

LARRY LITTLE 29 6-1 265　　　　　　　　　　　　Guard

Called "Big Man" by Dolphins and it has nothing to do with size, since he is one of smaller OGs around ... Considered the dominant OL in league and so voted for three years by NFL Players Association ... At best against the top defensive tackles ... "He has made it tough for me," admits Steelers' Joe Greene ... Does it all but is, well, super on sweeps ... Exceptional strength and speed to get to corner before a Mercury Morris ... Adept holder, rarely caught ... Born Nov. 2, 1945, in Groveland, Ga. ... Grew up in Miami ... Free agent from Bethune-Cookman and signed by San Diego, which traded him to Dolphins in 1969 for DB Mack Lamb, a high school teammate. One of bigger trading blunders in NFL history ... Given honorary degree by Biscayne College for civic affairs, including operation of camp for underprivileged children.

MERCURY MORRIS 28 5-10 195　　　　　　　Running Back

Super talent but getting rep as a glass house after injuries ruined his 1974 season ... Ran for 1,000 yards in 1972, 954 the following year ... Early-season injuries slowed him first three seasons .... Exceptionally strong for size, gets to corner quicker than anyone in league ... Has image as game-breaker, but in fact has run for more than 50 yards only three times . . . Has had endless hassles with Shula over splitting playing time with Jim Kiick . . . Fair blocker, mediocre receiver . . . Born Jan. 5, 1947, in Pittsburgh, Pa. . . . Set all-time NCAA career rushing record of 3,388 yards at West Texas State . . . Devoted weightlifter . . . One of game's stylish dressers . . . Outspoken and friendly.

NAT MOORE 23 5-10 180 — Wide Receiver

One of 10 Moores in league, doubtless the best one . . . Caught 37 passes for 605 yards as a rookie to rank sixth among AFC wide receivers . . . Did it on speed and fine moves; did it without running precise patterns . . . Should improve with experience . . . Runs the 40 in 4.4 . . . "He hurts you worse than Warfield," one NFL cornerman said last year . . . Born Sept. 19, 1951, in Tallahassee, Fla. . . . Transferred to University of Florida from Miami-Dade Community College and was an All-American as a senior . . . Dolphins' third-round pick in draft . . . Has fine hands . . . Drew some double coverage as 1974 season wore on . . . Brilliant potential.

JIM MANDICH 27 6-2 224 — Tight End

Developing into one of better receivers in NFL among TEs . . . Beat out veteran Marv Fleming last year and caught 33 passes, third highest among AFC tight ends . . . Still not the blocker Shula would like him to be, but improving . . . Lack of playing time caused him to seek trade two years ago . . . Good hands and runs well after the catch . . . Born July 30, 1948, in Cleveland . . . All-American at Michigan, where he stands second in career receptions and yardage . . . Second-round pick in 1970, but slow to convince Shula he could play regularly and caught only 15 passes his first three seasons . . . Plays a lot of basketball in Miami area during off-season.

JAKE SCOTT 30 6-0 190 — Safety

Dolphins' indestructible man and one of game's finest free safeties . . . Only compound fractures keep him on bench . . . Coming off of one of better seasons when he was fifth in NFL with eight interceptions . . . Plays game like it was war and is big hitter despite size, or lack thereof . . . In Pro Bowl last four seasons . . . Rides motorcycle, which Shula doesn't care for... Born July 20, 1945, in Greenwood, S.C., and mother taught high school English to Fran Tarkenton... Outstanding back at Georgia... Named MVP by Sport Magazine for 1973 Super Bowl... Head-hunter... Played reciever some early in Dolphin career... Holds NFL record for six fair catches in a game... Finished eighth in AFC with 11.1 average on punt returns... Spent one season in Canadian League.

DICK ANDERSON 29 6-2 196   Safety

Unsung hero of Miami's baffling zone defenses... Wicked tackler... Rep for rarely making mistake... Bald enough to be known as Mr. Clean by opposing players... Intercepted four passes and returned two for touchdowns in a 1973 game against Pittsburgh that moved former DB and coach Don Shula to observe: "He played as fine a game as I've ever seen a defensive back play"... Had eight interceptions in '73, tying for league lead, but dropped to one last season... Still made Pro Bowl and most All-NFL squads... Born Feb. 10, 1946, in Midland, Mich. ... Outstanding player in 1967 Blue-Gray game after starting for three years at Colorado... Younger brother, Bob, running back for Denver... Fine golfer.

JIM LANGER 27 6-2 255   Center

Generally regarded the top center in the NFL... Extremely quick off the ball... Best move is cut block on middle linebacker... Joins either guard, Larry Little or Bob Kuechenberg, to form league's toughest double-team... Another of celebrated Cleveland goofs, he was waivered by Browns in 1971 and immediately became Dolphin regular... Named the Dolphins' Best Offensive Lineman, no mean feat... Erudite... Good interview... Born May 16, 1948, in Little Falls, Minn. ... Captained baseball and football teams at South Dakota State... Set school records for most hits... Good basketball player... Off-season banker.

TOP ROOKIES

DARRYL CARLTON 22 6-5 260   Offensive Tackle
Dolphins considered him "top tackle in country and one of four

or five best prospects" ... Has fine size and quickness ... Started career at Tampa as DT ... Will be developed slowly unless old age overhauls Wayne Moore ... Going "to be a great player for a long time," say Dolphins.

FREDDIE SOLOMON 22 5-11 180　　　　　**Running Back**
Called by one scout "the quickest thing I've seen in 30 years" ... A quarterback at Tampa, but Don Shula will talk him into going at RB ... Could play defense ... Excellent prospect with 4.4 speed and super agility ... Ran for 3,229 yards and threw for 2,504 yards ... Size only reason not a No. 1.

COACH DON SHULA ... Once wrote a book called The Winning Edge after he discovered it ... Regarded as heir apparent to Vince Lombardi as the game's greatest coach although halo slipped a bit last year when Dolphins failed to win Super Bowl for third consecutive year ... First coach in NFL history to win 100 games inside 10 seasons ... Has a 56-13-1 regular-season mark in five years ... Tough, respected, genial man ... Says "I'm not a miracle worker. I'm as subtle as a punch in the nose. I've given the game everything I have because the whole idea is to somehow get an edge" ... Has got it often enough for a career mark of 127-36-5 ... Broke Baltimore contract and jumped to Miami in 1969 ... Zap, miracles ... Dolphins went 3-10-1 his first year and 10-4 the next ... "We were ready," said quarterback Bob Griese, "we were just looking for somebody to take us" ... Shula did.

CLUB HISTORY

In the spring of 1970, taking over a Miami team that had suffered four straight losing seasons and finished last in its division in two of those years, Don Shula had a thought.

"If you allow yourself to settle for anything less than No. 1, you're cheating yourself," he said. And preached to his troops. Immediately, the Dolphins quit settling for anything less than No. 1 and folks started talking about Don Shula and Vince Lombardi in the same sentence.

Certainly Shula has had the horses. Larry Csonka, Bob

Griese, Nick Buoniconti and Paul Warfield, among others. But, all the while more or less feuding with owner Joe Robbie, it has been Shula and his commitment to excellence that made the Dolphins.

They won Super Bowls in 1973 and 1974. And, despite last season's playoff loss to Oakland, they are still probably the No. 1 team in the NFL. Because Shula won't settle for less.

INDIVIDUAL DOLPHIN RECORDS

Rushing

Most Yards Game:	197	Mercury Morris, vs New England, 1973
Season:	1,117	Larry Csonka, 1972
Career:	5,900	Larry Csonka, 1968-74

Passing

Most TD Passes Game:	4	Bob Griese, vs New England, 1971
	4	Bob Griese, vs N.Y. Jets, 1969
	4	Bob Griese, vs Detroit, 1973
	4	John Stofa, vs Houston, 1966
Season:	21	Bob Griese, 1968
Career:	114	Bob Griese, 1968-74

Receiving

Most TD Passes Game:	4	Paul Warfield, vs Detroit, 1973
Season:	11	Paul Warfield, 1971
	11	Karl Noonan, 1968
Career:	33	Paul Warfield, 1970-74

Scoring

Most Points Game:	24	Paul Warfield, vs Detroit, 1973
Season:	117	Gary Yepremian, 1971
Career:	509	Garo Yepremian, 1970-74
Most TDs Game:	4	Paul Warfield, vs Detroit, 1973
Season:	12	Mercury Morris, 1972
Career:	44	Larry Csonka, 1968-74

BUFFALO BILLS

TEAM DIRECTORY: Pres.: Ralph Wilson; VP-GM: Robert Lustig; VP-Head Coach: Lou Saban; VP: Patrick McGroder; VP-Pub. Rel.: L. Budd Thalman; Dir. Player Pers.: Harvey Johnson; Dir. Pro Pers.: Bob Shaw; Treas.: Richard Morrison; Trainers: Eddie Abramoski, Bob Reese. Home: Rich Stadium, Buffalo, N.Y. (80,020).

O.J. Simpson rushed for 1,125 yards, third best in NFL.

SCOUTING REPORT

OFFENSE: Those are the new Buffalo Bills, right? The Juice ripping and plowing linebackers under as he goes off-tackle. Joe Ferguson improving every day as a passer. Enough team speed

66 THE COMPLETE HANDBOOK OF PRO FOOTBALL

for a pro track franchise. Uh-huh. Only the Bills finished 23rd in the NFL offensively. So the big question around the stove (you ever been in Buffalo?) is whether or not the Bills will move the football in 1975. Right, they'll move it. And move it. And ... you get the message.

Simpson played hurt all the way in 1974. Not the announced leg injuries, but a dozen hurts he didn't discuss. Coach Lou Saban, who probably panicked some when he threw frivolously and erringly a couple of times the previous year, untethered young Ferguson a bit with the result that his arm carried the Bills when Simpson's legs could not.

In addition, while the Bills had a fine offensive line, injuries cost them fullback Jim Braxton, who can block and move people inside when the urge to is upon him. Elsewhere, there is solidarity; not much flash, but results. Receivers J.D. Hill and Ahmad Rashad are burners. Tight end Paul Seymour lumbers and is really a tackle, but he makes the timely catch and blocks like Hurricane Althea. All of which is to say, Buffalo will move the football.

DEFENSE: To prove that statistics do lie (see above), the Bills ranked fifth in the league defensively. Only they're nowhere near that good. The three-man front is, beyond tough, old end Earl Edwards, pedestrian. And the linebacking, well, Pittsburgh got to Buffalo in the playoffs through the linebackers. Dave Washington is green; Jim Cheyunski is willing but way undersized and Bo Cornell, well, he used to be a running back. And still is.

The last line of defense is just fine, except for safety Tony Greene, who is super-fine and was the club MVP in 1974 and killed them in the playoffs because an injury kept him from playing. Privately, Saban says, "defensively, we've got people playing for us who've taken us as far as they can." Falling into this category are end Walt Patulski, most of the linebackers and whoever plays the strong safety. It is not that the Bills' defense is bad; it is that it's not good enough to win in the playoffs.

To correct that situation, the Bills drafted Nebraska linebackers Tom Ruud and Bob Nelson 1-2, and then chose seven other defenders. Whether or not they'll be able to help against teams that take it to Buffalo inside, and keep taking it there, is another question.

KICKING GAME: Bills tried two punters, Spike Jones and Marv Bateman, and neither inspired memories of Sammy Baugh. But Bateman came on late and will be adequate if not

BUFFALO BILLS 67

BILLS VETERANS ROSTER
HEAD COACH—Lou Saban. Assistant Coaches—Jim Ringo, Ed Cavanaugh, John Ray, Stan Jones, Bill Atkins

No.	Name	Pos.	Ht.	Wt.	NFL Exp.	College
60	Adams, Bill	G	6-2	254	3	Holy Cross
59	Allen, Doug	LB	6-2	225	2	Penn State
7	Bateman, Marv	P	6-4	210	4	Utah
34	Braxton, Jim	RB	6-1	240	5	West Virginia
22	Cahill, Bill	S	5-11	170	3	Washington
29	Calhoun, Don	RB	6-0	198	2	Kansas State
81	Chandler, Bob	WR	6-0	180	5	Southern California
50	Cheyunski, Jim	LB	6-1	220	8	Syracuse
30	Cornell, Bo	LB	6-2	215	5	Washington
42	Craig, Neal	S	6-1	190	5	Fisk
72	Croft, Don	DT	6-4	254	3	Texas-El Paso
68	DeLamielleure, Joe	G	6-3	254	3	Michigan State
73	Edwards, Earl	DT	6-7	256	7	Wichita State
12	Ferguson, Joe	QB	6-1	180	3	Arkansas
78	Foley, Dave	T	6-3	253	6	Ohio State
88	Gant, Reuben	TE	6-4	230	2	Oklahoma State
74	Green, Donnie	T	6-7	272	5	Purdue
43	Greene, Tony	S	5-10	170	5	Maryland
76	Hagen, Halvor	T	6-6	253	7	Weber State
28	Harrison, Dwight	CB	6-2	185	5	Texas A&I
47	Haslerig, Clint	RB	6-0	189	2	Michigan
21	Hayman, Gary	RB	6-1	198	2	Penn State
40	Hill, J.D.	WR	6-1	190	5	Arizona State
16	Hunter, Scott	QB	6-2	205	5	Alabama
20	James, Robert	CB	6-1	184	7	Fisk
51	Jarvis, Bruce	C	6-7	250	5	Washington
71	Kadish, Mike	T	6-5	270	3	Notre Dame
45	Kern, Rex	CB-S	6-1	190	5	Ohio State
37	Koy, Ted	LB	6-2	210	6	Texas
52	Krakau, Merv	LB	6-2	237	3	Iowa State
3	Leypoldt, John	K	6-2	230	5	None
17	Marangi, Gary	QB	6-1	196	2	Boston College
67	McKenzie, Reggie	G	6-4	242	4	Michigan
77	Means, Dave	DE	6-4	235	2	S.E. Missouri St.
53	Montler, Mike	C	6-4	253	7	Colorado
61	Parker, Willie	C-G	6-3	245	4	North Texas State
85	Patulski, Walt	DE	6-6	259	4	Notre Dame
27	Rashad, Ahmad	WR	6-2	200	4	Oregon
87	Seymour, Paul	TE	6-5	243	3	Michigan
32	Simpson, O.J.	RB	6-1	212	7	Southern California
55	Skorupan, John	LB	6-2	221	3	Penn State
86	Washington, Dave	LB	6-5	223	6	Alcorn A&M
75	Winans, Jeff	DE	6-5	265	3	Southern California
62	Yeates, Jeff	DT	6-3	240	2	Boston College

TOP FIVE DRAFT CHOICES

Rd.	Name	Pos.	Ht.	Wt.	Age	College
1	Tom Ruud	LB	6-3	223	22	Nebraska
2	Bob Nelson	LB	6-4	232	22	Nebraska
2	Glenn Lott	S	6-2	201	22	Drake
4	Tom Donchez	RB	6-2	216	22	Penn State
5	John McCrumbly	LB	6-2	253	23	Texas A&M

better. John Leypoldt (19-for-33) has quietly become one of the better placekickers around. Coverage-wise, as they say along Madison Ave., the Bills' special units aren't.

OUTLOOK: As The Juice goes, so ... Ferguson's passing isn't good enough to take a club to the playoffs—especially not one that faces a rugged schedule including five games against teams which made the 1974 playoffs. If Simpson enjoys another odyssey, the Bills will be there. If he does not, they will not. In short, Bills probably in a holding pattern until they acquire more overall talent to challenge the Pittsburghs and Oaklands, etc. Their highlight film is well-named. It's called "The First Step."

BILL PROFILES

O.J. SIMPSON 28 6-2 212   **Running Back**

What can you say? What Einstein was to calculus, he is to football ... May be game's finest runner ever ... Brilliant speed, moves, deception, whatever—except hands, which sometimes seem made of some metallic substance ... First runner ever to breach 2,000 yards, a feat which made him all-everything and gave him 1973 Hickok Award by biggest landslide in award's history ... Born in San Francisco, July 9, 1947 ... Worked on third movie this year, in Africa, with Telly Savalas ... Won Superstars, worth 38 grand. "I had the money spent before I went down there." Won baseball hitting—over USC's Anthony Davis, a Minnesota Twins' and N.Y. Jets' draftee—and ran 100 for first time in years, posting a 9.6 ... Yardage dropped off hugely in 1974—2,003 to 1,125—but he played hurt all season and still finished third in NFL.

JOE FERGUSON 25 6-1 180   **Quarterback**

Country boy ... One of league's worst dressers ... Shreveport high school successor of Terry Bradshaw and set handful of national scholastic passing records ... Tendency to get down on himself. "I put in so much time on my game, I feel like I should complete every pass," he says ... Bills began respecting him after O.J. Simpson was injured in Oakland opener and he guided team to win ... Born April 23, 1950, in Shreveport, La. ... Southwest Conference MVP as junior at Arkansas, but senior season total loss due to injuries and hassles with coach ... A veritable steal as a No. 3 pick ... Improved last year and ranked seventh in passing in AFC.

TONY GREENE 26 5-10 170   Free Safety

Might well have been Bills Most Valuable Player in 1974, O.J. notwithstanding ... For reasons unknown, Bills waited until final week of pre-season to move him to free safety, where he's best in business ... Smart player, runs secondary during game ... Tremendous leaper ... Excellent athlete ... One of four fastest on super-fast team ... 4.45 speed ... Studying for Masters degree ... Born Aug. 29, 1949, in Bethesda, Md. ... Led ACC in interceptions as Maryland senior, but wasn't drafted and signed as free agent ... Big hitter; excellent on pass coverage ... His absence due to injury hurt Bills grievously in playoffs.

JIM BRAXTON 26 6-1 243   Running Back

Off year on the basis of poor second-half, when he fumbled a lot and was overweight due to bad back that cut down his working time ... Called the Pillsbury Doughboy ... Smart player. O.J. Simpson claimed Braxton helped the club on the field because of ability to understand tempo of game and spot defensive tendencies ... Born May 23, 1949, in Vanderbilt, Pa. ... Called "Bubby" by black teammates ... Could be one of fine power runners in game, but has rep of not pushing self ... Bills drafted Penn State fullback Tom Donchez in bid to inspire Braxton ... All-America pick at West Virginia in 1970, but team lacked talent to exploit him. Spent one season at tight end ... 13th among AFC rushers with 543 yards ... Fine blocker.

EARL EDWARDS 29 6-7 256   Defensive End

Mean ... Defensive leader of club immediately after coming from San Francisco for journeyman back Randy Jackson and No. 3 draft pick in 1973 ... Can work inside, but one of the best at DE ... Exotic dresser. Owns haberdashery with teammate J.D. Hill ... Super hustler in practice and games ... Great inside move for DE ... All but ran Jet tackle Bob Svihus out of league in '73 game ... Born March 17, 1946, in Statebrough, Ga. ... Played some offense as 49er rookie and was with Edmonton in Canadian League two seasons ... Made 15 tackles against Drake while senior at Wichita State.

JOE DeLAMIELLEURE 24 6-3 254　　　　　　　　Guard

Overshadowed but not outplayed by opposite guard, Reggie McKenzie ... Had excellent 1974 season ... Quiet ... Brilliant drive blocker ... Bills' most underrated player ... Only weakness is in pulling ... Heart ailment caused him to flunk rookie physical and reason he wasn't drafted by Pittsburgh, but tests later revealed no problems ... Rarely ever missed a play in two years ... Born March 16, 1951, in Detroit ... Three-time All-Big Ten pick at Michigan and one of Bills' two first-round picks in 1973 ... Started every game as rookie ... Works for Buffalo sheriff's dept. in off-season ... Tremendous competitor ... Comes from family of 10 kids.

J.D. HILL 26 6-1 190　　　　　　　　Wide Receiver

Brilliant tools; not cerebral enough ... Very emotional, tends toward moodiness ... Flamboyant dresser with Sherlock Holmes outfit tops in his wardrobe ... Called "Heel" by Simpson ... Humorous and often center of attention in locker room ... Deadly blocker, with rep for cracking back. "When they know J.D. is coming, they're not looking for me," chuckles Simpson ... Born Oct. 30, 1948, in Stockton, Calif. ... MVP at Arizona State in 1970 and consensus All-American ... Does 100 in 9.3, 220 in 20.3 ... Senior Bowl MVP ... Works with disadvantaged kids ... Stats in 1974 improved in every area ... 32 receptions put him in AFC's top 20.

MIKE KADISH 25 6-5 274　　　　　　　　Defensive Tackle

Enjoying last laugh over scouts who rated him blubbery washout two years ago when he was cut by Miami even though a No. 1 draft pick ... Reported to Dolphin camp overweight and collapsed while trying to run six-minute mile ... Shuffled off to Bills for journeyman guard Irv Goode ... Turned it around last year as middleman in Bills' three-man defensive line ... Fine inside pass rusher ... Born May 27, 1950, in Grand Rapids, Mich. ... All-American defensive tackle

BUFFALO BILLS 71

who led Irish in tackles as senior . . . Has outplayed Bills' defensive end and Notre Dame buddy Walt Patulski, a Buffalo first choice . . . Will be pushed by second-year pro Jeff Winans and may move to DE.

REGGIE McKENZIE 25 6-4 242   **Guard**

Rep as one of world's truly nice guys; rep as one of NFL's best guards. Former true, latter not-so-true . . . Simpson's "Main Man" . . . Coming off mediocre year after being overly involved with labor problems as team player rep. Admits "I spent a lot of time in that area" . . . Very personable . . . Keeps locker-room loose and is bridge between black and white players . . . Fine pulling guard and wicked drive-blocker . . . Just fair pass blocker . . . Born July 27, 1950, in Detroit . . . Consensus two-time All-American at Michigan . . . Won starting job as rookie two years ago and played all year with bad ankles . . . Active in civic affairs in Buffalo . . . Works as public relations man.

JOHN SKORUPAN 24 6-2 220   **Linebacker**

Typical Penn State linebacker, which is to say, excellent . . . Loss at mid-season after tearing up knee against New England hurt Bills badly rest of way . . . Plays screens superbly . . . Close friend of quarterback Joe Ferguson . . . Has legs like chopsticks, but compensates well for lack of muscle . . . Born May 17, 1951, in Beaver, Pa. . . . Next-door neighbor of Joe Namath . . . Played on Cotton and Sugar Bowl teams as three-year regular at Penn State . . . Excellent against pass and gets it done against the run . . . If he stays free of injuries, should develop into one of better outside LBs in AFC . . . Club dancer.

TOP ROOKIES

TOM RUUD 21 6-3 223   **Linebacker**

Unanimous All-Big Eight last year at Nebraska . . . Wearing can't-miss tag for team badly in need of can't-miss LB . . . Tough on run, will have trouble in pros against the pass . . . Totaled 209 career tackles, including 104 as senior . . . Had three fumble recoveries and two interceptions as senior . . . Born July 26, 1953, in Bloomington, Minn.

72 THE COMPLETE HANDBOOK OF PRO FOOTBALL

BOB NELSON 21 6-4 232   **Linebacker**
Think Bills don't need help at LB?... Not as quick as Nebraska roomie Ruud, but stronger (they're called the Minnesota Twins)... Went in second round after fine Senior Bowl performance... Works in ice cream plant during summer... Business major... Made 198 tackles in three seasons... Born June 30, 1953, in Stillwater, Minn.

COACH LOU SABAN ... Has managed to rebuild Buffalo—twice ... Put together club that dominated AFL in 1964 and 1965 before surprising football people by taking Maryland job ... Bills fell apart while he was gone and he returned after five-year stint with Denver to wave the wand again ... Presto, a 4-9-1 year, then two 9-5 seasons ... Last one put Bills into AFC playoffs ... Low-key, conservative coach ... Had sense to give the ball to O.J. Simpson and let him keep it until Bills' offense could be remodeled to include passing game ... Fine handler of players ... Linebacker for Cleveland Browns in old AAFC for four seasons ... Unsuccessful head college coach for five years and still has not breached .500 mark in pros.

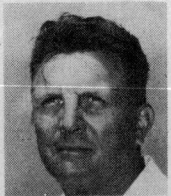

CLUB HISTORY

When you stop to consider the town and the fact that President William McKinley went there to get assassinated, the Buffalo Bills haven't fared that badly. As long as Lou Saban was around, that is.

Buffalo's fortunes have been tied to Lou, and vice versa. In 1964 and 1965, Saban led the Bills to AFL titles. But he left for poor performances at Maryland and later Denver; Cookie Gilchrist crumbled, and from 1967 through 1971, Buffalo won nine games.

Even the advent of The Juice couldn't redeem Buffalo, but Lou Saban did. In his second year back in town, the Bills went 9-5, matched it again last year and made the playoffs.

The quarterback is now Joe Ferguson instead of Jack Kemp and Cookie has been succeeded by The Juice, and the Bills' future is bright. As long as Lou Saban's around.

BUFFALO BILLS 73

INDIVIDUAL BILL RECORDS

Rushing

Most Yards Game:	250	O.J. Simpson, vs New England, 1973
Season:	2,003	O.J. Simpson, 1973
Career:	6,306	O.J. Simpson, 1969-74

Pasing

Most TD Passes Game:	4	Johnny Green, vs Oakland, 1960
Season:	14	Jack Kemp, 1967
	14	Dennis Shaw, 1972
Career:	77	Jack Kemp, 1962-69

Receiving

Most TD Passes Game:	3	Wray Carlton, vs Oakland, 1960
Season:	10	Elbert Dubenion, 1960-67
Career:	35	Elbert Dubenion, 1960-67

Scoring

Most Points Game:	30	Cookie Gilchrist, vs New York, 1963
Season:	128	Cookie Gilchrist, 1962
Career:	288	John Leypoldt, 1971-74
Most TDs Game:	5	Cookie Gilchrist, vs New York, 1963
Season:	15	Cookie Gilchrist, 1962
Career:	39	Elbert Dubenion, 1960-67

Cookie Gilchrist set Bills' mark for most TDs in game.

NEW ENGLAND PATRIOTS

TEAM DIRECTORY: Pres.: Robert Marr; GM-Head Coach: Chuck Fairbanks; Asst. GM: Peter Hadhazy; Dir. Player Pers.: Bucko Kilroy; Dir. Pub. Rel.: Pat Horne; Bus. Mgr.: Herman Bruce; Trainer: Tom Healion. Home: Schaefer Stadium, Foxboro, Mass. (61,279).

QB Jim Plunkett triggers AFC East's top-scoring offense.

SCOUTING REPORT

OFFENSE: Only Paul Revere's horse was swifter than the 1974 Patriot offense, and he probably didn't run as hard. The Pats should go even better in '75, which might be expected. Jim Plunkett didn't have one of his better years, but he played the second half with a torn knee cartilage and a horribly-pulled hamstring. "He hadn't reached his potential, but he still has the desire to," says coach Chuck Fairbanks. If Plunkett, possessed of one of the league's finer arms, realizes that potential, an offense that scored 348 points to rank behind only Oakland, could be better.

In backs Sam Cunningham and Mack Herron, the Pats have a diversified running game, and one needs only to reflect upon Miami to know what that means. Steve Corbett, a No. 1 pick in 1974 who missed the year with an injury, will improve an already good offensive line that lacks only depth. Shelby Jordan, also injured all of last year, will be back and Fairbanks says "he could become a fine tackle."

What the Patriots need, with Bob Windsor's knee ruined last year, is a fine tight end. They may have one in rookie Russ Francis, with Bob Adams a solid backup man. Depth is also a problem at receiver, where there is Randy Vataha, Daryl Stingley and damn little else. In toto, an offense that can hurt you, but can't stand to be hurt.

DEFENSE: It used to be tougher to run across Scollay Sq. than to thread through the Patriots, but no more. Only Pittsburgh ran against New England last year after Fairbanks went to the three-man defensive line. Going back to it may be more difficult. Tough nose guard Art Moore had what the club doctor said was the worst knee injury he's ever seen. Ray Hamilton is quick and fine in the middle against the passing teams. He wears down and can be had by run-oriented opponents. Julius Adams has become a fine defensive end. Oh, if he could only play in the secondary.

Behind a four-man linebacking setup peopled by such retreads as George Webster and heretofore unknowns as Sam Hunt there is mystery. If safety Rex Kern loses another step, will the tide rush in and overwhelm the Patriots? Who are Prentice McCray and Ron Bolton and why didn't they get run out of the league last year? In fact, they almost did. The Pats gave up a 56.1 completion percentage a year ago and only an unreal string of injuries hurt them worse than an opponent's ability to complete the third-down pitch. That may be more difficult this year, as rookie linebacker Rod Shoate, he of the 4.4 speed and larcenous heart, will move in at an outside linebacking post.

KICKING GAME: Southpaw sidewinder John Smith improved with age. Kept on the reserve list in 1973 through a paperwork trade in which he was a Pittsburgh Steeler for two days, Smith cashed 11 of 18 FG attempts last year. Dave Chapple's punting was less impressive. He is shaky. The Patriot special teams,

PATRIOTS VETERANS ROSTER

HEAD COACH—Chuck Fairbanks. Assistant Coaches—Hank Bullough, Red Miller, Jim Valek, Rollie Dotsch, Ron Erhardt, Ray Perkins, John Polonchek, Charlie Sumner, Larrye Weaver

No.	Name	Pos.	Ht.	Wt.	NFL Exp.	College
80	Adams, Bob	TE	6-2	222	6	Pacific
85	Adams, Julius	DE	6-4	260	5	Texas Southern
61	Adams, Sam	G	6-3	252	4	Prairie View
31	Ashton, Josh	RB	6-1	202	4	Tulsa
59	Barnes, Rodrigo	LB	6-1	215	3	Rice
27	Bolton, Ron	CB	6-2	170	4	Norfolk State
—	Carter, Kent	LB	6-3	235	2	Southern Cal
10	Chapple, Dave	P	6-1	195	5	Cal-Santa Barbara
54	Clark, Ernie	LB	6-3	225	3	Michigan State
62	Corbett, Steve	G	6-4	248	1	Boston College
35	Crosswhite, Leon	RB	6-2	215	3	Oklahoma
39	Cunningham, Sam	RB	6-3	224	5	Southern Cal
51	Damkroger, Maury	LB	6-2	230	2	Nebraska
68	DuLac, Bill	G	6-4	260	2	E. Michigan
58	Dumler, Doug	C	6-3	242	3	Nebraska
22	Durko, Sandy	S	6-1	186	5	Southern Cal
64	Gallaher, Allen	T	6-3	255	2	Southern Cal
55	Geddes, Bob	LB	6-2	240	3	UCLA
15	Graff, Neil	QB	6-3	200	2	Wisconsin
70	Gray, Leon	T	6-3	256	3	Jackson State
71	Hamilton, Ray	NT	6-1	245	3	Oklahoma
73	Hannah, John	G	6-2	265	3	Alabama
74	Hanneman, Craig	DE	6-4	245	4	Oregon State
42	Herron, Mack	RB	5-5	175	3	Kansas State
50	Hunt, Sam	LB	6-1	240	2	Stephen F. Austin
30	Jenkins, Ed	RB	6-2	210	3	Holy Cross
32	Johnson, Andy	RB	6-0	204	2	Georgia
—	Jordan, Shelby	T	6-7	260	1	Washington
52	King, Steve	LB	6-4	230	3	Tulsa
67	Lenkaitis, Bill	C	6-4	250	8	Penn State
72	Lunsford, Mel	DE	6-3	260	3	Central State
24	McCall, Bob	RB	6-0	205	2	Arizona
34	McCray, Prentice	CB	6-1	187	2	Arizona State
78	McGee, Tony	DE	6-4	245	5	Bishop
88	Marshall, Al	WR	6-2	190	2	Boise State
47	Massey, Jim	CB	5-11	198	2	Linfield
45	Mildren, Jack	S	6-1	200	4	Oklahoma
75	Moore, Arthur	NT	6-5	253	3	Tulsa
56	Morris, Jon	C	6-4	248	12	Holy Cross
57	Nelson, Steve	LB	6-2	230	2	N. Dakota State
77	Neville, Tom	T	6-4	253	11	Mississippi State
16	Plunkett, Jim	QB	6-2	212	5	Stanford
25	Sanders, John	S	6-1	187	2	South Dakota
87	Schubert, Steve	WR	5-10	185	2	Massachusetts
11	Shiner, Dick	QB	6-0	210	12	Maryland
65	Smith, Donnell	DE	6-4	252	4	Southern University
1	Smith, John	K	6-0	185	2	England
84	Stingley, Darryl	WR	6-0	195	3	Purdue
53	Tanner, John	LB	6-4	235	4	Tennessee Tech
18	Vataha, Randy	WR	5-10	170	5	Stanford
—	Webster, Ernie	G	6-4	245	1	Pittsburgh
90	Webster, George	LB	6-4	230	9	Michigan State
23	Wilson, Joe	RB	5-10	210	3	Holy Cross
86	Windsor, Bob	TE	6-4	225	9	Kentucky

TOP FIVE DRAFT CHOICES

Rd.	Name	Pos.	Ht.	Wt.	Age	College
1	Russ Francis	TE	6-6	240	22	Oregon
2	Rod Shoate	LB	6-1	211	22	Oklahoma
3	Pete Cusick	DT	6-1	255	22	Ohio State
4	Allen Carter	RB	5-11	208	22	Southern California
4	Steve Burks	WR-P	6-5	211	22	Arkansas State

NEW ENGLAND PATRIOTS

swift and usually arriving down-field under kicks in a rather foul mood, were not.

OUTLOOK: A team of "ifs." They'll make a run at the AFC East title if Plunkett can raise his completion average behind increasingly better protection; if the offensive line strength isn't lost to injury; if the secondary holds up, and if they don't hurt themselves with the foolish penalties that took a toll in 1974. And, of course, if the training room doesn't become an out-patient clinic as it did last season.

PATRIOT PROFILES

JIM PLUNKETT 27 6-2 210   Quarterback

Only Nixon had more trouble in '74... After good first-half of year, you-know-what fell in ... Had problems with quarterback coach Bill Nelsen, who subsequently left club... Played last four games with torn knee cartilage, repaired by off-season surgery, and torn hamstring... Completion percentage dropped, interceptions rose, and he finished ninth among AFC quarterbacks with poor 63.8 rating... Undisputed team leader due to unselfishness... Teammate says he's "one of few quarterbacks without ego problem"... Fine pocket passer... Scrambles on par with Namath... Won Heisman at Stanford and one of greatest college passers of all-time... Born Dec. 5, 1947, in San Jose, Calif.... Devoted to blind parents... First player taken in '71 draft... Rookie of Year... Improvement slowed since then.

DARYL STINGLEY 24 6-0 195   Wide Receiver

One of keys to Patriots' hope for improvement... Club desperately needs consistency at WR, especially since Randy Vataha has played out option... Solid rookie year in '73 when he made 23 catches after learning to quit running into occupied part of zones... Then broke arm in three places in third game last year and missed season... One of those can't-miss types... Speed merchant with hands... Moves will come... Born August 18, 1951, in Chicago... City's outstanding schoolboy athlete in 1968... Honor student... Third all-time receiver at Purdue... Third-round draft pick... Size (6-0) hurts him... Likes to run reverse and has 12.6 average.

78 THE COMPLETE HANDBOOK OF PRO FOOTBALL

JOHN HANNAH 24 6-2 265 — Guard

Patriots billing him as one of NFL's finest guards... He isn't, and won't be until his pass blocking improves... Gets overpowered too often... One of quicker guards off the ball... Born April 4, 1951, in Canton, Ga.... Superb career at Alabama, where he became one of handful of players Bear Bryant's called "the finest offensive lineman I ever coached"... Two-time All-American who scooped up every offensive lineman award in nation as a senior... Nicknamed Ham Hocks; for reasons unknown... Quickly made conversion from straight-ahead blocking of Alabama wishbone to pulling and drop-back assignments required in pros.

MACK HERRON 27 5-5 170 — Running Back

NFL's answer to Mickey Rooney... Listed as 5-5, barely 5-4... Broke Gale Sayers' total yardage record for a single season with 2,444 yards... Ninth in league in rushing (824), 10th in AFC in receiving (38 for 474), second in AFC in punt returns (14.8 average)... Terrorizes the slower DEs because of quick move outside... Born July 24, 1948, in Biloxi, Miss.... Brilliant senior year at Kansas State when led team in rushing, Big Eight in receiving and second in nation in scoring... Atlanta waited until sixth round to draft him because of size and he signed with Winnipeg of CFL, where he was runnerup MVP in 1972... Run out of CFL after being arrested for drug possession and picked up by Pats when scout Dick Steinberg, his college coach, discovered him selling jeans in Chicago store... Says he's now leading exemplary life and has become religious.

JULIUS ADAMS 27 6-3 257 — Defensive Tackle

Pats call him The Jewel... With good reason... "I can't believe the guy's not an all-pro," says Pat DE Craig Hanneman... Will be when he starts giving 100 percent every week... Fine two-gap (head-to-head) player... Excellent pass-rusher with fine inside move... Has rep as being tough to move out on run... Born April 26, 1948, in Macon, Ga.... Team hypochondriac... Four-year regular at Texas Southern... No. 2 draft pick... Played brilliantly in 1971 College All-Star Game... Pats tried him at linebacker during rookie season after he had problems making adjustment to pros ... Trial at DE a flop, but has prospered inside.

RAY HAMILTON 24 6-1 232   Defensive End-Tackle

Wound up at nose guard when Pats went to three-man defensive line and enjoyed good season ... Smallest defensive lineman in league ... Patriots list him at 6-1; he's under 6-0 ... Key to game are long arms, enabling him to make first move on tackle ... Excellent pass rush due to quickness ... Not overly strong ... Born Jan. 20, 1951, in Omaha, Nebr. ... Played five different positions as three-year regular at Oklahoma ... Pats stole him in 14th round of draft after he was bypassed because most teams projected him as a leadfoot linebacker ... Was started at DE as rookie ... Moved to middle guard when Arthur Moore was hurt and will be challenged for starting job in camp. Dependable hands, head ... Popular in locker room.

RANDY VATAHA 26 5-10 170   Wide Receiver

Everything argues against him being regular receiver in NFL except his hands, which a watchmaker would admire ... Gutty ... Played second-half of last season with a leg injury because Pats' receiver corps was decimated ... Small but, as the gag goes, slow ... Knows how to play, never runs route at DB ... As schoolboy, was conspicuous by lack of offers and wound up going to JC ... So much for recruiting. Transferred to Stanford and had brilliant career playing catch with Plunkett ... Drafted in 17th round by Rams and cut ... So much for scouting. Caught 51 passes to set Pat record as rookie ... Circus catch set up last-play win over Minnesota ... Born Dec. 4, 1948, in Santa Maria, Calif. ... Only caught 25 passes but got maximum mileage from them with sparkling 22.4 average.

BOB WINDSOR 32 6-4 225   Tight End

OT with hands ... Most heroic figure of 1974 when caught pass on Viking three, was hit and completely tore ligaments in knee, and powered way to end zone on one leg to beat Minnesota on last play of game ... Fair-to-good receiver ... Good-to-great blocker ... Born Dec. 19, 1942, in Washington, D.C. ... Went to JC where in one game scored four

TDs, rushed for 160 yards, and picked up 105 yards receiving and 150 returning kicks ... Only athlete to ever play both football and basketball at Kentucky ... One super year (49 catches) and two bad ones in five seasons with San Francisco before being traded to Pats, where he's been reliable at worst.

SAM HUNT 23 6-1 240   Linebacker

Came out of woodwork to help Pats with LB problem ... Plays inside in four-man setup ... A hitter ... Patriot management insists he has bright future ... Will get darker if he doesn't learn how to handle the pass ... Tough on run ... Holds position well ... Wears high-top shoes ... Looks like Sonny Liston; occasionally acts like him ... Four-year regular at Stephen F. Austin College, where he averaged 10 tackles a game during career ... Pats took a flyer with him in 15th round and came out smelling like a rose when he won starting job ... Defensive MVP in the-ah-Poultry Bowl ... Seven interceptions as a senior, three as pro rookie.

SAM CUNNINGHAM 25 6-3 224   Running Back

Bam ... That's the way he blocks, that's the way he runs, that's the sound his leg made when it was fractured in 10th game against Jets ... Still managed to finish 10th in NFL in rushing with 811 yards, catch 22 passes, block like hell and leave the general impression that this winter he just might be the best all-around fullback alive ... Made phenomenal improvement after knee woes hampered him during rookie season ... Born August 15, 1950, in Santa Barbara, Calif. ... From then on victim of poor coaching, as USC's John McKay wound up making a blocking back out of him as a senior ... A 9.8 sprinter called by USC track coach "the fastest man for 10 yards that I ever coached" ... Powerhouse blocker ... Dependable hands, head ... Popular in locker room.

TOP ROOKIES

RUSS FRANCIS 22 6-6 240   Tight End
Sat out senior year after dispute with new Oregon coach ... Super prospect who could be moved to tackle if regular TE Bob Windsor recovers from knee surgery ... Father pro wrestler and

he was tag-team partner in 50 bouts this year... Owns a pilot's license... Extraordinary athlete... Holds national prep record in javelin (259-9) and was drafted as pitcher by KC Royals.

ROD SHOATE 22 6-1 211   **Linebacker**
Considered No. 1 LB in country as Oklahoma junior... Had poor showing in post-season all-star games or would've been first-round pick... 4.4 speed... Size marginal for pros... Excellent hitter... "He's best linebacker ever to pull on an Oklahoma uniform," says Coach Barry Switzer... Consensus All-American.

COACH CHUCK FAIRBANKS... Brilliant 52-15-1 record in six years at Oklahoma propelled him into Patriot job after Penn State's Joe Paterno turned it down and he's been highly-successful, splitting 28 games in his two years... At 42, one of youngest coaches in league... An end for Michigan's national championship team in 1952... Handicapped by management that's traditionally been zany... A college assistant for eight years before polishing wishbone at Oklahoma... Rated good administrator... Has sought to bring oneness to club but is undermined by front office rep for tightness with dollar... Turned Pats into one of tougher teams in AFC last year and one that could've reached the playoffs save for a horrible string of serious injuries.

CLUB HISTORY

Somewhere there must be a portrait of a bent New England fan and the caption, "They ain't heavy, they're my Patriots." Such is the history of New England, nee Boston.

Disaster, in reflection, seems foretold. The first player signed was the eminently forgettable Clemson quarterback, Harv White. The Pats' first sellout was a horde of some 27,123. The first and only time the club played for a title, in the AFL in 1964, the Pats lost. 51-10. And when the Pats—long since short for patsy—became the first club to ever pay stockholders a dividend, the owners got the munificent sum of 15 cents a share.

But there have been a few silver linings. Babe Parilli's arm;

82 THE COMPLETE HANDBOOK OF PRO FOOTBALL

Gino Cappelletti's foot; Jim Nance's legs; Jim Plunkett's ability to withstand punishment.

The clouds? Last place three times. Over .500 only six times in 15 winters. The signing of only five top draft picks.

INDIVIDUAL PATRIOT RECORDS

Rushing

Most Yards Game:	208	Jim Nance, vs Oakland, 1966
Season:	1,458	Jim Nance, 1966
Career:	5,323	Jim Nance, 1965-71

Passing

Most TD Passes Game:	5	Vito Parilli, vs Buffalo, 1965
	5	Vito Parilli, vs Miami, 1967
Season:	31	Vito Parilli, 1964
Career:	132	Vito Parilli, 1961-67

Receiving

Most TD Passes Game:	3	Billy Lott, vs Buffalo, 1961
	3	Gino Cappelletti, vs Buffalo, 1964
	3	Jim Whalen, vs Miami, 1967
Season:	10	Jim Colclough, 1962
Career:	42	Gino Cappelletti, 1960-70

Scoring

Most Points Game:	28	Gino Cappelletti, vs Houston, 1965 (2 TD-4PATS-4 FG)
Season:	155	Gino Cappelletti, 1964 (7 TD-38 PATS-25 FG)
Career:	1,130	Gino Cappelletti, 1960-70
Most TDs Game:	3	Billy Lott, vs Buffalo, 1961
	3	Billy Lott, vs Oakland, 1961
	3	Larry Garron, vs Oakland, 1964
	3	Larry Garron, vs San Diego, 1966
	3	Gino Cappelletti, vs Buffalo, 1964
	3	Jim Whalen, vs Miami, 1967
	3	Sam Cunningham, vs Buffalo, 1974
	3	Mack Herron, vs Buffalo, 1974
Season:	12	Mack Herron, 1974
Career:	46	Jim Nance, 1965-71

NEW YORK JETS

TEAM DIRECTORY: Pres.: Philip Iselin; GM: Al Ward; Bus. Mgr.-Trav. Sec.: John Free; Dir. Player Pers.: Mike Holovak; Talent Scouts: Jim Royer, Ed Buckley, Carroll Huntress; Dir. Pub. Rel.: Frank Ramos; Asst. Dir. Pub. Rel.: Jim Trecker; Head Coach: Charley Winner; Trainer: Jeff Snedeker. Home: Shea Stadium, Flushing, N.Y. (60,000).

Joe Namath enters second decade at Jets' throttle.

SCOUTING REPORT

OFFENSE: The body is broken, but the spirit is indomitable, and most Sundays there is no finer quarterback than Joe Namath. That's most Sundays. Enough of them that with the running game lacking outside speed, Namath got the Jets some 279 points and a late surge that brought a 7-7 record. Alas, not enough of them to make up for defensive inadequacy and an in-

84 THE COMPLETE HANDBOOK OF PRO FOOTBALL

creasing tendency to force the ball to the receiver. Coming off the most accurate season of his career, Namath remains a liability in that his knees or whatever could go at any time. Not a healthy situation for a club trying to rebuild.

Part of that reconstruction took place last year when offensive line coach Bob Fry, fired by Pittsburgh for an alleged inability to teach fundamentals, forged the second-best pass blocking unit in the conference. The line, however, still doesn't block well enough for the run. An indication of the Jet offensive problems can be seen in the stat that shows they got a higher percentage of their yardage passing than any other AFC team.

The Jets still lack the kind of quick back who can get outside and reduce that statistic some, but the crux of the problem remains Namath. The receivers are there. In Jerome Barkum, David Knight, Eddie Bell and tight end Rich Caster, no club could ask for better targets. The question is: Do you put your chips on a quarterback so immobile he is the league's prime target?

DEFENSE: The Jets couldn't stop a determined running game with a howitzer. Short of Cleveland, they were the easiest club in the conference to possess the ball on, and everybody did. Which forced an imbalance in the Jet offense, of course. Most clubs didn't try anything very fancy. Just ran it inside the tackles, threw enough to keep the linebackers honest, and tapped the woebegone Jets for an even 300 points. Or more than given up by any team this side of Baltimore and Cleveland.

Things may get worse. Ends Mark Lomas and Ed Galigher are still being coveted by the WFL. Ends Billy Newsome and Jim Bailey came via trades, but Newsome didn't help New Orleans and Bailey was about to lose his job in Baltimore. First-year pro Carl Barzilauskas helped immeasurably at tackle and it's conceivable the Jets could go to a three-man front.

Which means the need to add another linebacker. Which won't help unless Godwin Turk, a third-round pick in 1974 who missed last season because of injuries, is as good as several scouts anticipated. Otherwise, the linebacking picture isn't too bright. St. Louis retread Jamie Rivers worked the middle adequately last year and vet Al Atkinson is still about, but flanking them are the sort of guys that lead you to believe you can almost hear Charley Winner's pleas for help. The secondary was victimized by a miserable pass rush and probably will be again.

KICKING GAME: It was lousy. Everything. Greg Gantt's punting, the kickoff returns, coverage, everything. No team in the

NEW YORK JETS 85

JETS VETERANS ROSTER

HEAD COACH—Charley Winner. Assistant Coaches—Dick Voris, Buddy Ryan, Sam Rutigliano, Ken Shipp, Bob Fry, Jim Spavital

No.	Name	Pos.	Ht.	Wt.	NFL Exp.	College
1	Adamle, Mike	RB	5-9	193	5	Northwestern
62	Atkinson, Al	LB	6-2	230	11	Villanova
76	Bailey, Jim	DT	6-6	255	6	Kansas
51	Baker, Ralph	LB	6-3	228	12	Penn State
83	Barkum, Jerome	WR	6-4	212	4	Jackson State
77	Barzilauskas, Carl	DT	6-6	280	2	Indiana
69	Belgrave, Earl	T	6-4	260	1	Ohio State
7	Bell, Ed	WR	5-10	160	6	Idaho State
68	Bernhardt, Roger	G	6-4	244	2	Kansas
40	Bjorklund, Hank	RB	6-1	200	4	Princeton
23	Bond, Jerry	S	6-3	210	1	Weber State
32	Boozer, Emerson	RB	5-11	205	10	Maryland E-S
86	Brister, Willie	TE	6-4	236	2	Southern U.
79	Browne, Gordie	T	6-5	265	2	Boston College
33	Burns, Bob	RB	6-3	212	2	Georgia
88	Caster, Richard	TE	6-5	228	6	Jackson State
90	Collins, Ed	WR	6-1	190	1	Rice
6	Demory, Bill	QB	6-2	195	3	Arizona
55	Ebersole, John	LB	6-3	235	6	Penn State
58	Ferguson, Bill	LB	6-3	225	3	San Diego State
85	Galigher, Ed	DT	6-4	260	4	UCLA
8	Gantt, Greg	P-K	5-11	188	2	Alabama
75	Hill, Winston	T	6-4	280	13	Texas Southern
20	Howell, Delles	CB	6-4	200	6	Grambling
3	Howfield, Bobby	K	5-9	180	8	None
43	Jackson, Jazz	RB	5-8	167	2	Western Kentucky
11	Jones, John	QB	6-1	195	1	Fisk
59	Kindig, Howard	C	6-6	260	10	Cal. State-L.A.
82	Knight, David	WR	6-1	182	3	William & Mary
53	Koegel, Warren	C	6-2	260	4	Penn State
5	Leahy, Pat	K	6-0	200	2	St. Louis
53	Lewis, Richard	LB	6-2	215	4	Portland State
57	Little, John	DE-DT	6-3	250	6	Oklahoma State
84	Lomas, Mark	DE	6-4	250	6	Northern Arizona
50	Mulligan, Wayne	C	6-3	250	6	Clemson
12	Namath, Joe	QB	6-2	200	11	Alabama
81	Neal, Richard	DE-DT	6-3	260	7	Southern
87	Newsome, Billy	DE	6-5	260	7	Grambling
22	Owens, Burgess	SS	6-2	200	3	Miami
37	Owens, Marv	WR	5-11	205	2	San Diego State
89	Piccone, Lou	WR	5-9	175	2	West Liberty State
25	Prout, Bob	S	6-1	190	2	Knox
78	Puetz, Garry	G	6-3	255	3	Valparaiso
66	Rasmussen, Randy	G	6-2	267	9	Kearney State
52	Reese, Steve	LB	6-2	232	2	Louisville
44	Riggins, John	RB	6-2	230	5	Kansas
54	Rivers, Jamie	LB	6-2	245	8	Bowling Green
63	Roach, Travis	G	6-2	260	2	Texas
71	Roberts, Gerry	DE	6-5	250	1	UCLA
74	Schmiesing, Joe	DT-DE	6-4	256	8	New Mexico State
46	Sowells, Rich	CB	6-0	185	5	Alcorn A&M
17	Steele, Larry	P	5-10	182	1	Santa Rosa J.C.
91	Sutton, Harold	LB	6-5	229	1	Temple
21	Tannen, Steve	S-CB	6-1	194	6	Florida
45	Thomas, Earlie	CB	6-1	190	6	Colorado State
56	Turk, Godwin	LB	6-3	230	2	Southern U.
35	Williams, James	RB	6-0	220	1	Cameron State
27	Wise, Phil	FS	6-0	190	5	Nebraska-Omaha
18	Woodall, Al	QB	6-5	194	7	Duke
70	Woods, Larry	DT	6-6	270	6	Tennessee State
72	Woods, Robert	T	6-3	255	3	Tennessee State
47	Word, Roscoe	CB	5-11	170	2	Jackson State

TOP FIVE DRAFT CHOICES

Rd.	Name	Pos.	Ht.	Wt.	Age	College
2	Anthony Davis	RB	5-8	180	23	Southern California
3	Richard Wood	LB	6-2	215	21	Southern California
5	Joe Wysock	G	6-4	250	23	Miami
6	Tom Alward	G	6-3	241	22	Nebraska
8	James Scott	WR	6-0	185	23	Henderson J.C.

AFC was as poor covering punts. And when the Jets had to replace Bobby Howfield with Pat Leahy, the placekicking went South, too. As far as the Jets returning kicks, forget it. In fact, the kicking game probably cost the Jets a couple of games.

OUTLOOK: Despair in the Big Apple, unless Namath would stay in one piece and have the sort of year he did a couple of times in the mid-1960s. Much depends on the rookies. Davis' speed is desperately needed and the linebacking could get a big shot in the leg from his USC teammate, Richard Wood. The improvement late last year won't be sustained.

JET PROFILES

RICHARD CASTER 26 6-5 228   Tight End

Smoothest and most dangerous TE in game ... Makes sky fall on the other guys and has 30 TD catches in five years ... Average of 19.6 per grab best in league among tight ends ... Had 38 catches on pass-happy club but ranked third on team ... Has the size and temperament to smack down feisty DBs ... Blocks like a WR but is improving ... Best-named wife in league—America ... Born Oct. 16, 1948, in Mobile, Ala. ... Teammate of Barkum's at Jackson State, where he also played receiver ... Deep speed gives strong safeties fits ... Fine tennis player ... Converted to TE in 1972 and went to Pro Bowl that season ... Been subject of trade talks.

WINSTON HILL 33 6-4 280   Offensive Tackle

Joe Namath's most reliable bodyguard ... Super pass-blocker ... Intelligent ... Jets like to run his tackle ... Perennial Pro Bowl, choice ... Has history of contract hassles with front office not ranked among most generous ... Played in 166 straight games ... Came to Jets after being cut by Baltimore coach Weeb Ewbank, who shortly followed him out of town ... Locker room leader on club given to cliques ... Has daughter named Hovlyn ... Texas state high school tennis champ for three years ... Born Nov. 23, 1941, in Gladewater, Tex. ... Owns ranch in Colorado ... Shut out tough Ordell Braase during Jets 1969 Super Bowl win ... Two-way All-American at Texas Southern.

NEW YORK JETS 87

JEROME BARKUM 25 6-4 212 — Wide Receiver

Jets call him "Gee"... Probably as in "gee whiz, there he goes again"... Coming off second straight fine season... Caught 41 passes, three less than in '73... Cornerbacks tightened up on him, with result average dropped from gaudy, conference-leading 18.4 to 12.8... Hit Pro Bowl in second season... Tough on slant-ins and deep stuff to flags... Great leaper... Clutch receiver... Not too fast (4.6) but quick... Born July 18, 1959, in Gulfport, Miss.... Cousin is Detroit DB Lem Barney... Has size to be good blocker... Would move to TE if Rich Caster hurt... Caught 128 passes in four seasons at Jackson State... Once grabbed 30 rebounds in high school basketball game.

EMERSON BOOZER 32 5-11 205 — Running Back

Superb competitor; bite your hand off for extra yard... Ranked 11th in AFC in rushing with 563 yards... Dropoff from career high 831 the year before... Excellent blocker who picks up blitz better than any back in football... High-kneed running style... Dislikes Namath but blocks for him "because I don't let personal feelings get involved in football"... Always known for "nose" for goal-line... Hampered almost every year by minor injuries... Born Fourth of July, 1943, in Augusta, Ga.... Drafted No. 6 out of Maryland Eastern Shore where he averaged 6.8 a pop for four years... Years have eaten up his speed, not his determination... Still has marginal hands... Topnotch banquet speaker... Has daily radio show.

RANDY RASMUSSEN 30 6-2 267 — Guard

Helped, but not much, to make Namath's knees what they are today... Actually, pass-blocking improved a lot over earlier years... Left guard for Jets for eight seasons... Best pulling guard Jets have ever had... Powerful drive blocker... Considered very coachable... Born May 10, 1945, in St. Paul, Neb.... All-NAIA at Kearney State (Neb.) for two years... Has helped turn young Robert Woods into competent offensive tackle, a hard task... Wife's name is LaWana... Farm boy turned suave and now is off-season broker... Big on banquet circuit... Good size... Age stealing speed and could be a year or two away from hanging them up.

88 THE COMPLETE HANDBOOK OF PRO FOOTBALL

JOHN RIGGINS 26 6-2 230 — Running Back

Just your average boy-next-door if the kid has a mohawk haircut and is flakier than dandruff... Has everything to be superstar but inclination... "John has the potential to be the greatest fullback ever to play this game," says Jet coach Charley Winner... Got 680 yards but still hasn't regained form of two years ago when he ran for 994 yards and led Jets in receiving... Good size and 9.8 speed... Took a long time deciding if he "wanted to play football any longer" prior to 1973 season, and sometimes doesn't... Almost quit over money dispute that year... Broke all of Gale Sayers' records at Kansas, where he rushed for 2,706 yards and countless coeds... Never missed a game or practice in college... Once told a team publicist his biggest thrill was seeing his picture on bubblegum cards.

EARLIE THOMAS 29 6-1 190 — Cornerback

When healthy, one of better cornerbacks in AFC... Only bright spot in Jet secondary that was inconsistent... Fine one-on-one defender... Has tendency to get lost some in zone situations... Born Dec. 11, 1945, in Denton, Tex.... Big play DB... Opposing quarterbacks usually work other side, cutting down on his interceptions... Two other Thomases, Emmitt of Kansas City and Skip of Oakland, combined for 15... Closes down well on run but not known as big hitter... Denver Golden Gloves champion while at Colorado State... Has master's degree in entomology (right, study of insects)... Brother Jim former San Francisco RB.

CARL BARZILAUSKAS 24 6-6 265 — Defensive Tackle

What more could anyone want than a DT nicknamed Brontosauras?... Finally put some muscle in Jets defensive line and juiced up one of worst rush lines in league... Tough kid who plays hurt... "The type of player we want," says Winner... Born March 19, 1951, in Waterbury, Conn.... Three-year regular at Indiana... Jets drafted him No. 1 a year ago after rating him best defensive lineman in nation... Uncle, Fritz, played for the Giants in early 1950s... Has the sort of size Jets have often lacked up front and runs the 40 in 5.0... Biggest virtue is strength and ability to shed blockers ... Makes typical rookie mistakes, but usually not more than once.

DAVID KNIGHT 24 6-1 182 — Wide Receiver

The new Raymond Berry ... No speed, size or strength ... All he can do is catch it ... Made 40 receptions last year and bumped Eddie Bell out of lineup ... Looks like Nutrament ad or choir boy in hippie church ... Fine knack at getting to ball and holding it, although you can hear his ribs rattle after solid hit ... Runs excellent patterns, uses head ... Not a bad blocker for wraith-like build ... Born Feb. 1, 1951, in Trieste, Italy ... Kind of receiver who makes passer look good with remarkable catches ... Polish belies lack of experience ... Out of that pro football incubator—William & Mary.

JOE NAMATH 32 6-2 200 — Quarterback

Finest dimples in league ... And on Any Given (sigh) Sunday, still the most dangerous QB in game ... Didn't have particularly good year in 1974 and led league in interceptions with 22 ... Four major operations have made knees more famous than Sophia Loren's anatomy and totally ruined his mobility ... Pro Football Register lists hobby as, well, golf ... Been in three movies and made too numerous TV appearances ... Only passer in pro history to throw for more than 4,000 yards in a season ... Despite l'affaire Super Bowl III, never been a consistent winner in big games ... "The finest athlete" Alabama's Bear Bryant "ever coached" ... Tide lost only three games and went to as many bowls during his career ... Got 400 grand to sign and caused NFL salaries to rise sharply ... Born May 31, 1943, in Beaver Falls, Pa.

AL WOODALL 29 6-5 195 — Quarterback

Heir apparent to Joe Namath's job ... Ironic in that he has similar injury problems ... Hurt last year and threw only eight passes ... Started six games in 1973 after Namath knocked out and gave indication could be promising NFL passer ... Completed better than 50 percent of his passes only two seasons he played with any regularity Born Dec. 7,

1945, in Erwin, N.C. . . . Played two years for Duke and then left school for Richmond of the Atlantic Coast Football League, which he led in passing . . . Jets' No. 2 pick in 1969 . . . In second year led Jets over Minnesota and Los Angeles . . . Poor year in '71 and spent most of '72 on cab squad . . . Very strong arm . . . Outstanding intelligence.

TOP ROOKIES

RICHARD WOOD 21 6-1 213   **Linebacker**
Key asset is quickness but average senior season cooled some scouts . . . Does 40 in 4.8 . . . May lack heft for pros . . . First three-time All-American at USC . . . Led USC in tackles as soph and junior . . . Nicknamed Batman for constantly moving arms . . . Drag racer . . . Brother, Jake, played for Detroit Tigers . . . Rated "smart" player.

COACH CHARLEY WINNER . . . Mostly a loser in head job with Cardinals and replaced father-in-law, Weeb Ewbank, last year . . . Had a 35-30-5 record in St. Louis . . . Never played pro . . . Trying to hang on until he can rebuild club through draft . . . Affable sort . . . Lost good control in St. Louis because of racial conflict that started before he got there . . . Best finish was second in Century Division with Cardinals . . . Has history of success as defensive coach but record didn't show it last year when Jets ranked 19th in the NFL . . . Was a bomber crewman and shot down over Germany in World War II, spending six weeks in POW camp . . . Must know similar feeling with Jets . . . Also an assistant at Baltimore, Washington.

CLUB HISTORY

Right away, everyone should've known the New York Jets, nee Titans, were doomed to mediocrity. Their first owner was a nasally play-by-play guy named Harry Wismer, who wound up running the club out of his West Side efficiency and blowing the payroll every other week.

Surprisingly enough, the Jets have since managed to convey a winner's image, largely due to Joe Namath putting his arm where his mouth had been in 1968 Super Bowl win over Baltimore.

Still, when all is said and done and Namath's conquests on

and off the field have turned to cold ashes, the Jets were and are mostly losers.

They've had three winning seasons in 15 years and Namath has lost four important games for every one he won. But there have been winners among them. Namath was worth 400 grand; Emerson Boozer, Matt Snell and gallant old Don Maynard only slightly less.

And would it all have been the same without Weeb Ewbank and his crewcut and foxy innocence and coachly wisdom?

INDIVIDUAL JET RECORDS

Rushing

Most Yards Game:	180	Matt Snell, vs Houston, 1964
Season:	948	Matt Snell, 1964
Career:	5,084	Emerson Boozer, 1966-74

Passing

Most TD Passes Game:	6	Joe Namath, vs Baltimore, 1972
Season:	26	Al Dorow, 1960
	26	Joe Namath, 1967
Career:	151	Joe Namath, 1965-74

Receiving

Most TD Passes Game:	3	Art Powell, vs Denver, 1960
Season:	3	Don Maynard, vs Denver, 1963
	3	Don Maynard vs San Diego, 1967
	3	Don Maynard, vs Miami, 1968
Career:	3	Richard Caster, vs Baltimore, 1972

Scoring

Most Points Game:	14	Art Powell, 1965
Season:	88	Don Maynard, 1960-72
Career:	19	Jim Turner, vs Buffalo, 1968 (1 PAT-6 FG)
Most TDs Game:	145	Jim Turner, 1968 (43 PATS-34 FG)
Season:	697	Jim Turner, 1964-70 (238 PATS-153 FG)

92 THE COMPLETE HANDBOOK OF PRO FOOTBALL

BALTIMORE COLTS

TEAM DIRECTORY: Pres.-Owner: Robert Irsay; VP-GM: Joseph Thomas; Treas.: Harriet Irsay; Dir. Player Pers.: Fred Schubach; Dir. Pro Pers.: Dick Szymanski; Pub. Dir.: Barry Jones; Head Coach: Ted Marchibroda; Trainer: Ed Block. Home: Memorial Stadium, Baltimore, Md. (60,000).

Lydell Mitchell's 72 catches led NFL.

SCOUTING REPORT

OFFENSE: Let's put it this way. A reporter who's covered the Colts longer than he'd like to admit says, "They couldn't score on me and you." Actually, that may not be true because the

BALTIMORE COLTS 93

Colts went out during the off-season and got themselves the makings of an offensive line, something they didn't have a year ago when quarterbacks Marty Domres and Bert Jones led the league in getting sacked. Plundered might be a better word.

Anyway, the Colts got fine tackle George Kunz from Atlanta and drafted guard Ken Huff, a good one who'll start. Elsewhere, up front there's mediocrity except at tight end, where there is the club receiver, Ray Chester, who hopefully is getting over the trauma of beginning his career with Oakland and Al Davis only to find himself in the clutches of Colt GM Joe Thomas. The Colts throw mostly to their backs and Lydell Mitchell led the NFL in receptions with 72. His average, however, was 7.2.

Offensively, the Colts are pretty much Mitchell, who does the running and most of the receiving. Domres and Jones do the quarterbacking. Sort of. Jones should be a good one; Domres will probably wind up watching, as he had the poorest rating of any AFC quarterback who threw more than 26 times. Glenn Doughty and Roger Carr are the targets, when they get open.

DEFENSE: The Colts have one, and it's coming along fine, thank you. Fred Cook and John Dutton started at the ends last year as rookies and sophomore tackle Joe Ehrmann began looking like all-pro material about halfway through the year. Jim Bailey worked next to Ehrmann and he was traded, so a handful of would-be replacements led by rookie Dave Pear could mean problems. In fact, lack of a rush—only the Chargers were worse among AFC teams in 1974—could hurt the Colts again this year.

Mike Curtis in the middle makes the linebacking solid at worst, but he is 32 and could be slowing. Flanking him are a pair of solid hitters, Tom MacLeod on the strong side, Stan White on the weak. In reserve are only new coach Ted Marchibroda's prayers. The Colt secondary is a good one, sparked by safety Bruce Laird and corner Nelson Muncey, but a poor rush put too much pressure on it last year and the enemy completed 57.7 of its passes, a figure matched only by San Diego.

KICKING GAME: Punter David Lee didn't excite too many Baltimore fans but is better than he looked last year. Toni Linhart, Austria's contribution to the NFL, went 12-for-20 on field goal tries and didn't miss an extra point, which was novel. The Colt special teams were neither particularly good nor particularly bad. All in all, fair.

OUTLOOK: Depends upon how players take out their reported dislike to Thomas. There is potential for improvement. Jones

COLTS VETERANS ROSTER

HEAD COACH—Ted Marchibroda. Assistant Coaches—
Maxie Baughan, George Boutselis, Whitey Dovell, Frank
Lauterbur, Pete McCulley, Jerry Smith

No.	Name	Pos.	Ht.	Wt.	NFL Exp.	College
88	Andrews, John	TE	6-3	227	4	Indiana
63	Barnes, Mike	DE	6-6	255	3	Miami (Fla.)
84	Berra, Tim	WR	5-11	185	2	Massachusetts
51	Bertuca, Tony	LB	6-2	225	2	Chico State
81	Carr, Roger	WR	6-3	200	2	Louisiana Tech
87	Chester, Raymond	TE	6-4	235	6	Morgan State
66	Collett, Elmer	G	6-4	240	9	San Francisco St.
72	Cook, Fred	DE	6-3	235	2	So. Mississippi
32	Curtis, Mike	LB	6-2	232	11	Duke
55	Dickel, Dan	LB	6-3	220	2	Iowa
14	Domres, Marty	QB	6-4	222	7	Columbia
35	Doughty, Glenn	WR	6-2	204	4	Michigan
78	Dutton, John	DE	6-6	260	2	Nebraska
76	Ehrmann, Joe	DT	6-5	260	3	Syracuse
33	Hall, Randy	CB	6-3	185	2	Idaho
7	Jones, Bert	QB	6-3	205	3	LSU
75	Kunz, George	T	6-6	268	7	Notre Dame
40	Laird, Bruce	S	6-0	185	4	American Int'l
49	Lee, David	P	6-4	230	10	Louisiana Tech
2	Linhart, Toni	K	5-11	178	3	Austria Vienna
52	MacLeod, Tom	LB	6-3	230	3	Minnesota
83	Mayo, Ron	TE	6-3	223	3	Morgan State
23	McCauley, Don	RB	6-1	214	5	North Carolina
57	Mendenhall, Ken	C	6-3	235	5	Oklahoma
26	Mitchell, Lydell	RB	5-11	204	4	Penn State
—	Mul-Key, Herb	RB	6-0	190	4	None
31	Munsey, Nelson	CB	6-1	185	4	Wyoming
50	Neal, Dan	C	6-4	240	3	Kentucky
68	Nelson, Dennis	T	6-5	260	6	Illinois State
30	Nettles, Doug	CB	6-0	177	2	Vanderbilt
25	Oldham, Ray	CB	6-0	200	3	M. Tennessee St.
38	Olds, Bill	RB	6-1	224	3	Nebraska
37	Orduna, Joe	RB	6-0	195	4	Nebraska
71	Palmer, Gery	T	6-4	255	1	Kansas
61	Pratt, Robert	G	6-3	255	2	North Carolina
56	Rhodes, Danny	LB	6-2	220	2	Arkansas
43	Rudnick, Tim	DB	5-10	185	2	Notre Dame
86	Scott, Freddie	WR	6-2	175	2	Amherst
60	Simonson, Dave	T	6-6	246	2	Minnesota
80	Smith, Ollie	WR	6-2	195	3	Tennessee St.
64	Taylor, David	T	6-4	254	3	Catawba
12	Troup, Bill	QB	6-5	220	2	South Carolina
67	Van Duyne, Bob	G	6-5	235	2	Idaho
21	Volk, Rick	S	6-3	195	9	Michigan
53	White, Stan	LB	6-1	225	4	Ohio State
74	Williams, Steve	DE	6-6	260	2	Western Carolina
65	Windauer, Bill	DT	6-3	245	3	Iowa

TOP FIVE DRAFT CHOICES

Rd.	Name	Pos.	Ht.	Wt.	Age	College
1	Ken Huff	G	6-4	260	22	North Carolina
3	Mike Washington	CB	6-3	190	22	Alabama
3	Dave Pear	DT	6-2	250	22	Washington
4	Marshall Johnson	RB	6-1	191	22	Houston
4	Paul Linford	DT	6-5	265	22	Brigham Young

can throw and should unseat Domres. A plus. The offensive line can't help but get better. Another plus. The defense will be a year older and wiser. Third plus. Still, Mitchell has to have running help, the receivers are routine and Jones is hardly polished goods. Well, the fans can always talk about John Unitas at the games.

COLT PROFILES

MIKE CURTIS 32 6-2 235   Middle Linebacker

Shuts down run better than any MLB in game ... Hits everything that moves on the field, including fan a couple of years ago ... Diamond in a shoddy setting, he managed to make Colt defense respectable in 1974 ... "Mike Curtis is the best middle linebacker in professional football," says Colt GM Joe Thomas ... "Joe Thomas is the worst (bleep) in professional football," says Curtis, or at least thinks it ... They had another run-in during off-season and Curtis says privately he'd like to be traded ... Born March 27, 1943, in Rockville, Md. ... Excellent against pass; has 17 interceptions in last five seasons ... MVP in Colts' Super Bowl V win over Dallas ... Perennial Pro Bowler ... No. 1 pick out of Duke, where he was also used as a fullback ... Colts used him there sparingly first year ... Married to ex-teammate Sam Ball's sister ... Called Mad Dog—but not to face.

RAY CHESTER 27 6-4 235   Tight End

Hard work could make him dominant tight end in game ... As is, he's merely one of the four best ... Came to Colts in trade for defensive end Bubba Smith after hassle over money with Raider owner Al Davis ... Seemed bum trade for both teams when Smith tore up knee and Chester had only 18 catches for Colts ... Rebounded well last year when he caught 37 passes, a figure topped by only two TEs in AFC ... Solid blocker ... Tremendously powerful open-field runner who once broke nine tackles on same play ... Born June 28, 1948, in Cambridge, Md. ... Highly versatile college player who worked four positions at Morgan State (Md.) ... NFL Rookie of Year in 1970 with Oakland.

96 THE COMPLETE HANDBOOK OF PRO FOOTBALL

BERT JONES 24 6-3 205 Quarterback

Valedictorian of quarterbacks, class of 1973 ... First player taken in '73 draft ... Son of former Cleveland receiver great Dub Jones ... Beat out Marty Domres to win starting job as rookie, lost it later in year, shared spot in 1974 ... Had decent season, ranking 10th among AFC quarterbacks ... Needs only experience ... One of league's stronger arms ... Excellent poise for third-year man ... "Especially for a quarterback, football is a thinking man's game," he says. "And I don't think you can play it if you're nervous" ... Durability proven after getting beat up last year due to lousy protection ... Born Sept. 7, 1951, in Ruston, La. ... Near unanimous All-American at LSU and was Sporting News Player of Year as a senior ... 53.0 completion average beefed up by throwing to backs ... Has to quit forcing passes.

JOE EHRMANN 26 6-5 260 Defensive Tackle

Should become one of fine DTs in league after learning that he couldn't overpower every guard across from him ... Anchored good defensive line last year ... "I found out two things," he says. "You can't be a football player without learning to accept pain. And after I got out-techniqued a few times, I discovered this game is more mental than physical" ... Started nine games as a rookie in 1973 and missed three because of a knee injury ... Born March 29, 1949, in Buffalo ... Three-year regular at Syracuse and was probably best defensive lineman in country senior season ... Fine pass-rusher ... Lost some speed due to torn-up knee at Syracuse that kept him out of 1971 season.

GLENN DOUGHTY 24 6-2 210 Wide Receiver

Well-named ... Fastest Colt ... Jumps well "but doesn't always come down with ball," says Baltimore writer ... Fair hands, moves ... Led club with 26 receptions in 1973 ... Best on short routes ... Born Jan. 30, 1951, in Detroit ... Rushed for 1,464 yards at Michigan despite being used mostly as a blocking back senior year ... Colts' second pick in 1972 and converted to receiver ... Won job as rookie ... "Glenn's one of the quality receivers in the NFL—he's on his way to the Pro Bowl," Colt coach Howard Schnellenberger said last year,

BALTIMORE COLTS 97

shortly before he was on his way to the unemployment office ... Excellent basketball player.

MARTY DOMRES 28 6-4 222   Quarterback

Poorest job last year among AFC regulars because of tendency to lean hard on short pass and throw too many interceptions ... Lives in $100,000 home, drives Mercedes, which isn't bad for QB with bad habit of abandoning pocket ... Tough ... Has to be because Colt QBs sacked more than any others in league in 1974 ... Impossible job of replacing John Unitas ... Now sharing job with probable successor, Bert Jones ... Born April 17, 1947, in Ithaca, N.Y. ... Studied anthropology under Margaret Mead ... Very bright ... Set 12 Ivy League passing records at Columbia and owns NCAA record for most total plays in career (1,133) ... Only average arm ... No TD passes in 1974 ... Stock broker ... One of most popular figures in Baltimore until last winter.

RICK VOLK 30 6-3 200   Safety

Tricky Ricky ... Only half as tricky in 1974, when interceptions dropped off from usual four to two ... Declining, but not as much as those around him ... Hurt by unsettled position of Colt secondary last two seasons ... Youngish-looking and was carded three years ago on anniversary ... Hard tackler but can be had on pass by speedburner ... Born March 15, 1945, in Toledo ... Went to Michigan as quarterback, but became one of finest defensive backs in Wolverine history ... Rep as clutch player ... Helped save Super Bowl V win over Dallas with interception ... Durable enough to have started 58 straight games in one stretch.

STAN WHITE 25 6-1 225   Linebacker

One of those linebackers of whom it is said "is always in wrong position but makes right play" ... Fine instinctive player ... Underrated hitter ... Better outside but has played middle when Mike Curtis was hurt ... Born Oct. 24, 1949, in Kent, Ohio ... Placekicker and two-year regular at Ohio State ... Colts got him in 17th round of 1972 draft and he came into own in 1973 when he led Colts in tackles (147) interceptions (4) and fumble recoveries (6), the latter a club record ... Fine special team player as a rookie ... Blitzes well ... Made only one interception last year, but returned it 52 yards for touchdown ... Teams with Curtis and Tom McLeod to give Colts strong linebacking trio.

LYDELL MITCHELL 26 5-11 205 — Running Back

Must've been guy man who invented merit raise had in mind ... Led NFL in receiving with 72 receptions although his 7.6 average was lowest among leaders and rushed for 757 yards. Again, 3.5 average was unimpressive ... Extremely durable ... Lacks breakaway speed—longest run was 31 yards—but is honest workman with good tools ... Born May 30, 1949, in Salem, N.J. ... Close friend of Franco Harris at Penn State ... Finished fifth in Heisman balloting as senior ... Instant hit with Colts, setting club single-season rushing record of 963 yards despite not playing in first three games ... Set three NCAA career records—single-season points (174), touchdowns (29) rushing touchdowns (26) ... Unanimous All-American.

JOHN DUTTON 24 6-6 260 — Defensive End

Bless the Colt scouting report on Dutton, which contained the following phrases prior to his being drafted No. 1 in 1974: "Great size, speed and athletic ability; has it all to be great pro; can defeat blockers; good against run; will get bigger" And, yes, Virginia, it all came true ... Regular as a rookie and didn't hurt club at all ... Smart player not often fooled, though lacks real experience ... Born Feb. 6, 1951, in Rapid City, So. Dakota ... Consensus All-American at Nebraska ... Fine discus thrower ... Got better as tough season wore on and is regarded by front office as all-pro material.

TOP ROOKIES

KEN HUFF 22 6-4 260 — Guard

Ranked top OL in country by two scouting combines ... Comes at time when club needs guards desperately ... All-American at

North Carolina and called by coach Bill Dooley "the best lineman I've ever been associated with"... Father a Navy captain... Psych major, which will help in Baltimore... Born Feb. 21, 1953, in Hutchinson, Kan.

MIKE WASHINGTON 22 6-3 190   **Defensive Back**
Big hitter... Made three All-America teams and was top DB in Southeastern Conference... Also played freshmen basketball at Alabama... Eight interceptions and seven blocked kicks for Tide during career... Colt scouting report on him: "Has excellent 4.6 speed in 40, a real hitter, great height and range... Can play either corner or safety."

COACH TED MARCHIBRODA... Replaces GM Joe Thomas in move that must've left players cheering for days... Moves into screwy situation with Thomas looking over one shoulder and owner Robert Irsay, who fired Howard Schnellenberger on the field last year, over the other... Legacy is lousy football team riddled by dislike of Thomas and curiosity at what Irsay might pull next... Served last nine years as assistant and offensive coordinator under George Allen at Washington... Was restricted because Allen ran offense... No. 1 draft pick of Steelers and quarterback they kept while ridding themselves of John Unitas... Played at St. Bonaventure and Detroit... Diplomatic type... Lacks Allen's charisma and phony image... Fine student of game... Considered strong tactician.

CLUB HISTORY

In some distant eon, a six-headed, no-legged, purple creature will open up a time capsule, pause over a history of the Baltimore Colts, and shake all six heads wearily in disbelief. Who'd ever believe the Colts?

Has ever a history been so rich, so pungent? First, John Unitas—what Sammy Baugh would've been if he'd had his druthers. Then the second-line legends, Hall of Famers all, Gino Marchetti and Jim Parker and Raymond Berry and Art Donovan.

Coaches the stripe of Weeb Ewbank and Don Shula; an owner with the gall of a Carroll Rosenbloom, who traded them en masse for the Los Angeles franchise.

Mediocrity their first six years, an NFL title won in sudden-death. Four more years of mediocrity; another NFL title. Super Bowl winners, Super Bowl losers. And, lately, more mediocrity.

In toto: Never a dull moment.

INDIVIDUAL COLT RECORDS

Rushing

Most Yards Game:	198	Norm Bulaich, vs N.Y. Jets, 1971
Season:	963	Lydell Mitchell, 1973
Career:	5,174	Lenny Moore, 1956-67

Passing

Most TD Passes Game:	5	Gary Cuozzo, vs Minnesota, 1965
Season:	32	John Unitas, 1959
Career:	287	John Unitas, 1956-72

Receiving

Most TD Passes Game:	3	Jim Mutscheller, vs Green Bay, 1957
	3	Raymond Berry, vs Dallas, 1960
	3	Raymond Berry, vs Green Bay, 1960
	3	Jimmy Orr, vs Washington, 1962
	3	Jimmy Orr, vs Los Angeles, 1964
Season:	14	Raymond Berry, 1959
Career:	68	Raymond Berry, 1955-67

Scoring

Most Points Game:	24	Lenny Moore, vs Chicago, 1958
	24	Lenny Moore, vs Los Angeles, 1960
	24	Lenny Moore, vs Minnesota, 1961
Season:	120	Lenny Moore, 1964
Career:	678	Lenny Moore, 1956-67
Most TDs Game:	4	Lenny Moore, vs Chicago, 1958
	4	Lenny Moore, vs Los Angeles, 1960
	4,	Lenny Moore, vs Minnesota, 1961
Season:	20	Lenny Moore, 1964
Career:	113	Lenny Moore, 1956-67

OAKLAND RAIDERS 101

OAKLAND RAIDERS

TEAM DIRECTORY: Gen. Partners: Al Davis (Managing), E.W. McGah, Wayne Valley; Exec. Asst.: Al LoCasale; Bus. Mgr.: Ken LaRue; Dir. Pub. Rel.: Tom Grimes; Head Coach: John Madden; Trainer: George Anderson. Home: Oakland Coliseum, Oakland Calif. (54,041).

Ken Stabler led the league with 26 TD passes.

SCOUTING REPORT

OFFENSE: If it gets any better this winter, Al Davis' hairline may quit receding, it's that potent. And it is the reason the Raiders went 12-2. The No. 1 unit in the league has no discernible weakness, although Davis would like a better all-purpose fullback and is trying to trade Marv Hubbard. He ran for 865 yards last winter, which gives you an idea of Oakland's strength.

Quarterback Kenny Stabler was the NFL Player of the Year and mastered two of the tougher chores of the profession: patience and bomb-throwing. He is a whiz on the 15-17 yard routes which make up much of the Raider passing game, has learned to exploit defensive weaknesses as well as the Khmer Rouge, and now throws the deep pass as well as all but a few quarterbacks in the league.

The line is awesome. Guard Gene Upshaw beats up most tackles and, with peerless deceit, holds the ones he can't brutalize. Art Shell is the game's most underrated tackle. Center Jim Otto aged rapidly last year, but there is a fine replacement in Dave Dalby, who looked good against Pittsburgh in the playoffs. The receivers are unmatched. Cliff Branch and wily Fred Biletnikoff combined for a league-high 102 catches. Behind them is Mike Siani, hurt last year, who had 45 catches in 1974. Bob Moore is a capable receiver and blocker who will be pushed by second-year pro Dave Casper. The offense could improve should Harold Hart, who had a 5.3 average in 1974, play to his brilliant potential.

DEFENSE: Oakland's flaw. Both Pittsburgh and Miami moved the ball well against the Raiders in the playoffs, and the club finished 16th in the league in total defense. Both of which may give Madden pause to ponder his Situation Substitution strategy. The line and the secondary are the Raiders' two weakest units. End Bubba Smith has never fully recovered from a knee injury and the good guards handle tackle Art Thoms.

The secondary only gave up 12 TD passes a year ago, but it's getting kind of long of tooth. The once-incomparable Willie Brown is 34 and the other reserves, Jimmy Warren and Ron Smith, are in their 30s. No. 1 draft pick Neal Colzie could replace Brown or challenge Skip Thomas at the other corner. Jack Tatum is the best safetyman going; George Atkinson's exploits don't quite match his Ali-like mouth.

Sandwiched between a good-but-not-great defensive line and a secondary suddenly questionable is a linebacking unit that's both good and bad. On the outside, Phil Villapiano gets the ink and Gerald Irons the quiet gratitude of his teammates. In the middle, veteran Dan Conners is the club's weakest link. But, as is usual with the Raiders, there is someone waiting in the wings. He's young vet Monte Johnson, who may replace Conners.

KICKING GAME: If they can shoot the Geritol into George Blanda's leg, which weakened early last year but was its tough,

OAKLAND RAIDERS 103

RAIDERS VETERANS ROSTER

HEAD COACH—John Madden. Assistant Coaches—Ollie Spencer, Tom Dahms, Bob Zeman, Tom Flores, John Robinson, Joe Scannella, Don Shinnick

No.	Name	Pos.	Ht.	Wt.	NFL Exp.	College
43	Atkinson, George	S	6-0	180	8	Morris Brown
40	Banaszak, Pete	RB	5-11	210	10	Miami
46	Bankston, Warren	TE-RB	6-4	235	7	Tulane
25	Biletnikoff, Fred	WR	6-1	190	11	Florida State
16	Blanda, George	QB-K	6-2	215	26	Kentucky
81	Bradshaw, Morris	WR	6-0	198	2	Ohio State
21	Branch, Cliff	WR	5-11	170	4	Colorado
24	Brown, Willie	DB	6-1	195	13	Grambling
64	Buehler, George	G	6-2	260	7	Stanford
61	Carr, Ray	DT	6-5	248	1	Newberry
87	Casper, Dave	TE	6-4	250	2	Notre Dame
84	Cline, Tony	DE	6-3	244	6	Miami
55	Conners, Dan	LB	6-1	230	12	Miami
50	Dalby, Dave	C-G	6-2	240	4	UCLA
28	Davis, Clarence	RB	5-10	195	5	Southern California
54	Dennery, Mike	LB	6-0	222	2	Southern Mississippi
73	Gay, Blenda	DE	6-5	250	1	Fayetteville State
18	Gaydos, Kent	TE	6-6	228	1	Florida State
8	Guy, Ray	K	6-3	190	3	Southern Mississippi
83	Hall, Willie	LB	6-2	220	3	Southern California
34	Hart, Harold	RB	6-0	206	2	Texas Southern
44	Hubbard, Marv	RB	6-1	225	7	Colgate
36	Hudson, Bob	RB	5-11	205	4	Northeastern, Okla.
86	Irons, Gerald	LB	6-2	230	6	Md.-Eastern Shore
6	Jakowenko, George	K	5-9	170	2	Syracuse
58	Johnson, Monte	LB	6-4	235	3	Nebraska
82	Jones, Horace	DE	6-3	255	5	Louisville
71	Korver, Kelvin	DT	6-6	270	3	Northwestern, Iowa
3	Lamonica, Daryle	QB	6-3	215	13	Notre Dame
70	Lawrence, Henry	T	6-4	268	2	Florida A&M
13	Lawrence, Larry	QB	6-1	208	2	Iowa
79	Medlin, Dan	G	6-3	260	2	North Carolina State
88	Moore, Bob	TE	6-3	220	5	Stanford
00	Otto, Jim	C	6-2	255	16	Miami
67	Paul, Harold	T	6-5	245	1	Oklahoma
85	Pitts, Frank	WR	6-3	199	11	Southern
78	Shell, Art	T	6-5	265	8	Maryland St. (ES)
49	Siani, Mike	WR	6-2	195	4	Villanova
60	Sistrunk, Otis	DT	6-4	255	4	None
77	Smith, Bubba	DE	6-7	265	8	Michigan State
23	Smith, Charlie	RB	6-0	205	8	Utah
27	Smith, Ron	DB	6-1	195	11	Wisconsin
12	Stabler, Ken	QB	6-3	215	11	Alabama
32	Tatum, Jack	S	5-11	200	5	Ohio State
—	Thaxton, Jim	TE	6-2	240	3	Tennessee State
26	Thomas, Alonzo	DB	6-1	205	4	Southern California
80	Thoms, Art	DT	6-5	260	7	Syracuse
63	Upshaw, Gene	G	6-5	255	9	Texas A&I
30	van Eeghen, Mark	RB	6-1	215	2	Colgate
75	Vella, John	T	6-4	255	4	Southern California
41	Villapiano, Phil	LB	6-2	222	5	Bowling Green
20	Warren, Jimmy	CB-S	5-11	175	12	Illinois
52	Weaver, Gary	LB	6-1	224	3	Fresno State

TOP FIVE DRAFT CHOICES

Rd.	Name	Pos.	Ht.	Wt.	Age	College
1	Neal Colzie	CB	6-2	200	22	Ohio State
2	Charles Phillips	S	6-2	200	22	Southern California
3	Louis Carter	RB	5-11	200	22	Maryland
5	Dave Humm	QB	6-2	180	22	Nebraska
7	James Daniels	S	6-1	185	23	Texas A&M

old self later on, everything will be excellent here. Ray Guy is one of the fine punters in the league. The coverage is swift and sure and old Ron Smith remains one of the dangerous return men in the NFL.

OUTLOOK: With Miami stricken by the loss of Warfield and Csonka, and with the Pittsburgh offense perhaps not so impressive as it appeared in the playoffs, the Raiders are the best team in the NFL. They should get another chance to prove it in January.

RAIDER PROFILES

FRED BILETNIKOFF 32 6-1 190   **Wide Receiver**

The Coyote (because he looks like one) ... Lost a lot of money in Oakland restaurant called The flanker. Could afford it because he is one of all-time great receivers ... Constant stomach problems—always vomits before games and missed two weeks of practice last year with stomach ailments ... 450 career catches makes him fourth among active players .. Had 42 in 1975 but failed to lead club for seventh straight year when his pupil, Cliff Branch, caught 60 balls ... Big-game performer, especially tough on mouthy defensive backs. Destroyed such types of Johnny Sample and Fred Williamson in critical games ... Born Feb. 23, 1943, in Erie, Pa. ... Exceptionally close to black Raiders ... Led NFL with 61 catches in 1971 ... All-American at Florida State.

DAN CONNERS 34 6-1 230   **Linebacker**

Rep for making strange statements, but well-liked by everyone ... Age has slowed him down ... Played out option two years ago and Raider boss Al Davis offered him to several teams, including Pittsburgh, for chattel mortgage on franchise concerned. No takers ... Coming off average year and probably weakest spot in strong Raider defense ... Will be challenged for middle LB job by Monte Johnson ... One of highest-scoring LBs in league history (five TDs) ... Born Feb. 6, 1941, in St. Mary's, Pa. ... Played in AFL All-Star Game in 1967-68-69 ... Three-year regular at defensive tackle at Miami (Fla.) ... Raiders' second pick in 1963.

OAKLAND RAIDERS

CLARENCE DAVIS 26 5-10 195 — Running Back

One of 16 Davises in NFL ... Probably the quietest ... Extraordinary strength for a running back probably his finest virtue ... Introverted ... Shot-put champion at Southern California, where his 2,323 yards rushing ranked him third to only O.J. Simpson and Mike Garrett ... Broke Simpson's national junior college record with 1,582 yards for East Los Angeles JC ... Extremely durable ... Fine blocker ... Good receiver ... Born June 28, 1949, in Birmingham ... Incorrectly underrated. Says Miami coach Don Shula, "He does so many things well he can hurt you before you know it's happening" ... Ranked 12th in AFC with 554 yards, but average fell off from 5.3 to 4.3 ... First time he'd been under 5.0 in four years.

MARV HUBBARD 29 6-1 225 — Running Back

Marvelous Marv ... Would be one of great runners in history—if you had to run straight ahead. Limited skills otherwise ... "Every linebacker in the league ought to get to cover Marv to build up confidence," says one veteran NFL LB ... Fifth in AFC in 1974 with typical 865-yard season ... But Raiders are still trying to trade him, as they did two years ago when all Al Davis wanted in return was Green Bay's John Brockington ... Born May 7, 1946, in Salamanaca, N.Y. ... Oakland's No. 11 pick in 1968, cut and resigned after year in Atlantic Coast League ... Bar brawler, lost airplane fight with teammate George Atkinson ... Very emotional after games ... Strong individualist ... Built own house, top-to-bottom ... Wears more than 20 pounds of equipment in games ... Fine back at Colgate ... Bad hands.

JIM OTTO 37 6-2 255 — Center

Classic example of what the aging process does to even the great ones ... Streak—shared with team's other greybeard George Blanda—of 210 straight league games is NFL record ... Only original Raider left ... 16th season probably one too many and he should lose job to young Dave Dalby, who played most of AFC title game against Steelers ...

Strong pro-management man during last year's strike ... Has lost rapport with rest of Oakland offensive linemen ... Until last season, missed only minutes of every Raider game ... Outstanding hustler ... Played in all 311 games of Raider history ... All-league center for every AFL all-star team and chosen to Hall of Fame AFL team of decade.

KEN STABLER 29 6-3 215   Quarterback

The Snake ... Probably the finest quarterback in the game ... Ranked second in NFL passing to Cincinnati's Ken Anderson ... Led league in touchdown passes with 26 ... Popular leader who inspired Raiders when he succeeded Daryl Lamonica early in 1973. "The Raiders put out for Stabler in a way they never quite did for Lamonica," says ex-Oakland defensive tackle Tom Keating ... Team took off flying when Stabler got job and many observers think Raiders are the best club in NFL despite AFC title-game loss to Pittsburgh ... Excellent play-caller and middle-distance passer; strong, gutty runner on occasion ... Asked to be traded before supplanting Lamonica ... Signed with Birmingham of WFL for reported $900,000, but contract was invalidated ... Born Christmas Day, 1946, in Foley, Ala. ... Pro Bowl choice for second year in 1974 ... Guided Alabama to national championship in 1965 ... Raiders' No. 2 pick that winter.

JACK TATUM 27 5-11 200   Free Safety

Talks softly, carries a big hit ... One of game's fiercest tacklers ... Underrated some ... Plays difficult position, as Raiders put pressure on free safety to come up quickly and make more than usual number of tackles ... Tackled Pittsburgh's Frenchy Fuqua on last-second play dubbed The Immaculate Reception when Franco Harris caught deflection and ran for TD that gave Steelers playoff win in 1972 ... Quite possibly the best free safety in league ... Made annual Pro Bowl appearance ... Born November 18, 1948, in Cherryville, N.C. ... Drafted No. 1 in 1971 after getting extraordinary amount of ink as safetyman at Ohio State ... Holds NFL record for 102-yard fumble recovery return against Green Bay in 1972.

OAKLAND RAIDERS

GENE UPSHAW 29 6-5 255   Guard

Could be league's finest guard ... Excellent puller ... Something of locker-room politician, but well-liked ... Extremely bright ... Ran for city council in Oakland ... Heavily involved in businesses ... Played in 114 straight games ... Older brother, Marv, is defensive end for Kansas City ... Very active in NFL Players Assn. ... Serves as effective buffer between white and black Raiders and is respected by both ... Born Aug 15, 1945, in Robstown, Tex. ... Played center, tackle and end at Texas A&I and was Oakland's first pick in 1967 ... Consistent Pro Bowl choice ... Called "one of the game's great holders," by Pittsburgh's Ernie Holmes. "Nobody ever catches slick Gene" ... Operates two Oakland nightclubs.

PHIL VILLAPIANO 26 6-1 222   Linebacker

Considered one of five best outside LBs in league but may be overrated ... Overshadows another fine outside LB on his own club, Gerland Irons ... Big hitter hated by tight ends, who consider him cheap-shot artist ... Had several field fights, including a couple with San Francisco's Ted Kwalick ... Coming off excellent year that put him in Pro Bowl for second straight season ... Head-hunter who made huge splash in rookie year on a Monday Night game during which Howard Cosell canonized him ... Born Feb, 26, 1949, in Long Branch, N.J. ... Dad is a high school athletic director ... No. 2 pick in 1971 after being Mid-American Conference Defensive Player of Year at Bowling Green.

CLIFF BRANCH 27 5-11 170   Wide Receiver

Whooooosh ... Potential to be game's most dangerous receiver ... 9.3 speed, Salome's moves, runs good patterns ... Doesn't have a pickpocket's hands, but they're better than at first suspected ... Got a chance to play in 1974 when Mike Siani tore a hamstring and needed surgery early in year ... Answered opportunity while its knuckles were still on the door and wound up fourth in the NFL with 60 receptions and led with 13 TD catches ... Sixth in league with 18.6 average ... Born August 1, 1948, in Houston ... Quiet, super-confident

... World class sprinter, setting world indoor record (9.3) in the 100 and tying it in 60 (5.9) ... All-purpose back at Colorado, but hampered in pros because the Buffs did not throw the ball much and track kept him out of spring practice ... Bomb from Stabler helped win playoff game with Miami.

TOP ROOKIES

NEAL COLZIE 22 6-2 205   **Defensive Back**
Rated best DB in nation as Ohio State senior ... Made eight interceptions in 1974 ... Led country in punt returns as a junior ... Could start at a corner as rookie and is heir apparent to Willie Brown ... Ohio State lost just three games during his career ... 15 career interceptions ... Florida High School Athlete of Year in 1970.

CHARLES PHILLIPS 22 6-2 215   **Defensive Back**
Sparked Southern California comeback against Notre Dame by intercepting three passes and returning one for TD ... Returned fumbles 98 and 83 yards for TDs against Iowa last year ... Fine speed and size for corner, but may be used initially at safety ... Made several All-America teams ... Fumble and interception returns for 302 yards during career is NCAA record.

COACH JOHN MADDEN ... Al Davis' alter ego but much better coach than generally thought ... Wild man on sidelines, likeable away from them ... Called "Pinky" by players because face reddens when excited ... Never had a losing season anywhere as a head coach ... Pro record of 58-19-7 ... Became Raider coach in 1969 at a callow 38 and was youngest coach in league ... Coach of Year in 1969 ... Somehow manages to coach with Davis peering steadily over shoulder and has won five straight AFC West titles ... Big enough (6-4, 230) to play tackle, which he played (as well as catcher) at Cal Poly. ... Played with Philly Eagles one season before knee injury ended playing career ... Smarter than he appears.

CLUB HISTORY

See Raiders win. See Al Davis smile. See Raiders lose the big one. See heads roll. See Al Davis howl. See Al Davis. See Al Davis. See ...

For all of time, mention of the Oakland Raiders will evoke the name Al Davis. Svengali of the NFL whose name is mentioned 21 times in first four pages of the club press guide.

No man save St. Vince ever stamped an NFL club the way Davis has branded Oakland. Its success is his—six straight AFC West titles and an AFL championship in 1964—its failures are his. The Raiders have not won the biggie.

"I spent a hundred years in Oakland one season," says ex-Raider Tom Keating, summing up most players' attitude to working for Davis.

But the club—sparked down the years by George Blanda and Daryle Lamonica and Jim Otto and Willie Brown—has the league's winningest percentage over the last 11 seasons with a record of 113-43-11.

Success, thy name is Davis.

INDIVIDUAL RAIDER RECORDS

Rushing
Most Yards Game:	200	Clem Daniels, vs N.Y. Jets, 1963
Season:	1,100	Marv Hubbard, 1972
Career:	5,103	Clem Daniels, 1961-67

Passing
Most TD Passes Game:	6	Tom Flores, vs Houston, 1963
	6	Daryle Lamonica, vs Buffalo, 1969
Season:	34	Daryle Lamonica, 1969
Career:	148	Daryle Lamonica, 1967-74

Receiving
Most TD Passes Game:	4	Art Powell, vs Houston, 1963
Season:	16	Art Powell, 1963
Career:	60	Fred Biletnikoff, 1965-74

Scoring
Most Points Game:	24	Art Powell, vs Houston, 1963
Season:	117	George Blanda, 1968
Career:	780	George Blanda, 1967-74 (351 PATS-143 FG)
Most TDs Game:	4	Art Powell, vs Houston, 1963
Season:	16	Art Powell, 1963
Career:	60	Fred Biletnikoff, 1965-74

110 THE COMPLETE HANDBOOK OF PRO FOOTBALL

DENVER BRONCOS

TEAM DIRECTORY: Chairman of Board: Gerald Phipps; Pres.: Allan Phipps; GM-Head Coach: John Ralston; Asst. GM-Dir. Player Pers.: Fred Gehrke; Dir. Scouting: Carroll Hardy; Dir. Pub. Rel.: Bob Peck; Trainer: Allen Hurst. Home: Denver Mile High Stadium, Denver, Colorado (51,706).

Otis Armstrong had 1,407 yards rushing, tops in NFL.

SCOUTING REPORT

OFFENSE: Somehow the Bronco offense, as good as it's been for two years, never seems quite enough to offset the Bronco defense, best described as a bunch of stiffs in search of a hole to fall in. Last year, little Otis Armstrong ran the ball better than anyone else; the club doctor held quarterback Charley Johnson together with tape and hope, and Denver scored 302 points. Or only eight more than the defense gave up.

Ol' Charley, 36 and holding these last few years, is a major question mark this year. He's tough enough but, after all, his X-rays are considered collector's items by the AMA and how long can he last? If he can't make it through the year, there will be trouble in the Rockies. Backup men Steve Ramsay and little-used John Hufnagel won't get coach John Ralston that AFC wild-card he's counting on this year because they can't throw or think or read defenses with Johnson.

But the Broncs will run. Armstrong proved sturdy enough to go inside, and the unknowns of the offensive line are better than they look and will be beefed up if tackle Marv Montgomery recovers from a knee injury that kept him out all of 1974. Receiver Haven Moses was excellent much of last year, but on the other side Ralston is left basically with Billy Van Heusen after trading Jerry Simmons to Atlanta for DB Clarence Ellis and losing the rights to Otto Stowe when he signed DE Phil Olsen. Last but certainly ... tight end Riley Odoms catches, runs and, best of all, blocks.

DEFENSE: Okay. Ah ... yes, defense. Well, the Broncos don't have much. Without the repeatedly injured Paul Smith at a tackle, the pass rush must depend on ends Lyle Alzado and Barney Chavous. Ralston swapped guard Larron Jackson to Atlanta for defensive tackle Greg Marx, and went for defense heavily in the draft by taking cornerback Louie Wright and tackle Charley Phillips 1-2. Ray May remains a fine outside linebacker, but doesn't get much help, and Randy Gradishar has a way to go in the middle, especially against the pass.

The secondary consists of a bunch of guys named Joe and there were only two NFL teams easier to throw against last year than Denver. Bill Thompson successfully made the switch from corner to strong safety, but it's downhill from there. Good passing clubs shredded the Broncos due to the inconsistent pass rush and secondary inefficiencies. In fact, almost 60 percent of the yardage the Broncos surrendered was made with the pass.

KICKING GAME: Things started badly for placekicker Jim Turner—he blew a shortie to cost Denver a win against Pittsburgh in the second game—and got worse. He made just 11 of 21 field goal tries and at 34 may be losing his leg. Billy Van Heusen isn't. He finished ninth in the NFL in punting, but generally poor coverage hurt the Denver kicking game.

BRONCOS VETERANS ROSTER

HEAD COACH—John Ralston. Assistant Coaches—Joe Collier, Richard "Doc" Urich, Bob Gambold, Myrel Moore, Max Coley, Jerry Frei, Kay Dalton

No.	Name	Pos.	Ht.	Wt.	NFL Exp.	College
77	Alzado, Lyle	DE	6-3	252	5	Yankton, S.D.
11	Anderson, Bobby	RB	6-0	208	5	Colorado
—	Andrews, Billy	LB	6-0	225	9	S.E. Louisiana
24	Armstrong, Otis	RB	5-10	196	2	Purdue
65	Arnold, LeFrancis	G	6-3	245	2	Oregon
87	Brown, Boyd	TE	6-4	216	2	Alcorn A&M
79	Chavous, Barney	DE	6-3	252	3	So. Carolina St.
54	Cindrich, Ralph	LB	6-1	230	4	Pittsburgh
76	Coleman, Steve	DE	6-4	252	2	Delaware State
53	Criter, Ken	LB	5-11	223	7	Wisconsin
74	Current, Mike	T	6-4	270	9	Ohio St.
55	Duranko, Pete	DT	6-2	250	9	Notre Dame
—	Echols, Reggie	DB-WR	6-2	190	1	UCLA
—	Ellis, Clarence	S	6-0	190	4	Notre Dame
86	Frazier, Marv	WR	6-0	180	1	Cheyney St.
52	Gradishar, Randy	LB	6-3	233	2	Ohio St.
63	Grant, John	DE	6-3	235	3	So. California
60	Howard, Paul	G	6-3	260	3	Brigham Young
16	Hufnagel, John	QB	6-1	194	2	Penn St.
57	Jackson, Tom	LB	5-11	220	3	Louisville
12	Johnson, Charley	QB	6-1	200	15	New Mexico St.
—	Johnson, Charlie	DB	6-1	190	0	Southern
26	Jones, Calvin	CB	5-7	169	3	Washington
72	Kampa, Bob	DT	6-4	245	3	California
32	Keyworth, Jon	RB	6-3	230	2	Colorado
44	Little, Floyd	RB	5-10	196	9	Syracuse
22	Lynch, Fran	RB	6-1	205	9	Hofstra
61	Lyons, Tom	G	6-2	230	5	Georgia
50	Maples, Bobby	C	6-3	250	11	Baylor
—	Marx, Greg	DT	6-4	260	2	Notre Dame
81	Masters, Billy	TE	6-5	240	9	LSU
56	May, Ray	LB	6-1	230	9	So. California
71	Minor, Claudie	T	6-4	280	2	San Diego St.
25	Moses, Haven	WR	6-2	208	7	San Diego St.
78	Montgomery, Marv	T	6-6	255	5	So. California
88	Odoms, Riley	TE	6-4	230	4	Houston
—	Olsen, Phil	DE	6-5	265	5	Utah State
66	O'Malley, Jim	LB	6-1	230	3	Notre Dame
—	Ellis, Clarence	S	6-0	190	4	Notre Dame
48	Pitts, John	S	6-4	218	9	Arizona St.
10	Ramsey, Steve	QB	6-2	210	6	North Texas St.
59	Rizzo, Joe	LB	6-1	220	2	Mer. Mar. Acad.
30	Ross, Oliver	RB	6-0	210	3	Alabama A&M
46	Rowser, John	CB	6-1	190	9	Michigan
64	Schnitker, Mike	G	6-3	245	7	Colorado
—	Sens, Mark	T	6-5	265	1	Colorado
75	Smith, Ed	DE	6-5	241	3	Colorado College
70	Smith, Paul	DT	6-3	256	7	New Mexico
36	Thompson, Bill	S	6-1	200	7	Maryland St.
15	Turner, Jim	K	6-2	205	12	Utah St.
23	Tyler, Maurice	S	6-0	188	4	Morgan St.
42	Van Heusen, Bill	WR-P	6-1	200	8	Maryland
—	Walton, Chuck	G	6-3	256	9	Iowa St.
—	Weatherley, Jim	C	6-3	245	1	Mt. San Antonio

TOP FIVE DRAFT CHOICES

Rd.	Name	Pos.	Ht.	Wt.	Age	College
1	Louie Wright	CB	6-2	195	22	San Jose State
2	Charles Smith	DE	6-5	245	21	North Carolina Central
3	Mike Franckowiak	QB	6-3	220	22	Central Michigan
3	Drew Mahalic	LB	6-4	225	22	Notre Dame
4	Steve Taylor	S	6-0	188	22	Georgia

DENVER BRONCOS 113

OUTLOOK: There isn't enough defensive talent on hand to move Denver up appreciably in the standings; certainly not enough to challenge Oakland in the AFC West. The Broncos could also have trouble staying ahead of an improving San Diego club. In general, too many question marks and not enough Otis Armstrongs.

BRONCO PROFILES

OTIS ARMSTRONG 24 5-10½ 190   **Running Back**

Legstrong would be more like it... Led NFL in rushing with 1,407 yards and topped it in the other two major categories, average (5.3) and single-game performance (183)... Had seven 100-yard games, including last four... Only fifth back in history to average better than 100 yards a game... Excellent receiver, caught 39 passes to finish 11th in AFC, fourth among backs... Major reason why Broncs were fifth best offensive team in NFL... Biggest assets as runner are instincts and quick first move... Born Nov. 15, 1950, in Chicago... Holds all Purdue rushing records... Second-round pick because considered marginal prospect due to lack of size... Says "obviously I'm big enough"... Well-liked by teammates and news media.

CHARLEY JOHNSON 36 6-1 200   **Quarterback**

Strung together like Six-Million Dollar Man, he's undergone an operation for almost each of his 15 years in league... Finished fifth among NFL passers... Nobody, but nobody, reads defenses better... Tough competitor who played almost entire 1970 season with broken collarbone... "There's no way Charley could've done more for us," says Bronco coach John Ralston... Has thrown for more than 22,000 yards in career... Lacks mobility and it has caused him to get hurt... Born Nov. 22, 1938, in Big Spring, Tex. ... Previously played for Houston and St. Louis, where he still holds most of the club passing records... Led New Mexico State to two Sun Bowl wins... Has Ph.D. in chemical engineering... Outstanding golfer.

RANDY GRADISHAR 23 6-3 233   Linebacker

Score one for Denver scouting department, as Gradishar, whose knees were reportedly too shaky to stand pro game, had good rookie season ... Moved into regular spot early in year after injuries to regulars ... Played middle but could move outside ... A hitter ... Had minor problems adjusting to pass, but played run well ... Lack of experience in middle has hurt him ... Always played wide side at Ohio State, where Woody Hayes called him "the finest linebacker we've ever had here" ... Says "I'm more comfortable in the middle, but I can play outside" ... Born March 3, 1952, in Warren, Ohio ... Underwent knee surgery after being hurt in 1973 Rose Bowl and several pro teams lost interest in him even though he didn't miss a game or a practice as senior.

LYLE ALZADO 26 6-3 265   Defensive End

What all good DEs are—mean ... Developed into fine pass rusher ... One of deadlier sets of forearms in game, but primary game is outside rush ... Among the quickest down linemen in game, has run 4.7 in 40 ... Just average against the run ... Under pressure last year on unit that finished 24th against the pass because of weak rush ... Born April 3, 1949, in Brooklyn ... Onetime regional Golden Gloves champ and won 27 straight as amateur ... Very strong, has bench pressed 500 pounds ... Has degree in special education and teaches handicapped children ... First player ever drafted from Yankton (So. Dak.) College ... Four-year regular.

FLOYD LITTLE 33 5-10 195   Running Back

Spirit's still willing, but the knees are weak and they may only last one more year ... Coming off poorest pro season. Lost job to Armstrong and gained only 312 yards. Worse, had a 2.7 average ... Excellent receiver and had 29 catches although splitting time ... Led NFL in rushing in 1971 with 1,133 yards and has topped 850 four times ... Works with various Denver youth groups ... Most popular Bronco ever ... Has lost some of outside speed, but remains elusive ... Owns clothing store with Chicago cornerback Nemiah Wilson ... Born Independence Day, 1942, in New Haven, Conn. ...

DENVER BRONCOS 115

College football's first bonafide three-year All-American in more than 15 years after leaving Syracuse in 1966 with Jim Brown's rushing records ... In prime was never on team which could fully exploit his talents.

MARV MONTGOMERY 27 6-6 255   Offensive Tackle

Was going to be one of the finest tackles in game until his leg went snap, crackle and pop against Steelers late in '73 season ... Now going to be a question mark ... Bone graft didn't speed healing process and he was largely a zero in 1974 ... Still has tools to be great. House-sized with quickness ... Broncs' No. 1 pick in 1971 after distinguished career at USC ... All-star technique at position Vince Lombardi called "the hardest in the game to master" ... Born Feb. 8, 1948, in Torrance, Calif., town known for producing poker players ... Learned to hold really well ... Transferred to Southern Cal as junior from Los Angeles Valley College ... Excellent pass blocker.

HAVEN MOSES 29 6-3 205   Wide Receiver

Big talent, bigger ego ... Never quite lived up to expectations although has had two solid years in row ... Caught 34 passes last year and owned rather gaudy 16.4 average ... Has speed, body control, size and leaping ability to be superstar ... Everything, apparently, but the ambition ... Not particularly effective blocker ... Catches well in a crowd, which doesn't necessarily mean he can't get open ... Born July 27, 1946, in Los Angeles ... One of top three receivers in country in '67 at San Diego State ... Drafted No. 1 by Buffalo, but traded to Broncs a year later for cornerback Dwight Harrison.

RILEY ODOMS 25 6-4 230   Tight End

Prototype of modern tight end ... Deep speed, locomotive power ... New John Mackey, of whom it was said, "the lucky ones fall off him" ... Hates comparison with Philly's Charlie Young, but it's inevitable since they're the two top TEs in game ... Caught 42 passes last year, good enough to lead AFC tight ends but only enough to give him distant view of Young, who caught 63 ... Pro Bowl ever since rookie year... Has too many drops... Likes to trample DBs, and does... Born March 1, 1950, in Luling, Tex.... All-American at Houston and Denver's first pick in 1972... A hit from the beginning and caught 21 passes as rookie while learning to block NFL linebackers.

PAUL SMITH 29 6-3 256 — Defensive Tackle

Funny thing happened to him on way to immortality... He tore up a knee to go with earlier shoulder and finger ailments... All of which must postpone Ralston's theory that "he's the finest defensive tackle in pro football today"... Maybe yesterday, which for Smith would be 1973, when he made Pro Bowl and was named Denver's top defensive player... Now must prove he can come back from injuries... If not, Ralston should try to cancel season, as Denver's defense all but nonexistent without him... One of best pass-rushers, he averaged 11 sacks a season prior to 1974... Born Aug. 13, 1945, in Ada, Okla.... First sophomore at New Mexico U. ever to be named Lineman of Year... A ninth-round pick in 1968.

BILLY VAN HEUSEN 29 6-1 200 — Receiver-Punter

Namath wouldn't want his knees, which have probably kept him from superstardom... Has had eight knee operations... Finished ninth in NFL in punting with 40.3 average... More importantly, hangs ball very well and is adept corner kicker whose accuracy saved Denver from two defeats... Fine receiver... Made only 16 receptions, but owned 26.3 average, best in league... Wants to play regularly and has asked to be traded... Born Aug. 27, 1946, in New Rochelle, N.Y.... Exceptional athlete... Played halfback, quarterback, flanker and defensive back at Maryland... Near-scratch golfer... One of most popular Broncos.

TOP ROOKIES

LOUIE WRIGHT 22 6-2 190 — Defensive Back

Almost every scout's choice as the best defensive back in the draft... Beaten deep once in three seasons at San Jose State and that one came on deflection... Has run 9.7 in 100, 21.8 in 220... Knocks down low-hanging clouds on leaps... Needs muscle

... Also question of ability to shut down the sweep ... Good football smarts.

CHARLES SMITH 22 6-6 260   **Defensive End**
Could be sleeper of draft ... One scout says "he has all-pro potential" ... Nickname Bubba ... Played for defensive line at North Carolina Central called The Gruesome Four ... No particular speed and could be moved inside as Broncos strive for stronger defense, and might have to replace Paul Smith.

COACH JOHN RALSTON ... Fine coach, lousy prognosticator ... After Denver was 0-1-1 said "we'll win the next 12 and make the Super Bowl" ... Club did neither and defense still has a way to go ... The Norman Vincent Peale of the NFL; never sees a silver lining because he overlooks clouds ... In only two years made a winner out of Broncos, something they hadn't been in their previous 14 winters ... Gregarious, ever-smiling ... Players say he talks too much ... Does very little game-day coaching, with assistants Max Coley and Joe Collier running the club ... Makes big buck as after-dinner speaker ... Became head coach and GM in 1972 ... Two years later club was respectable 7-5-2 and only a final-game loss to Oakland kept Denver from AFC West title ... Was 54-36-3 in nine years at Stanford, where he developed several fine quarterbacks ... Oakland-born, Ralston was a linebacker on two U. of California Rose Bowl teams.

CLUB HISTORY

There have been a few bright spots. Couple of winning exhibition seasons. The day management ceased its long civil war and Gerald Phipps got control of the club. The weather's nice some Sundays. Damn little pollution around Mile High Stadium.

And, of course, John (Keep Your Sunny Side Up) Ralston. You know about John Ralston, of course. Teeth never lacking for fresh air. The guy who pulled the Denver Broncos out of their 13-year hibernation.

Through dint of hard work and boundless optimism, Ralston has actually made the Denver Broncos—hold on—competitive. After years of enthusing only over Floyd Little's good moves and Lionel Taylor's hands, the Denver fans actually get to see winning football. About half the time.

118 THE COMPLETE HANDBOOK OF PRO FOOTBALL

Which ain't bad when in its 15-year existence, the ballclub failed to win more than five games on 12 occasions.

Long live Riley Odoms and Otis Armstrong and the rest. Denver turned the corner in 1973. Went 7-5-2 for first winning season. Can the Super Bowl be far behind?

INDIVIDUAL BRONCO RECORDS

Rushing
Most Yards Game:	183	Otis Armstrong, vs Houston, 1974
Season:	1,407	Otis Armstrong, 1974
Career:	5,878	Floyd Little, 1967-74

Passing
Most TD Passes Game:	5	Frank Tripucka, vs Buffalo, 1962
Season:	24	Frank Tripucka, 1960
Career:	51	Frank Tripucka, 1960-63

Receiving
Most TD Passes Game:	3	Haven Moses, vs Houston, 1973
	3	Bob Scarpitto, vs Buffalo, 1966
	3	Lionel Taylor, vs Buffalo, 1960
Season:	12	Lionel Taylor, 1960
Career:	50	Lionel Taylor, 1960-66

Scoring
Most Points Game:	21	Gene Mingo, vs Los Angeles, 1960
Season:	137	Gene Mingo, 1962 (4 TD-32 PATS-27 FG)
Career:	399	Gene Mingo, 1960-65 (11 TD-117 PATS-72 FG)
Most TDs Game:	3	Floyd Little, vs Cincinnati, 1973
	3	Floyd Little, vs Minnesota, 1972
	3	Haven Hoses, vs Houston, 1973
	3	Bob Scarpitto, vs Buffalo, 1966
	3	Don Stone, vs San Diego, 1962
	3	Lionel Taylor, vs Buffalo, 1960
	3	Otis Armstrong, vs Houston, 1974
	3	Jon Keyworth, vs Kansas City, 1974
Season:	13	Floyd Little, 1972, 1973
Career:	50	Lionel Taylor, 1960-66
	50	Floyd Little, 1967-74

SAN DIEGO CHARGERS 119

SAN DIEGO CHARGERS

TEAM DIRECTORY: Pres.: Eugene Klein; GM-VP: Harland Svare; Asst. to Pres. Player Pers.: John Sanders; Bus. Mgr.: Bob Hood; Dir. Pub. Rel.: Jerry Wynn; Head Coach: Tommy Prothro; Trainer: Ric McDonald. Home: San Diego Stadium, San Diego, Calif. (52,568).

Don Woods runs behind blocking of Doug Wilkerson.

SCOUTING REPORT

OFFENSE: Coach Tommy Prothro says "if the rookies develop quickly and our young veterans improve greatly, we can be contenders. But realistically, you can't count on it." Right, because the Chargers have half-a-team—the offensive half. The offensive line is called The Unknown Soldiers, but led by tackle Russ Washington, it's a dandy. And, of course, there is Don Woods,

120 THE COMPLETE HANDBOOK OF PRO FOOTBALL

who should improve on his 1,162 yards rushing because last year he got them all in 10 games.

However, there are other problems. Like at quarterback, where Dan Fouts is injury prone and unreliable and second-year pro Jesse Freitas is merely greener than spinach. Neither took charge and that may be the reason the Chargers lacked confidence inside the other guys' 20.

San Diego had the seventh-ranked offense in the league a year ago, but still managed fewer points than all but one team in the AFC. This in spite of Woods' running and the explosive blocking of rookie fullback Bo Matthews. Woods will get running help from Bears' retread Jim Harrison, 240 pounds of muscle, but Gary Garrison probably will have to carry the receiving load alone, as he did last year by catching 41 passes. Jerry LeVias seems over the hill and lost his job to rookie Harrison Davis, who had trouble getting off the line and had only 18 catches.

DEFENSE: You San Diegans remember defense, don't you? What you do when the other folks have the ball? And what the Chargers did worse than any team in the NFL last year when they gave up a horrendous 4,830 yards. For that reason, the Chargers' first seven draftees were defenders. Five of them will probably start—tackles Gary Johnson and Louie Kelcher, cornerback Mike Williams, linebacker Ken Bernich and free safety Mike Fuller. That's bad. Worse is the absolute need for decent seasons from vets Coy Bacon and Bob Brown up front.

The linebacking is Goode and bad. Don Goode was probably the defensive MVP and should improve on the strong side. Floyd Rice was fair on the weak side and the middle was a disaster after vet Fred Forsberg was hurt early-on. MLB Chuck Anthony was a rookie last year and it showed. Chris Fletcher was the club's top DB last year at strong safety, but he can be shuffled to free safety or a corner as the situation dictates.

The Charger defense, bolstered by the hiring of ex-Portland Storm boss Dick Coury as linebacker coach, can hardly help but improve. But it is still a draft away from severely handicapping the offense, and until it quits doing that the Chargers will not be contenders. No one has to tell coach Tommy Prothro. "I hope our fans don't anticipate too much too quickly," he says.

KICKING GAME: The Chargers don't have much. Ray Wersching hit on just six of 16 field-goal attempts and was one of the reasons the Chargers failed to score more. Punter Dennis Partee had a 40.0 average, seventh in the AFC, kicked extra points and went one-for-five trying field goals.

SAN DIEGO CHARGERS 121

CHARGERS VETERANS ROSTER

HEAD COACH—Tommy Prothro. Assistant Coaches—John David Crow, Jackie Simpson, Earnel Durden, Bobb McKittrick, Howard Mudd, Rudy Feldman, Dick Coury, George Dickson

No.	Name	Pos.	Ht.	Wt.	NFL Exp.	College
59	Anthony, Charles	LB	6-1	230	2	USC
79	Bacon, Coy	DE	6-4	270	8	Jackson State
40	Beauchamp, Joe	S	6-0	188	10	Iowa State
85	Beirne, Jim	WR	6-2	206	8	Purdue
45	Berry, Reggie	S	5-11	185	4	Long Beach State
73	Boatwright, Bon	DT	6-5	262	2	Oklahoma State
21	Bonner, Glen	RB	6-2	202	2	Washington
78	Brown, Bob	DT	6-5	290	10	Arkansas A&M
46	Colbert, Danny	S	5-11	167	2	Tulsa
88	Cotton, Craig	TE	6-4	225	6	Youngstown
87	Davis, Harrison	WR	6-4	219	2	Virginia
52	Douglas, Jay	C-T	6-6	260	3	Memphis State
86	Dunbar, Jubilee	WR	6-0	196	3	Southern U.
39	Dunlap, Len	CB	6-2	198	5	North Texas State
44	Fletcher, Chris	S	5-10	182	6	Temple
56	Forsberg, Fred	LB	6-1	225	7	Washington
14	Fouts, Dan	QB	6-3	193	3	Oregon
17	Freitas, Jesse	QB	6-1	203	2	San Diego State
27	Garrison, Gary	WR	6-1	195	10	San Diego State
54	Gersbach, Carl	LB	6-1	230	6	West Chester State
50	Goode, Don	LB	6-2	234	2	Kansas
69	Gordon, Ira	G	6-3	265	6	Kansas State
82	Grannell, Dave	TE	6-4	230	2	Arizona State
34	Harrison, Jim	RB	6-4	238	5	Missouri
23	Hoey, George	CB	5-10	180	5	Michigan
13	Horn, Don	QB	6-2	195	9	San Diego State
24	Howard, Bob	CB	6-2	177	5	San Diego State
26	Jones, Clint	RB	6-0	205	8	Michigan State
71	Lazetich, Pete	DE	6-3	245	4	Stanford
25	LeVias, Jerry	WR	5-9	177	7	SMU
65	Markovich, Mark	G-C	6-5	256	2	Penn State
41	Matthews, Bo	RB	6-4	230	2	Colorado
55	Mauck, Carl	C	6-4	243	7	Southern Illinois
53	Myrtle, Chip	LB	6-2	225	8	Maryland
76	Owens, Terry	T	6-6	260	10	Jacksonville State
80	Parris, Gary	TE	6-2	226	3	Florida State
29	Partee, Dennis	K	6-1	209	8	SMU
57	Rice, Floyd	LB	6-3	223	5	Alcorn A&M
74	Rowe, Dave	DT	6-7	265	9	Penn State
89	Stewart, Wayne	TE	6-7	230	6	California
83	Sweet, Joe	WR	6-2	196	4	Tennessee State
77	Teerlinck, John	DT	6-5	245	2	Western Illinois
35	Thomas, Bob	RB	5-10	202	5	Arizona State
38	Thompson, Tommy	RB	6-1	205	2	Southern Illinois
75	Tipton, Dave	DE	6-6	240	5	Stanford
68	Vertefeuille, Brian	T	6-3	252	2	Idaho State
70	Washington, Russ	T	6-7	289	8	Missouri
15	Wersching, Ray	K	5-11	210	3	California
63	Wilkerson, Doug	G	6-3	256	6	North Carolina Central
47	Williams, Sam	CB	6-2	192	2	California
33	Woods, Don	RB	6-1	210	2	New Mexico

TOP FIVE DRAFT CHOICES

Rd.	Name	Pos.	Ht.	Wt.	Age	College
1	Gary Johnson	DE	6-2	257	23	Grambling
1	Mike Williams	CB	5-10	180	21	Louisiana State
2	Louie Kelcher	DT	6-5	291	20	Southern Methodist
2	Fred Dean	LB	6-3	224	23	Louisiana Tech
3	Mike Fuller	S	5-10	188	22	Auburn

122 THE COMPLETE HANDBOOK OF PRO FOOTBALL

OUTLOOK: Club on the rise, but like a skyscraper—slowly. The offense isn't able to carry the defense because it lacks the primary requisite, seasoned and steady quarterbacking. The defense hangs on the rookies, which in the NFL is simply a good way to hang. All in all, the Chargers are a year away from contention. Maybe a light year.

CHARGER PROFILES

DON WOODS 24 6-2 200   **Running Back**

Made the Brinks job look like a candy-store heist after Chargers got him for $100 waiver price from Green Bay... Second-leading runner in NFL to Denver's Otis Armstrong with 1,162 yeards and 5.1 average... Packers cut him and kept somebody named Eric Torkelson because they "didn't like his blocking and tendency to fumble;" later admitted error... Got 157 yards against Miami for second-best one-game effort in AFC... Six games over 100 yards... More than adequate replacement for retired Mike Garrett... Deceiving speed to outside... "There weren't any better backs last year," said Los Angeles coach Chuck Knox... Born Feb. 17, 1951, in Denton, Tex.... Transferred to New Mexico U. from New Mexico Highlands... Wishbone quarterback at New Mexico under Rudy Feldman, a Charger assistant who triggered waiver claim ... Fine receiver who finished among top 35 in AFC with 26 catches and 13.4 average.

Bo Matthews adds power to ground game.

SAN DIEGO CHARGERS

DON GOODE 24 6-2 224 — Linebacker

One of Chargers' two first round picks a year ago—back Bo Matthews was the other ... Second half of last season, was team's top defensive player ... Tremendous build ... Joined strikers as a rookie until discovering he wasn't going to get paid, at which time he returned to camp ... Outstanding potential ... Born June 21, 1951, in Houston ... "He's like a boxer, when he hits people he stops 'em in their tracks," described Charger player personnel director Tom Miner ... Nicknamed Sugar ... Called "an explosive hitter" by Kansas coach Don Fambrough and proved it as a rookie ... Played strong side for Chargers ... African studies student.

CHRIS FLETCHER 26 5-11 185 — Defensive Back

On a team that had the sort of defense displayed at the Alamo, he was one of two solid performers (Goode was the other) ... Best defensive back on club ... Worked at strong safety last year, but may go to free safety or a corner this fall depending upon where Chargers are hurting the worst ... Had four interceptions in 1974 after winning starting job early in season ... Forte is consistency and the ability to forget being burned ... Part-time starter in 1973 after missing '72 season due to knee injury ... Returned kicks in 1971 and 1972 but now too valuable—Chargers finished 26th in team defense—for those chores ... Born Christmas day, 1948, in Morristown, N.J. ... Active in Black Athletes Foundation ... Three-year starter at Temple.

JESSE FREITAS 23 6-1 190 — Quarterback

Had incredible camp until veterans reported and may have been psyched by presence of regular Dan Fouts ... Recovered poise late and started final three games after Fouts broke thumb passing ... Led Chargers to their best win of year, 17-0 in Denver ... Will challenge the erratic Fouts for regular job ... Poor runner ... Sets up very well for young quarterback ... Coach Tom Prothro says he "sees receivers very well for his experience" ... Born Sept. 19, 1951, in San Mateo,

Calif. ... Rode bench behind Jim Plunkett at Stanford for two years before transferring to San Diego State, where he was the nation's total offense and passing leader in 1973 ... Lack of height made him Chargers' sixth draft pick.

DAN FOUTS 24 6-3 195   Quarterback

Rep as a "glass house" ... Broken thumb knocked him out of three games last year after he won starting job ... Shoulder injury cost him pre-season and four league games previous year ... Regarded as inaccurate under pressure ... Like the little girl with the curl, when he's good ... and so forth ... Born June 10, 1951, in San Francisco ... Oregon passing and total offense leader. "He's the toughest individual and best college passer I've ever seen," said Oregon coach Dick Enright ... Ranked 11th in AFC in quarterback ratings and had a 48.5 percent completion average ... Poor runner ... Big interest in politics ... Will be pressed to hold job this year.

GARY GARRISON 31 6-2 193   Wide Receiver

Probably most underrated receiver in game ... Called The Ghost for ability to run after catch ... Ranked fifth in AFC with 41 receptions despite fact Chargers had no threat on the other side and he was constantly double-teamed ... The solid professional the Chargers have so few of ... Shoulder injury limited him to five starts in 1973 and he only had 13 catches, but has topped 40 in each of his nine other season ... Born Jan. 21, 1944, in Amarillo, Tex. ... Runnerup to Len Dawson as NFL Man of the Year in 1973 ... Ranks fourth among active receivers with 375 receptions ... Had 148 catches last two seasons at San Diego State ... Banker and horse trainer in off-season.

RUSS WASHINGTON 28 6-6 290   Offensive Tackle

Most valuable Charger, which ain't saying a lot but got him into Pro Bowl ... Few peers as a pulling tackle ... Amazingly quick for a man his size ... Runs the 40 in 4.9 ... Just coming into his own and nucleus around which decent offensive line was built by Prothro ... Fine athlete who stars as a receiver in after-practice touch games ...

SAN DIEGO CHARGERS

Born Dec. 17, 1946, in Kansas City ... Fourth player selected in 1968 draft after making All-Big Eight three years while at Missouri ... Played some offensive tackle and fullback at Missouri ... Pursuing acting career ... Outstanding pass blocker ... One of last players to leave practice field ... May well develop into game's dominant offensive lineman.

COY BACON 32 6-4 270   Defensive End

One of great names in game next to Fair Hooker (Arch Pork?) ... In ninth season, playing on past rep and will be pushed hard by two high draft picks, Gary Johnson and/or Lou Kelcher ... His name mentioned by Chargers in trade discussions provoked widespread yawning ... A powerhouse a few years ago; now fringe player ... Born Aug. 30, 1943, in Cadiz, Ky. ... Inauspicious start in football as mediocre player at Jackson State and in Continental League ... Bloomed after signing with Dallas as free agent in 1967 ... Went to Rams in 1968 for a fifth-round draft pick and made Pro Bowl in 1971 and 1972 ... Recreation supervisor in San Diego ... Ran 80 yards with interception in 1973 ... Still regarded as a hitter.

SAM WILLIAMS 23 6-1 186   Cornerback

Another of the 1974 rookies San Diego hopes will lead Chargers from NFL wilderness ... Played all 14 games at a corner after being drafted in 12th round ... A big hitter who will get a look at strong safety in camp ... Rarely beaten ... So aggressive he started a fight last year in front of the Kansas City bench ... Born July 22, 1952, in Cameron, Tex. ... Transferred to California after two seasons at New Mexico Highlands and immediately drew attention of pro scouts ... Quiet ... Very strong for slender build ... Called "one of the good young cornerbacks" by Denver coach John Ralston ... Will start somewhere in secondary in 1975.

TOP ROOKIES

GARY JOHNSON 23 6-2 260   Defensive End
Certain starter on poorest defensive unit in league ... Nicknamed Big Hands ... How big are they? Well, he says "sometimes I can't even get them in my pockets." ... MVP in

East-West and Senior Bowl games . . . Great strength and good quickness . . . "The best defensive lineman in football," said Grambling coach Eddie Robinson . . . Made some All-America teams as a sophomore.

MIKE WILLIAMS 22 5-10 180 **Defensive Back**
Will challenge veteran Bobby Howard for cornerback job . . . Outstanding DB in SEC as LSU senior . . . Made All-American at safety after playing corner first two years . . . Fine speed . . . Size makes him a bit questionable but should add weight . . . Had 25-yard plus average returning kickoffs . . . Also returned punts.

COACH TOMMY PROTHRO . . . In the vernacular, has it all . . . Smarts (life master in bridge), size (6-3, 270), experience (16 years in major college ranks, three in pros) . . . In fact, has so much size that club paid his way to a fat farm in off-season to get his weight down . . . Said in 1974 when he took Charger job, "I have no illusions about being a miracle worker" . . . Miracle called for and his shrewd reconstruction of club could bring it about in, say, 1976 season . . . 104-55-5 at Oregon State and UCLA . . . Only 14-12-2, though, with Los Angeles Rams and bounced . . . Father, Doc, onetime manager of Philadelphia Phillies . . . Star blocking back as player at Duke . . . Gregarious and respected by everyone associated with Chargers.

CLUB HISTORY

Remember when Bambi scared people in the NFL and Jack Kemp wasn't a congressman and there were guys like Keith Lincoln and Paul Lowe running behind guys like Ron Mix, and remember when people didn't snicker when someone mentioned the Chargers? Remember?

They can in San Diego. Barely. For the Chargers, the feast came early when they reached the AFL championship game in six of their first seven seasons.

But the famine goes on and on. There are no more Lance Alworths and the Chargers have won more than five games only once in five years in the NFL.

Sid Gillman took his ulcers to Houston when it began to go downhill, and uncertain ownership and lousy drafts have left fans leering slightly when the Chargers are mentioned.

SAN DIEGO CHARGERS 127

INDIVIDUAL CHARGER RECORDS

Rushing

Most Yards Game:	206	Keith Lincoln, vs Boston, 1964
Season:	1,162	Don Woods, 1974
Career:	4,963	Paul Lowe, 1961-67

Passing

Most TD Passes Game:	5	John Hadl, vs Denver, 1968
Season:	27	John Hadl, 1968
Career:	201	John Hadl, 1962-72

Receiving

Most TD Passes Game:	4	Lance Alworth, vs Denver, 1968
Season:	14	Lance Alworth, 1965
Career:	81	Lance Alworth, 1962-70

Scoring

Most Points Game:	24	Lance Alworth, vs Denver, 1968
Season:	106	Dennis Partee, 1968 (43 PATS-22 FG)
Career:	500	Lance Alworth, 1962-70
Most TDs Game:	4	Lance Alworth, vs Denver, 1968
Season:	15	Lance Alworth, 1964
Career:	83	Lance Alworth, 1962-70

Lance Alworth made his marks.

KANSAS CITY CHIEFS

TEAM DIRECTORY: Pres.: Lamar Hunt; Ex. VP-GM: Jack Steadman; Asst. GM: Jim Schaaf; Sec. Treas.: Ron Combest; Pub. Rel. Dir.: Bob Sprenger; Head Coach: Paul Wiggin; Trainer: Wayne Rudy. Home: Arrowhead Stadium, Kansas City, Mo. (78,138).

Woody Green was bright spot in Chiefs' running game.

SCOUTING REPORT

OFFENSE: Old. Geritol, hardening-of-the-arteries old. And, worse, in the wrong places. At quarterback, where Len Dawson is immobile, prone to injury because of it, and pushing too hard to quit a winner. And one can only wonder why Hank Stram let the offensive line go to hell. Surrounding all-pro center Jack

Rudnay is mostly decay and bad pass-protectors in the persons of guards Ed Budde and George Daney and tackle Jim Tyrer. The other tackle is second-year man Charlie Getty, but he had heavy rookie problems in 1974.

The receivers aren't in much better shape. Otis Taylor is a brilliant talent, but would rather be someplace else. Elmo Wright looks best doing an occasional strut-step in the end zone. Barry Pearson is dependable. Behind him, zilch. Woody Green is going to be a delight, but elsewhere at running back there is journeyman Ed Podolak, on the verge of being run out of town because fans got tired of him being Stram's offense, and aging Wendell Hayes.

The draft brought a tight end, where Gary Butler holds forth with no need of help. And, sigh, there's the quarterback picture. Time may well have run out on Dawson; Mike Livingston's forte is inconsistency, and young David Jaynes may have a chronic sore arm.

DEFENSE: Older than the offense and 25th out of 26 a year ago. Where to begin? Chiefs traded unhappy Curly Culp and wound up with mediocre pass rush supplied largely by improving end Wilbur Young. On the other side, Marvin Upshaw is pedestrian and Buck Buchanan ain't nearly what he used to be, with result people run up the pipe on Chiefs. Also not what they once were are two of the three linebackers. Bobby Bell has slowed noticeably. Willie Lanier keeps talking about quitting and the thoughts have to affect him. Jim Lynch is a good one; but one, or two, isn't enough. Young vet Clyde Werner will put some serious heat on Bell in camp if he's recovered from foot surgery. Whenever Lanier does pack it in, Lynch will have to move to the middle, weakening two positions. Chiefs needed a linebacker out of the draft and didn't get one.

The secondary is more settled and is getting too much pressure from the lack of a competent rush. All-pro Emmitt Thomas got that way by leading the league in interceptions. He is also right up there in getting burned. Jim Kearney has also threatened to quit and is getting along. On the left corner, Nate Allen is a journeyman and Jimmy Marsalis sits, at some sort of odds with the front office. Kearney's safety cohort Mike Sensibaugh is a reliable one.

Depth is also a problem defensively. The line is paper thin. Tackle John Matuszak, who still insists on straightening up with the snap too often, isn't Curley Culp but can go the route. Buchanan could use a breather, and may get a long one if reserve Tom Keating's free spirit is acceptable to new coach Paul Wig-

CHIEFS VETERANS ROSTER

HEAD COACH—Paul Wiggin. Assistant Coaches—Chet Franklin, Bob Schnelker, Joe Spencer, Vince Costello, Tom Pratt, Tom Bettis, Steve Ortmayer

No.	Name	Pos.	Ht.	Wt.	NFL Exp.	College
48	Allen, Nate	CB	5-10	170	5	Texas Southern
—	Atkins, Dave	RB	6-1	210	2	Texas El Paso
—	Avery, Ken	LB	6-0	227	9	Southern Mississippi
78	Bell, Bobby	LB	6-4	228	13	Minnesota
84	Briggs, Robert	DE	6-4	258	7	Heidelberg
83	Brunson, Larry	WR	5-11	180	2	Colorado
86	Buchanan, Buck	DT	6-7	270	13	Grambling
71	Budde, Ed	G	6-5	265	13	Michigan State
82	Butler, Gary	TE	6-3	235	3	Rice
9	Carlson, Dean	QB	6-3	210	4	Iowa State
65	Condon, Tom	G	6-3	240	2	Boston College
60	Daney, George	G	6-4	240	8	Texas El Paso
16	Dawson, Len	QB	6-0	190	19	Purdue
69	DeBernardi, Fred	DE	6-6	250	2	Texas El Paso
76	Drougas, Tom	T	6-4	267	4	Oregon
24	Ellison, Willie	RB	6-2	210	9	Texas Southern
77	Getty, Charlie	T	6-4	260	2	Penn State
56	Graham, Tom	LB	6-2	235	4	Oregon
27	Green, Woody	RB	6-1	205	2	Arizona State
80	Hamilton, Andy	WR	6-3	190	3	LSU
73	Hill, Dave	T	6-5	260	13	Auburn
52	Humphrey, Tom	C	6-6	260	2	Abilene Christian
12	Jaynes, Dave	QB	6-2	212	2	Kansas
32	Jones, Doug	S	6-2	202	3	San Fernando Valley
46	Kearney, Jim	S	6-2	206	11	Prairie View A&M
74	Keating, Tom	DT	6-2	247	12	Michigan
31	Kinney, Jeff	RB	6-2	215	4	Nebraska
—	Kratzer, Dan	WR	6-3	194	3	Missouri Valley
63	Lanier, Willie	LB	6-1	245	9	Morgan State
10	Livingston, Mike	QB	6-4	212	8	Southern Methodist
—	Lohmeyer, John	DE	6-4	229	2	Emporia State
51	Lynch, Jim	LB	6-1	235	9	Notre Dame
40	Marsalis, Jim	CB	5-11	194	7	Tennessee State
79	Matuszak, John	DE	6-8	275	3	Tampa
30	Miller, Cleophus	RB	5-11	202	2	Arkansas (Pine Bluff)
70	Nicholson, Jim	T	6-6	261	2	Michigan State
47	Osley, Willie	CB	6-0	195	2	Illinois
57	Palewicz, Al	LB	6-1	215	3	Miami (Fla.)
85	Pearson, Barry	WR	5-11	185	4	Northwestern
75	Peay, Francis	G	6-5	250	10	Missouri
14	Podolak, Ed	RB	6-1	205	7	Iowa
—	Polen, Bruce	DB	5-11	180	1	William Penn
15	Reardon, Kerry	S	5-11	180	5	Iowa
—	Roman, Nick	DE	6-3	245	7	Ohio State
20	Sensibaugh, Mike	S	5-11	192	5	Ohio State
3	Stenerud, Jan	K	6-2	187	9	Montana State
87	Strada, John	TE	6-3	230	2	William Jewell
43	Thomas, Bill	RB	6-2	225	4	Boston College
18	Thomas, Emmitt	CB	6-2	192	10	Bishop
50	Thornbladh, Bob	LB	6-1	220	2	Michigan
89	Taylor, Otis	WR	6-3	215	11	Prairie View A&M
81	Upshaw, Marvin	DE	6-4	260	8	Trinity
72	Walton, Wayne	T	6-5	255	4	Abilene Christian
54	Werner, Clyde	LB	6-3	230	6	Washington
44	Wilson, Jerrel	P	6-2	222	13	So. Mississippi
17	Wright, Elmo	WR	6-0	190	5	Houston
99	Young, Wilbur	DE	6-4	285	5	William Penn

TOP FIVE DRAFT CHOICES

Rd.	Name	Pos.	Ht.	Wt.	Age	College
2	Elmore Stephens	TE	6-3	235	23	Kentucky
3	Cornelius Walker	DT	6-1	245	21	Rice
6	Morris LaGrand	RB	6-1	212	22	Tampa
6	Dave Wasick	LB	6-3	220	22	San Jose State
8	Wayne Hoffman	T	6-4	230	23	Oklahoma

KANSAS CITY CHIEFS 131

gin. Back of the ends there is nothing but hard times. Much the same situation with the linebackers and secondary.

KICKING GAME: Seems to have gone downhill with rest of the club. Once the best, Jan Stenerud was victim of more-distant goalposts and hit just six of 14. Jerrel Wilson is the best punter in the AFC. Conversely, Chiefs' special teams were poorest, sadly lacking overall speed.

OUTLOOK: A real struggle for Chiefs to stay out of AFC West basement and play .500 ball. Green will juice up the offense playing an entire season, but if gallant old Len D. isn't right, forget it because the defense is sagging.

CHIEF PROFILES

WOODY GREEN 23 6-0 198   **Running Back**

Cornerstone upon which Chiefs will try to rebuild from rubble left by Hank Stram ... Could be one of the league's best inside-outside runners this year ... Question concerning his ability to withstand the beating inside ... Fractured a shoulder his senior year at Arizona State, reinjured it the third exhibition game and then was hurt again in the seventh league game and had off-season surgery ... Needs more muscle and is trying to get it lifting weights ... Brilliant acceleration outside if hole is closed ... Gained 509 yards last year despite missing almost half the year ... Exceptional reader of blocking ... 4.5 speed ... Born July 20, 1952, in Warren Ohio ... Broke Dallas defensive back Mel Renfro's prep records at Jefferson High in Portland, Ore., and was consensus two-time All-American at Arizona State, where he rushed for 3,806 yards and 33 touchdowns.

LEN DAWSON 40 6-0 190   **Quarterback**

Another of the old-folks which caused the fall of KC ... Still, at 40 one of the better QBs around ... Club needs his leadership as well as his arm, since Mike Livingston doesn't provide either ... Stayed out of Stram firing—"At this stage, I don't want to make enemies"—after being healthy in 1974 following season in which injuries kept him out of eight games ... Desperately "wants to go out a winner" ... All-time NFL passing leader with 27,616 yards ... Lost job as sports director of KC television station after Stram fired ... Born June 20, 1935, in Alliance, Ohio ... No. 1 draft choice of Pittsburgh in 1959 after distinguished career at Purdue ... Traded to Cleveland, cut, signed by Dallas Texans of AFL in 1962 and led them to title.

JACK RUDNAY 28 6-3 240 — Center

Only effective player on KC offensive line that last year leaked like a flophouse roof ... Called "most underrated center in pros" until got enough attention in 1973 to make Pro Bowl ... Great at cutting middle linebacker ... So great, in fact, that Dick Butkus once told him, straight-faced, "I'm going to kill you" ... Strong snapper, pass-blocker ... Born Nov. 21, 1947, in Cleveland ... Probably will die sometime in September in KC if he doesn't get some help up front ... Gives teammates hell on field for mistakes ... Center and defensive tackle at Northwestern ... Works with retarded children and sells real estate in off-season ... Back injury kept him out of his rookie season in 1969 ... One of the best-liked players in locker room.

EMMITT THOMAS 32 6-2 195 — Cornerback

Led league in interceptions with 12—and in getting burned ... Gambler who makes big play one game, goes to stake the next ... Led league in 1969 with nine steals and is second best interceptor still active in AFC ... Chiefs flip-flop him to work opposition's top receiver ... Had longest return—75 yards against Minnesota—of 1974 ... Fine basketball player ... Born June 3, 1943, in Angleton, Tex. ... Free agent from Bishop (Tex.) College ... Has averaged more than five thefts a year over nine seasons ... Three-year starter in Pro Bowl ... Super speed (4.3 in 40) ... Not particularly tough, but a cagey tackler ... Involved in government program getting jobs for unemployed kids ... Good golfer.

KANSAS CITY CHIEFS 133

JIM KEARNEY 32 6-2 205   **Strong Safety**

A bit long in the tooth, but the definitive old pro ... Loss of a step may cost him his job as Doug Jones will pressure him in camp ... Rarely burned ... Has three kids of own and recently adopted his sister's four ... Liquor salesman in off-season ... Extremely durable over the years—KC playing-hurt champ ... Born Jan. 21, 1943, in Wharton, Tex. ... Threatened to retire in 1974 if didn't get big raise. Didn't—didn't quit, either ... Otis Taylor's college quarterback at Prairie View, but wrong color for pros and converted ... Super steady until last year ... Spent two years at Detroit, cut, signed as free agent by Chiefs in 1968 ... Owns piece of two NFL records for interception return yardage ... Plays mean saxophone.

MIKE LIVINGSTON 29 6-4 212   **Quarterback**

Presumably will pressure Dawson for starting job, although there's a theory he lacks necessary assertiveness for front-line QB job ... Inconsistent as regular, although at one point in 1974, Chiefs had gone 13-4-1 with him under center ... Tough runner, but cut down scrambling a year ago after Stram started griping about it ... Born Nov. 14, 1945, in Dallas ... Broke most of Don Meredith's passing records at SMU and was Chiefs' No. 2 pick in 1968 draft ... Coming off miserable season in which the only AFC quarterback ranked below him was Marty Domres of Baltimore ... Completed only 46.8 percent and had a poor 7.1 interception rate ... Has yet to prove himself a capable starter

JIM LYNCH 30 6-1 235   **Linebacker**

Helped make Willie Lanier a household name, but gets little ink ... Strength is consistency ... Played the right side in every Chiefs' game since 1968, but will get a look in the middle when Lanier quits, although that's doubtful ... Probably lacks muscle to play inside, but is one of the league's harder hitters ... Born Aug. 28, 1945, in Kansas City ... Shook down the thunder as captain of 1966 national championship team at Notre Dame and is considered one of the all-time Irish greats ... Won Maxwell Award as nation's outstanding player as senior ... With Lanier's status shaky and Bobby Bell

134 THE COMPLETE HANDBOOK OF PRO FOOTBALL

over the you-know-what, could be defensive key during Chiefs' rebuilding process.

ED PODOLAK 27 6-1 204 — Running Back

Nominated most likely to follow Hank Stram out of KC after fans sent up constant chant of "Hi diddle diddle, Podolak up the middle"... Bad thumb injury cost him five games and he wound up having a year almost as poor as Stram's... Yardage down from 721 to 386, he was victim of stilted offense, which became familiar to opponents, and over-use... Gutsy runner but lacks good move and speed to outside... Business entrepreneur (bank, resort, real estate firm, local radio show) and criticized for it... Deeply involved with NFLPA as vice president... Born Sept. 1, 1947, in Atlantic, Iowa... Quarterback at Iowa, switched to tailback fourth game of senior year and set single-season rushing record of 937 yards... KC's most eligible bachelor.

WILBUR YOUNG 26 6-6 285 — Defensive End

Possibly one of the next truly great defensive linemen... "He's only a few minutes away from greatness," says Pittsburgh pro scout Tim Rooney... Wears uniform No. 99... Born April 20, 1949, in New York City... No. 2 pick of Chiefs in 1971 out of small William Penn College... Came to rookie camp weighing 300 and was still quick... Used to have rep for making the dumb play; no more... Hobby is tailoring and he makes clothes for teammates... Holds league title for largest thighs... Won starting job in 1973 training camp and last year was Chiefs' top pass rusher... Credits KC defensive line coach Tom Platt with success... Will have to be a fort for weak KC defensive line this season.

OTIS TAYLOR 33 6-3 215 — Wide Receiver

No longer The Man in KC after poor year in which he caught only 24 balls and ranked fourth on the second passingest team in AFC... Bitter last couple of years in which he's said repeatedly "they aren't throwing to me"... Still has brilliant tools and perhaps the finest pure receiver talent in the game... Used a lot at tight end as KC made heavy use of two TE set ... Calcium deposit on elbow benched him for two games ... Has attitude problem and could go under new management ... Born Aug. 11, 1942, in Houston ... Legend at Prairie View, where his No. 17 was the first jersey ever retired ... Horseback riding enthusiast ... Ranks fourth—379 catches—among active AFC receivers ... Has caught over 50 passes four times in 10 years ... One of league's most exciting receivers ... Super hands.

TOP ROOKIES

ELMORE STEPHENS 22 6-3 220 **Tight End**
Since KC draft might one day be called Hank Stram's Revenge, no one particularly enthused about Stephens ... Not much size for a TE and no particularly impressive stats ... Led Kentucky in receiving twice ... Speed questionable ... Played defense and a freshman ... Wasn't ranked by scouting combines as a prospective first-round choice.

CORNELIUS WALKER 22 6-3 250 **Defensive Tackle**
Chiefs gambling on this Rice grad ... Will have to recover from knee surgery before camp ... Might've been better off playing baseball after hitting .500 in high school ... Pool shark ... Mobility may not be up to pro standards ... Seems too small for defensive line; too slow for LB.

COACH PAUL WIGGIN ... Successor to Henry Stram when "Hank Must Go" campaign in KC overwhelmed front office ... In lamentable position as will have no control whatsoever over scouting and management decisions ... Was defensive coordinator for San Francisco unit that was pretty uncoordinated ... Also ran one of shakier defensive lines in league ... DE for Cleveland for 11 honorable seasons and candidate for Cleveland Brown job that went to Forrest Gregg ... All-American tackle at Stanford ... Onetime brilliant rugby player ... Wears crewcut ... Inherits team that uses more Geritol than Gatorade ... Biggest headaches will be restructuring OL and finding successor to aging Len Dawson.

CLUB HISTORY

For a long, long time, little Henry Stram was up to date in Kansas City. Now Stram isn't even in Kansas City. And somewhere in between is the rise and fall of the Chiefs, who won a Super Bowl in 1970 on Len Dawson's arm and Jan Stenerud's foot, only to have wound up second behind Oakland in the AFC West, lo, these last six winters.

Henry made the Chiefs. Developed Dawson, Mike Garrett, Abner Haynes, Otis Taylor, Willie Lanier and all the rest of the once-brilliant cast. And, ultimately, Henry ruined the Chiefs. Time slipped up and smacked KC over the head. Last year the Chiefs—the once proud Chiefs—got old in a hurry and Henry got fired.

But it was nice while it lasted. Three AFL titles. Two trips to the Super Bowl and one championship there. Dawson throwing, Taylor catching them one-handed, Stenerud kicking them into the low-hanging clouds. Lanier's ferocity, Haynes' elusiveness. And, finally, Stram's demise.

INDIVIDUAL CHIEF RECORDS

Rushing

Most Yards Game:	192	Mike Garrett, vs N.Y. Jets, 1967
Season:	1,087	Mike Garrett, 1967
Career:	3,837	Abner Haynes, 1960-65

Passing

Most TD Passes Game:	6	Len Dawson, vs Denver, 1964
Season:	30	Len Dawson, 1964
Career:	232	Len Dawson, 1962-74

Receiving

Most TD Passes Game:	4	Frank Jackson, vs San Diego, 1964
Season:	12	Chris Burford, 1962
Career:	55	Chris Burford, 1960-67

Scoring

Most Points Game:	30	Abner Haynes, vs Oakland, 1961
Season:	129	Jan Stenerud, 1968
Career:	845	Jan Stenerud, 1967-74
Most TDs Game:	5	Abner Haynes, vs Oakland, 1961
Season:	19	Abner Haynes, 1962
Career:	58	Abner Haynes, 1960-65

KANSAS CITY CHIEFS 137

Kicker Jan Stenerud is Chiefs' all-time leading scorer.

WINNING PLAYS

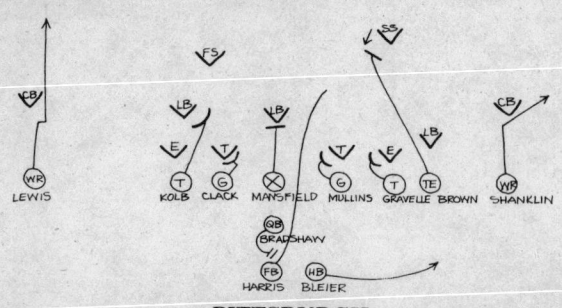

PITTSBURGH

The champion Steelers call it P-10 and center Ray Mansfield calls it "our bread and butter." The Steelers run a fullback-oriented offense dealing heavily in power. "When we get into trouble, we go to P-10," Mansfield said after the play worked very well against Oakland. P-10 is an option play for fullback Franco Harris. There is little deception, the quarterback not even taking a full pivot before handing off. The strength of the play depends upon isolating the middle linebacker. As Mansfield explains, "The key is the center's block on the middle linebacker. I take him whichever direction he wants to go and Franco reads my block." In this case, tight end Larry Brown seals off the strong safety and weakside tackle Jon Kolb the weakside linebacker.

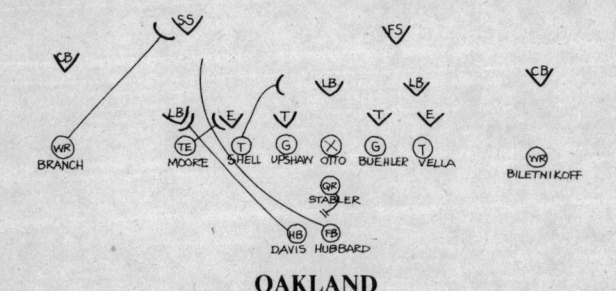

OAKLAND

Any discussion of the Oakland running game must begin and end with muscle. The Raider ground game is early-Neanderthal. "Take a look at the size of our linemen," says back Marv Hubbard. "With studs like them stuffing people, we don't need to do anything fancy." In this instance, the Raiders don't. Tight end Bob Moore and strong side tackle Art Shell combine on the defensive end and tackle; halfback Clarence Davis drives the linebacker to the outside and Hubbard plows through. Should center Jim Otto seal off the middle linebacker, Shell is free to go downfield after the weak safety.

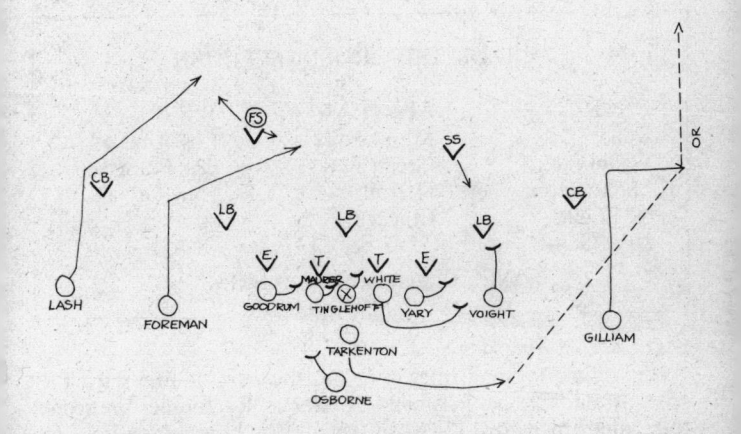

MINNESOTA

As it became apparent in Super Bowl IX, the Vikings throw almost all their passes off a roll-out. This is necessary because of Fran Tarkenton's lack of height. If Fran stays in the pocket he can't see over the linemen, so he prefers to roll. This cuts off half the field but also puts acute pressure on one-half of the defense. Their favorite play comes with Chuck Foreman in the slot on the weakside. Foreman goes about ten yards deep and looks for a gap in the zone between the linebacker and safety. Meanwhile, flanker John Gilliam is one-on-one with the cornerback since the strong safety must respect the tight end. Gilliam drives off 15 yards, then breaks sharply to the sideline. The Vikes frequently burn their opponents deep with Gilliam breaking outside, then turning the pattern upfield. Another possibility is keyed off the movement of the free safety. If he stays back, respecting the deep post move of the other wide receiver (Jim Lash), Foreman should be clear down the middle. If the safety closes on Foreman, Lash should have the inside route to the post to himself.

INSIDE THE NFC

By RAY DIDINGER
Philadelphia Bulletin

PREDICTED ORDER OF FINISH

EAST	CENTRAL	WEST
Dallas	Minnesota	Los Angeles
Washington	Green Bay	San Francisco
Philadelphia	Detroit	New Orleans
St. Louis	Chicago	Atlanta
N.Y. Giants		

NFC Champion: Los Angeles

Let's face it, gang, these are not the best of times for the once-proud National Football Conference. Remember the scene following Super Bowl I? Green Bay's Vince Lombardi admitting with modest reluctance that the AFL's Kansas City Chiefs were not in a class with the NFL big boys. My, how things have changed.

The American Football Conference is now the dominant force in Pete Rozelle's playground. The AFC has won six of the last seven Super Bowls, the past three in contests so one-sided the nation greeted the outcome with an alarming yawn.

The shift in power is evident all the way down both 13-team conferences. Last season just five NFC teams (Los Angeles, St. Louis, Washington, Dallas, Minnesota) had winning records. Conversely, only four AFC teams had losing records.

The NFC players are aware of it and the talk psyched them into an upset of the AFC Stars in last January's Pro Bowl. Maybe that signals a slowing of the current trend.

Los Angeles, even with unproven James Harris at quarterback, must be favored to with the NFC. With the exception of their secondary, the Rams can match personnel with any club in football. Ironically, their only problem might be their lack of opposition in the Western Division. After tip-toeing through San Francisco, New Orleans and Atlanta for half the schedule, they could have trouble preparing for tougher tests in the playoffs.

NFC INTRO 141

Even though the Vikings have been manhandled in the last two Super Bowls, they are still the team to beat in the Central Division. Detroit will try to finish second for the sixth straight year ahead of Green Bay and Chicago, clubs currently rebuilding under Bart Starr and Jack Pardee.

The most competitive division is the East where only one club (the 2-12 Giants) finished with a losing record last year. The early favorite is deeper-than-ever Dallas. The Cowboys missed the playoffs for the first time in eight years last season but that shouldn't happen again. Last year's surprise champion, St. Louis, appears in an open scramble with always-dangerous Washington and improving Philadelphia for second place and the wild card spot.

Can there be another Super Bowl for Fran Tarkenton?

142 THE COMPLETE HANDBOOK OF PRO FOOTBALL

LOS ANGELES RAMS

TEAM DIRECTORY Pres.: Carroll Rosenbloom; Exec. VP-GM: Don Klosterman; Asst. to Pres.: Steve Rosenbloom; Dir. Player Pers.: Mark Duncan; Administrative Asst.: Jack Teele; Bus. Mgr.: William John; Dirs. of Pub. Rel.: Jack Geyer, Jerry Wilcox; Head Coach: Chuck Knox; Trainers: Gary Tuthill, George Menefee. Home: Los Angeles Memorial Coliseum, Los Angeles, Calif. (92,000).

James Harris was the No. 2 passer in NFC.

SCOUTING REPORT

OFFENSE: According to league statistics, the Rams were only the ninth best offensive team in the NFL last season, which just proves how deceptive statistics can be. The Rams are an outstanding offensive machine, even with relatively unproven James Harris at quarterback. "I'm not saying I'm Superman," Harris said when he became LA's No. 1 man, "but with this team, I don't have to be." He's right. The Rams can surround Harris with a solid, experienced line, led by All-Pro guard Tom Mack; no less than seven top-notch runners, and an assortment of quality receivers, including tight end Bob Klein, Jack Snow, Harold Jackson and budding novelist Lance Rentzel.

Their principal weapon is still—as it was even during John Hadl's super year in '73—the running of Lawrence McCutcheon, who rushed for 1,097 yards as a rookie and upped his total to 1,109 last year, best in the NFC. His performance was particularly impressive since he was under pressure following the trade of Hadl and injury to his running partner Jim Bertelsen (whose yardage fell from 854 to 419).

Rams have plenty of depth in backfield, though, with John Cappelletti, Cullen Bryant, Tony Baker and Les Josephson ready to step in. And note that Harris, after getting his big chance, finished as the second-leading passer in the NFC. He might not be Superman but he isn't exactly Clark Kent, either.

DEFENSE: Next to Pittsburgh's Steel Curtain, there is no front seven (defensive line and linebackers) in football better than the Rams. Against the run, they are almost unbeatable, limiting their opponents to just 68 first downs and 1,308 yards last year, both NFC lows. They recorded 44 sacks, an NFC high. They allowed just four TDs on the ground, another NFC low. They have the perfect blend of speed (Fred Dryer and Larry Brooks) and strength (Merlin Olsen and Jack Youngblood) up front. Olsen, who talked of retirement, had one of his best seasons in '74. "Merlin is like the state fair," said Saints' Archie Manning. "He gets bigger and better every year."

The linebackers hit hard and, thanks to the effectiveness of the front four, they can take deep drops on passing situations. That paid off in the playoff win over Washington when both Isiah Robertson and Jack Reynolds intercepted passes in the fourth quarter. The other outside linebacker, Ken Geddes, doesn't get much publicity but handles everything that comes his way. The only real question mark is the secondary, which was burned for 16 TD passes last season, fourth most in the NFC. That shouldn't happen to a defense which registers 44 sacks. Dave Elmendorf and Charlie Stukes each had seven interceptions but the unit lacks cohesion. The key could be at safety where young Bill Simpson moved in at mid-season and showed promise.

RAMS VETERANS ROSTER

HEAD COACH—Chuck Knox. Assistant Coaches—Ed Alsman, Leeman Bennett, Tom Catlin, Jack Faulkner, Ray Malavasi, Ken Meyer, Elijah Pitts, Ray Prochaska, Jim Wagstaff

No.	Name	Pos.	Ht.	Wt.	NFL Exp.	College
35	Baker, Tony	RB	5-11	215	8	Iowa State
56	Baska, Richard	LB	6-3	225	1	UCLA
45	Bertelsen, Jim	RB	5-11	205	4	Texas
90	Brooks, Larry	DT	6-3	255	4	Virginia St.
32	Bryant, Cullen	RB	6-1	218	3	Colorado
11	Burke, Mike	P-K	5-10	188	2	Miami (Fla.)
22	Cappelletti, John	RB	6-1	217	2	Penn State
44	Clark, Al	CB	6-0	185	5	Eastern Michigan
73	Cowan, Charlie	T	6-4	265	15	New Mexico Highlands
88	Curran, Pat	TE	6-3	238	7	Lakeland
55	Curry, Bill	C	6-2	235	11	Georgia Tech
—	Dempsey, Tom	K	6-1	265	7	Palomar J.C.
37	Drake, Bill	S	6-1	195	3	Oregon
89	Dryer, Fred	DE	6-6	240	7	San Diego State
42	Elmendorf, Dave	S	6-1	195	5	Texas A&M
46	Fink, Mike	CB	5-11	185	2	Missouri
36	Geddes, Ken	LB	6-3	235	5	Nebraska
4	Guthrie, Grant	K	6-1	225	3	Florida State
12	Harris, James	QB	6-4	210	6	Grambling
63	Horton, Greg	G	6-4	245	1	Colorado
29	Jackson, Harold	WR	5-10	175	8	Jackson State
16	Jaworski, Ron	QB	6-2	185	2	Youngstown State
51	Johnson, Sam	LB	6-3	225	1	Arizona State
76	Jones, Cody	DT	6-5	240	2	San Jose State
62	Jones, Tom	G	6-3	255	1	Northern Iowa
34	Josephson, Les	RB	6-1	207	11	Augustana (S.D.)
52	Kay, Rick	LB	6-4	235	2	Colorado
54	Kelso, Al	C	6-6	255	1	Washington
80	Klein, Bob	TE	6-5	235	7	Southern California
65	Mack, Tom	G	6-3	250	10	Michigan
39	McCoy, Mike	S-CB	5-11	180	1	Western Kentucky
30	McCutcheon, Lawrence	RB	6-1	205	3	Colorado State
24	McGee, Willie	WR	5-11	178	1	Alcorn A&M
41	McMillan, Eddie	CB	6-0	190	3	Florida State
15	Milan, Don	QB	6-3	200	1	Cal Poly (SLO)
67	Nelson, Bill	DT	6-7	270	5	Oregon, State
83	Nelson, Terry	TE	6-2	230	2	Arkansas AM&N
74	Olsen, Merlin	DT	6-5	270	14	Utah State
57	Peterson, Jim	LB	6-5	240	2	San Diego State
21	Plummer, Tony	S	5-11	190	6	Pacific
20	Preece, Steve	S	6-1	195	7	Oregon State
27	Ray, David	K	6-0	195	7	Alabama
19	Rentzel, Lance	WR	6-2	202	10	Oklahoma
64	Reynolds, Jack	LB	6-1	232	6	Tennessee
58	Robertson, Isiah	LB	6-3	225	5	Southern U.
17	Sanger, Rich	P	6-0	215	1	Nebraska
61	Saul, Rich	C-G	6-3	235	6	Michigan State
71	Scibelli, Joe	G	6-0	255	15	Notre Dame
33	Scribner, Rob	RB	6-0	200	3	UCLA
48	Simpson, Bill	S	6-1	180	2	Michigan State
84	Snow, Jack	WR	6-2	190	11	Notre Dame
66	Stein, Bob	LB	6-3	235	7	Minnesota
78	Stokes, Tim	T	6-5	252	2	Oregon
47	Stukes, Charlie	CB	6-3	212	9	Maryland State
26	Walker, Donnie	S	6-2	180	3	Central State (Ohio)
75	Williams, John	T	6-3	256	8	Minnesota
85	Youngblood, Jack	DE	6-4	255	5	Florida
53	Youngblood, Jim	LB	6-3	239	3	Tennessee Tech

TOP FIVE DRAFT CHOICES

Rd.	Name	Pos.	Ht.	Wt.	Age	College
1	Mike Fanning	DT	6-6	260	22	Notre Dame
1	Dennis Harrah	T	6-5	257	22	Miami
1	Doug France	T	6-5	260	22	Ohio State
2	Monte Jackson	CB	5-10	189	22	San Diego State
2	Leroy Jones	DE	6-6	250	24	Norfolk State

LOS ANGELES RAMS 145

KICKING GAME: Not in keeping with club's overall excellence. Place-kicker David Ray led league in field goals and points two years ago but faded last season, converting only nine field goals and missing six extra points. The arrival of Tom Dempsey from Philadelphia—owner of the longest field goal in NFL history (63 yards)—has to be an improvement. Punter Michael Burke ranked a lowly 11th in the conference. Cullen Bryant excelled on special teams, leading Rams in punt returns and breaking a kickoff 84-yards for touchdown.

OUTLOOK: No one in Western Division has a chance at unseating the Rams and, since arrival of Chuck Knox, the club has drawn progressively closer to the Super Bowl. If he can get another good season out of James Harris and Merlin Olsen, the Rams might play their first championship game in 20 years.

RAM PROFILES

JIM BERTELSEN 25 5-11 205 **Running Back**

Hampered by hyperextension of his knee last season, his rushing total dwindled to 419 yards, lowest of three-year pro career ... "I think the knee bothered me subconsciously more than anything else," he said. "It didn't bother me to run and cut but I felt it when I was tackled" ... Still showed flashes of his old form late in the season, rushing for two TDs vs. Atlanta ... An outstanding blocker, credited with helping Lawrence McCutcheon to back-to-back 1,000-yard seasons ... "Bertelsen has helped me a lot. His block is usually the one that springs me" McCutcheon said ... Born Feb. 25, 1950, in St. Paul, Minn., attended University of Texas, where he gained 2,510 yards, scored 33 TDs ... "The finest football player I've ever coached," said Texas coach Darrell Royal of Bertelsen.

FRED DRYER 29 6-6 240 **Defensive End**

One of football's most delightful flakes, Dryer prefers sleeping in his Volkswagen bus to settling in a permanent home ... Showed up at last year's Super Bowl with teammate Lance Rentzel posing as reporters in 1930s garb ... "Fred is a human UFO," joked ex-teammate Fran Tarkenton ... Beneath the zany exterior, Dryer is a fine defensive end, specializing in a strong rush ... Only defensive lineman in NFL history to record two safties via quarterback sack in the same game (vs. Green Bay, Oct. 21, 1973) ... Relies on great quickness rather than strength ... Born July 6, 1946, in Hawthorne, Calif., and attended San Diego State ... Originally a No. 1 pick by N.Y. Giants, but he never adjusted to the Big City ... "Ever try to surf in the East River?" he asked.

JAMES HARRIS 28 6-4 210   Quarterback

When John Hadl was dealt to Green Bay, Harris became Rams' No. 1 QB for last half of '74 season ... Showed no nervousness in his first start, hitting 12 of 15 passes for 276 yards and three touchdowns vs. 49ers ... Performance ranked him second to Sonny Jurgensen among NFC passers ... "Passing's my meal ticket," Harris says. "I'm not going to miss a man who's open and there's almost always somebody out there who's open" ... Born July 20, 1947, in Monroe, La., attended Grambling where one scout called him "A black Joe Namath" ... Drafted eighth by Buffalo, he became first black QB to start an NFL opener (1969) ... Wavied by Buffalo in 1972, Harris dropped out of football (working in Washington in Department of Commerce's Office of Minority Enterprise) until Rams signed him as free agent ... Capped last season by being voted MVP in Pro Bowl.

HAROLD JACKSON 29 5-10 175   Wide Receiver

Again led all Ram outside receivers in receptions (30) last seasons ... A 9.5 sprinter with excellent hands and a deceptively good move to the sideline ... Appears frail but is actually one of the most durable athletes in the league ... "He has that way of 'giving' with a tackle," says Dallas' Cliff Harris. "You figure you're gonna drill him but it's like hitting a ghost" ... Started on LA cab squad in '68, went to Philadelphia in trade and returned to Rams in Roman Gabriel deal two years ago ... Celebrated his return to Rams with outstanding '73 season, catching 40 passes for 874 yards and career-high 13 touchdowns ... Best game vs. Dallas with seven catches for 238 yards, four TDs ... Born Jan. 6, 1946, in Hattiesburg, Miss., attended Jackson State ... Lives in Hattiesburg in off-season, operating a clothing store.

LOS ANGELES RAMS   147

TOM MACK 31 6-3 250   Guard

"Gives an outstanding performance, week after week," says coach Chuck Knox about Tom Mack. "You grade the films and just marvel over the man's consistency. He never misses an assignment" ... A starter in last year's Pro Bowl, the eighth time he's appeared in the post-season contest in the last nine years ... Has made numerous All-Pro and All-Conference teams in past two seasons ... Born Nov. 1, 1942, in Cleveland, son of the late Ray Mack, former Cleveland Indians baseball player ... Set several swimming records at Cleveland Heights High ... Attended U. of Michigan, winning All-American honors as a senior.

LAWRENCE McCUTCHEON 25 6-1 205   Running Back

Led NFC in rushing last season, piling up 1,109 yards in 236 carries ... Only back in the conference to go over 1,000 yards for season ... Broke his own Ram one-season yardage ma k (1,097) which he set in '73 ... "He's destined to break many more records before he's through," says teammate Merlin Olsen. "Lawrence will be one of the best runners ever" ... Joined Rams in '72 but played in only three games, without carrying the ball ... Rushed for 100 yards or more four times last season ... Best efforts: 140 yards vs. Atlanta; 139 vs. N.Y. Jets ... Born June 2, 1950, in Plainview, Tex. ... Attended Colorado State, where he topped 1,000 yards twice and was voted Western Athletic Conference's outstanding back.

MERLIN OLSEN 34 6-5 270   Defensive Tackle

An all-time great defensive lineman, Olsen has played 13 NFL seasons and been voted onto the Pro Bowl squad 13 straight times, an unprecedented feat ... Last season was presented Philadelphia's Maxwell Club Bert Bell Award as pro football's outstanding player, an honor he termed his "greatest thrill" ... "I accept this award for all guys in the trenches, all the defensive linemen in pro football," he said. "This award indicates people are finally recognizing there is a game played away from the football" ... Born Sept. 15, 1940, in Logan, Utah, attended Utah State where he was Phi Beta Kappa ... A great interview, Olsen is perhaps the most articulate man in football ... Spent off-season making movie with Joe Don Baker.

JACK REYNOLDS 27 6-1 232   Linebacker

Formerly middle linebacker understudy to Myron Pottios and Marlin McKeever, Reynolds blossomed as a starter in '73 ... Sat out '71 with knee injury that put career in jeopardy ... Won nickname "Headhunter" with his reckless, savage play on special teams ... "I think that open-field hitting is fun," Reynolds says. "To me, the bomb squads ARE football" ... Born Nov. 22, 1947, in Cincinnati, he attended Tennessee, where he and Steve Kiner gave Vols two of best linebackers in college football ... Rams' first draft choice in 1970 ... Now lives in California and sells jeeps in off-season.

ISIAH ROBERTSON 26 6-3 225   Linebacker

Made The Big Play in Rams' NFC playoff win over Redskins, cutting in front of Larry Brown to intercept a Sonny Jurgensen pass, then returning it 59 yards for the clinching touchdown ... Won recognition as rookie in '71, roaming spectacularly from sideline to sideline, crunching runners, intercepting four passes ... "I want them to know who's the best," he said ... Settled down into "team defense" player in recent seasons and is even more valuable ... Born Aug. 17, 1949, in New Orleans, attended Southern University where he picked off 11 passes, won All-American mention ... Rams' first draft pick in '71, using a choice acquired from Washington ... "One of my trades finally got the best of me," said George Allen following playoff defeat.

JACK YOUNGBLOOD 25 6-4 255   Defensive End

"I played alongside some great defensive linemen with the original Fearsome Foursome," says Merlin Olsen, "but Jack Youngblood is as good as any. And he's still improving" ... The former Florida All-American understudied Deacon Jones as a rookie in '71 and says the experience helped him immeasurably ... First became a starter in '73 and went directly to the Pro Bowl ... Repeated Pro Bowl appearance last season ... His strength perfectly complements Fred Dryer's quickness at the other end ... "Jack has unlimited physical potential," says coach Chuck Knox. "He could develop into the finest all-around defensive end there is" ... Born Jan. 26, 1950, in Jacksonville, Fla.

TOP ROOKIES

MIKE FANNING 21 6-6 260   **Defensive Tackle**
First of three first-round selections by Rams... Named to four All-American teams as senior at Notre Dame... Combines strength of heavyweight wrestler (he was 18-0 and qualified for NCAA finals as junior) with 5.1 speed for the 40... Says scout Norm Pollum: "He should be in the star category. He hits a good blow and sheds quickly... Has very good lateral moves."

DENNIS HARRAH 21 6-5 257   **Offensive Tackle**
Another first-round pick... First offensive lineman Rams have taken on first round since All-Pro Tom Mack in 1966... Has all the makings: tremendous size and 4.8 speed in the 40... All-American at U. of Miami... "An excellent prospect who will be an NFL starter," predicts personnel director Mark Duncan... Keeps in shape by working summers as a grave digger back in Charleston, W. Va.

COACH CHUCK KNOX... Under Knox, the Rams have drawn progressively closer to the Super Bowl... In his first year, 1973, he lifted the Rams from a 6-7-1 record to 12-2 and first place in the Western Division. They lost their first playoff game to Dallas... Last season the Rams advanced to the NFC finals, only to lose to the Vikings... "If you like to project such things," Knox said, "A similar improvement would put us in the Super Bowl this year"... Born April 27, 1932, in Sewickley, Pa., son of an Irish steel worker, he played football at tiny Juniata College... Broke into pro football as offensive line coach with N.Y. Jets before joining Detroit in similar capacity until Rams called... "Chuck is the best of both worlds," says Merlin Olsen, "a coach you can respect and like at the same time."

CLUB HISTORY

The Rams were founded in Cleveland in 1937 but didn't attract much attention until 1945 when they drafted a T-formation quarterback, Bob Waterfield of UCLA. Not only did he guide the Rams to their first winning season (9-1) but he also steered them past Washington, 15-14, in the NFL championship game.

The following year, Dan Reeves moved the team to Los Angeles and it seemed the players couldn't adjust to all the nice weather, slumping to 6-4-1.

Not until Clark Shaughnessy became coach did they climb back into contention. In 1949, Waterfield teamed with a rookie QB, Norm Van Brocklin, and great receivers Tom Fears and Elroy Hirsch to give the Rams football's most explosive offense. They lost in their next two title shots (to the Eagles and Cleveland) before finally winning their first league championship since moving west, upsetting Cleveland, 24-17, on a 73-yard Van Brocklin to Fears pass.

The Rams suffered through some bleak years in the early '60s but George Allen re-established the winning climate and Chuck Knox has put them in the playoffs the last two years.

INDIVIDUAL RAM RECORDS

Rushing
Most Yards Game:	247	Willie Ellison, vs New Orleans, 1971
Season:	1,109	Lawrence McCutcheon, 1974
Career:	5,417	Dick Bass, 1960-69

Passing
Most TD Passes Game:	5	Bob Waterfield, vs N.Y. Bulldogs, 1949
	5	Norm Van Brocklin, vs Detroit, 1950
	5	Norm Van Brocklin, vs N.Y. Yanks, 1951
	5	Roman Gabriel, vs Cleveland, 1965
Season:	25	Roman Gabriel, 1967
Career:	154	Roman Gabriel, 1962-72

Receiving
Most TD Passes Game:	4	Bob Shaw, vs Washington, 1949
	4	Elroy Hirsch, vs N.Y. Yanks, 1951
	4	Harold Jackson, vs Dallas, 1973
Season:	17	Elroy Hirsch, 1951
Career:	53	Elroy Hirsch, 1949-57

Scoring
Most Points Game:	24	Elroy Hirsch, vs N.Y. Yanks, 1951
	24	Bob Shaw, vs Washington, 1949
	24	Harold Jackson, vs Dallas, 1973
Season:	130	David Ray, 1973 (40 PATS-30 FG)
Career:	573	Bob Waterfield, 1945-52
Most TDs Game:	4	Elroy Hirsch, vs N.Y. Yanks, 1951
	4	Bob Shaw, vs Washington, 1949
	4	Harold Jackson, vs Dallas, 1973
Season:	17	Elroy Hirsch, 1951
Career:	55	Elroy Hirsch, 1949-57

SAN FRANCISCO 49ERS 151

SAN FRANCISCO 49ERS

TEAM DIRECTORY: Pres.-GM: Louis Spadia; VP-Pers.: Jack White; Asst. to Pres.: Art Johnson; Chief Scout: John Michelosen; Pub. Rel. Dir.: George McFadden; Head Coach: Dick Nolan; Trainers: Chuck Krpata, Frank Egenhoff. Home: Candlestick Park, San Francisco, Calif. (61,000).

Wilbur Jackson spurred 49ers' rushing with 705 yards.

SCOUTING REPORT

OFFENSE: The 49ers experimented with no less than five—count 'em, five—quarterbacks through the first half of last season. Head coach Dick Nolan predicted it would be difficult replacing retired vet, John Brodie, but he never guessed it could be that difficult. Two kids, Joe Reed and Dennis Morrison, got a shot at the job but they didn't last. Two vets, Steve Spurrier and Norman Snead, tried and failed. The one quarterback who took charge was an obscure 13th-round draft pick from Wichita, Tom Owen. He led the 49ers to four wins in their last five games and, although he threw 15 interceptions, showed enough potential to rate as the No. 1 QB for this season. Reed and Morrison are gone and Nolan has kept Spurrier and Snead on as insurance.

Owen has several things easing his way into the NFL: a fine group of receivers and a better-than-average offensive line. The wide receivers are Danny Abramowicz, who catches everything thrown his way, and Gene Washington, a threat to score on every play. Tom Mitchell is a reliable tight end. Last year's top draft pick, Wilbur Jackson had a fine rookie year, rushing for 705 yards, and Larry Schreiber bounced back from knee surgery with 634 yards so the backfield is young and able.

DEFENSE: Through the last five weeks last season, the 49ers were the most effective defensive team in the NFC, shutting out Chicago and Atlanta, holding Green Bay to just two field goals and limiting Cleveland to one touchdown in a 7-0 loss. Okay, so maybe those four teams aren't the mightiest offensive machines in the league, but the 49ers must have been doing something right to shut them down so completely. The 49ers were strongest defending against the pass, ranking third (behind Atlanta and Washington) in the NFC. They also picked off 20 enemy passes, placing fifth in that department.

The emergence of Ralph McGill at safety, where he led the club with five interceptions, helped, as did the return to form by middle linebacker Frank Nunley who spent parts of the previous two seasons on the bench. Jimmy Johnson, now 37, did his usual gutsy job at cornerback, intercepting three passes and forcing running plays as well as ever. Bob Hoskins overcame Hodgkins Disease and had the finest season of his five-year pro career at tackle. Cedrick Hardman had flashes at end. The retirement of OLB Dave Wilcox leaves a hole that must be filled.

KICKING GAME: 49ers ran out of patience with Bruce Gossett and used a third-round draft pick for Maryland's booming kicking specialist, Steve Mike-Mayer. Scouts say Steve is better than his brother, Nick, of Atlanta. Punter Tom Wittum who led NFC in '73, finished a close second last year.

49ERS VETERANS ROSTER

HEAD COACH—Dick Nolan. Assistant Coaches—Dick Stanfel, Don Heinrich, Doug Scovil, Lew Erber, Bob Holloway, Ed Beard, Rich Brooks

No.	Name	Pos.	Ht.	Wt.	NFL Exp.	College
46	Abramowicz, Danny	WR	6-0	193	9	Xavier
79	Banaszek, Cas	T	6-3	255	8	Northwestern
77	Barrett, Jean	T-C	6-6	254	3	Tulsa
88	Beasley, Terry	WR	5-10	182	3	Auburn
65	Beisler, Randy	G-T	6-5	247	10	Indiana
72	Belk, Bill	DE-DT	6-4	248	8	Maryland St. (ES)
50	Belser, Ceaser	LB	6-0	205	8	Arkansas AM&N
80	Bettiga, Mike	WR	6-3	193	2	Humboldt State
75	Blue, Forest	C	6-6	265	8	Auburn
71	Fahnhorst, Keith	T	6-6	255	2	Minnesota
30	Gossett, Bruce	K	6-1	229	12	Richmond
43	Hall, Windlan	S	5-11	175	4	Arizona State
86	Hardman, Cedrick	DE	6-4	258	6	North Texas State
63	Hardy, Ed	G	6-4	242	3	Jackson State
59	Harper, Willie	LB	6-2	219	3	Nebraska
53	Hart, Tommy	DE	6-4	248	8	Morris Brown
74	Hindman, Stan	DT	6-4	245	8	Mississippi
47	Hollas, Hugo	S	6-0	190	5	Rice
20	Holmes, Mike	CB-S	6-2	193	2	Texas Southern
56	Hoskins, Bob	DT	6-3	251	6	Wichita State
54	Hull, Tom	LB	6-3	229	2	Penn State
40	Jackson, Wilbur	RB	6-1	215	2	Alabama
37	Johnson, Jimmy	CB	6-2	185	15	UCLA
48	Johnson, Sammy	RB	6-0	223	2	North Carolina
78	Krueger, Rolf	DE-DT	6-4	253	7	Texas A&M
49	McGill, Ralph	CB-S	5-11	183	4	Tulsa
58	McKoy, Billy	LB	6-3	226	5	Purdue
84	Mitchell, Tom	TE	6-3	215	9	Bucknell
45	Moore, Manfred	RB	6-0	194	2	Southern California
57	Nunley, Frank	LB	6-2	234	9	Michigan
14	Owen, Tom	QB	6-1	195	2	Wichita State
66	Penchion, Bob	G	6-6	252	4	Alcorn A&M
69	Peoples, Woody	G	6-2	252	8	Grambling
32	Phillips, Mel	S	6-2	191	10	North Carolina A&T
76	Rhode, Len	T	6-4	248	16	Utah State
60	Sandifer, Bill	DT	6-6	278	2	UCLA
33	Saunders, John	CB-S	6-2	196	4	Toledo
35	Schreiber, Larry	RB	6-0	209	5	Tennessee Tech
16	Snead, Norman	QB	6-4	215	15	Wake Forest
11	Spurrier, Steve	QB	6-2	200	8	Florida
44	Taylor, Bruce	CB	6-0	189	6	Boston University
52	Vanderbundt, Skip	LB	6-3	223	7	Oregon State
18	Washington, Gene	WR	6-2	185	7	Stanford
67	Watson, John	G	6-4	245	5	Oklahoma
85	West, Robert	WR	6-3	218	4	San Diego State
24	Williams, Del	RB	6-0	195	2	Kansas
13	Wittum, Tom	K-P	6-1	190	3	Northern Illinois

TOP FIVE DRAFT CHOICES

Rd.	Name	Pos.	Ht.	Wt.	Age	College
1	Jimmy Webb	DT	6-6	248	23	Mississippi State
2	Greg Collins	LB	6-3	228	22	Notre Dame
3	Jeff Hart	T	6-5	266	21	Oregon State
3	Steve Mike-Mayer	K	6-0	180	27	Maryland
3	Wayne Baker	DT	6-6	260	22	Brigham Young

OUTLOOK: 49ers suffered their second straight losing season but their strong finish offered hope for '75. However, the four closing wins all came over clubs with records worse than theirs, which makes the optimism suspect. Quarterback situation holds key to season. If Owen continues developing, 49ers are a good bet for second place.

49ER PROFILES

FORREST BLUE 29 6-5 262   Center

Appeared in his fourth straight Pro Bowl last season, has started in three... Durable lineman, has missed only one game since 1969... 49ers' first draft pick in 1968 following All-American career at Auburn... Helped establish present standards of the big, mobile center... "It used to be that teams would put their weakest blocker at center; they thought they could hide him," says Dick Nolan. "But with Forrest, we gave ourselves strength in the middle; we let him lead the way"... Born Sept. 7, 1945, in Marfa, Tex., grew up in Tampa, Fla.... Scored one pro TD, running 25 yards with fumble vs. New England in '71.

DAN ABRAMOWICZ 30 6-1 195   Wide Receiver

Extended his streak of having caught at least one pass in 105 straight games through end of last season... Streak almost ended in 12th week of season on snowy day in Cleveland when Danny didn't catch his first pass until 18 seconds remained in game... "I would have hated to see it end because of lousy weather conditions," he said... Old mark was 96 straight games, set by Lance Alworth... Danny dropped three passes before finally holding one vs. Detroit to tie the record... "My teammates honored me by presenting me with a game ball with handles taped on it," he said... Born June 13, 1945, in Steubenville, O., attended Xavier, where he set numerous receiving records... Drafted 17th by Saints, who actually cut him his rookie year, but he refused to leave camp... Hung on long enough to make club.

SAN FRANCISCO 49ERS 155

CEDRICK HARDMAN 26 6-4 251　　　　　　　Defensive End

Top pass rusher has accounted for over 60 quarterback sacks in five-year pro career ... Plays in streaks, can be awesome one week, indifferent the next ... Played in 1971 Pro Bowl and was considered a budding superstar ... His inconsistency has diminished some of the superlatives ... Born Oct. 4, 1948, in Houston, Tex. ... Attended Carver High School there, played three sports and excelled as a baseball pitcher ... Went to North Texas State as 5-11, 185-pound defensive back but grew into a position on line alongside Mean Joe Greene ... Cedrick explains his physical development simply enough: "I ate a lot" ... Works in record promotion in off-season.

BOB HOSKINS 29 6-3 251　　　　　　　Defensive End

Inspiring comeback story of 1974 season ... Battled courageously to overcome Hodgkin's Disease, a form of cancer which causes progressive enlargement of lymph glands, spleen and liver ... Underwent two operations and endured a month of radiation treatment before returning to football ... Radiation treatments caused him to lose his hair but Hoskins took it good-naturedly: "I look like Isaac Hayes" ... Amazingly, Hoskins had his finest season in '74, grading out 94 percent, highest of any 49er lineman ... Born Sept. 16, 1945, in Highland, Ill., attended Wichita ... A real find for 49ers, who drafted him in 16th round in 1969 ... "Hodgkins didn't slow Bob down," says Oakland guard Gene Upshaw, "he gave me all I could handle. I've been playing against him since '70 and he was never better."

JIMMY JOHNSON 37 6-2 187　　　　　　　Cornerback

Physical marvel, still playing football's most demanding position in his late 30s ... Voted to NFC Pro Bowl squad for sixth time in past seven years ... "Jim amazes me," says Dick Nolan. "He never seems to age. He still has the body and endurance of a rookie" ... Has been a starter in 49er secondary for 13 years ... Played 1971 season with broken arm, winning George Halas Award as league's Most Courageous Player ... Picked off three passes last season, upping his career interception total to 44 ... Born March 31, 1938, in Dallas, brother of Olympic decathlon champ Rafer Johnson ... Track and football star at UCLA, he made Dean's List his last two years.

WILBUR JACKSON 23 6-1 205   Running Back

Stepped in as rookie and gave 49ers the swift running threat they sought for many years ... Gained 705 yards on 174 attempts, eighth in NFC ... Injured in Coaches' All-American game but made strong comeback ... "He works like the devil," says Dick Nolan. "When he picks up five yards he wonders why he didn't get 10" ... Born Nov. 19, 1951, in Ozark, Ark., where he lives in the off-season ... Starred at Alabama, although coach Bear Bryant's tendency to rotate backs kept his yardage deceptively low ... Three-year rushing total with Crimson Tide was only 1,537 yards, but he accomplished it on just 212 carries, an average of 7.2 yards per attempt.

GENE WASHINGTON 28 6-1 188   Wide Receiver

Lack of stability at quarterback has caused Washington's receiving stats to drop past two years ... Last season he caught 29 passes for 615 yards (21.2 avg.) and six touchdowns, far short of his usual productivity when working with John Brodie ... "I never had a moment's hesitation throwing the ball to Gene," said Brodie. "Even if he was double-teamed, I knew he'd make the catch. He has more fluidity than any receiver I ever saw" ... Born Jan. 14, 1947, in Tuscaloosa, Ala., attended Stanford and set virtually all the receiving records ... Has done considerable movie and TV work and won critical praise for his lead role in an otherwise undistinguished motorcycle epic, "The Black Six."

TOM OWEN 25 6-1 195   Quarterback

Stepped in as 49ers' No. 1 quarterback down stretch and led team to four wins in last five games ... Completed 88 of 184 attempts for 1,327 yards and 10 touchdowns ... Inexperience caused him to throw 15 interceptions, third most in NFC ... Enters season listed as starter ahead of vets Steve Spurrier and Norman Snead ... Born Sept. 1, 1952, in Shreveport, La. ... Three-year starter at Wichita, where

SAN FRANCISCO 49ERS 157

he threw for 1,300 yards and eight TDs as a senior... Scrambles well enough but is better if given time to set up in pocket... A 13th-round draft choice who showed encouraging progress during training camp... "Tom might lack experience," says Dick Nolan, "but he knows how to win."

Cedrick Hardman is one of league's best pass rushers.

TOP ROOKIES

JIMMY WEBB 23 6-5 248   **Defensive End**
No, this isn't the Jimmy Webb who wrote "MacArthur Park" and "By the Time I Get to Phoenix"... This Jimmy Webb was an All-American at Mississippi State and was the 49ers' first-round draft choice... Born in Jackson, Miss., majored in veterinary medicine... Scouting report says: "Attacks every play with great determination. Quick reactions, good speed and lateral action. Makes good use of his strength."

GREG COLLINS 22 6-3 228   **Linebacker**
49ers' second-round draft pick... Starting middle linebacker at Notre Dame, was first team All-American last season... Led Irish in tackles and minutes played each of past two years... Born in Troy, Mich., where he was standout junior hockey player... Scouting report says: "Very smart defensive analyst. Moves to ball quickly and powerfully. Studies game situations with intelligence and concentration."

COACH DICK NOLAN: There was talk about the Bay Area last season that Dick Nolan was on his way out, but the 49ers' strong finish kept him in office... Entering his eighth year as head coach and only Buck Shaw (nine years) endured longer at the 49er helm... Named NFL Coach of the Year in 1970 after leading the 49ers to their first divisional title... Born March 26, 1932, in Pittsburgh... Played both offensive and defensive halfback at U. of Maryland... Played pro football with New York Giants, Chicago Cardinals and Dallas Cowboys... Began coaching during his final playing season (1962) and Tom Landry appointed him Cowboys' defensive coordinator in 1966... Nolan was hired to give the 49ers a winner in '68 and he came through.

CLUB HISTORY

The 49ers, like their native city, have a history that is colorful, charming and, occasionally interrupted by disasters like earthquakes and Towering Infernos. The 49ers, for example, had outstanding personnel over the years including quarterbacks Frankie Albert and Y.A. Tittle, runners Joe Perry and Hugh (The King) McElhenny, and receivers Billy Wilson, Gordy Soltau and R.C. (Alley-Oop) Owens. But, until 1970, they never won so much as a division title.

And, although they won three straight Western Division crowns (1970-72), they never could win the conference, losing out each time to Dallas. The last time was particularly heartbreaking as Roger Staubach threw two TD passes in the final 1:30 to stun them, 30-28. "The toughest loss of my career," said 49er QB John Brodie. The 49ers haven't had a winning season since that game but, by now, maybe the shock has worn off. If they get desperate, they could always bring back Red Hickey's shotgun offense.

INDIVIDUAL 49ER RECORDS

Rushing

Most Yards Game:	174	Joe Perry, vs Detroit, 1958
Season:	1,049	Joe Petty, 1954
Career:	8,689	Joe Perry, 1948-60, 1963

Passing

Most TD Passes Game:	5	Frank Albert, vs Cleveland (ACC), 1949
	5	John Brodie, vs Minnesota, 1965
	5	Steve Spurrier, vs Chicago, 1972
Season:	30	John Brodie, 1965
Career:	214	John Brodie, 1957-73

Receiving

Most TD Passes Game:	3	Alyn Beals, vs Brooklyn (ACC), 1948
	3	Rlyn Beals, vs Chicago (ACC), 1949
	3	Gordy Soltau, vs Los Angeles, 1951
	3	Bernie Casey, vs Minnesota, 1962
	3	Gene Washington, vs San Diego, 1972
Season:	14	Alyn Beals (ACC), 1948
Career:	49	Alyn Beals, 1946-52
	49	Billy Wilson, 1951-60

Scoring

Most Points Game:	26	Gordy Soltau (3 TDs-5 PATS-1 FG) vs Los Angeles, 1951
Season:	114	Gordy Soltau (6 TDs-48 PATS-10 FG), 1953
Career:	737	Tommy Davis (347 PATS-130 FG), 1959-69
Most TDs Game:	4	Bill Kilmer, vs Minnesota, 1961
Season:	14	Alyn Beals (ACC), 1948
Career:	80	Joe Perry, 1948-60

NEW ORLEANS SAINTS

TEAM DIRECTORY: Pres.: John Mecom Jr.; Asst. to Pres.: Fred Williams; Exec. VP: Richard Gordon Jr.; VP-Admin.: Harry Hulmes; Dir. Pub. Rel.: Larry Liddell; Dir. Promotions: Bill Treuting; Bus. Mgr.-Treas.: Eddie Jones; Dir. Player Pers.: Bob Whitman; Head Coach: John North; Trainer: Dean Kleinschmidt. Home: Tulane Stadium, New Orleans, LA (80,997).

Archie Manning must return to top form for Saints to win.

SCOUTING REPORT

OFFENSE: The Saints' offense sagged last season while Archie Manning skipped four games with assorted ailments. Each of his subs, Bobby Scott and Larry Cipa, managed to win a game, a

NEW ORLEANS SAINTS 161

fact which encouraged head coach John North. However, a healthy Manning is still the best weapon the Saints have and he must come through if New Orleans hopes to have its first winning season. He will be aided this year by the addition of No. 1 draft pick, Larry Burton, a wide receiver with great speed.

Burton's deep threat will complement the Saints' other receivers, Bob Newland and 6-5 Joel Parker, who impressed with 41 catches as a rookie. New Orleans is solid at tight end with Paul Seal coming off a sparkling first year and vet John Beasley in reserve.

The Saints' most impressive rookie last year was fullback Alvin Maxon, who paced the club in rushing (714 yards) and receiving (42 catches), although he didn't break into the starting lineup until the fourth game. Jess Phillips has first crack at the halfback spot but swift Ron McNeill could nudge him out. The biggest question mark is the line, which was populated by unknowns last year. North strengthened his club in this area, drafting Ohio State's Kurt Schumacher and Auburn's Lee Gross in the first two rounds. Both could be starters by September.

DEFENSE: "Last season, our defense kept us in most all of our games. It never completely fell apart, even in the face of some discouraging situations," noted North. The Saints had their finest defensive season, ranking seventh in the NFC overall. They blanked St. Louis, held Atlanta to a field goal and limited Los Angeles to seven points in impressive performances. Saints traded their best all-around lineman, Billy Newsome, to the Jets for No. 1 draft choice but North feels second-year man Andy Dorris can fill in. He drafted two rookies, Elois Grooms and Charlie Hall, early, just in case.

Joe Owens, who led the club with 11 sacks, should again serve as a pass rush specialist. The linebacker corps is unheralded but effective with rugged Joe Federspiel flanked by Wayne Colman and Jim Merlo. The secondary is better than average with Ernie Jackson, Bivian Lee and last year's rookie surprise, Terry Schmidt, vying for starting jobs. Tom Myers, the heady fourth-year man who calles defensive signals, is developing at free safety. The only weak link is strong safety where Johnny Fuller is the best of an undistinguished crew.

KICKING GAME: Saints' biggest weapon in this area is also their smallest, 5-5 Howard Stevens, who ranked among league leaders in punt and kickoff returns. He's clever and fearless. Kicker Bill McClard has range (tried two field goals beyond 50

SAINTS VETERANS ROSTER

HEAD COACH—John North. Assistant Coaches—Bob Cummings, Wimp Hewgley, Robert Ledbetter, Lamar McHan, Jim "Red" Phillips, Doug Shively, Bud Whitehead, Billy Ray Barnes

No.	Name	Pos.	Ht.	Wt.	NFL Exp.	College
20	Alderson, Tim	S	6-2	198	1	Minnesota
89	Anderson, Frosty	WR	5-11	175	1	Nebraska
63	Baumgartner, Steve	DE	6-7	260	3	Purdue
85	Beasley, John	TE	6-3	228	8	California
16	Blanchard, Tom	P	6-0	190	5	Oregon
21	Boyd, Greg	S	6-2	201	3	Arizona
38	Butler, Bill	RB	6-0	210	4	Kansas State
46	Childs, Henry	TE	6-2	223	2	Kansas State
13	Cipa, Larry	QB	6-3	209	2	Michigan
55	Coleman, Don	LB	6-2	222	2	Michigan
59	Colman, Wayne	LB	6-1	220	8	Temple
86	Davis, Dave	WR	6-0	175	5	Tennessee State
47	DeGrenier, Jack	RB	6-1	225	2	Texas-Arlington
51	Didion, John	C	6-4	255	7	Oregon State
69	Dorris, Andy	DE	6-4	230	3	New Mexico State
58	Federspiel, Joe	LB	6-1	235	4	Kentucky
24	Fuller, Johnny	S	6-0	185	8	Lamar
83	Garrett, Len	TE	6-3	230	5	New Mexico Highland
80	Havrilak, Sam	WR	6-2	195	7	Bucknell
30	Jackson, Ernie	CB	5-10	175	4	Duke
53	Kingrea, Rick	LB	6-1	230	5	Tulane
50	Kupp, Jake	G	6-3	248	12	Washington
67	LaPorta, Phil	T	6-4	256	2	Penn State
39	Lawson, Odell	RB	6-2	205	5	Langston
11	Lee, Bivian	CB	6-3	200	5	Prairie View
8	Manning, Archie	QB	6-3	215	5	Mississippi
87	Martin, Curtis	TE	6-3	220	1	LSU
28	Maxson, Alvin	RB	5-11	205	2	SMU
19	McClard, Bill	K	5-10	202	4	Arkansas
27	McNeill, Rod	RB	6-2	219	2	USC
57	Merlo, Jim	LB	6-1	225	3	Stanford
54	Middleton, Richard	LB	6-2	228	2	Ohio State
74	Moore, Derland	DT	6-4	260	3	Oklahoma
25	Moore, Jerry	S	6-3	208	5	Arkansas
73	Morring, John	T	6-6	255	5	Tampa
76	Morrison, Don	T	6-5	260	5	Texas-Arlington
37	Myers, Tom	S	5-11	184	4	Syracuse
41	Newland, Bob	WR	6-2	190	5	Oregon
72	Owens, Joe	DE	6-2	250	6	Alcorn State
88	Parker, Joel	WR	6-5	212	2	Florida
34	Phillips, Jess	RB	6-1	210	8	Michigan State
82	Pollard, Bob	DE-DT	6-3	250	2	Weber State
75	Price, Elex	DT	6-3	260	3	Alcorn State
66	Rasley, Rocky	G	6-3	255	6	Oregon State
40	Schmidt, Terry	CB	6-0	177	2	Ball State
12	Scott, Bobby	QB	6-1	200	4	Tennessee
84	Seal, Paul	TE	6-4	222	2	Michigan
70	Sloan, Bonnie	DE	6-5	260	2	Austin Peay
29	Spencer, Maurice	DB	6-0	175	2	N. Carolina Central
22	Stevens, Howard	RB	5-5	165	3	Louisville
65	Thompson, Dave	C-T	6-4	260	5	Clemson
49	Wicks, Bob	WR	6-3	205	3	Utah State
79	Zanders, Emanuel	G	6-1	263	2	Jackson State

TOP FIVE DRAFT CHOICES

Rd.	Name	Pos.	Ht.	Wt.	Age	College
1	Larry Burton	WR	6-1	190	23	Purdue
1	Kurt Schumacher	T	6-3	260	22	Ohio State
2	Lee Gross	C-G	6-3	245	22	Auburn
3	Andrew Jones	RB	6-2	213	22	Washington State
3	Elois Grooms	DE	6-4	240	22	Tennessee Tech

NEW ORLEANS SAINTS 163

yard last year, made both) but isn't consistent. Punter Tom Blanchard led NFC (42.1 avg.) and had longest boot in league last year, 71 yards. He's a plus.

OUTLOOK: John North has won 10 games in two seasons with the Saints and seems to be putting some promising pieces together. Saints could surprise and play .500 ball this season if Manning bounces back with a strong year. If not, well, the Saints won't go marching anywhere with Bobby Scott or Larry Cipa leading the offense.

SAINT PROFILES

WAYNE COLMAN 29 6-1 220   **Linebacker**

Among the most underrated outside linebackers in the NFC ... Colman had his finest pro season last year, starting all 14 games on the right side ... Always seems to have a half-dozen guys fighting for his job at camp, but he consistently comes out ahead ... Made one interception last season, saving 14-13 win over Atlanta ... Came up with seven solo tackles, three assists in upset over Philadelphia ... Win was sweet for Colman, who was waived by Eagles in '69 ... Born April 13, 1946, at Ventnor, N.J., attended Temple University where he excelled at defensive end ... Enjoys water sports ... Was member of Atlantic City Beach Patrol during high school days and still spends his off-seasons rowing, surfing and fishing along the New Jersey shore.

JOE FEDERSPIEL 25 6-1 235   **Linebacker**

"Who's this guy Federspiel?" one of the Eagles wanted to know last year. "He sounds like the accordian player in a Polka band." ... The Eagles learned who Joe Federspiel was quickly enough as he headed up a tough Saints' defense which turned Philadelphia away at the goal line for a 14-10 win ... Joe might not be a household word yet but he's earning respect in a hurry ... "He's as hard a hitter as we've got," said coach John North. "He doesn't have great size but he can really pop" ... Born May 6, 1950, in Louisville, attended U. of Kentucky ... First drew scouts' attention at North-South Shrine game where he was voted the South's MVP.

ARCHIE MANNING 26 6-3 210   Quarterback

Archie's coming off an unsettling season in '74 ... He split quarterbacking duties with two others and made it clear he doesn't like sitting on the bench ... Injured his knee vs. Chicago early, then missed the last two games with mononucleosis ... Underwent knee surgery in off-season and says he's ready to reclaim No. 1 status ... Played brilliantly in win over Philadelphia, driving Saints 78 yards in seven plays to the winning touchdown with a minute to go ... Key play was Archie's 23-yard third down scamper ("That broke our backs," said Eagle coach Mike McCormack) ... Born May 19, 1949, in Cleveland, Miss., became Southern fold hero during All-American career at Ole Miss.

TOM MYERS 24 5-11 185   Safety

Bounced back from stomach and knee surgery to win a full-time job as Saints' free safety last season ... Missed two games with ankle injury but excelled while he was on the field ... Intercepted three passes, returned them for 43 yards ... Best game came vs. Denver when he made six solo tackles and three assists, then set up a touchdown by returning an interception to one-yard line ... "Tommy's got a great future," said coach John North. "He can find that ball and that's what a free safety must do" ... Born Oct. 24, 1950, at Cohoes, N.Y. ... Attended Syracuse, where he was captain and All-American in 1971 ... Broke Floyd Little's school record for punt return yardage (436) as a junior ... Calls defensive signals.

JESS PHILLIPS 28 6-1 210   Running Back

Started all 14 games at halfback, then underwent knee surgery in off-season ... Counted on for another strong year ... Second to Alvin Maxon in rushing last year with 566 yards in 174 attempts (3.2 avg.) and two touchdowns ... One of his TDs was the game winner vs. Philadelphia ... Best game came vs. Atlanta when he carried ball 16 times for 63 yards in Saints' 14-13 win ... Still holds New Orleans record for most rushing attempts (198) set in '73 ... Born Feb. 28, 1947, in Beaumont, Tex. ... Attended Michigan State where he played defensive back... Stayed on defense his rookie year with Cincinnati before Paul Brown switched him to offense. He immediately became Bengals' top rusher in '69 and '70.

BOB POLLARD 26 6-3 255 — Defensive Tackle

Another underrated defensive player, Pollard's great strength is consistency... "Bob seldom has a bad game," said John North. "Week after week, he does an outstanding job for us."... Led all Saints' linemen with 98 tackles last year and had seven quarterback sacks for the second straight season ... Best games: vs. Chicago, ten tackles, and vs. Atlanta, seven tackles, three assists and one sack... Born Dec. 30, 1948, at Beaumont, Tex., started at Texas Southern but transferred to Weber State for final two collegiate seasons... Has played both tackle and end on defense, could go either way this year.

HOWARD STEVENS 25 5-5 165 — Running Back

A favorite with New Orleans fans, Stevens refused to believe the scouts and coaches who said he was too small to play in the NFL... Was Saints' 16th round draft pick in '73 and won spot on roster with daring deeds on special teams... Was valuable spot player again last season, gaining 190 yards on 43 carries, an average of 4.4 yards per attempt, best of any New Orleans' running back... Often used by John North to spark Saints' offense... "Howard's a dynamic little runner," Archie Manning said. "He comes into a game and shakes everybody up"... Placed among NFC leaders in punt returns (10.2 avg.) and kickoff returns (22.7 avg.)... Born Feb. 9, 1950, in Harrisonburg, Va., attended Louisville.

ALVIN MAXON 23 5-11 205 — Running Back

The find of the year for the Saints... Was club's eighth-round draft pick from SMU as scouts doubted he had size to make it as NFL fullback... Maxon amazed everyone, piling up 714 yards on 165 attempts, including a team record 148 yards in one game vs. St. Louis... Longest burst of season was 66 yards for TD vs. Cards... Did not break into starting lineup until fourth game but John North doesn't know when he'll ever be dislodged ... "He gave us a great running threat but people don't realize what a job he did blocking and catching the ball (his 42 receptions also paced the club)," said North ... Born Nov. 12, 1951, in Beaumont, Tex., attended SMU where he broke most of Kyle Rote's records.

TERRY SCHMIDT 23 6-0 177   **Cornerback**

Schmidt was at cornerback when Saints opened last season and San Francisco quarterback Joe Reed decided to test the rookie from Ball State immediately ... Reed threw his first pass in that direction and Schmidt intercepted ... Picked off four passes in first nine games and returned one 27 yards for touchdown vs. Denver ... Missed final five games with injured foot ... Voted first-team All-Rookie by Pro Football Writers ... Born May 28, 1952, at Columbus, Ind. ... An honor student in science in college, Schmidt was both a football and academic All-American ... Plans career in dentistry where he can begin drilling teeth instead of receivers.

PAUL SEAL 23 6-4 215   **Tight End**

Another rookie who came through for Saints ... Seal was club's second-round draft pick after being Most Valuable Player in his senior year at University of Michigan ... Edged out veteran John Beasley for starting job during season and displayed great promise ... Caught 32 passes for 466 yards and three touchdowns ... Also scored once on end-around play ... Made sensational 23-yard reception from Archie Manning at eight-yard line vs. Philadelphia, setting up winning touchdown ... Defender he beat on the play was Eagle safety Randy Logan, who grew up with Seal in Detroit and was a teammate at Michigan ... "Paul's a great athlete," Logan said. "I've been watching him make catches like that for years. That's the first time he's done it to me, though" ... Born Feb. 27, 1952, in Detroit.

TOP ROOKIES

LARRY BURTON 23 6-1 190   **Wide Receiver**
Saints' first first-round pick ... Gave up football for a time to prepare for Olympic Games in Munich ... Returned to Purdue

gridiron last season where he won mention on numerous All-American teams... Averaged 18 yards per catch... Has run 9.1 100 and 4.2 40... "Speed's my thing," Burton says... Expected to give Saints the game-breaking threat they've needed.

KURT SCHUMACHER 22 6-3 260   Offensive Tackle
Saints' second first-round pick, acquired from N.Y. Jets... Starting tackle in three Rose Bowls for Ohio State... Won All-American, All-Big 10 honors as a senior... Very quick off ball and scouts are impressed with his hustle in throwing downfield blocks... Tremendously strong in upper body and surprisingly quick (4.9 speed)... Pulls, traps well... Born Dec. 26, 1952, in Cleveland.

COACH JOHN NORTH: When the ABC-TV cameras focused on Saints' coach John North during 40-3 loss to Dallas two years ago, Howard Cosell said, There's John North... a man staring into a bleak future"... At the time, it might have seemed so since Saints were coming off a 62-7 loss in the previous week's opener... But North has turned things around in New Orleans... Although the club has managed just ten wins in two years under North, the caliber of personnel has improved dramatically and the Saints are giving every opponent a tough time... North, a native of Gillian, La., played end at Vanderbilt and three seasons as a receiver with Baltimore before becoming a coach... He spent eight years as receiver coach in Detroit before taking an assistant's job at LSU. From there, he joined the Saints as an assistant and was named the successor when J.D. Roberts was fired in 1973 pre-season.

CLUB HISTORY

In 1967, the New Orleans Saints came into the NFL like few other franchises. Owner John W. Mecom was jogging on the sidelines in his football shoes. A jazz band, led by Al Hirt and Pete Fountain, was wailing in the end zone. The honky-tonk crowd from Bourbon Street filled the stands and when rookie John Gilliam took the opening kickoff 94 yards for a Saints' touchdown, it was instant Mardi Gras.

The Saints eventually lost the game to Los Angeles but there was enough excitement for everybody. That's pretty much the way things have gone for the Saints. They have been in the NFL eight years, never won more than five games in a season but always managed to provide some thrills. Who could forget Tom Dempsey's 63-yard field goal on the final play, beating Detroit in 1970? And who could forget the 51-42 win over St. Louis in which Billy Kilmer threw six touchdown passes? The Saints have won 10 games in two years under head coach John North and it appears better times are ahead.

INDIVIDUAL SAINT RECORDS

Rushing

Most Yards Game:	148	Alvin Maxson, vs St. Louis, 1974
Season:	761	Andy Livingston, 1969
Career:	1,219	Jess Phillips, 1973-74

Passing

Most TD Passes Game:	6	Bill Kilmer, vs St. Louis, 1969
Season:	20	Bill Kilmer, 1969
Career:	47	Bill Kilmer, 1967-70

Receiving

Most TD Passes Game:	3	Dan Abramowicz, vs San Francisco, 1971
Season:	7	Dan Abramowicz, 1968, 1969, 1972
Career:	37	Dan Abramowicz, 1967-72

Scoring

Most Points Game:	18	Walt Roberts, vs Philadelphia, 1967
	18	Dan Abramowicz, vs San Francisco, 1971
Season:	99	Tom Dempsey, 1969 (33 PATS-22FG)
Career:		Charlie Durkee, 1967-68, 1971-72 (87 PATS-52 FG)
Most TDs Game:	3	Walt Roberts, vs Philadelphia, 1967
	3	Dan Abramowicz, vs San Francisco, 1971
Season:	8	Andy Livingston, 1969
Career:	37	Dan Abramowicz, 1967-72

ATLANTA FALCONS

TEAM DIRECTORY: Chairman of the Board: Rankin Smith; Pres.: Frank Wall; GM: Pat Peppler; Dir. of Player Pers.: Tom Braatz; Pub. Rel. Dir.: Wilt Browning; Head Coach: Marion Campbell; Trainer: Jerry Rhea. Home: Atlanta-Fulton County Stadium, Atlanta, Ga. (58,850).

Tommy Nobis anchors Falcons' defense in 10th season.

170 THE COMPLETE HANDBOOK OF PRO FOOTBALL

SCOUTING REPORT

OFFENSE: A disaster area in '74 and might not be much better this year. Last season, Falcons scored just 111 points, fewest ever by an NFL team in a 14-game schedule. They managed only 12 touchdowns, one on a punt return, another on an interception. That means the offense produced 10 touchdowns. Since then, their problems have compounded with some suspect front office juggling. They traded the best blocker, George Kunz, and the best fullback, Art Malone.

Meanwhile, they used their first pick in the draft to secure California's Steve Bartkowski for No. 1 quarterback. The Falcons told their fans Bartkowski is in the same class as Jim Plunkett and Terry Bradshaw but even Plunkett and Bradshaw suffered through painful periods of adjustment on graduating to the NFL. And many scouts remain unconvinced that Bartkowski is that good. "He was just the best of a poor crop this year," is the way one scout put it. In any case, the Falcons clearly have much rebuilding to do offensively and if Bartkowski learns any lessons this year, they will undoubtedly be painful ones.

DEFENSE: The Falcons ranked a lowly 15th in league's overall defense, including a shocking 26th (last) against the run. Everyone agrees Atlanta has better talent than that but last season with the offense not scoring any points and coughing up 55 turnovers (31 interceptions, 24 fumbles), the defense spent inhuman stretches of time on the field. "They were worn down, mentally and physically," explained head coach Marion Campbell.

All-Pro defensive end Claude Humphrey rose above all the adversity and had his finest season (16 sacks, five blocked kicks, eight blocked passes) while the other end, John Zook, is an established star. But if the offense doesn't improve significantly this year—and that seems unlikely—the defense might suffer a similar letdown. One area of strength is the deep secondary with safety Ray Brown (NFC leader with eight interceptions). Tommy Nobis, despite his injury problems, remains one of the better middle linebackers and a forceful on-the-field leader. The question is, how do you inspire your teammates to force turnovers when they know their offense won't do anything but give the ball right back?

KICKING GAME: The soundest area on the entire club. Nick Mike-Mayer dropped off from his rookie scoring binge (112

FALCONS VETERANS ROSTER

HEAD COACH—Marion Campbell. Assistant Coaches—Fred Bruney, Eddie Khayat, Al Lavan, Marv Matuszak, Bill Nelsen, Bill Walsh, Jimmy Orr, John Raush

No.	Name	Pos.	Ht.	Wt.	NFL Exp.	College
68	Bailey, Larry	DT	6-4	238	2	Pacific
63	Bebout, Nick	T	6-5	260	3	Wyoming
50	Brezina, Greg	LB	6-1	221	8	Houston
34	Brown, Ray	S	6-2	202	5	W. Texas St.
82	Burrow, Ken	WR	6-0	191	5	San Diego St.
38	Byas, Rick	DB	5-9	180	2	Wayne St.
41	Dodd, Al	WR	6-0	178	8	N.W. Louisiana St.
32	Easterling, Ray	S	6-0	192	4	Richmond
89	Francis, Wallace	WR	5-11	190	3	Arkansas AM&N
66	Fritsch, Ted	C	6-2	242	4	St. Norbert
67	Gabel, Paul	G	6-4	252	1	Penn. State
84	Geredine, Thomas	WR	6-2	189	3	N.E. Missouri St.
65	Gotshalk, Len	G	6-4	259	5	Humboldt St.
—	Greer, Charles	DB	6-0	205	7	Colorado
43	Hampton, Dave	RB	6-0	202	8	Wyoming
58	Hansen, Don	LB	6-2	228	9	Illinois
56	Havig, Dennis	G	6-2	256	5	Colorado
27	Hayes, Tom	CB	6-1	198	5	San Diego St.
87	Humphrey, Claude	DE	6-5	265	8	Tennessee St.
68	Jackson, Larron	G	6-3	260	5	Missouri
6	James, John	P	6-3	200	4	Florida
—	Jenkins, Alfred	WR	5-10	172	1	Morris Brown
20	Kendrick, Vince	RB	6-0	223	2	Florida
22	Lawrence, Rolland	CB	5-10	179	3	Tabor
69	Lewis, Mike	DT	6-4	261	5	Arkansas AM&N
77	Manning, Rosie	DT	6-5	255	4	N.E. Oklahoma
50	Maree, Ron	G	6-6	272	1	Purdue
83	Mialik, Larry	TE	6-1	226	4	Wisconsin
12	Mike-Mayer, Nick	PK	5-9	187	3	Temple
55	Miller, Jim	G	6-3	240	5	Iowa
86	Mitchell, Jim	TE	6-1	236	7	Prairie View
52	Mitchell, Ken	LB	6-1	224	3	Nevada, Las Vegas
31	McGee, Molly	RB	5-10	184	2	Rhode Island
11	McQuilken, Kim	QB	6-2	203	2	Lehigh
80	Neal, Louis	WR	6-4	215	3	Prairie View
60	Nobis, Tommy	LB	6-2	243	10	Texas
51	Palmer, Dick	LB	6-2	232	6	Kentucky
44	Ray, Eddie	RB	6-2	240	6	L.S.U.
53	Ryczek, Paul	C	6-2	230	2	Virginia
61	Sandeman, Bill	T	6-5	260	10	Pacific
—	Simmons, Jerry	WR	6-1	190	11	Bethune-Cookman
64	Smith, Royce	G	6-3	250	4	Georgia
73	Smith, Steve	T	6-5	250	9	Michigan
24	Stanback, Haskel	RB	6-0	210	2	Tennessee
7	Sullivan, Pat	QB	5-11	201	4	Auburn
74	Tilleman, Mike	DT	6-7	278	9	Montana
81	Tinker, Gerald	WR	5-9	170	2	Kent St.
57	Van Note, Jeff	C	6-2	247	7	Kentucky
79	Walker, Chuck	DT	6-3	261	12	Duke
59	Warwick, Lonnie	LB	6-2	240	11	Tennessee Tech
71	Zook, John	DE	6-5	249	7	Kansas

TOP FIVE DRAFT CHOICES

Rd.	Name	Pos.	Ht.	Wt.	Age	College
1	Steve Bartkowski	QB	6-4	215	22	California
2	Ralph Ortega	LB	6-2	220	22	Florida
3	Woody Thompson	RB	6-1	219	23	Miami
4	John Nessel	G	6-6	257	22	Penn State
5	Greg McCrary	TE	6-1	216	23	Clark

points to 39) but it wasn't his fault. The Falcons didn't get across midfield very often and he only attempted 16 field goals, compared to 38 the previous season. Punter John James is as good as any and Gerald Tinker showed promise as a kick returner.

OUTLOOK: Falcons' grim future was apparent at last season's final game when just 10,020 fans turned out at Atlanta Stadium (48,000 no shows). Prospects for this year appear equally bleak. If Bartkowski is the real thing, it will still take three or four years for him to develop. If he's not, Falcons might not equal last year's total of three wins.

FALCON PROFILES

RAY BROWN 26 6-2 202   Safety

Led NFC with eight interceptions last season, giving him four-year career total of 19 ... Scored his first NFL touchdown ever, picking off a Norm Snead pass, returning it 59 yards vs. Giants ... "They flip-flopped their receivers," Brown said, explaining the play, "but I had the feeling they would try the same pattern" ... As usual, Brown guessed right ... Born Jan. 12, 1949, in Ft. Worth, Tex., attended West Texas State ... Was Atlanta's sixth-round draft pick for '71 but did not make active roster until mid-season ... Intercepted three passes over final seven games of his rookie year, convincing coaches he belonged ... Holds all Falcon punt return records.

DAVE HAMPTON 28 6-0 202   Running Back

After two outstanding seasons in 1972-73 (when he rushed for 995, then 997 yards), Hampton slumped last year ... He carried the ball only 127 times and gained 464 yards, his lowest output since his final year (1971) in Green Bay ... Hampered by injuries much of the season, Hampton was healthy for the finale and showed flashes of his old form, carrying ball 23 times for 96 yards and the winning touchdown as Falcons beat Green Bay ... A key performer if Atlanta is to climb back into contention ... Born May 7, 1947, in Ann Arbor, Mich., attended U. of Wyoming ... Originally drafted by Packers, who used him primarily on kickoff returns (he returned three for TDs in three years).

ATLANTA FALCONS 173

CLAUDE HUMPHREY 31 6-5 265 — Defensive End

While the rest of the club sagged in '74, Claude Humphrey had the finest season of his seven-year career ... "I'm playing better than ever," he admitted after sacking Chicago QB Gary Huff five times in 13-10 Falcon victory ... Overall, Humphrey finished with 16 sacks, 68 individual tackles and 25 assists ... He also batted down eight passes (for second straight year), blocked four field goals and one extra point ... "In a year like this, you find out what an athlete is really made of," praised coach Marion Campbell ... Born June 29, 1944, in Memphis, attended Tennessee State ... Spends off-season entering his prize Doberman Pinscher, Jade's Commanche Barchet, in major dog shows.

NICK MIKE-MAYER 25 5-8 180 — Kicker

His college coach, Wayne Hardin of Temple University, began calling Mike-Mayer "The Million Dollar Leg" in only his sophmore year ... Writers laughed at first, figuring it as another Hardin con job, but Mike-Mayer justified his coach's enthusiasm ... Drafted by Atlanta two years ago, Nick almost ate himself out of football at his first training camp, packing on 12 extra pounds and pulling a muscle ... But Falcons stayed with him and the rookie delivered, kicking 26 field goals, scoring 112 points, earning a spot on the NFC Pro Bowl squad ... Born March 1, 1950, in Bologna, Italy, son of a world-famous Hungarian soccer star ... His brother, Steve, kicked for Maryland and was third-round draft pick of San Francisco.

JIM MITCHELL 27 6-1 236 — Tight End

One of the unheralded tight ends in football but still regarded among the best ... Consistent performer who has started since his rookie year, 1969 ... Had his best season in 1970, catching 44 passes for 650 yards and six touchdowns ... "Jim could do even better," ex-coach Norm Van Brocklin said at the time, "if we had faster wide receivers who could pull that secondary deep and stretch the zones a little more. As it is, they can sag off on Jim" ... Born Oct. 19, 1947, in Shelbyville, Tenn., attended Prairie View A&M where he made

174 THE COMPLETE HANDBOOK OF PRO FOOTBALL

the Southwestern Athletic Conference all-star team four straight years.

TOMMY NOBIS 31 6-3 243   **Linebacker**

Last of the original (1966) Falcons... Was club's No. 1 draft pick after two All-American seasons at U. of Texas and stepped right in at middle linebacker... Has been there ever since... A vicious competitor who, like Humphrey, refused to quit when '74 season hit the skids... Led club with 129 solo tackles, including 15 in a gallant effort in lopsided 42-7 loss to Miami... "That Tommy Nobis is one great football player," said Don Shula afterwards. "He was still giving it 110 percent at the final gun. That's what this game is all about." ... Born Sept. 20, 1943, in San Antonio, Tex.... Appeared in five Pro Bowls, three times voted Falcon MVP... A great hockey fan, seldom misses an Atlanta Flames home game.

JOHN ZOOK 27 6-5 248   **Defensive End**

A wild, reckless character who enjoys skydiving and other assorted death-defying leisure activities... Once had his main chute fail and barely opened his emergency in time to save himself... He landed in a farm pasture, startling several grazing cows... Enjoys the country life, spends his offseasons camping by lakes and fishing... During season, Zook is among the top pass rushers in pro football... "I feel good making All-Pro," said Claude Humphrey, "but I feel bad when John doesn't get it, he deserves it too"... Born Sept. 24, 1947, in Garden City, Kan., attended U. of Kansas ... Was originally drafted by Los Angeles but came to Atlanta through Philadelphia in complicated three-way trade.

JEFF VAN NOTE 29 6-2 247   **Center**

Was Falcons' eleventh draft pick in '69 after twice being named All-Southeast Conference linebacker at U. of Kentucky... Falcons wanted to convert him to center, so they farmed him out to Huntsville, Ala., of the Continental Football League where he spent a year learning the position... Returned to Falcons in '70, won a regular job and has

ATLANTA FALCONS 175

developed into a top NFL center ... Last year was chosen for first Pro Bowl appearance ... "I went to the Pro Bowl disliking just about everybody connected with the game," Van Note said. "I knew most of the guys only as opponents and I didn't like them. Particularly the Dallas and Los Angeles players. But I found out they were the nicest guys you'd ever hope to meet" ... Born Feb. 7, 1946, in South Orange, N.J.

GERALD TINKER 24 5-9 170   Wide Receiver

Falcons' top draft pick (second round) for last season ... Did not win regular job at wide receiver but could move in this year as he gains experience and learns to run more precise patterns ... Helped Falcons immediately on special teams, however, placing third in NFL in punt returns and eighth in kickoff returns ... Returned 14 punts for 195 yards (13.9 avg.) and one 72 yard touchdown ... Took 29 kickoffs back 704 yards (24.3 avg.), including a 59-yarder ... Born Jan 19, 1951, in Miami, attended Kent State ... Speed is part of his family ... His father ran track in Europe during World War I; his sister, Joyce, was considered "fastest girl in world" when she was just 12 ... Gerald won gold medal at 1972 Olympics as member of U.S. 400-meter relay team ... Has run 9.1 100.

KEN BURROW 27 6-0 191   Wide Receiver

Beginning his fifth season with Atlanta after bouncing back from neck surgery to lead Falcon pass-catchers in 1974 ... His 34 receptions netted 544 yards and one touchdown ... Played for St. Louis Cardinals' coach Don Coryell while at San Diego State ... An early-round 1967 draft selection of the Los Angeles Dodgers as power-hitting catcher ... Was big winner on the Hollywood game show "Gambit" ... Spent the first nine games of the '73 season gathering in a team-leading 31 receptions for 567 yards and seven touchdowns before suffering cervical nerve root injury against Philadelphia ... Underwent surgery twice within six months ... Born March 29, 1948, in Richmond, Calif. ... An amateur photographer who enjoys surfing near his home in Encinata, Calif. ... Has a B.S. degree in criminal justice.

TOP ROOKIES

STEVE BARTKOWSKI 21 6-4 215   Quarterback
This U. of California hot shot better be good after the deal Atlanta made to acquire him ... Falcons traded George Kunz, a superb offensive tackle, and their No. 1 pick to Baltimore for their leadoff spot in the NFL draft ... "That's how badly we wanted Steve," said Frank Wall. "He's out of the same mold as a Jim Plunkett or Terry Bradshaw" ... Had impressive stats at Cal but pro scouts are widely split on his potential. Some feel he could be a colossal bust ... If he is, Falcons are in big trouble.

RALPH ORTEGA 21 6-2 220   Linebacker
Falcons' second-round draft pick from U. of Florida ... Born in Havana, Cuba, where his father was a senator during the Batista regime ... Came to U.S. in 1959 ... Older brother, Tony, played at Auburn ... Jarring tackler, credited with 279 solo tackles in college, forcing 14 fumbles, recovering eight himself ... Also had 12 QB sacks, intercepted three passes, returning them for 75 yards, including 29-yard TD vs. Florida State.

COACH MARION CAMPBELL: Took over for his old buddy and ex-teammate Norm Van Brocklin at mid-season and, although Falcons won only one game under him, president Frank Wall liked Campbell enough to rehire him for this year ... "Marion has been with us since 1969," Wall said. "He knows what we need to win and, I believe, he knows how to get it" ... Campbell did an impressive job as an assistant, reshaping the Atlanta defense from one of the NFL's worst to one of the best in 1973 ... Born May 25, 1929, in Chester, S.C., and was outstanding tackle at U. of Georgia ... All-Pro defensive end with 49ers, then with Philadelphia in 1959 and 1960 when Eagles shocked experts by winning world championship ... Nicknamed "The Swamp Fox" after Revolutionary War hero Francis Marion.

CLUB HISTORY

The Atlanta Falcons were born in 1965 when someone in the NFL office realized the football-crazy South might support an expansion franchise. The notion was born out when on Christmans Eve—just five months after the franchise was awarded—the Falcons had to cut off season ticket sales at 45,000.

Not everything went smoothly at first. The training camp—the Blue Ridge Assembly YMCA camp in Asheville, N.C.—was a joke and so were most of the players who showed up. The roster was burdened with names like Preston Ridlehuber and Wade Traynham and in two years under Norb Hecker the club won just four games.

Norm Van Brocklin replaced Hecker in 1968 and led the Falcons to their first winning season (7-6-1) in '71. The cantankerous Dutchman had them in contention (9-5) in 1973 until the final month of the season. Last year the club crumbled and Van Brocklin was fired, leaving his chief aide, Marion Campbell, to pick up the pieces.

INDIVIDUAL FALCON RECORDS

Rushing

Most Yards Game:	161	Dave Hampton, vs Los Angeles, 1972
Season:	997	Dave Hampton, 1973
Career:	2,455	Dave Hampton, 1972-74

Passing

Most TD Passes Game:	4	Randy Johnson, vs Chicago, 1969
Season:	16	Bob Berry, 1970
Career:	57	Bob Berry, 1968-72

Receiving

Most TD Passes Game:	2	14 times. Last time, Ken Burrow vs Philadelphia, 1973
Season:	7	Ken Burrow, 1973
Career:	20	Jim Mitchell, 1969-74

Scoring

Most Points Game:	15	Nick Mike-Mayer, vs Los Angeles, 1973
Season:	112	Nick Mike-Mayer, 1973
Career:	151	Nick Mike-Mayer, 1973-74
Most TDs Game:	2	31 times. Last time, Eddie Ray, Kan Burrow, vs Philadelphia, 1973
Season:	11	Eddie Ray, 1973
Career:	24	Art Malone, 1970-74

178 THE COMPLETE HANDBOOK OF PRO FOOTBALL

DALLAS COWBOYS

TEAM DIRECTORY: Board Chairman: Clint Murchison Jr.; Pres.-GM: Tex Schramm; VP, Player Dev.: Gil Brandt; Treas.: Don Wilson; Pub. Rel. Dir.: Curt Mosher; Bus. Mgr.: Joe Bailey; Player Pers. Dir.: Dick Mansperger; Head Coach: Tom Landry; Trainer: Don Cochren. Home: Texas Stadium, Dallas, Texas (65,101).

Roger Staubach slipped in '74 but remains Cowboys' gun.

SCOUTING REPORT

OFFENSE: The Cowboys were, statistically speaking, the strongest offensive team in football last season. Which is surprising considering quarterback Roger Staubach had a subpar year and Calvin Hill missed three games, falling below the 1,000-yard mark rushing for the first time since 1971. That testifies to Dallas' depth, which permits the Cowboys to reach back for people like Clint Longley, Robert Newhouse and Charley Young.

However, this year Calvin Hill is gone and his loss is not temporary. Newhouse, until now strictly a spot player, must step into Hill's demanding halfback spot and prove he can carry the ball 25 to 30 times a game without fumbling and without injury. Cowboys coaches believe he can do it. If he fails, Young, coming off an impressive rookie season, would get the next call. Broncbusting Walt Garrison is still entrenched at fullback.

The loss of Hill also puts more pressure on Staubach, now 33, who might find it more necessary to throw the football. Roger, who seldom threw interceptions early in his career, has been victimized 30 times the past two seasons. His receivers are among the best with young Drew Pearson (62 catches) and Golden Richards providing outside speed and tight end Billy Joe DuPree improving considerably on his pass routes.

DEFENSE: A puzzling blend in '74. The Cowboys ranked second stopping the run but a shockingly low 14th against the pass. The forward line, led by ferocious outside rushers Ed (Too Tall) Jones and Harvey Martin, sacked the quarterback 37 times (second only to the Rams in the NFC) but Dallas intercepted a conference low 13 passes. The Cowboys gave up just eight touchdowns on the ground but were burned for 17 through the air.

Part of the blame can be placed on the secondary, which missed cornerback Mel Renfro for three games—but part must be attributed to middle linebacker Lee Roy Jordan and outside man Dave Edwards, both in their second NFL decade and a step slower than they once were. With that in mind, the Cowboys drafted for help in their deep seven. Three of their top four picks were linebackers: Randy White, Tom Henderson and Bob Breunig. White, a 6-4, 250-pounder with the speed of a halfback, is the projected replacement for Jordan.

To fill out the secondary, the Cowboys drafted four defensive backs (Oklahoma's Randy Hughes is the best) and signed Hise Austin, a 6-4, 195-pound cornerback from the World Football

COWBOYS VETERANS ROSTER

HEAD COACH—Tom Landry. Assistant Coaches—Ermal Allen, Mike Ditka, Ed Hughes, Jim Myers, Dan Reeves, Alvin Roy, Gene Stallings, Ernie Stautner, Jerry Tubbs

No.	Name	Pos.	Ht.	Wt.	NFL Exp.	College
64	Arneson, Jim	C-G	6-3	252	3	Arizona
—	Austin, Hise	CB	6-4	210	2	Prairie View A&M
31	Barnes, Benny	CB	6-1	192	4	Stanford
10	Carrell, Duane	P	5-10	185	2	Florida State
63	Cole, Larry	DE	6-4	250	8	Hawaii
21	Dennison, Doug	RB	6-1	195	2	Kutztown State
89	DuPree, Billy Joe	TE	6-4	228	3	Michigan State
52	Edwards, Dave	LB	6-1	226	13	Auburn
62	Fitzgerald, John	C	6-5	255	5	Boston College
15	Fritsch, Toni	K	5-7	185	4	None
84	Fugett, Jean	TE	6-3	226	4	Amherst
32	Garrison, Walt	RB	6-0	205	10	Oklahoma State
34	Green, Cornell	S	6-3	212	14	Utah State
77	Gregory, Bill	DT	6-5	252	5	Wisconsin
43	Harris, Cliff	S	6-0	190	6	Ouachita
22	Hayes, Bob	WR	5-11	190	11	Florida A&M
1	Herrera, Efren	K	5-9	185	2	UCLA
86	Houston, Bill	WR	6-3	208	2	Jackson State
87	Howard, Ron	TE	6-4	215	2	Seattle
59	Hutcherson, Ken	LB	6-1	220	2	Livingston State
72	Jones, Ed	DE	6-9	260	2	Tennessee State
55	Jordan, Lee Roy	LB	6-1	226	13	Alabama
60	Killian, Gene	G	6-4	250	2	Tennessee
—	Kokolus, Harry	K	5-10	184	2	Iowa
74	Lilly, Bob	DT	6-5	260	15	Texas Christian
19	Longley, Clint	QB	6-1	193	2	Abilene Christian
51	Manders, Dave	C	6-2	250	11	Michigan State
79	Martin, Harvey	DE	6-5	252	3	East Texas State
37	Morgan, Dennis	RB	5-11	200	2	Western Illinois
73	Neely, Ralph	T	6-6	255	11	Oklahoma
44	Newhouse, Robert	RB	5-10	205	4	Houston
76	Niland, John	G	6-3	255	10	Iowa
61	Nye, Blaine	G	6-4	255	8	Stanford
88	Pearson, Drew	WR	6-0	183	3	Tulsa
58	Peterson, Cal	LB	6-3	220	2	UCLA
75	Pugh, Jethro	DT	6-6	250	11	Elizabeth City State
20	Renfro, Mel	CB	6-0	192	12	Oregon
83	Richards, Golden	WR	6-0	183	3	Hawaii
12	Staubach, Roger	QB	6-3	197	7	Navy
40	Strayhorn, Les	RB	5-10	205	3	East Carolina
57	Walker, Louie	LB	6-1	216	2	Colorado State
71	Wallace, Rodney	T	6-5	255	4	New Mexico
78	Walton, Bruce	T	6-6	252	4	UCLA
46	Washington, Mark	CB	5-10	186	6	Morgan State
41	Waters, Charlie	S	6-1	193	6	Clemson
70	Wright, Rayfield	T	6-6	260	9	Fort Valley State
30	Young, Charles	RB	6-1	210	2	North Carolina State

TOP FIVE DRAFT CHOICES

Rd.	Name	Pos.	Ht.	Wt.	Age	College
1	Randy White	LB	6-4	245	22	Maryland
1	Tom Henderson	LB	6-2	214	22	Langston
2	Burton Lawless	G	6-4	253	21	Florida
3	Bob Breunig	LB	6-2	236	22	Arizona State
4	Pat Donovan	DE	6-5	240	22	Stanford

DALLAS COWBOYS 181

League. Austin played previously with Green Bay. Tom Landry doesn't have to worry about his free safety. Hard-hitting Cliff Harris is coming off his best year but Cornell Green, now 35, could be slipping at strong safety.

KICKING GAME: Cowboys went through three kickers last season but came up with a find, signing UCLA product Efren Herrera as a free agent. Herrera shows poise and promise. Toni Fritsch, the Austrian, has accuracy and distance but is troubled by recurring muscle pulls. Punter Duane Carrell seems set.

OUTLOOK: Cowboys missed the playoffs for the first time in nine years in '74 and the frustration is still there. With loss of Hill and absence of Craig Morton, Dallas is thinner offensively than in the past but the off-season infusion of defensive talent makes the Cowboys a contender once again.

COWBOY PROFILES

WALT GARRISON 31 6-0 205   **Running Back**

Gutty fullback from Oklahoma State who has played steadily for nine years with Cowboys ... Ranks third among all-time Cowboy rushers and fifth for all-time receivers ... Rushed for 429 yards last season and caught 34 passes, more than any Dallas back ... Spends off-season wrestling and roping steers on pro rodeo circuit and has ranch hand's toughness ... "Walt's the kind of guy who never shows up on the injury report," says Tom Landry. "He's played when nobody else would have tried" ... Born July 23, 1944, in Denton, Tex. ... Relaxes by whittling, a hobby that cost him 16 stitches in a finger just before a game three years ago.

CLIFF HARRIS 26 6-0 185   **Safety**

Hardest hitting free safety in NFC ... Even his own teammates fear him ... Golden Richards gave Harris a crash helmet with flashing red light and battery-powered siren to wear in practice ... "I just want to know when Cliff's coming my way," Richards explained ... Signed as free agent out of tiny Ouachita Baptist College ... Born Nov. 12,

182 THE COMPLETE HANDBOOK OF PRO FOOTBALL

1948, in Fayetteville, Ark. . . . Harris led Cowboys with three interceptions last season, also returned 26 punts . . . Best game came vs. Giants when he recovered fumble, intercepted pass, knocked ball away from Bob Tucker in end zone in fourth quarter . . . "Cliff has been our best defensive player all year," Landry said . . . Played in his first Pro Bowl last year.

LEE ROY JORDAN 34 6-1 218   Linebacker

In an age when middle linebackers are bigger and stronger than ever, Jordan continues to excel due to his keen knack of reading plays and his leech-like tackling . . . Two years ago, the former Alabama All-American made 21 tackles in a game vs. Philadelphia, prompting Tom Landry to call it, "the best day any linebacker ever had for the Cowboys" . . . The following week, he intercepted three Ken Anderson passes in the first quarter as Dallas whipped Cincinnati . . . "He just seems to be in the right place at the right time," Anderson said . . . Born April 4, 1941, in Excel, Ala. . . . "To me," Jordan says, "football is like a day off. I grew up picking cotton on my daddy's farm and nobody asked for your autograph or put your name in the paper for that."

BLAINE NYE 29 6-4 251   Guard

Once obscured by Niland's publicity, Nye is at last being discovered . . . "The past few years everybody wants to know how I feel about not getting any publicity," Nye jokes. "Actually, I've become famous from people asking me how it feels not to be famous" . . . Chosen for last year's Pro Bowl ahead of Niland . . . Already a first-rate guard but should improve further . . . Born March 29, 1946, in Ogden, Utah . . . Attended Stanford . . . Listed as one of top 13 intellectuals in pro sports by Esquire Magazine . . . Has completed work for Masters Degree in physics from U. of Washington and Masters in Business Administration from Stanford . . . "Physics and football are unrelated," Nye says, "except that football tends to pay for the cost of physics graduate school."

DALLAS COWBOYS 183

JOHN NILAND 31 6-3 245 — Guard

Unlike most offensive linemen, Niland doesn't use his hands when he's blocking... "Too much chance of getting called for a penalty," Niland says... He prefers to butt-block, using his head and shoulders... Weight-lifting has built his neck up to 20 inches but the constant butting usually leaves his forehead and nose gashed during the season... "It's worth it when you win," Niland says... Born Feb. 29, 1944, in Quincy, Mass., went to U. of Iowa... A six-time Pro Bowl participant, Niland has ideal attitude for offensive lineman: "I enjoy going out there on Sunday afternoon and knocking the heck out of somebody."

DREW PEARSON 24 6-0 175 — Wide Receiver

Named after the famous late Washington political columnist, Drew is making a name for himself... Signed as a free agent out of Tulsa two years ago, Pearson surprised coaches by making roster, then moved right into starting lineup... Caught 22 passes that year and scored on an 83-yarder vs. Rams in playoffs... Last year, he caught 62 passes (2nd in NFC) for a conference-high 1,087 yards... "He can get open, he can get deep in a hurry and he's a great fluid receiver," says Tom Landry... Born Jan. 12, 1951 in South River, N.J. ... Caught 10 passes in one game vs. Eagles last year... Also caught a 32-yard TD pass vs. Giants, then passed 46 yards to Golden Richards for another in same game... "I used to be a quarterback in college," he pointed out.

MEL RENFRO 33 6-0 190 — Cornerback

Renfro intercepted just one pass last season, which is not unexpected since quarterbacks are reluctant to throw his way... "I stay away from Renfro," says John Hadl. "I don't like fooling with him. He's the best in the league"... Has picked off 43 passes in 11-year career, returned three for touchdowns... "There couldn't possibly be a better cornerback in football," says coach Gene Stallings. "Watch him force a running play. He's like a cutting horse, darting in and out. I've never seen anything like him, on film or anywhere else" ... Born Dec. 30, 1941, in Houston ... Attended Oregon, where he starred in football and track ... Ran 9.6 100, 13.8 in high hurdles and did 25-11½ in long jump.

ROGER STAUBACH 33 6-3 197　　　　　　　Quarterback

The former Heisman Trophy winner from Navy had a difficult season in '74 ... His TD pass total slipped from 23 in '73 to just 11, and he threw 15 interceptions ... Cowboys hope for Jolly Roger to make a big comeback this season ... "Roger is too fine a competitor to stay down long" Tom Landry said ... Still managed to set two Dallas club records: most completions in a season (190) and most attempts (360) ... "He'll be the Cowboys quarterback for however long he wants to play," says Miami's Bob Griese ... Born Feb. 5, 1942, in Cincinnati ... Voted MVP of Dallas' victory in Super Bowl VI ... Has written his autobiography, entitled "First Down, Lifetime to Go" ... active in Fellowship of Christian Athletes.

RAYFIELD WRIGHT 30 6-6 255　　　　　　　　　Tackle

A starter in the Pro Bowl for the fourth straight year, there is little doubt Wright is one of the best offensive tackles in football ... "I think Rayfield is pretty much a composite of an All-Pro tackle," says Viking Carl Eller. "He has size, strength, quickness. The big thing in Rayfield's favor is he has so much range" ... "There's nobody in the league who could replace him," says Tom Landry ... Born Aug. 23, 1945, in Griffin, Ga., where he became an Eagle scout and earned 21 merit badges ... A remarkable athlete, he lettered in football, basketball and track at Ft. Valley State College where he ran the 440 in 50 seconds flat and played briefly in the secondary.

TOP ROOKIES

RANDY WHITE 22 6-4 250　　　　Defensive End/Linebacker
Second man picked in the draft ... Everybody's All-American as defensive end at Maryland, White won Outland Trophy and Vince Lombardi Award as the nation's top collegiate lineman ... White can bench press 450 pounds, run 4.5 40 ... Cowboys

hope to convert him to middle linebacker, groom him as Lee Roy Jordan's successor... "He has all the traits you look for," said Dallas scout Red Hickey. "Quickness, balance, toughness, agility, desire and smarts."

TOM HENDERSON 22 6-2 214 Linebacker
Cowboys used their second first-round pick to grab this sleeper ... Henderson played at a small college, Langston, and has just marginal pro size, but Dallas' scouts raved about him ... Says Red Hickey: "He's one of the tremendous athletes in the country. He's quick, he's agile, he's fast, he blocks punts, picks 'em up and runs 'em in for touchdowns, he chases people down from behind. He's all over the field."

COACH TOM LANDRY ... It is almost impossible to imagine the Dallas Cowboys without Tom Landry standing at the bench, arms folded, staring cooly onto the field... He was the Cowboys' head coach when they came into the league in 1960 and he has built them into a pro football power that last season missed the post-season playoffs for the first time in nine years... A former star at the U. of Texas, Landry later played and coached with the New York Giants... During World War II, Landry flew 30 B-17 missions over Germany with the Eighth Air Force... Many people who watch Landry from the stands consider him unemotional and placid. His players disagree. "Tom," says John Niland, "can chew you out with the best of them"... "This game is played with the heart," Landry says. "You don't have to drink or swear or hit people in the face when they're not looking, but you do have to be tough to win."

CLUB HISTORY

Who would have guessed, watching the expansion Dallas Cowboys struggle through their first season (0-11-1 in 1960) that one day Tom Landry would build a dynasty in silver-and-blue? That's what he did, taking a bunch of castoffs (Jim Mooty, Gary Wisener, John Gonzaga, Sonny Gibs, etc.) and replacing them with All-Pros (Bob Lilly, Calvin Hill, John Niland, Mel Renfro). The Cowboys started with a too-small quarterback, Eddie LeBaron, a too-old halfback, L.G. Dupre, and too-slow receivers, Fred Dugan and Jim Doran, and worked their way up.

They broke even (7-7) in 1965, giving the hint of things to come. The following year with Dandy Don Meredith passing to Bob Hayes and Lance Rentzel, the Cowboys finished 10-3-1 and barely lost to the great Packers (34-27) in an exciting title game. That marked the first of eight straight appearances in the post-season playoffs, highlighted by a 24-3 victory over Miami in Super Bowl VI in January, 1972.

INDIVIDUAL COWBOY RECORDS

Rushing

Most Yards Game:	153	Calvin Hill, vs San Francisco, 1974
Season:	1,412	Calvin Hill, 1973
Career:	6,217	Don Perkins, 1961-68

Passing

Most TD Passes Game:	5	Eddie LeBaron, vs Pittsburgh, 1962
	5	Don Meredith, vs N.Y. Giants, 1966
	5	Don Meredith, vs Philadelphia, 1966 and 1968
	5	Craig Morton, vs Philadelphia, 1969
	5	Craig Morton, vs Houston, 1970
Season:	24	Don Meredith, 1966
Career:	135	Don Meredith, 1960-68

Receiving

Most TD Passes Game:	4	Bob Hayes, vs Houston, 1970
Season:	14	Frank Clarke, 1962
Career:	71	Bob Hayes, 1965-74

Scoring

Most Points Game:	24	Dan Reeves, vs Atlanta, 1967
	24	Bob Hayes, vs Houston, 1970
	24	Calvin Hill, vs Buffalo, 1971
	24	Duane Thomas, vs St. Louis, 1971
Season:	107	Danny Villanueva, 1966
Career:	456	Bob Hayes, 1965-74
Most TDs Game:	4	Dan Reeves, vs Atlanta, 1967
	4	Bob Hayes, vs Houston, 1970
	4	Calvin Hill, vs Buffalo, 1971
	4	Duane Thomas, vs St. Louis, 1971
Season:	16	Dan Reeves, 1966
Career:	76	Bob Hayes, 1965-74

WASHINGTON REDSKINS

TEAM DIRECTORY: Pres.: Edward Bennett Williams; First VP: Jack Kent Cooke; VP-Treas.: Milton King; VP-GM-Head Coach: George Allen; Pub. Dir.: Michael Menchel; Pers. Dir.: Tim Temerario; Trainer: Joe Kuczo. Home: Robert F. Kennedy Stadium, Washington, D.C. (54,398).

Billy Kilmer has led 'Skins to playoffs four straight years.

SCOUTING REPORT

OFFENSE: "It's George Allen's theory," says another NFC coach, "that he wins games with his defense. All he wants his offense to do is get him about 14 points and not make any big mistakes. The defense will take care of the rest." If that's true, the Redskin offense has presented George with some nice bonuses in recent seasons. Last year, for example, Washington was the top scoring and top passing team in the NFC, completing 61 percent of its attempts for 2,978 yards and 22 touchdowns (all conference highs).

The only problem is that Allen's top passer (after the retirement of Sonny Jurgensen) is Billy Kilmer, 35, who is—if you believe NFL longevity statistics—already living on borrowed time. But foxy George has a relatively fresh quarterback in the wings, ex-Giant and ex-WFLer Randy Johnson. And young Joe Theismann awaits a crack at the job.

The Skins still have the same cast of gifted receivers, Jerry Smith, Roy Jefferson and the incomparable Charley Taylor, making game-winning catches. However, there is concern over Washington's running attack, which has faded badly in recent years with tailback Larry Brown hobbling on sore legs. If Duane Thomas ever gets his head on straight, he could be the answer. Moses Denson filled in nicely for Charley Harraway at fullback.

DEFENSE: Allen's pride-and-joy had another typical year, leading the NFC in total defense, interceptions and takeaways (40). They allowed only seven touchdowns on the ground, second best in the league, posted one shutout (42-0 over Chicago) and held three other opponents without a touchdown. Eight times they held the other team to less than 100 yards rushing. Twice they returned interceptions for touchdowns, including a 24-yarder by cornerback Mike Bass for the winning score vs. the Giants.

They scored another touchdown when Chris Hanburger recovered a Roman Gabriel fumble in the end zone, sparking the Skins to a come-from-behind victory. "We don't go on the field hoping to keep the other team from scoring," explained tackle Diron Talbert. "We go out planning to score ourselves. We're what you might call an offensive defense." The front four is strong and deep with Talbert, Bill Brundige and Manny Sistrunk at tackle, Verlon Biggs and Ron McDole at end. The outside linebacker spots are the guts of the unit manned by Hanburger, an established All-Pro, and ex-Packer Dave Robinson, still making all the plays at 34. The only area of doubt is in the

WASHINGTON REDSKINS 189

REDSKINS VETERANS ROSTER

HEAD COACH—George Allen. Assistant Coaches—Charlie Waller, Bill Austin, Dick Bielski, Joe Walton, LaVern Torgeson, Ralph Hawkins, Jim Hilyer, Kirk Mee, Paul Lanham

No.	Name	Pos.	Ht.	Wt.	NFL Exp.	College
—	Aldridge, Allen	DE	6-6	250	4	Prairie View
41	Bass, Mike	CB	6-0	190	8	Michigan
86	Biggs, Verlon	DE	6-4	275	11	Jackson State
4	Bragg, Mike	P	5-11	186	8	Richmond
43	Brown, Larry	RB	5-11	195	7	Kansas State
77	Brundige, Bill	DT	6-5	270	6	Colorado
26	Brunet, Bob	RB	6-1	205	6	Louisiana Tech
—	Carroll, Joe	LB	6-1	225	3	Pittsburgh
40	Cunningham, Doug	RB	6-0	195	9	Mississippi
44	Denson, Moses	RB	6-1	215	2	Maryland St. (ES)
59	Dusek, Brad	LB	6-2	214	2	Texas A&M
31	Evans, Charlie	RB	6-1	220	5	Southern California
37	Fischer, Pat	CB	5-9	170	15	Nebraska
46	Grant, Frank	WR	5-11	181	3	So. Colorado State
55	Hanburger, Chris	LB	6-2	218	11	North Carolina
84	Hancock, Mike	TE	6-4	220	3	Idaho State
56	Hauss, Len	C	6-2	235	12	Georgia
—	Hermeling, Terry	T	6-5	255	5	Nevada-Reno
27	Houston, Ken	S	6-3	198	9	Prairie View
—	Howard, Leroy	CB	5-11	179	1	Bishop
25	Hull, Mike	RB	6-3	220	8	Southern California
66	Imhof, Martin	DE	6-6	256	3	San Diego State
80	Jefferson, Roy	WR	6-2	195	11	Utah
—	Johnson, Carl	G-T	6-4	255	3	Nebraska
61	Johnson, Dennis	DT	6-4	260	2	Delaware
—	Johnson, Randy	QB	6-3	205	9	Texas A&I
21	Jones, Larry	CB	5-10	170	2	N.E. Missouri State
17	Kilmer, Billy	QB	6-0	204	14	UCLA
—	Kuziel, Bob	C	6-5	255	1	Pittsburgh
73	Laaveg, Paul	G	6-4	250	6	Iowa
24	Malinchak, Bill	WR	6-1	200	10	Indiana
79	McDole, Ron	DE	6-4	265	15	Nebraska
53	McLinton, Harold	LB	6-2	235	7	Southern
—	Minor, Lincoln	RB	6-2	211	2	New Mexico
3	Moseley, Mark	K	6-0	205	4	Austin State
57	O'Dell, Stu	LB	6-1	220	2	Indiana
—	Overmyer, Bill	LB	6-3	220	2	Ashland
23	Owens, Brig	S	5-11	190	10	Cincinnati
—	Parson, Ray	TE-T	6-5	239	3	Minnesota
52	Pergine, John	LB	6-1	225	7	Notre Dame
88	Reed, Alvin	TE	6-5	235	9	Prairie View
—	Reppond, Mike	WR	6-0	185	2	Arkansas
—	Ressler, Glenn	G	6-3	250	11	Penn State
—	Robinson, Craig	T	6-4	250	2	Houston
34	Robinson, Darwin	RB	6-1	190	1	Dakota State
89	Robinson, Dave	LB	6-3	245	13	Penn State
—	Rogers, Mel	LB	6-2	233	4	Florida A&M
51	Rycek, Dan	C	6-3	245	3	Virginia
30	Salter, Bryant	S	6-5	196	5	Pittsburgh
62	Schoenke, Ray	G	6-4	250	12	Southern Methodist
64	Sistrunk, Manny	DT	6-5	265	5	Arkansas AM&N
87	Smith, Jerry	TE	6-3	208	11	Arizona State
38	Smith, Larry	RB	6-3	220	7	Florida
—	Speyrer, Cotton	WR	6-0	175	4	Texas
74	Starke, George	T	6-5	249	3	Columbia
20	Stone, Ken	S	6-1	179	3	Vanderbilt
63	Sturt, Fred	G	6-4	255	2	Bowling Green
78	Sweeney, Walt	G	6-4	254	13	Syracuse
72	Talbert, Diron	DT	6-5	255	9	Texas
42	Taylor, Charley	WR	6-3	210	12	Arizona State
7	Theismann, Joe	QB	6-0	184	2	Notre Dame
47	Thomas, Duane	RB	6-2	215	5	West Texas State
67	Tillman, Rusty	LB	6-2	230	5	No. Arizona
29	Vactor, Ted	CB	6-0	185	6	Nebraska
58	Varty, Mike	LB	6-1	220	1	Northwestern
—	Wyatt, Alvin	DB	5-10	185	5	Bethune-Cookman

TOP FIVE DRAFT CHOICES

Rd.	Name	Pos.	Ht.	Wt.	Age	College
5	Mike Thomas	RB	5-11	190	22	Nevada-Las Vegas
6	Mark Doak	T	6-4	265	24	Nebraska
9	Dallas Hickman	DE	6-2	235	23	California
11	Ardell Johnson	CB	5-11	190	22	Nebraska
11	Jerry Hackenbruck	DT	6-5	245	22	Oregon State

middle where Harold McLinton and Rusty Tillman have both fallen short of expectations. The secondary is trusty, although you have to wonder how much longer Pat Fischer, 35 can keep going at cornerback.

KICKING GAME: Typically, Redskin special teams had their share of big plays, breaking a punt and kickoff for touchdowns and leading league with 25.9 average on kickoff returns. Mark Moseley, who failed earlier in Philadelphia and Houston, gave Skins some clutch kicking. Punter Mike Bragg had an off-year but should come back.

OUTLOOK: Under Allen, Redskins have reached post-season playoffs four straight years but his loyal troops are growing older. This will be a pivotal year in Washington. Does the Over-the-Hill Gang have enough left for one last assault on the Super Bowl or will it be passed by younger clubs like Philadelphia and St. Louis?

REDSKIN PROFILES

MIKE BASS 30 6-0 190   **Cornerback**

One of steadier cornerbacks in game . . . Very physical player . . . Has unusual strength and frequently uses it to overpower a smaller wide receiver . . . Made big play, stripping ball from Dallas' Drew Pearson near goal line in closing minutes of Redskins' win last season . . . "The ball was on target, I thought I had him beat," Pearson said, "but Bass just made a helluva play" . . . Born March 31, 1945, in Ypsilanti, Mich. . . . Attended U. of Michigan . . . Late bloomer in NFL . . . Was 12th draft pick of Green Bay in '67, was cut, and failed to stick on Detroit cab squad before catching on with Skins in '69.

LARRY BROWN 27 5-11 204   **Running Back**

Struggled through second straight sub-par season . . . Rushed for only 430 yards on 163 attempts (2.6 avg.) and just three touchdowns . . . Hobbled by leg injuries, Brown's production tapered off in '73 to 860 yards on 273 tries . . . Was NFL Player of the Year in '72, rushing for 1,216 yards, scoring 12 touchdowns, leading Redskins to Super Bowl . . . Only Redskin to ever rush for 1,000 yards in a season, a feat he has ac-

WASHINGTON REDSKINS 191

complished twice (he gained 1,125 yards in '72) ... Born Sept. 19, 1947, in Clairton, Pa. ... Attended Kansas State where he was used as a blocking back for Mack Herron ... Wasn't given much hope in pro ball until Skins' coach Vince Lombardi saw him at camp ... "I like the kid," Lombardi said. "He's got guts."

PAT FISCHER 35 5-9 170   Cornerback

"They keep saying Pat Fischer is too small but until I can find somebody better, he'll play for me," says George Allen ... Fischer defies all football logic: he's too old, too small, a step too slow, yet he continues to turn the league's best receivers inside-out ... "I can't figure the man out," says the Eagles' 6-8 Harold Carmichael. "I stand next to him, he comes up to my belt buckle, but when I reach for a pass, he's right with me" ... Born Jan. 2, 1940, in Omaha, graduated from U. of Nebraska ... Originally a 17th-round draft pick by St. Louis, claimed as free agent by Washington ... Second to Paul Krause among active NFC interceptors with 47.

KEN HOUSTON 30 6-3 198   Safety

George Allen saw Houston playing for Oilers and knew he would fit into Skins' secondary ... Allen sent Oilers five players for Houston and the trade is one of Allen's best ... Had great season for Oilers in '71, intercepting nine passes to top AFC, returning them for 220 yards and four touchdowns, an NFL record ... His career total of nine TDs on intercepts is also a league high ... Born Nov. 12, 1944, in Lufkin, Tex., attended Prairie View ... Played two years with Redskins and was voted first-team All-NFC both times ... "Kenny is a very smart player," Allen says. "He's never out of position and he anticipates plays well."

CHRIS HANBURGER 34 6-2 218   Linebacker

"We've run plays designed to take Hanburger away from the ball," said Dallas' Roger Staubach, "and he still comes in to tackle the runners for a loss. His instincts are unbelievable" ... Everyone ranks Hanburger among top outside linebackers in the game ... Selected for seven Pro Bowls and numerous All-Pro teams ... NFC's Defensive Player of

192 THE COMPLETE HANDBOOK OF PRO FOOTBALL

the Year in '72 ... Master of the "big play" ... Scored third touchdown of his career last season in a crucial spot ... With Redskins losing to Philadelphia, Hanburger pounced on Roman Gabriel fumble in end zone to spark Washington's come-from-behind victory ... "When Chris fell on that ball, I could see our club sag," Mike McCormack said. "It was like they said, 'That damn Hamburger did it to us again.'" ... Born Aug. 13, 1941, at Ft. Bragg, N.C., attended University of North Carolina.

BILLY KILMER 35 6-0 204   Quarterback

Joined Skins in '71 as back-up for Sonny Jurgensen but, due to Sonny's injury problems, spent last four years as club's No. 1 quarterback ... Although critics insist Kilmer has limited physical skills, the former UCLA tailback has guided Skins to post-season playoffs four straight times ... Throws wobbly passes from peculiar-looking stances but he gets the ball there ... A savage competitor ... "He'd bite your head off for a first down," says Dallas' Charlie Waters ... Born Sept. 5, 1939, in Topeka, Kan. ... Was third-ranked passer in NFC last season ... Played brilliantly in two Monday Night appearances: hit 17-of-23 passes for 223 yards and two TDs vs. Denver and 19-of-29 for 269 yards and three TDs vs. Los Angeles.

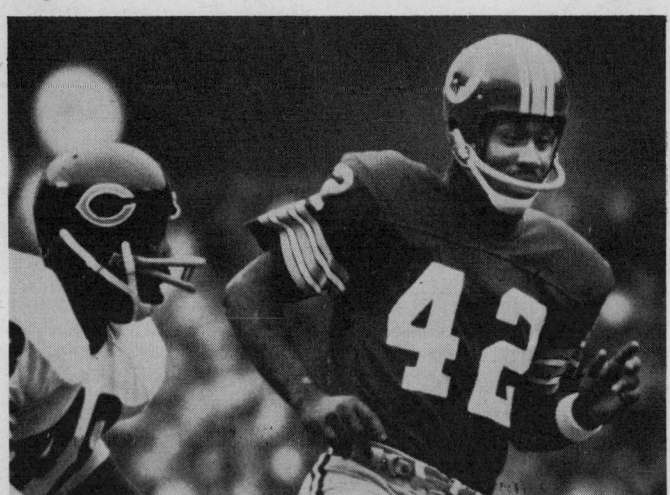

Charley Taylor threatens NFL's all-time receiving marks.

WASHINGTON REDSKINS 193

ROY JEFFERSON 31 6-2 195 — Wide Receiver

One of Washington's most feared offensive weapons is quick slant pass to Jefferson ... Jefferson is deceptively strong and catches ball well moving into the middle ... Caught 43 passes last season, topped all Redskins in yards averaged per catch (15.2) ... Born Nov. 9, 1943, in Texarkana, Ark., attended University of Utah ... Drafted by Pittsburgh then dealt to Baltimore and Washington in '71 ... One of NFL's flashiest dressers ... Favors hand-crafted leather shoulder bags and knee-high fur boots ... Spends off-season working as youth services specialist for Metro Area Transit Authority in Washington.

RON McDOLE 35 6-4 265 — Defensive End

Typifies Allen's "Over-the-Hill Gang" ... Cast off by two clubs (St. Louis, Houston), played eight years with Buffalo but everyone figured he was washed up when Allen traded for him in '71 ... Has given Allen four solid seasons at left end ... In first year with Skins, McDole intercepted three passes, returning one for touchdown ... Born Sept. 9, 1939, in Toledo, attended University of Nebraska ... "A real hustler," says Miami tackle Norm Evans. "You have to block him every second or he'll get to the ball" ... Last year he sacked Roger Staubach once, batted down two of his passes—one of which Staubach caught only to be dropped by McDole for 13-yard loss.

CHARLEY TAYLOR 33 6-3 210 — Wide Receiver

Again topped all skins in pass receptions (54) ... Tops all active NFL receivers in career catches (582) ... "I keep waiting for Charley to slow down, to lose a step one of these years but he never does," says Bill Kilmer. "If anything, he's improving with age ... like wine" ... Was Skins' No. 1 draft pick out of Arizona State in '64, became starting halfback immediately ... Was voted NFL's Rookie of the Year, set league record for backs with 53 pass receptions that season ... All-time Redskin leader in pass receptions and touchdowns (84) ... Born Sept. 28, 1941, in Grand Prairie, Tex. ... "He's the toughest man in the league for me to cover," says Dallas' Charlie Waters.

TOP ROOKIES

MIKE THOMAS 22 5-10 188 **Running Back**
As usual, Redskins didn't have a pick until the fifth-round but Allen may have helped himself... Thomas was rated among the 10 best running back in this year's college crop with his lack of height the only mark against him... Sparkplug of Nevada-Las Vegas' high scoring offense... Fine speed, good hands.

MARK DOAK 6-3 245 **Offensive Tackle**
Skins' sixth-round pick from University of Nebraska... Scouts say he has a chance to make it... Good techniques and good upper body strength... Might need some refining on his pass protection but with Washington, Doak will be given time to develop.

COACH GEORGE ALLEN... People around pro football kid about George Allen... They laugh about the way he distributes a dozen game balls after each win... About how he serves ice cream and cake to his players after a victory... How he hangs cornball slogans around the lockerrooms... But while other coaches laugh, George Allen wins... He is, in fact, the winningest coach in the NFC (career mark: 89-32-5)... Allen is an almost maniacal worker, spending as much as 18 hours per day in his office, reviewing films and scanning personnel around the league... He was born April 29, 1922, in Detroit and attended the University of Michigan... Started in NFL as Chicago Bear defensive coordinator in 1958... Has written six books, but has never authored a winning Super Bowl script.

CLUB HISTORY

The Redskins are a storybook full of great names from the past. Like Sammy Baugh who joined them their first year in Washington (after moving from Boston) and led them to the NFL championship. Baugh not only was the greatest passer of his time but was also a superb safety on defense (first man ever to intercept four passes in one game) and a booming punter (led league four straight seasons).

WASHINGTON REDSKINS

Slingin' Sammy played for the Redskins for 15 years and five times guided them to championship games. The Redskins had other Hall of Famers like Cliff Battles, Turk Edwards, Wayne Millner and Bill Dudley. The club went sour late in the '50s, winning just two games in 1960-61.

In 1969, Edward Bennett Williams hired Vince Lombardi, who gave the Redskins one winning season before he died. In 1971, Williams turned the club over to George Allen, who stocked his roster with old veterans and other people's malcontents and guided the Skins to the playoffs four straight years.

INDIVIDUAL REDSKIN RECORDS

Rushing

Most Yards Game:	191	Larry Brown, vs N.Y. Giants, 1972
Season:	1,216	Larry Brown, 1972
Career:	5,460	Larry Brown, 1969-74

Passing

Most TD Passes Game:	6	Sam Baugh, vs Brooklyn, 1943
	6	Sam Baugh, vs St. Louis, 1947
Season:	31	Sonny Jurgensen, 1967
Career:	255	Sonny Jurgensen, Eagles 1957-63, Redskins 1964-73

Receiving

Most TD Passes Game:	3	Hugh Taylor (5 times)
	3	Jerry Smith, vs Los Angeles, 1967
	3	Jerry Smith, vs Dallas, 1969
	3	Hal Crisler (once)
	3	Joe Walton (once)
	3	Pat Richter, vs Chicago, 1968
	3	Larry Brown, vs Philadelphia, 1973
Season:	12	Hugh Taylor, 1952
	12	Charley Taylor, 1966
	12	Jerry Smith, 1967
Career:	73	Charley Taylor, 1964-74

Scoring

Most Points Game:	24	Dick James, vs Dallas, 1961
	24	Larry Brown, vs Philadelphia, 1973
Season:	114	Curt Knight, 1971
Career:	546	Bobby Mitchell, 1958-68
Most TDs Game:	4	Dick James, vs Dallas, 1961
	4	Larry Brown, vs Philadelphia, 1973
Season:	15	Charley Taylor, 1966
Career:	84	Charley Taylor, 1964-74

PHILADELPHIA EAGLES

TEAM DIRECTORY: Pres.: Leonard Tose; GM: Jim Murray; Bus. Mgr.: Leo Carlin; Dir. Player Pers.: Herman Ball; Dir. Pub. Rel.: Jim Gallagher; Head Coach: Mike McCormack; Trainer: Otho Davis. Home: Veterans Stadium, Philadelphia, Pa. (65,954).

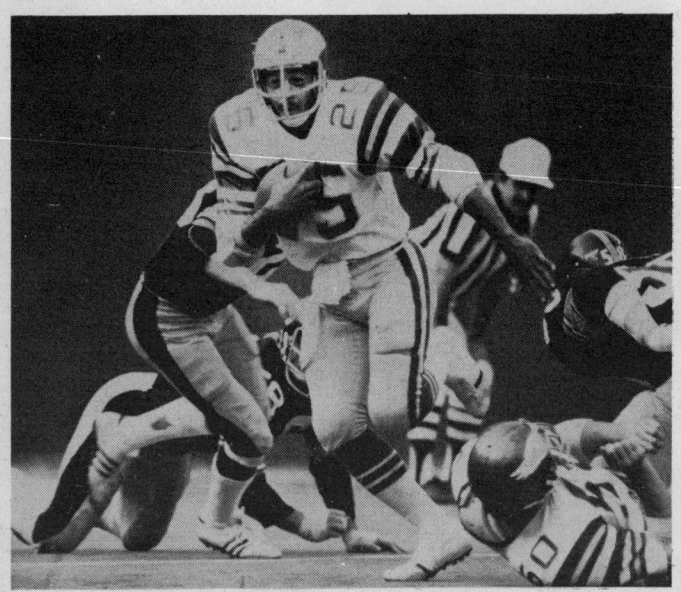

Tom Sullivan topped NFL rushers with 11 TDs.

SCOUTING REPORT

OFFENSE: The Eagles, who had the most potent passing team in the NFC two years ago, badly slumped last season. Many blamed the regression on quarterback Roman Gabriel, who was hailed as "The Messiah" when he arrived in '73 and was booed to the bench last year. Sure, Gabriel failed to equal his extraordinary first year, but to blame the entire offensive letdown on him is neither fair nor accurate. Most of the Eagles offensive problems began when both fullbacks, Norm Bulaich and Po James, were sidelined with injuries.

Without a capable fullback to spearhead their I-formation,

tailback Tom Sullivan, who rushed for 968 yards the previous year, was held to 760. Overall, the Eagles rushed for fewer yards than any NFC club (25th in league) enabling defenses to lay back and wait for Gabe to throw the ball. Mike McCormack has made sure that won't happen again, trading for two good fullbacks, Art Malone and John Tarver.

If the Birds get their I-formation rolling again, Gabriel should be able to re-open the air lanes to brilliant receivers Harold Carmichael and tight end Charles Young, who led the NFC with 63 catches. Of course, if Gabriel can't move the team, McCormack would not hesitate to call on young Mike Boryla who started the final three games last season and won them all.

DEFENSE: While the offense, which figured to be potent, turned feeble last year, the defense responded with some gallant efforts. In the first five weeks the defense produced 20 turnovers to lift the Eagles to a 4-1 start. And after six straight losses, it was the defense that forced five fumbles and an interception to upset Green Bay and ignite a sweep of the final three games.

"When our defense is playing well," said Mike McCormack, "there's not enough gold in Fort Knox to put a value on them." They key to last year's dramatic improvement was middle linebacker Bill Bergey, acquired at great expense from Cincinnati. Instantly, the fans adopted him as a folk-hero and his teammates, inspired by Bergey's bruising example, began copying his intimidating style of play. The unit became known as "Bergey's Brawlers" and people around the league took notice.

"Those dudes are playing mean," said the Steelers' Joe Greene, whose name is synonymous with the word. Basically, it is a young group with a bright future. The front four was improved further with the signing of WFL returnee Carter Campbell. The outside linebackers are Steve Zabel, who led the team in tackles, and underrated John Bunting, who was graded higher than any defensive player by coaches. The secondary allowed just nine TD passes, second best in the league. Cornerback Joe Lavender and Randy Logan, entering their third seasons, are future All-Pros. The other cornerback, John Outlaw, led the club by breaking up 17 passes. Free safety Bill Bradley ties the unit together.

KICKING GAME: Tom Dempsey is still the top long-range field goal threat in football. But he has been traded to Los Angeles. The Eagles went to training camp searching for a replacement. Punting could be a problem, too. Punter Merritt

EAGLES VETERANS ROSTER

HEAD COACH—Mike McCormack. Assistant Coaches—Boyd Dowler, John Idzik, Dick LeBeau, John Mazur, Walt Michaels, John Sandusky

No.	Name	Pos.	Ht.	Wt.	NFL Exp.	College
31	Bailey, Tom	RB	6-2	211	5	Florida St.
66	Bergey, Bill	LB	6-3	253	7	Arkansas St.
10	Boryla, Mike	QB	6-3	200	2	Stanford
28	Bradley, Bill	S-P	5-11	190	7	Texas
36	Bulaich, Norm	RB	6-1	218	6	Texas Christian
95	Bunting, John	LB	6-1	220	4	North Carolina
78	Cagle, Jim	DT	6-5	255	2	Georgia
—	Campbell, Carter	DE	6-4	248	5	Weber State
17	Carmichael, Harold	WR	6-8	225	5	Southern U.
21	Chesson, Wes	WR	6-2	189	5	Duke
8	Coleman, Al	S	6-0	183	7	Tennessee St.
75	Cullars, Willie	DE	6-5	250	2	Kansas State
67	Dobbins, Herb	T	6-4	260	2	San Diego St.
—	Dorton, Wayne	G	6-1	250	1	Arkansas State
61	Dunstan, Bill	DT	6-4	250	3	Utah State
5	Gabriel, Roman	QB	6-4	220	14	No. Carolina St.
56	Halverson, Dean	LB	6-2	230	7	Washington
33	Jackson, Randy	RB	6-0	220	4	Wichita St.
27	James, Ron	RB	6-1	202	4	New Mexico St.
64	Jones, Joe	DE	6-6	250	5	Tennessee St.
37	Kersey, Merritt	P	6-1	205	2	West Chester
72	Key, Wade	G	6-5	245	6	S.W. Texas St.
65	Kirksey, Roy	G	6-1	255	5	Maryland St. (ES)
87	Kramer, Kent	TE	6-4	235	9	Minnesota
30	Lavender, Joe	CB	6-4	190	3	San Diego St.
55	LeMaster, Frank	LB	6-2	224	2	Kentucky
41	Logan, Randy	S	6-1	195	3	Michigan
63	Luken, Tom	G	6-3	253	4	Purdue
26	Malone, Art	RB	6-0	216	6	Arizona St.
22	Marshall, Larry	S	5-10	195	4	Maryland
—	McGuire, Larry	DE	6-4	243	1	Widener
50	Morriss, Guy	C	6-4	245	3	Texas Christian
48	Oliver, Greg	RB	6-0	205	3	Trinity (Tex.)
20	Outlaw, John	CB	5-10	180	7	Jackson St.
24	Parker, Artimus	S	6-3	215	2	Southern Calif.
77	Patton, Jerry	DT	6-3	265	4	Nebraska
82	Picard, Bob	WR	6-1	195	3	E. Washington
7	Reaves, John	QB	6-3	210	4	Florida
45	Reeves, Marion	CB	6-1	195	2	Clemson
52	Reilly, Kevin	LB	6-2	220	3	Villanova
—	Shubert, Eddie	LB	6-2	233	1	Drexel
76	Sisemore, Jerry	T	6-4	250	3	Texas
—	Sitterle, Allen	T	6-4	260	1	No. Carolina St.
85	Smith, Charles	WR	6-1	185	2	Grambling
73	Stevens, Richard	T	6-4	245	6	Baylor
—	Stewart, Darryll	CB	6-1	179	1	Oklahoma State
25	Sullivan, Tom	RB	6-0	190	4	Miami
79	Sutton, Mitch	DT	6-4	265	2	Kansas
49	Tarver, John	RB	6-3	220	4	Colorado
71	Wynn, Will	DE	6-4	245	3	Tennessee St.
86	Young, Charles	TE	6-4	238	3	Southern Calif.
89	Zabel, Steve	LB	6-4	234	6	Oklahoma
80	Zimmerman, Don	WR	6-3	195	3	N.E. Louisiana

TOP FIVE DRAFT CHOICES

Rd.	Name	Pos.	Ht.	Wt.	Age	College
7	Bill Capraun	T	6-5	253	22	Miami
8	Jeff Bleamer	T	6-4	250	21	Penn State
10	Ken Schroy	CB	6-2	190	22	Maryland
11	Keith Rowen	G	6-3	240	22	Stanford
12	Richard Pawlewicz	RB	6-2	220	21	William & Mary

Kersey caught on as a free agent but had two blocked and averaged just 36.1 yards, poorest in the conference.

OUTLOOK: Eagles have made steady progress under Mike McCormack, winning five games in '73 and seven last year. They are on the verge of becoming a contender, needing only a beefed-up running game to make a run at the East Division crown. The Eagles are probably still a year away but they bear watching.

EAGLE PROFILES

BILL BERGEY 30 6-3 245   **Linebacker**

"Bill is gonna give the fans of Philadelphia the kind of linebacker play they haven't seen since the days of Chuck Bednarik," coach Mike McCormack predicted when the Eagles acquired Bergey from Cincinnati prior to last season ... Bergey more than lived up to his billing ... Topped the Eagles in solo tackles and interceptions (five) and provided leadership the club had lacked ... "When Bill hits somebody and we hear that leather pop, it jacks us all up," says teammate Jerry Patton ... Bergey is an extremely physical player who enjoys the heavy hitting ... "I like to hit a man hard," Bergey says. "I want him to think, 'Oww ... that must have been Bergey again.'" ... Born Feb. 9, 1945, in South Dayton, N.Y. ... Attended Arkansas State.

BILL BRADLEY 28 5-11 190   **Safety**

Playing in more disciplined defense which limits the amount of roaming he can do, Bradley's interception totals have dropped to six in past two seasons ... He picked off 20 the two previous years ... Still regarded as one of top ball hawks in the league ... "He's like a phantom," Sonny Jurgensen once said. "He appears out of nowhere." ... A prep school legend as a boy in Palestine, Tex. ... Born Jan. 24, 1947 ... Played three positions, including quarterback, at U. of Texas ... Returns punts for Eagles, holds for placekicks and can punt if necessary ... Nicknamed "Soupy," a spoof of his college nickname, "Super Bill."

HAROLD CARMICHAEL 25 6-8 225   Wide Receiver

Led NFC in pass receptions in '73 with 67 catches ... Placed third in '74 with 56 receptions for 649 yards and eight touchdowns ... Played only part-time his first two years as both wide receiver and tight end ... "Harold is a whole new dimension in football," says assistant coach Dick LeBeau, a former cornerback. "He has great size, strength and speed (4.7). One-on-one, a cornerback is helpless against him." ... Former basketball star at Southern University ... Born in Jacksonville, Fla., Sept. 22, 1949 ... Great natural athlete ... Can catch punts one-handed and throw a football from end zone to end zone.

ROMAN GABRIEL 35 6-4 220   Quarterback

Had disappointing season last year after great start with Eagles in '73 ... Completed 57 percent of his passes, but yardage (1,867) and touchdowns (nine) were well off his expected output ... Slowed by injuries (hip pointer, bruised ribs) last year and absorbed 35 sacks, eight in one game vs. St. Louis ... Sat out final three games as rookie Mike Boryla took over ... "Gabe is still our number one quarterback," McCormack announced ... Born Aug. 5, 1940 in Wilmington, N.C. ... Played at North Carolina State ... No. 1 draft pick by Rams in '62, played 11 years with Los Angeles ... Voted the league's MVP following the 1969 season ... A devoted exponent of Kung Fu, practicing several hours every day.

JOE LAVENDER 26 6-4 190   Cornerback

Nicknamed "Big Bird" because of his long, sleek build ... Established himself as a top NFL cornerback last season, breaking up six passes and intercepting another ... Returned that interception 37 yards for touchdown vs. Colts ... Sparked Eagles to big win over Dallas, recovering fumble, racing 98 yards for touchdown ... "Bird is one of those guys who makes the big plays," says McCormack. "People don't like to throw the ball his way" ... A native of Rayville, La. ... Born Feb. 10, 1949, he attended San Diego State, where he played basketball and football ... Only player in league who wears

PHILADELPHIA EAGLES 201

glasses on the field... "Bird is steadily gaining in confidence," says assistant coach John Mazur. "With experience, he could be an All-Pro."

TOM SULLIVAN 25 6-0 190 — Running Back

Sleeper uncovered by McCormack two years ago... Was Eagles' 15th-round draft pick from U. of Miami in '72, spent rookie season on special teams... McCormack made him his No. 1 tailback in 1973... Sullivan responded by rushing for 968 yards... Last season, "Silky" gained 760 yards on the ground and rushed for 11 touchdowns, most in the league... A fine receiver... Has caught 93 passes in three pro seasons... A native of Jacksonville, Fla.... Born March 5, 1950... Spends off-season traveling and painting... "He's the hardest worker on our club," says McCormack. "He not only loves to play football, he loves to practice, too."

WILL WYNN 26 6-4 245 — Defensive End

Made the tough switch from right defensive end to the left side last season and coaches were pleased with the results... Made 62 solo tackles, including eight behind the line of scrimmage... Finished second to Joe Jones in sacks with four... Ran 87 yards with John Hadl fumble for second touchdown of his career last year... "I don't know why," Wynn says, "but the ball just seems to bounce my way"... Born in Darlington, S.C., Jan. 15, 1949... Captained standout Tennessee State team in '72... Happy-go-lucky bachelor... Drives a bright orange Cadillac with an Eagle and his uniform number painted on the door. A fierce competitor on the field... Ejected from Giant game last year for fighting with tackle John Hill.

CHARLES YOUNG 24 6-4 242 — Tight End

Generally regarded as the best tight end in football... Came on after slow start last year to top all NFC receivers with 63 receptions for 696 yards and three touchdowns... Best game came in monsoon rains at New Haven vs. Giants where he caught nine passes for 103 yards and one touchdown... "He's an incredible athlete," said rookie quarterback Mike Boryla that day. "We were slipping around in the mud and

Charlie was gliding like Secretariat on a dry track"... Young brashly predicted greatness for himself when the Eagles picked him from Southern Cal... "I'm gonna revolutionize the (tight end) position," Young said. "I can run like a scatback, block like a tackle and catch like, well, like myself. On a 10-unit scale, I'm a full 10"... Young is a native of Fresno, Cal., born Feb. 5, 1951.

STEVE ZABEL 27 6-4 238   Linebacker

Playing confidently and living up to great potential that prompted the Eagles to draft him No. 1 from U. of Oklahoma in 1970... Led club in total tackles (108), breaking club record in process... Had 14 tackles vs. Colts, made two interceptions... Impressed everyone with remarkable recovery from ruptured Achilles tendon suffered in '73... Born in Minneapolis on Mar. 20, 1948... Operates night club in South Jersey... Spent off-season serving as Delaware Valley chairman of Multiple Sclerosis drive... Originally drafted as tight end but coaches felt his natural aggressiveness was best suited for defense.

MIKE BORYLA 23 6-3 200   Quarterback

Helped salvage Eagles' season... Replaced Roman Gabriel for final three games and produced three wins... Rookie from Stanford showed remarkable poise... Completed 59 percent of passes, threw for five touchdowns... "I figured he'd toss and turn all night before his first start," said roommate Steve Zabel, "but, heck, he was asleep before lights out. I don't think he knows what nerves are"... Born in Long Island, N.Y., Mar. 6, 1951... Son of Vince Boryla, former star and coach of basketball's N.Y. Knicks... Originally drafted by Cincinnati but Eagles acquired him via trade prior to camp... "At this stage of his career," says assistant coach Boyd Dowler, "Mike compares very favorably to my old teammate, Bart Starr. I'd give Mike an edge on his stronger arm."

TOP ROOKIES

BILL CAPRAUN 21 6-4 250   Offensive Tackle
Eagles, who didn't have a pick until the seventh round, were

delighted to find Capraun still available ... "When we saw he was still on the board in the fifth round, we started holding our breath," McCormack said. "When our turn came and he was still there, we couldn't believe it" ... Big, tough blocker was overshadowed at U. of Miami, playing on same line as All-American Dennis Harrah.

JEFF BLEAMER 22 6-4 250   **Offensive Tackle**
Chosen on eighth round ... Bleamer is another offensive tackle candidate ... Played full-time in senior year at Penn State ... Called by Maryland All-American Randy White "the toughest tackle I faced all year" ... Born June 22, 1953, and raised in Allentown, Pa., where he attended Dieruff High ... Plans career in forestry.

COACH MIKE McCORMACK ... Friends and football co-workers advised Mike McCormack not to take the head coaching job in Philadelphia two years ago. "They told me, 'You don't want to get stuck with that can of worms,'" McCormack recalls ... But McCormack took the job and in just two seasons transformed a perennial loser into an exciting, competitive team ... Led Eagles to five wins in '73, upped that to 7-7 last year, the club's first non-losing season since 1966 ... Played and coached under the most respected football minds ... An All-Pro offensive tackle for the Cleveland Browns under Paul Brown ... Later became offensive line coach in Washington under Vince Lombardi and George Allen ... "I didn't copy any of them," McCormack says, "but I'm sure some ideas rubbed off."

CLUB HISTORY

The Eagles have enjoyed only one sustained period of success, in the late 1940s when a thick-legged fullback from LSU named Steve Van Buren carried them to three division titles and two world championships. Until the "Moving Van" joined the club in 1944, the Eagles managed just one winning season (1943, when they merged with Pittsburgh to form the 'Steagles').

After the departure of Van Buren, the Eagles floundered through the '50s until they acquired quarterback Norm Van Brocklin from Los Angeles in 1958. Two years later, they upset

Green Bay for the world championship with Van Brocklin directing the offense and Chuck Bednarik, a 33-year-old physical marvel, playing both ways (center and linebacker) the full 60 minutes.

Van Brocklin retired after winning the title and the following year his back-up man, Sonny Jurgensen, pitched the Birds within a half-game of repeating as East Division champs. Since then, it's been a rebuilding process which is finally showing some results under head coach Mike McCormack who last season guided the Eagles to a 7-7 finish, their best in eight years.

INDIVIDUAL EAGLE RECORDS

Rushing

Most Yards Game:	205	Steve Van Buren, vs Pittsburgh, 1949
Season:	1,146	Steve Van Buren, 1949
Career:	5,860	Steve Van Buren, 1944-51

Passing

Most TD Passes Game:	7	Adrian Burk, vs Washington, 1954
Season:	32	Sonny Jurgensen, 1961
Career:	111	Norman Snead, 1964-70

Receiving

Most TD Passes Game:	4	Joe Carter, vs Cincinnati, 1934
	4	Ben Hawkins, vs Pittsburgh, 1969
Season:	13	Tommy McDonald, 1960 and 1961
Career:	66	Tommy McDonald, 1957-63

Scoring

Most Points Game:	25	Bobby Walston, vs Washington, 1954
Season:	114	Bobby Walston, 1954
Career:	881	Bobby Walston, 1951-62
Most TDs Game:	4	Joe Carter, vs Cincinnati, 1934
	4	Clarence Peaks, vs St. Louis, 1958
	4	Tommy McDonald, vs N.Y. Giants, 1959
	4	Ben Hawkins, vs Pittsburgh, 1969
Season:	18	Steve Van Buren, 1945
Career:	77	Steve Van Buren, 1944-51

ST. LOUIS CARDINALS 205

ST. LOUIS CARDINALS

TEAM DIRECTORY: Managing General Partner: William Bidwell; Dir. Oper.: Joe Sullivan; Dir. Player Pers.: George Boone; Dir. Pro Scouting: Larry Wilson; Pub. Dir.: Joe Rhein; Head Coach: Don Coryell; Trainer: John Omohundro. Home: Busch Memorial Stadium, St. Louis, Mo. (51,392).

Jim Hart was voted NFC's Outstanding Player.

SCOUTING REPORT

OFFENSE: There is a tendency to dismiss the Cardinals' showing of last season as a fluke. Particularly on offense, where they scored 13 of their 36 touchdowns from at least 40 yards out.

206 THE COMPLETE HANDBOOK OF PRO FOOTBALL

Their average TD play was a 28-yarder, which must be some kind of league record. Figure they just caught a year full of lucky breaks? If you check the figures closer, you might change your mind.

The Cardinals, besides being an explosive offensive team, were also the most consistent in the conference. For one thing, the line allowed QB Jim Hart to be sacked just 16 times, fewest in the NFC. For another, the Cards only committed 17 turnovers (eight interceptions, nine fumbles), the best ball-control figure in the league. No, the Cardinal offense is not a mirage... They are, as Howard Cosell likes to say, for real.

Of course, for the Big Red to be as effective this season they will need another strong year from Hart, who could do no wrong in '74. He threw for 20 TDs (most in NFC), cut down on his interceptions, was voted NFC Offensive Player of the Year and began leading the offense with great confidence. The Cards are also counting on another big year from Terry Metcalf, who led the club in every offensive category except passing. Making sure Metcalf stays healthy is an unheralded but strong line led by super tackle, Dan Dierdorf.

DEFENSE: The showing of the Big Red defense last season was an even bigger surprise than the improved offense. The Cards gave early indications of being stingier in their opening game, holding the high-scoring Eagles to a field goal in a 7-3 win. In fact, the Eagles never did score a touchdown on the Cards last season, losing 13-3 in a rematch as the Big Red sacked Roman Gabriel eight times.

Overall, the Card defenders allowed almost 1,000 fewer yards and 147 fewer points than in '73. On the plus side, they upped their sacks and interceptions by six apiece. It might be hard for casual fans to understand this improvement since the St. Louis defense is hardly stocked with big-name players. "From a pure talent standpoint," admits coach Don Coryell, "we cannot stand up to most of the good teams in the NFL." But the Cards get the job done with fiery hustlers like Bob Rowe and Ron Yankowski on the line backed up by vet Larry Stallings, Mark Arneson and Pete Barnes.

Cards are hoping massive Dave Butz, their No. 1 pick in '73, recovers from knee injury which sidelined him all of last season. The secondary, once a shooting gallery for enemy quarterbacks, is showing promise with Norm Thompson (six intercepts) and All-NFC Roger Wehrli at the corners and Ken Reaves and Clarence Duren at safety.

ST. LOUIS CARDINALS 207

CARDINALS VETERANS ROSTER

HEAD COACH—Don Coryell. Assistant Coaches—Jim Champion, Joe Gibbs, Harry Gilmer, Sid Hall, Jim Hanifan, Wayne Sevier, Ray Willsey

No.	Name	Pos.	Ht.	Wt.	NFL Exp.	College
18	Albert, Sergio	K	6-3	195	2	U.S. International
61	Allison, Henry	G	6-3	255	3	San Diego State
57	Arneson, Mark	LB	6-2	220	4	Arizona
25	Bakken, Jim	K	6-0	200	14	Wisconsin
54	Banks, Tom	C-G	6-2	245	4	Auburn
59	Barnes, Pete	LB	6-1	240	9	Southern
79	Bell, Bob	DE	6-4	250	5	Cincinnati
51	Brahaney, Tom	C	6-2	250	3	Oklahoma
—	Briscoe, Marlin	WR	5-11	175	8	Omaha
70	Brooks, Leo	DT	6-6	240	6	Texas
83	Brunson, Mike	WR	6-0	185	2	Arizona State
62	Butz, Dave	DT	6-7	290	2	Purdue
88	Cain, J.V.	WR	6-4	225	2	Colorado
65	Crum, Bob	DE	6-5	240	2	Arizona
26	Crump, Dwayne	CB	5-11	180	3	Fresno State
72	Dierdorf, Dan	T	6-3	280	5	Michigan
66	Dobler, Conrad	G	6-3	255	4	Wyoming
41	Duren, Clarence	S	6-1	190	3	California
60	Finnie, Roger	G-T	6-3	250	7	Florida A&M
63	George, Steve	DT	6-5	265	2	Houston
—	Ginn, Hubert	RB	5-10	185	6	Florida A&M
85	Gray, Mel	WR	5-9	175	5	Missouri
30	Hammond, Gary	WR	5-11	185	3	Southern Methodist
17	Hart, Jim	QB	6-1	210	10	Southern Illinois
50	Hartle, Greg	LB	6-2	225	2	Newberry
55	Iman, Ken	C	6-1	240	15	S.E. Missouri State
34	Jones, Steve	RB	6-0	200	3	Duke
12	Keithley, Gary	QB	6-3	215	3	Texas-El Paso
69	Kindle, Greg	T	6-4	265	2	Tennessee State
52	LeVeck, Jack	LB	6-0	225	3	Ohio
73	McMillan, Ernie	T	6-5	265	15	Illinois
21	Metcalf, Terry	RB	5-10	185	3	Long Beach State
58	Miller, Terry	LB	6-2	220	6	Illinois
27	Moss, Eddie	RB	6-0	215	3	S.E. Missouri State
53	Neils, Steve	LB	6-2	215	2	Minnesota
35	Otis, Jim	RB	6-0	225	6	Ohio State
36	Reaves, Ken	S	6-3	210	10	Norfolk State
14	Roberts, Hal	P	6-1	180	2	Houston
75	Rowe, Bob	DT	6-4	270	9	Western Michigan
74	Rudolph, Council	DE	6-4	245	4	Kentucky State
38	Scales, Hurles	CB	6-1	200	2	North Texas State
11	Shaw, Dennis	QB	6-2	210	6	San Diego State
81	Smith, Jackie	TE	6-4	230	13	Northwest Louisiana
67	Stallings, Larry	LB	6-1	230	13	Georgia Tech
28	Stringer, Scott	CB	5-11	180	2	California
82	Thomas, Earl	WR	6-2	215	5	Houston
43	Thompson, Norm	CB	6-1	180	5	Utah
45	Tolbert, Jim	CB-S	6-4	210	9	Lincoln, Mo.
22	Wehrli, Roger	CB	6-0	190	7	Missouri
20	Willard, Ken	RB	6-2	215	11	North Carolina
56	Withrow, Cal	C	6-0	240	6	Kentucky
78	Yankowski, Ron	DE	6-5	235	5	Kansas State
64	Young, Bob	G	6-1	270	10	Howard Payne

TOP FIVE DRAFT CHOICES

Rd.	Name	Pos.	Ht.	Wt.	Age	College
1	Tim Gray	CB	6-1	200	22	Texas A&M
2	Jim Germany	RB	5-11	200	22	New Mexico State
5	Harvey Goodman	T	6-4	260	22	Colorado
6	Larry Jameson	DT	6-6	255	22	Indiana
8	John Adams	DT	6-5	265	22	West Virginia

KICKING GAME: Jim Bakken enters his 14th season coming off a good year in '74, winning games with last-second field goals. Cards save Bakken's leg by carrying young Sergio Albert as kickoff specialist. Hal Roberts had so-so punting year (38.7) as rookie. Metcalf, who led league in kickoff returns last year, is threat every time he touches ball.

OUTLOOK: Cards jumped off to fast start last year, winning first seven games. They had problems thereafter (3-4) as opponents began taking them seriously. As Don Coryell admits, "We won't surprise our opponents as we did last year." Cards gained confidence and a winning attitude in '74 which will make them dangerous this season. However, it is unlikely they can repeat as East Division Champs.

Versatile Terry Metcalf had 2,058 yards total offense.

CARDINAL PROFILES

DAN DIERDORF 26 6-3 275 — Offensive Tackle

Finally gaining recognition after five strong pro seasons ... Voted into last year's Pro Bowl, an honor he called "my greatest thrill in sports" ... Possesses awesome strength and is improving techniques all the time ... Thoroughly dominated Minnesota's Carl Eller in NFC playoff game, prompting Eller to remark, "That's the toughest anyone has played me in years" ... Voted to seven All-American teams during his career at Michigan ... Born June 29, 1949 in Canton, O. ... Occassionally used as defensive tackle in goal-line situations ... "Dan's a natural leader who puts forth tremendous effort," says Card line coach Jim Hanifan. "A superb drive blocker." Jim Hart calls him, "the best pass blocker in football."

MEL GRAY 26 5-9 175 — Wide Receiver

The game-breaking receiver with 9.2 speed had his biggest year in '74, catching 39 passes for 770 yards and six touchdowns ... Feels rules change limiting bump-and-run coverage helped him ... "Before, they all came up and cut me early," Gray says. "That threw our timing off and if the linebacker was blitzing, he'd sack the quarterback. Now they've got to get a good hit on me the first time because once I'm past them, I'm gone" ... A great trackman at Missouri, was voted outstanding athlete in 1970 Big Eight championships, winning the 100, 220, long jump and placing in the triple jump ... Born Sept. 28, 1948, in Fresno, Ca.

TERRY METCALF 23 5-10 185 — Running Back

Scouts originally thought Metcalf too small to endure the punishment but he has proved them wrong ... A brilliant open-field runner ... Led Cards in rushing (718 yards), receiving (50 catches), punt returns (13.1 avg.), kickoff returns (an NFC high 31.2 avg.) and touchdowns (eight) ... "Without Terry, we could never have won the division," says Jim Hart. "When we needed offense, I just got the ball to Terry and he did the rest" ... Born Sept. 24, 1951, in Seattle, Wash. ... A product of Long Beach State ... Gained 50 yards on his very

210 THE COMPLETE HANDBOOK OF PRO FOOTBALL

first NFL carry, a draw play against the Eagles ... "I reached for him and he was gone," said the Eagles' Bill Bradley. "I said, 'Who is that guy?'"

JIM HART 31 6-1 215   Quarterback

Once the target of St. Louis boobirds, Hart has put two outstanding seasons back-to-back ... Last year was voted the NFC's Outstanding Player after guiding the Big Red to first divisional championship in 26 years ... Hart threw more TD passes (20) than any quarterback in NFC and his interception percentage (2.1) was the lowest ... A product of Southern Illinois, he signed as a free agent in 1966, stepped in as replacement for Charley Johnson who was called to Army duty ... Impressive from the start, Harry Gilmer once said Hart "would be better than Johnny Unitas" ... Lost his job in 1971-72 under coach Bob Hollway ... Restored to No. 1 status by Don Coryell and has blossomed ... "For the first time, Hart believes in himself," says George Allen ... Born April 29, 1944, in Evanston, Ill.

JIM OTIS 27 6-0 220   Running Back

Finally established himself last season ... Rushed for 664 yards as Big Red's first-team fullback ... Almost retired prior to camp, feeling his career was going nowhere ... Set rushing and scoring records at Ohio State but failed in trials with New Orleans and Kansas City before Cards claimed him ... "I'm not a hanger-on," Otis told Coryell last year. "If I'm not gonna play, tell me now and I'll quit" ... Coryell convinced him to stick around and it paid off ... Durable runner who seldom fumbles ... Strong blocker ... Nicknamed "Milk Shake" due to weight problem ... Born April 29, 1948, in Celina, O.

JACKIE SMITH 35 6-4 235   Tight End

Still considered the premier tight end in pro football by folks in St. Louis ... Pass-receiving total dropped off slightly last year, from 41 in '73 to 25 in '74, but Card coaches point out that Jim Hart was throwing more to his wide receivers, Mel Gray and Earl Thomas, than ever before ... Currently ranks as second-leading active receiver in pro football, behind Charlie Taylor ... Smith tops all Cardinal receivers with

ST. LOUIS CARDINALS 211

459 lifetime catches, 37 of those for touchdowns ... Born Feb. 23, 1940, in Columbia, Miss. ... Product of Northwest Louisiana ... Ferocious blocker, extremely difficult to tackle after catch.

BOB ROWE 30 6-4 270 — Defensive Tackle

Durable defensive lineman from Western Michigan ... Has missed only one start in last five years ... Aggressive pass rusher, led eight-sack onslaught against Eagle QB Roman Gabriel last year, dropping Gabe three times himself ... Once blocked three field goals in a single game vs. Baltimore in '72 opener and was named AP Defensive Player of the Week ... "Bob got caught up in our success," coach Don Coryell said last year. "When we got off to such a fast start, you could see Bob getting better and better. He's a natural leader, someone our young defensive players can look up to." ... Born May 23, 1945, in Flint, Mich.

ROGER WEHRLI 27 6-0 190 — Cornerback

Considered by many the finest cornerback in the league ... Named to most All-Pro teams following season ... Helped Cards to vital mid-season victory over Washington by intercepting Sonny Jurgensen pass and returning it 53 yards for touchdown, the first via interception in Wehrli's six year pro career ... A local hero, born Nov. 26, 1947 in New Point, Mo. ... Played college ball at Missouri ... Named top St. Louis sports figure of 1971 by Elks Club ... Has been a starter ever since his rookie year ... Spent one season at free safety (1972), then switched back to corner ... "As good on man-to-man coverage as any cornerback around," says Billy Kilmer of Washington.

RON YANKOWSKI 28 6-5 240 — Defensive End

Contributed one of biggest plays of season to Cards' title drive, scooping up fumble by Redskin QB Billy Kilmer, then racing 71 yards to touchdown in 17-10 victory ... "I didn't know I had that much speed," Yankowski said later ... Had fine career at Kansas State (batting down 15 passes in two years) but some scouts felt he might lack bulk to make it in NFL ... Broke into starting lineup as a rookie and displayed outstanding potential ... Missed four games with bad knee in '72, but played entire '73 season with thumb in cast ... Good pass rusher with, as Coryell puts it, "a nose for the football" ... Born Oct. 23, 1946, in Arlington, Mass.

TOP ROOKIES

TIMOTHY GRAY 22 6-1 200   **Cornerback**
Big Red's top draft pick was consensus All-Southwest Conference player at Texas A&M, second team All-American ... Possesses 4.6 speed in the 40 and has reputation as a tough, aggressive hitter ... Broke up five passes as a senior, no interceptions ... Says Card draft master Joe Sullivan: "We feel he can come in and help us right now. He has all the skills ... He has character and leardership."

JIM GERMANY 21 5-11 200   **Running Back**
Cards' second draft choice was All-Missouri Valley and conference Back of the Week twice in a row ... Led conference in rushing and scoring as a senior at New Mexico State (1,096 yards, 14 TDs) and his five touchdowns vs. Texas-Arlington last year were an NCAA high ... Has 4.6 speed.

COACH DON CORYELL ... "He just has that knack," defensive tackle Bob Rowe says. "There are some people who can walk into a bad situation and turn it around. Coach Coryell is that type of person" ... The 50-year-old head coach's record attests to that ... Coyrell was 23-5-1 in three years at Whittier College, then 104-19-2 in 12 years at San Diego State before coming to the Cardinals in 1973 ... His first season was a disappointment, 4-9-1, but he didn't panic. "I could tell," he says, "we were making progress." Last year his Cardinals won their first seven games and finished atop the NFC's rugged East Division with a 10-4 record, their best mark since 1948 ... "Better times," he promised following a playoff loss to Minnesota, "are ahead." Born in Seattle, a graduate of U. of Washington.

ST. LOUIS CARDINALS 213

CLUB HISTORY

The Cardinals got their start back in 1921 in the bustling bootleg town of Chicago as John (Paddy) Driscoll decided to buck George Halas' big, bad Bears in the pro football market. In 1925, under a coach named Norman Barry, the Cards went 11-2-1 and won their first NFL title. The next year, the Cards dropped below .500 and Norman Barry was gone. That was typical of the early Cardinals who went through 11 different head coaches in the first two decades.

The only one to show any staying power was Jim Conzelman, who assembled a sensational backfield—Paul Christman, Elmer Angsman, Pat Harder and Charlie Trippi—and defeated the Eagles for the championship in 1947. The Cards sputtered through the '50s, managing only one winning season (7-5, in '56) despite the individual brilliance of Ollie Matson. The club moved to St. Louis in 1960 and, after several near-misses, finally captured the Eastern Division title last season under Coach Don Coryell and quarterback Jim Hart, NFC player of the Year.

INDIVIDUAL CARDINAL RECORDS

Rushing
Most Yards Game:	203	John David Crow, vs Pittsburgh, 1960
Season:	1,071	John David Crow, 1960
Career:	3,608	John Roland, 1966-72

Passing
Most TD Passes Game:	6	Jim Hardy, vs Baltimore, 1950
	6	Charley Johnson, vs Cleveland, 1965
	6	Charley Johnson, vs New Orleans, 1969
Season:	28	Charley Johnson, 1963
Career:	108	Charley Johnson, 1961-69

Receiving
Most TD Passes Game:	5	Bob Shaw, vs Baltimore, 1950
Season:	15	Sonny Randle, 1960
Career:	60	Sonny Randle, 1959-66

Scoring
Most Points Game:	40	Ernie Nevers, vs Chicago, 1929
Season:	117	Jim Bakken, 1967 (36 PATS-27 FG)
Career:	1,074	Jim Bakken, 1962-74 (381 PATS-221 FG)
Most TDs Game:	6	Ernie Nevers, vs Chicago, 1929
Season:	17	John David Crow, 1962
Career:	60	Sonny Randle, 1959-66

214 THE COMPLETE HANDBOOK OF PRO FOOTBALL

NEW YORK GIANTS

TEAM DIRECTORY: Pres.: Wellington Mara; VP-Treas.: Timothy Mara; VP-Sec.-GM: Raymond Walsh; Dir. Operations: Andy Robustelli; Dir. Pro Pers.: Jim Trimble; Asst. Dir. Pro Pers.: Emlen Tunnell; Dir. Pub. Rel.: Ed Croke; Head Coach: Bill Arnsparger; Trainer: John Johnson. Home: Shea Stadium, Flushing, N.Y. (60,000).

Top rookie John Hicks leads Doug Kotar around end.

SCOUTING REPORT

OFFENSE: Clearly, the Giants have to score more than they scored last year if they hope to scramble out of the East Division basement. Only once in 14 games did they score more than 21 points; six other times they were held to one touchdown or less. "You can't win in this league with that kind of offense," said head coach Bill Arnsparger.

However, the raw materials are there; it is only a matter of fitting them together. In Craig Morton, they have an experienced quarterback who—with some help—has shown he can win. The Giants have a fine assortment of runners including Joe Dawkins, who topped the club in rushing and receiving last year; Doug Kotar, who impressed as a rookie, and speedy Leon McQuay.

The key, however, is Ron Johnson who was slowed by injuries in '74 and finished the season puzzled and unhappy. If Johnson comes back this year and flashes that 1,000-yard form again, it could turn the whole club on. Bob Tucker leads the receivers, although Walker Gillette and Bob Grim made some big catches last season. The Giants have added needed speed to their outside receiver corps, drafting Danny (Lightning) Buggs of West Virginia.

DEFENSE: Bill Arnsparger came to New York hailed as a defensive genius. Last season's debut was particularly embarrassing to him since the Giants finished as the worst defensive team in the conference and 24th worst in the league (edging out Kansas City and San Diego). Giants gave up 299 points (most in NFC) and a shockingly-high 22 touchdown passes, five more than the next-worst team, New Orleans.

Unlike the offense, the ingredients for improvement don't seem to be on hand. Nose-guard John Mendenhall was Giant's best defensive player and Arnsparger is counting on end Jack Gregory snapping out of his slump. Ex-Eagle Gary Pettigrew, who was impressive in a brief look before suffering an injury, could help. The linebacker corps is active but on the smallish side with Pat Hughes, Ron Hornsby and Brian Kelley all hovering around 225 pounds. Giants' biggest linebacker is Brad Van Pelt who, at 6-5, 235, still hasn't shown the aggressiveness needed to handle the run. "He still plays like a free safety (which he was at Michigan State)," says one pro coach.

Obviously, a secondary which yielded 22 TD passes needs shoring up and there is hope Henry Stuckey, who impressed Arnsparger at Miami, could help at corner back. On the positive side, Chuck Crist, a former basketball star at Penn State, shows promise at strong safety.

KICKING GAME: Giants drafted Tennessee's Ricky Townsend to upgrade them in this area. David Jennings hit some booming

216 THE COMPLETE HANDBOOK OF PRO FOOTBALL

GIANTS VETERANS ROSTER

HEAD COACH—Bill Arnsparger. Assistant Coaches—Floyd Peters, John Symank, Ray Wietecha, Marty Schottenheimer, Ted Plumb, Ed Rutledge

No.	Name	Pos.	Ht.	Wt.	NFL Exp.	College
45	Athas, Pete	CB	5-11	185	5	Tennessee
—	Bond, Sid	T	6-4	270	1	Texas Christian
37	Brooks, Bobby	CB	6-1	195	2	Bishop College
—	Buchanon, Carlton	DT	6-3	250	1	S.W. Okla. State
61	Chandler, Karl	G	6-5	250	2	Princeton
88	Clune, Don	WR	6-3	195	2	Pennsylvania
24	Crist, Chuck	S	6-2	205	4	Penn State
—	Christoff, Larry	TE	6-4	227	1	Rutgers
33	Crosby, Steve	RB	5-11	205	2	Fort Hays College
—	Curbow, Kelley	T	6-5	255	1	Missouri
26	Dawkins, Joe	RB	6-2	220	6	Wisconsin
12	DelGaizo, Jim	QB	6-1	190	4	Tampa
66	Dvorak, Rick	DE	6-4	235	2	Witchita State
62	Enderle, Dick	G	6-2	250	7	Minnesota
—	Fersen, Paul	T	6-5	260	2	Georgia
—	Gaines, Palmer	RB	6-1	210	1	Delaware State
84	Gillette, Walker	WR	6-5	200	6	Richmond
83	Glass, Chip	TE	6-4	235	7	Florida State
2	Gogolak, Pete	K	6-1	190	12	Cornell
81	Gregory, Jack	DE	6-5	255	9	Delta State
27	Grim, Bob	WR	6-0	200	9	Oregon State
72	Hasenohrl, George	DT	6-1	260	2	Ohio State
85	Herrmann, Don	WR	6-2	205	7	Waynesburg
74	Hicks, John	G	6-2	258	2	Ohio State
52	Hill, John	T	6-2	245	4	Lehigh
78	Hilton, Roy	DE	6-6	240	11	Jackson State
67	Hornsby, Ron	LB	6-3	228	5	Southeast Louisiana
56	Hughes, Pat	LB	6-2	225	6	Boston University
70	Hyland, Bob	C	6-2	255	9	Boston College
22	Jackson, Honor	CB	6-2	195	4	Pacific
75	Jacobson, Larry	DT	6-6	260	4	Nebraska
13	Jennings, Dave	P	6-4	205	2	St. Lawrence
30	Johnson, Ron	RB	6-1	205	7	Michigan
55	Kelley, Brian	LB	6-3	222	3	California Lutheran
44	Kotar, Doug	RB	5-11	205	2	Kentucky
43	Lockhart, Carl	S	6-2	175	11	North Texas State
—	May, John	DE	6-3	250	1	Central Conn. State
25	McQuay, Leon	RB	5-9	195	2	Tampa
64	Mendenhall, John	DT	6-1	255	4	Grambling
15	Morton, Craig	QB	6-4	210	11	California
73	Mullen, Tom	G	6-3	245	2	S.E. Missouri State
71	Pettigrew, Gary	DT	6-5	255	10	Stanford
76	Pietrzak, Jim	DT	6-5	260	2	Eastern Michigan
39	Powers, Clyde	S	6-1	195	2	Oklahoma
80	Reed, Henry	LB	6-3	230	5	Weber State
82	Rhodes, Ray	WR	5-11	185	2	Tulsa
57	Selfridge, Andy	LB	6-3	220	4	Virginia
54	Singletary, Bill	LB	6-2	230	2	Temple
18	Small, Eldridge	CB	6-1	190	4	Texas A&I
20	Stienke, Jim	CB	5-11	182	3	S.W. Texas State
48	Stuckey, Henry	CB	6-1	180	4	Missouri
19	Summerell, Carl	QB	6-4	208	2	East Carolina
—	Thomas, Bernard	DT	6-4	250	1	Western Michigan
38	Tucker, Bob	TE	6-3	230	6	Bloomsburg State
63	Van Horn, Doug	T	6-3	245	9	Ohio State
10	Van Pelt, Brad	LB	6-5	235	3	Michigan State
—	Wafer, Carl	DT	6-3	250	2	Tennessee State
—	Watkins, Larry	RB	6-2	230	7	Alcorn A&M
—	White, Jeff	K	5-10	175	2	Texas El Paso
69	Young, Willie	T	6-0	255	10	Grambling
34	Zofko, Mickey	RB	6-1	195	5	Auburn

TOP FIVE DRAFT CHOICES

Rd.	Name	Pos.	Ht.	Wt.	Age	College
2	Allen Simpson	T	6-5	265	24	Colorado State
3	Danny Buggs	WR	6-3	188	22	West Virginia
4	Robert Gibkin	CB	6-2	205	21	Houston
7	Jim Obradovich	TE	6-2	255	22	Southern California
8	John Tate	LB	6-2	228	22	Jackson State

punts as a rookie but was erratic and had two blocked. Place-kicker Pete Gogolak has slipped into the mediocre category after 11 pro seasons and no longer is the 40-to-50-yard threat he once was.

OUTLOOK: A team top-heavy with "ifs." Giants could be dangerous offensively IF all the pieces fall together. And they could be respectable defensively IF Arnsparger weaves some of his Miami magic. But in the East Division, "ifs" aren't good enough. Another losing season.

GIANT PROFILES

JOE DAWKINS 27 6-2 223   Running Back

Came to Giants via trade from Denver Broncos prior to last season and developed into club's steadiest offensive threat ... Led Giants in rushing with 561 yards on 156 carries (3.6 avg.), in pass receptions with 46 for 332 yards and in touchdowns, six ... Previously played with Houston Oilers (1970-71) and Denver (1972-73) ... Best season was his final one in Denver when he rushed for 706 yards, filling in for injured Bob Anderson ... Born Jan. 27, 1948, in Los Angeles ... Younger brother of Don McCall, former San Diego running back ... Attended U. of Wisconsin, where he was used primarily as a blocker, rushing for just 816 yards in two years.

DOUG KOTAR 24 5-10 205   Running Back

Chunky surprise package was one of few bright spots in gloomy Giant season ... Kotar was originally signed as a free agent by Pittsburgh, who traded him to New York for Leo Gasienica, a minor-league QB ... Went 68 yards for touchdown first time he touched ball for Giants in pre-season game vs. Jets ... Scored on 12-yard run later in same game, dragging four tacklers into end zone ... Rushed for 280 yards in last two pre-season games to win regular job ... Hampered by injuries, Kotar gained only 396 yards during regular season, but showed great potential ... Born June 11, 1951, in Canonsburg, Pa., attended U. of Kentucky ... "When you look at Kotar, it doesn't look like he even belongs in pro football until you see all the things he can do," says Coach Bill Arnsparger.

218   THE COMPLETE HANDBOOK OF PRO FOOTBALL

JACK GREGORY 30 6-5 250   Defensive End

A first-rate defensive lineman who excells at rushing the passer... Came to Giants in 1972 after playing out his option in Cleveland and had his finest season ever... Had league-high of 21 quarterback sacks which tripled the output of the Giants' entire defensive unit for '71 ... That spectacular performance came as Gregory was used as "rover" in ex-coach Jim Garrett's defensive system... Settled down to playing conventional end position past two seasons and has played solidly... Born Oct. 3, 1944, in Okolona, Miss., attended Delta State... "When Jack gets up for a game, there isn't a better defensive end in the league," said former Giant great Jim Katcavage.

RON JOHNSON 27 6-1 205   Running Back

Coming off the unhappiest year of his pro career... Plagued by injuries, including a fractured hand which caused him to play with a cast at end of season... Gained only 218 yards in 97 carries (2.2 avg.)... Was openly critical of the way he was handled by Bill Arnsparger, particularly following his benching in loss to Chicago... "I'm not some guy who just came into the league," Johnson said. "I'm a damned good football player. I can play for somebody. This season, to say the least, has been the worst of my life"... Born Oct. 17, 1947, in Detroit, attended U. of Michigan... When Johnson's healthy, there are few better running backs... Has topped 1,000 yards rushing twice (1970 and '72)... Best season was '72, when he rushed for 1,182 yards, caught 45 passes and scored 14 touchdowns.

SPIDER LOCKHART 32 6-2 175   Safety

Has been a starter in Giant secondary since his rookie year, 1965... Originally an obscure 13th-round draft pick out of North Texas State, Spider won a regular job at left cornerback in his first season... Switched to free safety the past eight years and is one of the league's steadiest deep men... "I respect Spider," says Eagles' Harold Carmichael. "He talks to you a lot on the field, he pops off, but he plays a good, clean game"... Has 40 career interceptions, ranking him third on all-time Giant list behind Emlen Tunnel and Jimmy Patton ... Born April 6, 1943, in Dallas... Played in two Pro Bowls and

NEW YORK GIANTS

was All-NFL in '68, intercepting eight passes, returning two for touchdowns.

JOHN MENDENHALL 26 6-1 255 — Defensive Tackle

Scouts thought Mendenhall might be too short to make it in the NFL but Giants took a chance and it paid off ... Drew raves from opponents around the league, particularly in Dallas ... "He seemed to make half the tackles and we were keying on him," said guard John Niland. "He literally hops out of the way of blocks" ... "It's probably one of the few cases when we build our game plan around a defensive tackle and it still doesn't work," said Roger Staubach ... "Best tackle in our conference? He's the best in the league," said Calvin Hill ... Born Dec. 3, 1948, in Cullen, La., attended Grambling ... "Mendenhall is the backbone of New York's defense," said KC's Francis Peay. "His pursuit is fantastic."

CRAIG MORTON 32 6-4 215 — Quarterback

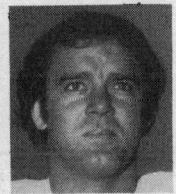

Joined Giants in mid-season trade after spending his first nine years with Dallas Cowboys ... Played in his first game for Giants vs. Cowboys, losing 21-7 ... After acquiring Morton, Giants went 1-7, three of those losses coming in the final seconds ... Morton's best game was vs. Jets, completing 21 passes, two for touchdowns but Giants lost in sudden death ... Also threw for two TDs in 23-21 loss to St. Louis ... "I've lived with frustration a long time," Morton said, "I don't mind it so much now" ... Born Feb. 5, 1943, in Campbell, Calif., attended U. of California where he was an All-American ... Led Cowboys to Super Bowl V but was goat when he threw last-minute interception to Mike Curtis, leading to decisive field goal.

BOB TUCKER 30 6-3 230 — Tight End

Cinderella in shoulder pads ... Tucker was dropped by Patriots and Eagles, bounced around in semi-pro leagues for two seasons before signing with Giants as free agent in '70 ... Immediately shot past four veterans to No. 1 status by scoring two TDs in pre-season game vs. Eagles, the club that said he wasn't ready for the NFL ... Caught 40 passes as rookie and led NFC with 59 receptions his second year ... In five pro seasons, Tucker has caught 245 passes and scored 21 touchdowns ... "Trying to tackle him in the open field is like diving in front of a train," said Eagle safety Bill Bradley ... Born June 8, 1945, in Hazelton, Pa., attended Bloomsburg State where he set three NAIA receiving records.

JOHN HICKS 24 6-2 260   Offensive Guard

Giants' No. 1 draft pick last season, won starting job at guard and was voted NFC's Rookie of Year, beating out 49ers' Wilbur Jackson by one vote ... Highly-emotional player, Hicks will jump up cheering after a good block and embrace his teammates after touchdowns ... Clearly outplayed Dallas' Jethro Pugh in Giants' upset vicotry ... Threw key block on Claude Humphrey, springing Doug Kotar to 55-yard TD run vs. Atlanta ... "Coming off the ball, Hicks is as good as any guard I've seen," said Eagles' coach Mick McCormack. "He's fast and very strong. And he has that added touch of meanness that makes for an outstanding offensive lineman" ... Born March 21, 1951, in Cleveland, won All-American honors at Ohio State.

LEON McQUAY 25 5-10 195   Running Back

An explosive, exciting runner, McQuay joined Giants last season after spending three years with Toronto of the Canadian Football League ... Placed third among NFC's kickoff returners with 27.8 avg. and a long runback of 72 yards ... Contributed as spot performer at halfback, carrying ball 55 times for 240 yards (4.4 avg.) ... Born March 19, 1950, in Tampa, McQuay attended U. of Tampa where he rewrote record books, even though he left school in junior year to sign with CFL. Had 3,039 yards rushing and 37 touchdowns in abbreviated college career ... All-CFL his first year, rushing for 917 yards on 138 tries (7.1 avg.) with nine TDs ... Has 4.4 speed for 40 yards.

TOP ROOKIES

AL SIMPSON 22 6-5 255   Offensive Tackle
Giants' first pick in second round ... Standout offensive lineman from Colorado State was put in same class as first rounders Dennis Harrah and Darryl Carlton by scouts ... Projected as a

starter by Bill Arnsparger who says, "With Simpson and Hicks, we have the nucleus of an offensive line for many years to come."

DANNY BUGGS 22 6-3 190   **Wide Receiver**
A great bargain for the Giants, who found Buggs still available on the third round ... Many scouts had Buggs, out of West Virginia U., listed as the best wide receiver in the draft, placing him ahead of first-round choice Larry Burton ... Nicknamed "Lightning" because of his great speed ... "He's the best receiver I've seen this year," said Herb Adderley, the great ex-Packer cornerback who does color commentary on college football. "If he doesn't make it, nobody will."

COACH BILL ARNSPARGER ... Joined Giants last year after serving four years as Don Shula's top aide in Miami, where he helped assemble the Dolphins' now famous "No Name" defense ... Too many people expected miracles and none were forthcoming as Giants won just two games and finished last in NFC East ... However, many of the losses were by less than a touchdown and three occurred in the closing seconds so the club's real improvement was obscured ... "The Giants will be a very competitive football team this season," said Dallas' Tom Landry. "I have great respect for Bill Arnsparger ... he won't be in fifth place for long" ... Born Dec. 16, 1926, in Paris, Ky., where he played at Paris High under Blanton Collier ... Played college football at Miami of Ohio under Woody Hayes.

CLUB HISTORY

The Giants used to stand tall in the National Football League. Purchased by Tim Mara in 1925 for a mere $500, the Giants became one of the most successful operations in sport.

They developed a winning tradition under Steve Owen, who won eight division titles in 22 years, and whose team represented the Eastern Division in the first NFL championship game in 1933 when it lost to the Chicago Bears, 23-21. But the Giants beat the Bears in 1934, 30-13, to reign as champions.

A succession of stars made the Owen era, such as Ken Strong, Tuffy Leemans, Mel Hein, Ward Cuff, Ed Danowski, Hank Soar, Frank Reagan, Eddie Price and Jim Lee Howell, who succeeded Owen in 1954 and directed the Giants to a world championship in 1956—the year the Giants moved from the Polo Grounds to Yankee Stadium.

Under Howell, the names changed—now it was Charlie Conerly, Kyle Rote, Frank Gifford, Sam Huff, Andy Robustelli and Alex Webster.

In 1961, Allie Sherman took over as coach and Y.A. Tittle came from San Francisco and the Giants won three straight division titles. But the Maramen, who saw Sherman replaced by Alex Webster in 1969, and Webster by Bill Arnsparger in 1974, haven't won anything since. Worse, they've spurned New York City—out of necessity they're playing at Shea Stadium now ... on the way to a new home in New Jersey.

INDIVIDUAL GIANT RECORDS

Rushing

Most Yards Game:	218	Gene Roberts, vs Chi, Cardinals, 1950
Season:	1,182	Ron Johnson, 1972
Career:	4,638	Alex Webster, 1955-64

Pasing

Most TD Passes Game:	7	Y.A. Tittle, vs Washington, 1962
Season:	36	Y.A. Tittle, 1963
Career:	173	Charley Conerly, 1948-61

Receiving

Most TD Passes Game:	3	Frank Liebel vs Philadelphia, 1945
	3	Gene Roberts, vs Chicago Bears, 1949
	3	Gene Roberts, vs Green Bay, 1949
	3	Bob Schnelker, vs Washington, 1954
	3	Del Schofner, vs Washington, 1961 and 1962
	3	Del Schofner, vs Philadelphia, 1961
	3	Del Shofner, vs Dallas, 1962
	3	Joe Walton, vs Washington, 1962
	3	Joe Walton, vs Dallas, 1962
	3	Rich Houston, vs Green Bay, 1971
	3	Ron Johnson, vs Philadelphia, 1972
Season:	13	Homer Jones, 1967
Career:	48	Kyle Rote, 1951-61

Scoring

Most Points Game:	24	Ron Johnson, vs Philadelphia, 1972
Season:	107	Pete Gogolak, 1970 (32 PATS-25 FG)
Career:	646	Pete Gogolak, 1966-74 (268 PATS-126 FG)
Most TDs Game:	4	Ron Johnson, vs Philadelphia, 1972
Season:	17	Gene Roberts, 1949
Career:	78	Frank Gifford, 1952-60, 1962-64

MINNESOTA VIKINGS

TEAM DIRECTORY: Chairman of Board: Bernard Ridder Jr.; Pres.: Max Winter; Asst. to Pres.: Mike Lynn; VP-Treas.: H.P. Skoglund; VP: Ole Haugsrud; Bus. Mgr.: Harley Peterson; Player Pers. Dir.: Jerry Reichow; Dir. Pub. Rel.-Promotions: Merrill Swanson; Head Coach: Bud Grant; Trainer:-Fred Zamberletti. Home: Metropolitan Stadium, Minneapolis, Minn. (48,503).

Chuck Foreman carries Minnesota offense.

SCOUTING REPORT

OFFENSE: The last time we saw the Minnesota offense, it was writhing helplessly on the floor of Tulane Stadium under the enormous might of the Pittsburgh defense in Super Bowl IX. The running game netted just 17 yards on 21 carries. The passing game fared little better as Francis Tarkenton had three passes intercepted and eight others swatted down at the line.

The question is, was that just one bleak afternoon or a glimpse into the Vikings' future? It was probably a bit of both. Surely, the Viking offense cannot be contained that thoroughly every week—not with a great threat like Chuck Foreman in the backfield, carrying the ball and circling over the middle for passes. But Super Bowl IX does indicate that defenses are wising up to Fran Tarkenton. The Steelers built their defense to contain Fran's favorite play, the sprint-out pass. "On third-down, he'll sprint right nine times out of ten," said Steeler safety Glen Edwards.

Pittsburgh shut Francis off early, then spent the rest of the day swarming on Foreman. Later, there was speculation Fran's passing arm is fading. All of which leaves the Vikings' offense a bigger question mark than it has been anytime in recent years. The line, led by the strong right side pairing of Ed White and Ron Yary, can handle most front fours. It is not as bad as it looked against Mean Joe Greene and friends.

DEFENSE: The Vikes used their first two draft picks to acquire defensive linemen of considerable potential, Mark Mullaney of Colorado State and Art Riley of Southern Cal. It could mark the end of the old "Purple People" era. That once-great front four is showing signs of age, particularly at the ends where Carl Eller (33) and Jim Marshall (37) no longer terrorize opposing quarterbacks. Alan Page is still the NFC's premier tackle, despite the double-and-triple teaming he must battle on every play. The other tackle spot is an open scramble between Doug Sutherland, Bob Lurtsema, Gary Larsen and Riley.

The linebacking is a blend of two generations with sturdy Jeff Siemon anchoring the group in the middle. The older pair of outside linebackers includes Roy Winston and Wally Hilgenberg. The younger set is Fred McNeill and Matt Blair. The vets are losing ground in the fight to retain their jobs.

The secondary played well throughout '74, allowing just eight TD passes, fewest in football. Nate Wright proved himself a top-flight cornerback, leading the club with six interceptions. The right corner will be contested between incumbent Jackie Wallace and big-play specialist Bobby Bryant, who sat out last year with a broken arm. The safeties, Jeff Wright and Paul Krause, are smart, dependable.

KICKING GAME: Best phase of Viking special teams last year was punt coverage which held opposing returners to just 7.7

MINNESOTA VIKINGS 225

VIKINGS VETERANS ROSTER

HEAD COACH—Bud Grant. Assistant Coaches—Neill Armstrong, Jerry Burns, Jack Patera, John Michels, Bus Mertes, Jocko Nelson

No.	Name	Pos.	Ht.	Wt.	NFL Exp.	College
67	Alderman, Grady	T	6-2	247	16	Detroit
56	Anderson, Scott	C	6-4	234	2	Missouri
17	Berry, Bob	QB	5-11	185	11	Oregon
21	Blahak, Joe	DB	5-10	188	3	Nebraska
59	Blair, Matt	LB	6-5	229	2	Iowa State
71	Boone, Dave	DE	6-3	248	2	Eastern Michigan
30	Brown, Bill	RB	5-11	222	15	Illinois
24	Brown, Terry	S	6-2	205	6	Oklahoma State
20	Bryant, Bobby	CB	6-1	170	7	South Carolina
14	Cox, Fred	K	5-10	200	13	Pittsburgh
84	Craig, Steve	TE	6-3	231	2	Northwestern
52	Cureton, Gregg	LB	6-2	223	1	Tennessee
—	Danmeier, Rick	K	5-11	214	1	Sioux Falls, S.D.
45	Dixon, Alan	RB	5-11	200	1	Harding
11	Eischeid, Mike	P	6-0	190	9	Upper Iowa
81	Eller, Carl	DE	6-6	247	12	Minnesota
44	Foreman, Chuck	RB	6-2	207	3	Miami
42	Gilliam, John	WR	6-1	195	9	South Carolina St.
68	Goodrum, Charles	T-G	6-3	256	3	Florida A&M
58	Hilgenberg, Wally	LB	6-3	229	12	Iowa
85	Holland, John	WR	6-0	190	2	Tennessee State
89	Kingsriter, Doug	TE	6-2	222	3	Minnesota
22	Krause, Paul	S	6-3	200	12	Iowa
77	Larsen, Gary	DT	6-5	255	12	Concordia
82	Lash, Jim	WR	6-2	199	3	Northwestern
65	Lawson, Steve	G	6-3	265	5	Kansas
75	Lurtsema, Bob	DE-DT	6-6	250	9	Western Michigan
49	Marinaro, Ed	RB	6-2	212	4	Cornell
70	Marshall, Jim	DE	6-4	240	16	Ohio State
55	Martin, Amos	LB	6-3	228	4	Louisville
66	Maurer, Andy	G	6-3	275	6	Oregon
33	McClanahan, Brent	RB	5-10	202	3	Arizona State
80	McCullum, Sam	WR	6-1	203	2	Montana State
54	McNeill, Fred	LB	6-2	229	2	UCLA
41	Osborn, Dave	RB	6-0	208	11	North Dakota
88	Page, Alan	DT	6-4	245	9	Notre Dame
29	Poltl, Randy	S	6-3	190	2	Stanford
32	Reed, Oscar	RB	6-0	222	8	Colorado State
78	Riley, Steve	T	6-5	258	2	So. California
50	Siemon, Jeff	LB	6-2	230	4	Stanford
64	Sunde, Milt	G	6-2	250	12	Minnesota
69	Sutherland, Doug	DT	6-3	250	6	Wisc. St. (Superior)
10	Tarkenton, Fran	QB	6-0	190	15	Georgia
53	Tingelhoff, Mick	C	6-2	240	14	Nebraska
83	Voigt, Stu	TE	6-1	225	6	Wisconsin
25	Wallace, Jackie	DB	6-3	197	2	Arizona
72	Ward, John	G	6-4	250	4	Oklahoma State
15	Wells, Mike	QB	6-5	225	1	Illinois
62	White, Ed	G	6-2	280	7	California
60	Winston, Roy	LB	5-11	222	14	Louisiana St.
23	Wright, Jeff	S	5-11	190	5	Minnesota
43	Wright, Nate	CB	5-11	180	7	San Diego St.
73	Yary, Ron	T	6-5	255	8	USC

TOP FIVE DRAFT CHOICES

Rd.	Name	Pos.	Ht.	Wt.	Age	College
1	Mark Mullaney	DE	6-5	242	22	Colorado State
2	Art Riley	DT	6-4	255	21	Southern California
4	Harold Henson	RB	6-3	240	22	Ohio State
4	Bruce Adams	WR	6-1	180	22	Kansas
5	Robert Miller	RB	5-11	204	22	Kansas

yards per runback. That was aided by Mike Eischeid, who averaged only 36 yards per punt, 12th in the NFC. Placekicker Fred Cox is no boomer but he did manage 12 field goals, including a last-second game winner in Dallas.

OUTLOOK: Vikings hardly looked like a juggernaut while losing their third straight Super Bowl but you've got to respect them for getting that far. They remain the favorite in the talent-thin Central Division but they can no longer overpower their opponents as they once did. Vikes should make the playoffs again but they may huff-and-puff more than usual.

VIKING PROFILES

CARL ELLER 33 6-6 247   **Defensive End**

Consensus All-Pro and NFC starter in Pro Bowl once again last year, but overall the season was not one of his best... Went without a sack in three post-season playoff games... Still capable of the big game on occasion but doesn't dominate the line of scrimmage the way he once did... Won George Halas Award in 1971 as NFL's best defensive player... Born Feb. 25, 1942, in Winston-Salem, N.C.... Was two-way starter at tackle (along with Chiefs' Bobby Bell) at University of Minnesota... Very interested in movie-making and has already acted in several films... Called "Moose" by teammates.

CHUCK FOREMAN 24 6-2 216   **Running Back**

One of the game's coming superstars... Voted NFL's Rookie of the Year two seasons ago, Foreman proved there's no such thing as sophomore jinx in '74... Opened season by scoring three TDs vs. Green Bay and never slowed down... Led entire league with 15 touchdowns (nine rushing, six on passes) and set club mark with 53 pass receptions in a season... Led NFC in rushing for first half of season but skipped final two league games to rest a sore knee... Finished with 777 yards... "Foreman is their whole offense, we've got to stop him to win," said Pittsburg's Glen Edwards before Super Bowl... Born Oct. 26, 1950, in Frederick, Md., attended University of Miami... "Chuck has a big man's power and a little man's

MINNESOTA VIKINGS 227

moves," says teammate Jeff Siemon. "He's the perfect pro running back."

PAUL KRAUSE 33 6-3 200   Safety

Started his fourth straight Pro Bowl last year after another fine season at free safety ... Intercepted two passes, giving him career total of 64, third on the all-time NFL list, just four behind Hall of Famer Night Train Lane ... Krause tops all active pro players in interceptions ... Had spectacular NFL debut with Washington in 1964, picking off 12 passes his rookie year, winning All-Pro honors ... Born Feb. 19, 1942, in Flint, Mich. ... Was All-Big Ten receiver at Iowa ... Appeared on way to a promising baseball career until shoulder injury hampered him ... "Krause is an amazing athlete," said Pittsburgh's Lynn Swann. "He doesn't look that big or that fast but he goes to the football like a magnet" ... Raises cattle in Minnesota in his spare time.

DAVE OSBORN 32 6-0 208   Running Back

Answered critics who said he was washed up by having his best season in four years in '74 ... Carried ball 131 times for 514 yards and four touchdowns ... Had two 96-yard games, two 98-yard games last season ... Scored winning TD in NFC title game vs. Rams on one-yard plunge ... The league's only regular running back in his 11th year ... "I'm in great physical condition," Osborn says. "I'll play as long as the coach thinks I have some value. If not as a starter, then as a back-up man or special teamer" ... Born March 18, 1943, in Cando, N.D., attended North Dakota U. ... Enjoys chopping wood around the house to stay in shape.

ALAN PAGE 30 6-4 245   Defensive Tackle

Thought by many to be premier defensive tackle in NFC ... Was named league's Most Valuable Player in 1971, first time a defensive player ever won the award ... Has good strength but relies mostly on quickness to beat his man ... Named All-Pro for fourth time last season and played in his seventh straight Pro Bowl ... "He's a problem," said

Pittsburgh center Ray Mansfield. "He can roll over you like a tank or dart around you like a skate board"... Won praise from Steeler linemen after Super Bowl IX, making nine tackles and one sack... Born Aug. 7, 1945, in Canton Ohio... Attended Notre Dame where he studied political science... "Alan's skills have helped all defensive linemen," says teammate Gary Larsen, "because, thanks to him, we're finally getting recognition."

JEFF SIEMON 25 6-2 230   Linebacker

Vikes drafted Siemon in first round in '72, predicting he could step in immediately and be their regular middle linebacker... He has not disappointed the coaches... First gained national attention leading Stanford defense in Rose Bowl upsets of Ohio State and Michigan... "I never saw a young guy play the middle with such complete confidence," Card QB Jim Hart said. "Everybody talks about the Viking front four but Siemon pulls the whole defense together."... Born June 2, 1950, in Bakersfield, Calif.... Played brilliantly in defeat in Super Bowl IX... Made game-high 15 tackles vs. Pittsburgh including three behind the line of scrimmage, prompting Steeler back Rocky Bleier to remark, "I thought Siemon was twins."

FRAN TARKENTON 35 6-0 190   Quarterback

Once considered a scrambler, Fran has mellowed with age... He now prefers the roll-out (or sprint-out) pass, leaving the scrambling to younger QBs... His career stats in pass attempts (4,800), completions (2,658), yards (35,846) and touchdowns (266) are second only to Johnny Unitas... Barring injury, Tarkenton could overtake Unitas in every category by the end of the '77 season... Has never missed a game in 14-year career due to injury... "Sure, I work at not getting hurt," Fran says. "I say my prayers every night"... Born Feb. 3, 1940, in Richmond, Va.... Won All-American honors at Georgia... Very popular with his teammates; treated his offensive line to dinner at Antoine's in New Orleans prior to Super Bowl IX... "The man has class," said guard Ed White. "Joe Kapp took us to places where we had to drink beer out of pitchers."

MINNESOTA VIKINGS

ED WHITE 28 6-2 280 — Guard

Strongest man on Vikings and enjoys proving it in arm-wrestling matches ... Once pinned two teammates (Osborn, Dale Hackbart) at the same time to the delight of QB Joe Kapp ... "If I'm ever in a barroom brawl," Kapp said, "White's my first draft choice" ... Very quiet and scholarly-looking away from the locker room, enjoys painting for relaxation ... Born April 4, 1947, in La Mesa, Calif. ... Was All-American defensive tackle at California ... "If Ed keeps developing, he'll be an All-Pro guard very soon," says Bud Grant. "Straight ahead, he can handle anyone."

RON YARY 29 6-6 255 — Tackle

All-Pro and Pro Bowl starter four straight years ... Highly regarded by the league's coaches ... "He's so strong, he can control a man with his upper body and turn him completely away from the play," says Eagle coach Mike McCormack. "In films, you'll see Yary fire out and the defensive end just disappear" ... Had tough time in Super Bowl IX working against Pittsburgh's L.C. Greenwood, who harassed Fran Tarkenton most of the day ... First player chosen in '68 pro draft, first offensive lineman to have that distinction ... Born Aug. 16, 1946, in Chicago ... Attended Southern Cal where he was an All-American and winner of Outland Trophy as top collegiate lineman in '67.

TOP ROOKIES

MARK MULLANEY 6-5 255 — Defensive End

Tough, strong as a bull defensive end from Colorado State was Vikings' first-round draft pick ... Seen as eventual replacement for veteran ends Jim Marshall (37) and Carl Eller (32) ... Scouts very high on Mullaney's potential, particularly as a pass rusher ... Figures to benefit working with Marshall and Eller, who can show him the tricks of the trade.

ART RILEY 22 6-4 248 — Defensive Tackle

Chosen on the second round from Southern Cal. ... An All-

Pacific 8 choice at defensive tackle ... Made 68 tackles as a senior ... Named Pac 8 Player of the Week after Trojans' 34-10 rout of league runnerup Stanford ... Quick and extremely agile, Riley played on same Thornridge High (Phoenix, Ill.) basketball team with Indiana star Quinn Buckner.

COACH BUD GRANT ... Generally portrayed as a cold, humorless man with a head so cluttered with X's and O's he has room for nothing else ... "Bud Grant and Tom Landry had a personality contest and they both finished second," said Don Meredith ... It's actually a bad rap ... Grant is a bright, witty man with a genuine weakness for practical jokes around the office ... But on the sideline he is all business ... "To me, football is a game of controlled emotion," Grant says. "A head coach cannot afford the luxury of emotion. If he panics or loses his poise, his team follows" ... The Vikes have followed Grant to three Super Bowls and averaged 10 victories a year since he joined them in 1967 ... A great athlete, Grant played pro football with the Philadelphia Eagles and pro basketball with the Minneapolis Lakers before signing with Winnipeg of the Canadian League.

CLUB HISTORY

The Vikings entered the NFL in a most impressive fashion in 1961, upsetting Chicago, 37-13, in their very first regular-season game. "I knew it was too good to last," said guard Grady Alderman, claimed from Detroit in the expansion pool. "We just didn't have very many good players." The Vikes only won two more games that first season but they scared most clubs with their unpredictable offense, led by a scrambling rookie quarterback, Fran Tarkenton.

They managed one winning season (8-5-1 in '64) under Norm Van Brocklin, but they lacked consistency. The management switched to Bud Grant in 1967 and one year later he had them above .500 again. They haven't had a losing season since and in the past seven years the Vikes have won their division title six times. Last January, they made their third Super Bowl appearance. They haven't won the Big One yet but there will be other chances.

MINNESOTA VIKINGS 231

INDIVIDUAL VIKING RECORDS

Rushing

Most Yards Game:	155	Dave Osborn, vs Green Bay, 1967
	155	Clinton Jones, vs Atlanta, 1971
Season:	972	Dave Osborn, 1967
Career:	5,757	Bill Brown, 1962-74

Passing

Most TD Passes Game:	7	Joe Kapp, vs Baltimore, 1969
Season:	22	Francis Tarkenton, 1962 and 1964
Career:	163	Francis Tarkenton, 1961-66, 1972-74

Receiving

Most TD Passes Game:	3	Jerry Reichow, vs Chicago, 1961
	3	Charlie Ferguson, vs Chicago, 1962
	3	Gene Washington, vs Cleveland, 1969
Season:	11	Jerry Reichow, 1961
Career:	23	Bill Brown, 1962-74
	23	Gene Washington, 1967-72

Scoring

Most Points Game:	18	Bill Brown, vs Los Angeles, 1972; 7 others
Season:	125	Fred Cox, 1970
Career:	1,142	Fred Cox, 1963-74
Most TDs Game:	3	Bill Brown, vs Los Angeles, 1972; 6 others
Season:	16	Bill Brown, 1964
Career:	73	Bill Brown, 1962-74

Joe Kapp's seven TD passes in game is team record.

GREEN BAY PACKERS

TEAM DIRECTORY: Pres.: Dominic Olejniczak; VP: Richard Bourguignon; Sec.: John Torinus; Treas.: Fred Towbridge; GM-Head Coach: Bart Starr; Corp. GM: Bob Harlan; Corp. Bus. Mgr.: Tom Miller; Dir. Pro Pers.: Dick Corrick; Dir. College Scouting: Lloyd Eaton; Pub. Rel.: Chuck Lane and Lee Remmel; Trainer: Domenic Gentile. Home: Lambeau Field, Green Bay, Wis. (56,267).

After three years, John Brockington missed 1,000.

SCOUTING REPORT

OFFENSE: Packers had their moments—both good and bad—under John Hadl last year. The good was quite good, evidenced by three straight wins, including a 19-7 upset of the Vikings in

GREEN BAY PACKERS   233

Minnesota. The bad was embarrassingly so, particularly the 36-14 loss in Philadelphia in which the Packers fumbled the ball away five times, three by Hadl himself. No one can be quite sure how effective Hadl will be this season. Packer coaches feel Hadl will be improved since he has the whole camp to blend into the offense. There are other observers who say Hadl's arm is shot and the Rams unloaded him at just the right time.

It might not make all that much difference. If Bart Starr installs the old Green Bay power offense this year, Hadl might be able to quarterback the entire season with his arm in a sling. Fullback John Brockington, coming off his first sub-1,000-yard season, figures to be the primary weapon of Starr's offense with MacArthur Lane providing balance. A man who bears watching is last year's top draft pick, 240-pound fullback Barty Smith, who was injured and played in only eight games. Green Bay could use help at wide receiver where Steve Odom, Barry Smith and John Staggers had only two touchdowns among them last year. Tight end Rich McGeorge is probably the best receiver in the bunch.

DEFENSE: While the offense ranked a lagging 21st last season, the defense kept the Pack respectable, placing sixth in the NFL. Once again, they were tough to pass against as cornerbacks Willie Buchanon and Ken Ellis and safeties Al Matthews and Jim Hill swallowed enemy receivers up in their green-and-gold zones. The deep four received considerable help from the three linebackers, Jim Carter, Fred Carr and Ted Hendricks. "Together, they were the finest linebacker unit in the league last year," said Starr. Carr, at 29, has lost none of his speed on the outside, still catching wide receivers and halfbacks from behind in the open field.

The Pack added another quality defensive player in the draft, taking Ohio State cornerback Steve Luke on the fourth round. Luke was overshadowed by his All-American teammate Neal Colzie but has much the same raw ability. Along the front four, the Pack has plenty of bulk but lacks quickness. They could use one lineman with speed to compliment 280-pound Mike McCoy and 270-pound Aaron Brown, who do a good job shutting down the run but have trouble getting across the line of scrimmage.

KICKING GAME: Chester Marcol led all pro football scorers with 94 points and 25 field goals and, at 26, has not yet reached his prime. Packers feel he's the best in the league. Punting was problem last year when vet Ron Widby was injured. Randy Walker filled in but Widby is back to fight for his job.

PACKERS VETERANS ROSTER

HEAD COACH—Bart Starr. Assistant Coaches—Dave Hammer, Paul Roach, Jim Colbert, John Meyer, Zeke Bratkowski, Leon McLaughlin, Lew Carpenter, Bob Lord

No.	Name	Pos.	Ht.	Wt.	NFL Exp.	College
52	Acks, Ron	LB	6-2	225	8	Illinois
42	Brockington, John	RB	6-1	225	5	Ohio State
74	Brown, Aaron	DE	6-5	270	9	Minnesota
28	Buchanon, Willie	CB	6-0	190	4	San Diego St.
53	Carr, Fred	LB	6-5	240	8	Texas-El Paso
50	Carter, Jim	LB	6-3	245	6	Minnesota
10	Concannon, Jack	QB	6-3	200	10	Boston College
58	Cooney, Mark	LB	6-4	222	2	Colorado
86	Donohoe, Mike	TE	6-3	230	6	San Francisco
48	Ellis, Ken	CB	5-10	195	6	Southern U.
71	Fanucci, Mike	DE	6-4	242	4	Arizona St.
68	Gillingham, Gale	G	6-3	265	10	Minnesota
25	Goodman, Les	RB	5-11	206	3	Yankton, S.D.
12	Hadl, John	QB	6-1	214	14	Kansas
21	Hall, Charlie	CB	6-1	190	4	Pittsburgh
77	Hayhoe, Bill	T	6-8	260	7	So. Calif.
51	Hefner, Larry	LB	6-2	230	4	Clemson
56	Hendricks, Ted	LB	6-7	220	7	Miami
39	Hill, Jim	S	6-2	195	7	Texas A&I
72	Himes, Dick	T	6-4	260	8	Ohio State
55	Jenke, Noel	LB	6-1	225	5	Minnesota
31	Jones, Spike	P	6-2	195	6	Georgia
30	Krause, Larry	RB	6-0	208	6	St. Norbert
36	Lane, MacArthur	RB	6-1	220	8	Utah State
23	Leigh, Charlie	RB	5-11	206	7	None
62	Lueck, Bill	G	6-4	235	8	Arizona
13	Marcol, Chester	K	6-0	190	4	Hillsdale
43	Mason, Dave	DB	6-0	195	3	Nebraska
29	Matthews, Al	S	5-11	190	6	Texas A&I
54	McCarren, Larry	C	6-3	240	3	Illinois
76	McCoy, Mike	DT	6-5	285	6	Notre Dame
81	McGeorge, Rich	TE	6-4	230	6	Elon
70	Nystrom, Lee	T	6-5	258	3	MacAlester
84	Odom, Steve	WR	5-8	165	2	Utah
73	Okoniewski, Steve	DT	6-4	252	4	Montana
85	Payne, Ken	WR	6-1	185	2	Langston
75	Pureifory, Dave	DE	6-1	250	4	Eastern Mich.
—	Purvis, Bart	G	6-4	240	1	Maryland
87	Roche, Alden	DE	6-4	255	6	Southern U.
—	Redmond, Rudy	DB	6-1	190	7	U. of Pacific
79	Schuh, Harry	T	6-3	260	11	Memphis State
52	Schmitt, John	C	6-4	250	12	Hofstra
80	Smith, Barry	WR	6-1	190	3	Florida State
33	Smith, Barty	RB	6-3	240	2	Richmond
45	Smith, Perry	CB	6-1	195	3	Colorado St.
67	Snider, Malcolm	G-T	6-4	250	7	Stanford
22	Staggers, Jon	WR	5-10	180	6	Missouri
17	Tagge, Jerry	QB	6-2	215	4	Nebraska
26	Torkelson, Eric	RB	6-2	194	2	Connecticut
59	Toner, Tom	LB	6-3	235	3	Idaho St.
61	Van Dyke, Bruce	G	6-2	255	10	Missouri
18	Walker, Randy	P	5-10	177	2	N.W. La.
20	Widby, Ron	P	6-4	220	8	Tennessee
83	Williams, Clarence	DE	6-5	255	6	Prairie View
65	Wortman, Keith	G	6-2	250	4	Nebraska
60	Zaunbrecher, Godfrey	C	6-2	240	5	La. State

TOP FIVE DRAFT CHOICES

Rd.	Name	Pos.	Ht.	Wt.	Age	College
2	Bill Bain	G	6-4	280	23	Southern California
3	Willard Harrell	RB	5-8	182	22	Pacific
4	Steve Luke	CB	6-2	205	21	Ohio State
7	Tony Giaquinto	WR	6-3	185	23	Central Conn. State
9	Jay Hodgin	RB	5-11	205	22	South Carolina

OUTLOOK: Pack has a number of established players but they finished last season crumbling and demoralized. Big question is how long will it take Bart Starr to pull the club back together again? They have the personnel to climb to second in Central Division but the heavy price paid for Hadl makes long-range rebuilding job difficult.

PACKER PROFILES

JOHN BROCKINGTON 26 6-1 225 **Running Back**

Slipped below 1,000 yards for first time in four seasons last year, gaining 833 yards on 266 attempts ... Still placed second to Lawrence McCutcheon in NFC ... Totaled 3,276 yards rusing first three pro seasons becoming only back in NFL history to top 1,000 yards first three years ... Caught career high 43 passes in '74 for 314 yards ... Born Sept. 7, 1948, in Brooklyn, N.Y. ... Attended Ohio State where he once held school rushing record with 1,041 yards as All-American senior ... Combines speed (4.5 in 40) with crushing power ... "The critical area for me is five yards past the line," he says. "If I get past the linebackers, I'm up against guys who weigh maybe 180 pounds. When I get that far, it's a mismatch." ... Admits he emulates Jim Brown: "I want to be as consistent as he was. He was there every Sunday, killing people on every play."

WILLIE BUCHANON 24 6-0 190 **Cornerback**

Packers' No. 1 draft choice for 1972, did not disappoint, winning a regular spot as the left corner immediately ... Shared club lead with four interceptions that year and was named Defensive Rookie of the Year by Associated Press and NEA ... Broken leg suffered vs. Los Angeles his second year cut short that season but he came back strong in '74 ... Born in Oceanside, Calif. ... Attended San Diego State where he was a consensus All-American under coach Don Coryell, now at St. Louis ... Dazzled scouts with his showing in post-season college games, particularly East-West Shrine game where he shut out Mike Siani of Oakland and made two interceptions ... Has great reactions and blazing (9.4) speed ... "I'm glad he wasn't around when I was throwing the ball," says coach Bart Starr.

FRED CARR 29 6-5 235　　　　　　　　　　　Linebacker

Among the most respected outside linebackers in football... "A great, great athlete," says Eagle coach Mike McCormack. "I saw one film where he caught a halfback who had a 20-yard lead on him. When he caught the ball, Carr wasn't even in the picture but he chased him down"... Great speed for big man (4.6 in 40; 10.2 for 100)... Packs' first draft pick in '68 out of Texas-El Paso where he also played for UTEP's NCAA championship basketball team... Born Aug. 19, 1946, in Phoenix... Played in three Pro Bowls and voted Most Valuable Player in 1971 post-season game.

JIM CARTER 26 6-3 233　　　　　　　　　　　Linebacker

Colorful, outspoken middle linebacker moved out legendary Ray Nitschke in 1971 and has impressed consistently ever since... Voted Packs' most valuable defensive player in '73 and appeared in his first Pro Bowl... "One of the best pursuit middle linebackers playing today," said Burt Gustafson, ex-Packer linebacker coach... Born Oct. 18, 1948, in St. Paul, Minn. ... Attended U. of Minnesota where he played fullback, captained squad as senior... An all-state hockey player in high school, Carter was a star defenseman on Minnesota U. hockey club... Talked seriously of signing with World Hockey Association's Minnesota Fighting Saints two years ago, sending a shudder through every 170-pound WHA forward... Manages Left Guard Supper Club in Eau Claire, Wis., during off-season.

GALE GILLINGHAM 31 6-3 265　　　　　　　　　　　Guard

Considered by many pro football insiders to be every bit as good as all-time Green Bay great Jerry Kramer... Started his fourth straight Pro Bowl last year and was voted onto assorted All-Pro teams for fifth time in illustrious career... Hits a terrific blow on running plays... "He hit me harder than I've been hit in years," said Eagle linebacker Bill Bergey. "Once, on the goal line, he hit me and I didn't know where I was for three plays"... Born Feb. 3, 1944, in Madison, Wis. ... Attended U. of Minnesota... Packs' first-round draft pick in 1966... Switched to defensive tackle in '72 but injured

GREEN BAY PACKERS 237

his knee in second game, missed rest of season and went happily back to offense last year.

CHESTER MARCOL 25 6-0 190 — Kicker

Topped all scorers in pro football last season with 94 points, including a league-high 25 field goals and 19-for-19 PAT efficiency ... Only third player in NFL history to accumulate 300 or more points (304) in his first three seasons (others were Jan Stenerud and Gino Cappelletti) ... Kicked four field goals in one game last year for fourth time in his career ... Nicknamed "The Polish Messiah" by his teammates ... Born Oct. 24, 1949, in Opole, Poland, emigrated here in 1965 ... Attended Hillsdale College where he set NAIA record with 62-yard field goal ... Packs' second draft choice in '72, topped NFL in scoring as rookie with 128 points and 33 field goals.

MIKE McCOY 26 6-5 280 — Defensive Tackle

Massive Mike is showing improvement as all-around defensive lineman ... Always strong against the run, he's developing moves enabling him to put pressure on quarterback ... Led Pack in QB sacks in '73 with six, including three in one game vs. Bears ... In same game, he made nine tackles and recovered a fumble ... Has excellent strength, surprising quickness and lateral pursuit but never quite achieved the greatness predicted for him ... Born Sept. 6, 1948, in Erie, Pa. ... Became state high school wrestling champion ... Attended Notre Dame where he was consensus All-American ... Was Packs' number one draft pick in 1970 ... Has 5.1 speed in 40.

TED HENDRICKS 27 6-7 220 — Linebacker

Signed a WFL contract and was considered expendable by Baltimore ... Traded to Green Bay for another outside linebacker, Tom MacLeod ... Came through with one of his finest seasons in Green Bay ... Topped club with five interceptions, including one which he returned 44 yards ... Blocked three extra points, four field goals and two punts ... Played for NFC in Pro Bowl, one of few players to play for both conferences in the post-season classic ... Was All-American defensive end at U. of Miami where he was nicknamed "Mad

Stork" due to his height and slender frame ... Lack of bulk is deceptive as Hendricks is one of the stronger linebackers in pro football ... Majored in mathematics in college, solves trigonometry problems for relaxation.

RICH McGEORGE 26 6-4 235   Tight End

Scouts had McGeorge pegged for superstardom when Pack drafted him in first round in 1970 ... Had great collegiate career at Elon College where he caught 224 passes for 3,486 yards and 31 TDs in four seasons ... Was AP Small College All-American ... Played sparingly as rookie and serious kneed injury cut short his '72 season after just two games ... Has yet to show any consistency, although he has good speed and fine hands ... Born Sept. 14, 1948, in Roanoke, Va. ... A solid blocker, McGeorge adds muscle to Packer run blocking and could be receiving threat if club comes up with a capable passer.

JOHN HADL 35 6-1 208   Quarterback

Suffered one of worst—and most sudden—collapses in pro football history ... Voted NFC Player of the Year in '73, leading Los Angeles to divisional championship ... Wound up on bench early last season with an ailing arm and was traded at mid-season to Green Bay for five future draft choices ... Started impressively with Pack, guiding them to three straight wins over Chicago, Minnesota and San Diego ... "This is like the coming of the Messiah," said safety Al Matthews ... But the optimism was a bit premature for Hadl fumbled three times the next week in a loss to the Eagles ("My worst game ever," he called it) and Green Bay finished the year, losing to the 49ers and Atlanta without scoring another touchdown ... Born Feb. 15, 1940, in Lawrence, Kan. ... Attended U. of Kansas where he was All-American twice and All-Big Eight three times.

TOP ROOKIES

BILL BAIN 22 6-3 268   Guard

Packers' top draft pick in second round ... Most versatile performer from Southern Cal, Bain has played at both guard and tackle and been on the strongside and weakside at various times due to injuries along the line ... *Time* magazine and *Sporting*

News All-American ... Started college career at U. of Colorado before transferring.

WILLARD HARRELL 5-10 175   **Running Back**
Packers' third-round draft pick from U. of Pacific ... A real steal in the third round ... Several independent scouting groups had him classified as the second best running back in the entire crop (behind Walter Payton) ... Pack plans to use him as a kick returner.

COACH BART STARR ... Bart Starr needs no introduction to the football fans of Green Bay ... He symbolizes the might of the great Packer dynasty almost as much as Vince Lombardi ... "Bart is the best quarterback in football," Lombardi once said. "Not the best passer, not the best runner ... but the best quarterback. There's a difference" ... Starr was a cool, methodical field general, who picked his spots carefully and got the most out of his offensive weapons ... Led the Pack to five NFL titles and two Super Bowl victories in seven years ... Holds the league record for passing efficiency, completing 57.42 percent of his attempts over a 16-year career ... He also holds league mark for most consecutive passes without an interception (294) ... Retired in 1971, stayed on as assistant for two years before retiring to private business ... "I'm coming back," Bart says, "to make the Packers a winner again."

CLUB HISTORY

The Packers, historically, have been a team of excesses. When they were good—as they were in their early years and again in the '60s—the were almost unbeatably good. But when they were bad—as they were throughout the '50s—they were horrid. Only in the past two years under Dan Devine did they hit any level that might be called mediocrity and the Green Bay fans couldn't tolerate that.

Devine has been replaced by Bart Starr, the ex-quarterback, who represents a return to the golden age of Vince Lombardi. The club was founded by Curly Lambeau, who was working for the local Indian Packing Company. His bosses helped bankroll the franchise and, as a way of repaying them, he named the team "the Packers" and a Green Bay institution was founded.

The Packers won the world championship three straight

years (1929-31) with Hall of Famers Cal Hubbard, Johnny Blood, Clark Hinkle and Arnie Herber. The team slipped dismally in the '50s before Lombardi took over in 1959 and led them to five league championships in seven years, including triumphs in Super Bowls I and II.

INDIVIDUAL PACKER RECORDS

Rushing
Most Yards Game:	186	Jim Taylor, vs N.Y. Giants, 1961
Season:	1,474	Jim Taylor, 1962
Career:	8,207	Jim Taylor, 1958-66

Passing
Most TD Passes Game:	5	Cecil Isbell, vs Cleveland, 1942
	5	Don Horn, vs St. Louis, 1969
Season:	24	Cecil Isbell, 1942
Career:	152	Bart Starr, 1956-71

Receiving
Most TD Passes Game:	4	Don Hutson, vs Detroit, 1945
Season:	17	Don Hutson, 1943
Career:	99	Don Hutson, 1935-45

Scoring
Most Points Game:	33	Paul Hornung, vs Baltimore, 1961
Season:	176	Paul Hornung, 1960
Career:	823	Don Hutson, 1935-45
Most TDs Game:	5	Paul Hornung, vs Baltimore, 1961
Season:	19	Jim Taylor, 1962
Career:	105	Don Hutson, 1935-45

Paul Hornung still holds Packer scoring marks.

DETROIT LIONS

TEAM DIRECTORY: Owner-Pres.: William Clay Ford; Exec. VP-GM; Russell Thomas; Sen. VP: Edwin Anderson; Asst. GM: Rogers Lehew; Dir. Marketing Ser.-Bus. Mgr.: Lyall Smith; Pub. Dir.: Elliott Trumbull; Treas.: Newton Peters; Player Pers. Dir.: Jerry Neri; Head Coach: Rick Forzano; Head Trainer: Kent Falb. Home: Pontiac Metropolitan Stadium, Pontiac, Mich. (80,000).

Eagles haul in Ron Jessie after one of 54 receptions.

SCOUTING REPORT

OFFENSE: Lions managed a 7-7 record and a respectable offense with virtually no running attack. Detroit's ground game was 24th in the NFL and ran up less yards (1,433) than any NFC team except Philadelphia. Part of the problem is the lack of a breakaway threat. Top rusher Altie Taylor is a good tough-yardage back but doesn't have the speed to get outside. The others—Steve Owens, Jimm Hooks, Jimmie Jones—are fullback-types. Eighth-round draftee Leonard Thompson, a 9.7 sprinter from Oklahoma State, might help.

Another problem is the offensive line, which could use bulking up. Lions used two of their first three draft picks to acquire blockers, guard Lynn Boden and tackle Craig Hertwig. In the 11th round, the Lions went for Ohio State's beefy center, Steve Myers. With that kind of added muscle, the Lions might clear some people out of the way this year.

The passing game is well-established with two capable quarterbacks, Bill Munson and Greg Landry, and three impressive receivers, Ron Jessie, Larry Walton and Charlie Sanders. Last season, Jessie proved himself the class receiver in the Central Division with 54 catches for 761 yards.

DEFENSE: Lions have lacked a good pass rush ever since the departure of Alex Karras and Roger Brown in the late '60s. They have drafted defensive linemen first for three straight years, but the situation hasn't improved. Last year, Detroit had fewer sacks (24) than any NFC team, which put undue pressure on the secondary.

The line wasn't exactly a brick wall against the run, either. It ranked 20th in the league in that department. Herb Orvis is the one quality player up front, with some vets (Larry Hand, Jim Mitchell) and youngsters (Ernie Price, Billy Howard) plugging the leaks in the dike. Coaches hope Doug English, No. 2 draft pick from Texas, might develop into a star. The linebacking is set with Ed O'Neil coming off a strong rookie year, flanked by rangy Charlie Weaver, experienced Paul Naumoff and third-year man Jim Laslavic.

The secondary is the backbone of the defense. The cornerbacks, Levi Johnson and Lem Barney, intercepted nine passes between them last year, and the Lions feel they drafted another good one in Purdue's Fred Cooper. Free safety Dick Jauron has made the conversion from offense successfully, and if Mike Weger could rebound from his injury and return to strong safety, the backfield would be set.

KICKING GAME: Errol Mann had outstanding season in '74, becoming the top scorer in Lion history. As accurate as ever, Mann has lost none of his distance. Herman Weaver slipped

DETROIT LIONS 243

LIONS VETERANS ROSTER

HEAD COACH—Rick Forzano. Assisstant Coaches—Bruce Beatty, Raymond Berry, Joe Bugel, Wally English, Jim Carr, Jerry Glanville, Fritz Shurmur, Rey Dempsey, Floyd Reese

No.	Name	Pos.	Ht.	Wt.	NFL Exp.	College
20	Barney, Lem	CB	6-0	190	9	Jackson State
81	Blair, T.C.	TE	6-4	220	2	Tulsa
68	Bonica, Chuck	G	6-1	255	1	Ohio State
87	Brady, John	TE	6-3	215	1	Washington
24	Bussey, Dexter	RB	6-1	195	2	Texas-Arlington
46	Capria, Carl	S	6-3	185	2	Purdue
51	Cunningham, Dick	LB	6-2	240	7	Arkansas
29	Davis, Ben	CB	5-11	180	8	Defiance
65	Davis, Jimmie	G	6-5	250	1	Alcorn A&M
60	Dennis, Guy	G-C	6-2	255	7	Florida
54	Flanagan, Ed	C	6-3	245	11	Purdue
76	Freitas, Rockne	T	6-6	270	8	Oregon State
39	Frohbose, Bill	S	6-0	185	1	Miami
74	Hand, Larry	DE	6-4	250	11	Appalachian State
58	Hennigan, Mike	LB	6-2	210	3	Tennessee Tech
30	Hooks, Jim	RB	5-11	225	3	Central State
70	Howard, Billy	DT	6-4	245	2	Alcorn A&M
45	Jarvis, Ray	WR	6-0	195	5	Norfolk State
26	Jauron, Dick	S	6-0	190	3	Yale
89	Jessie, Ron	WR	6-0	185	5	Kansas
23	Johnson, Levi	CB	6-3	190	3	Texas A&I
64	Jolley, Gordon	T	6-5	250	4	Utah
31	Jones, Jimmie	RB	5-10	205	2	UCLA
66	Kowalkowski, Bob	G	6-3	240	10	Virginia
11	Landry, Greg	QB	6-4	210	8	Massachusetts
53	Laskey, Bill	LB	6-3	230	10	Michigan
52	Laslavic, Jim	LB	6-2	230	3	Penn State
—	Lickiss, Hugh	LB	6-4	230	1	Simpson
12	Mann, Errol	K	6-0	200	8	North Dakota
83	Mitchell, Jim	DT	6-3	245	6	Virginia State
19	Munson, Bill	QB	6-2	210	12	Utah State
50	Naumoff, Paul	LB	6-1	215	9	Tennessee
55	O'Neil, Ed	LB	6-3	245	2	Penn State
80	Orvis, Herb	DT	6-5	240	4	Colorado
36	Owens, Steve	RB	6-2	215	6	Oklahoma
86	Pickard, Bob	WR	6-0	185	2	Xavier
72	Price, Ernie	DE	6-4	255	3	Texas A&I
14	Reed, Joe	QB	6-1	195	4	Mississippi State
88	Sanders, Charlie	TE	6-4	225	8	Minnesota
82	Sanders, Ken	DE	6-5	240	4	Howard Payne
84	Small, John	LB	6-4	260	6	Citadel
42	Taylor, Altie	RB	5-10	200	7	Utah State
21	Thrower, Jim	S-CB	6-2	195	6	East Texas State
44	Wakefield, Mark	WR	6-4	195	1	Tampa
49	Walton, Larry	WR	6-0	185	7	Arizona State
59	Weaver, Charlie	LB	6-2	220	5	Southern California
18	Weaver, Herman	P	6-4	210	6	Tennessee
28	Weger, Mike	S	6-2	200	8	Bowling Green
47	West, Charlie	S-CB	6-1	200	8	Texas-El Paso
67	White, Daryl	G	6-3	250	2	Nebraska
40	Wyatt, Doug	S	6-1	195	6	Tulsa
17	Wyche, Sam	QB	6-4	220	7	Furman
75	Yarbrough, Jim	T	6-5	265	7	Florida

TOP FIVE DRAFT CHOICES

Rd.	Name	Pos.	Ht.	Wt.	Age	College
1	Lynn Boden	G	6-5	270	21	South Dakota State
2	Doug English	DT	6-5	250	21	Texas
4	Craig Hertwig	T	6-8	260	23	Georgia
6	Fred Cooper	CB	5-11	190	23	Purdue
6	Horace King	RB	5-10	200	22	Georgia

244 THE COMPLETE HANDBOOK OF PRO FOOTBALL

from career-high punting average in '73 to career low (38 yards) last season. Still doesn't get ball away quickly enough, evidenced by his six career blocks.

OUTLOOK: Lions have finished second in Central Division six straight seasons but might have trouble repeating this year. Not good enough to overtake the Vikings, the Lions will have to struggle to hold off Green Bay for runner-up spot. If Rick Forzano can't get the ground game moving, Lions might slip to third.

LION PROFILES

LEM BARNEY 29 6-0 190   Cornerback

Drafted second by Lions in 1967 and immediately tabbed for superstardom. "Lem is gonna break all Night Train Lane's records," said then-coach Joe Schmidt. "He has the potential to be every bit as good as Train"... His rookie year was sensational as he intercepted 10 passes (returned three for touchdowns), made all-pro and was voted Rookie of the Year... Intercepted 32 passes his first four seasons but just 14 in the past four (he had four last year)... Born Sept. 8, 1948, in Gulfport, Miss. ... Attended Jackson State ... Has scored 12 TDs in pro career (seven on interceptions, one kickoff return, two punt returns, two field goal attempt returns).

DICK JAURON 24 6-0 190   Safety

One of the great running backs in history of Ivy League, Jauron set 10 Yale records, rushing for 2,941 yards and 27 touchdowns ... Drafted seventh by Lions in '73, switched to free safety during camp when defense was racked with injuries ... Was so impressive he won a regular job... As a rookie, intercepted three passes in one game vs. Chicago, one of which he returned 95 yards for touchdown ... Last year had one interception and 26-yard return ... Born Oct. 7, 1950, in Swampscott, Mass. ... Led NFC in punt returns last season with 17 for 286 yards (16.8 avg.) ... Brilliant mind, Jauron won Scholar-Athlete Award of National Football Foundation while at Yale.

DETROIT LIONS 245

RON JESSIE 27 6-0 185 — Wide Receiver

Touted as a coming star for three years, Jessie finally put it together last season, catching 54 passes (fourth in NFC) for 761 yards and three touchdowns ... That more than doubled his previous best year (24 catches in '72) and was the best for a Lion receiver since Pat Studstill's 67 catches in '66 (still the club record) ... Born Feb. 4, 1948, in Yuma, Ariz. ... Attended Kansas ... Originally drafted by Dallas, traded to Detroit in '72 ... Caught ten passes in one game vs. Minnesota last year ... Also caught six for 149 yards and one touchdown vs. Rams ... Made clutch 45-yard reception in last 29 seconds to set up the winning TD vs. Cincinnati.

LEVI JOHNSON 24 6-3 190 — Cornerback

While Lem Barney was compared to Night Train Lane, Levi Johnson was compared to Barney when Lions drafted him in third round in '73 ... Like Barney, he has not disappointed ... Made NFL All-Rookie team in first year, leading Detroit with five interceptions ... Topped Lions in interceptions again last season, picking off five which he returned for 139 yards (27.8 avg.) and two touchdowns ... Born Oct. 23, 1950, in Corpus Christi, Tex. ... Attended Texas A&I where he set the school record with 22 interceptions ... Was working at free safety his first year until Dick Jauron moved over from offense ... Prefers one-on-one challenge at cornerback.

GREG LANDRY 28 6-4 210 — Quarterback

Has seen just spot duty past two seasons after being club's No. 1 quarterback for four years and starting 41 straight games (a Lion record) ... Knee injury suffered in '73 has hampered him considerably ... Started final three games last year in relief of injured Bill Munson, beating Cincinnati and losing to Denver and Philadelphia ... Completed 49 of 82 passes (60 percent) but didn't move around with his familiar confidence, allowing himself to be sacked 11 times ... When healthy, Landry ranks with Bears' Bobby Douglass among top running QBs in football ... Has rushed for 2,048 yards in his career, and his 55 TD passes tie him for second place on all-time Lion list behind Bobby Layne ... Born Dec. 18, 1946, in Nashua, N.H., attended Massachusetts.

ERROL MANN 34 6-0 200　　　　　　　　　　　　　　Kicker

Last year, Mann passed Doak Walker to become the all-time leading scorer in Lion history with 548 points (123 field goals and 179 extra points) ... One of football's most accurate kickers, Mann's lifetime field goal percentage is 72 percent ... Has led Lions in scoring six straight seasons since being signed as free agent in 1969 after failing in brief stints with Denver, Cleveland and Green Bay ... Won two games for Lions last season with last-second field goals vs. Green Bay and the Giants ... "Frankly, I'd rather not be placed in that position," Mann said. "The other guys beat themselves bloody for 59 minutes ... "I shouldn't be the hero for one swing of my leg" ... Born June 27, 1941, in Breckenridge, Minn. ... Attended U. of North Dakota.

BILL MUNSON 34 6-2 210　　　　　　　　　　　　Quarterback

On the verge of completing his greatest season, Munson was sidelined three weeks from the end of '74 schedule ... Was still chosen Lions' offensive MVP in vote of the players ... Completed almost 57 percent of his passes (166 of 292) while having only seven (2.4 percent) intercepted, ranking him second in NFC in the turnover department ... Passed for 237 yards vs. Green Bay and was brilliant in upset win over Minnesota (Lions' first victory over Vikes in 13 tries) ... Munson completed 22 passes for 276 yards vs. Minnesota ... "It may not be a big deal to Minnesota but it was a big deal to us," Munson said. "I was so tight before the game you wouldn't believe it" ... Born Aug. 11, 1941, in Sacramento, Calif. ... Attended Utah State where he threw only three interceptions as a senior to lead the nation.

HERB ORVIS 28 6-5 240　　　　　　　　　　　　Defensive Tackle

Rapidly developing defensive player, regarded highly by league coaches ... Lions' No. 1 draft pick in '72 and press snickered, recalling Detroit's earlier disasters choosing defensive linemen first ... Orvis proved a notable exception ... Started two games as a rookie, then became a regular in '73, placed second on club in tackles and voted defensive

DETROIT LIONS

MVP... Born Oct. 17, 1946, in Petoskey, Mich.... Attended U. of Colorado where he was two-time All-American, recording 39 quarterback sacks... Spent two years in Army, served in Germany and played for service teams which won European championships... "Herb is an outstanding prospect," said Eddie Khayat. "He's a hitter and he's a leader."

CHARLIE SANDERS 29 6-4 225   Tight End

Came along as rookie in '68 and set standard for the modern tight end, combining size, speed, blocking and catching ability... Hasn't lost much in his seven seasons... Last year he caught 42 passes, equalling his previous best set in '69... Has career total of 250 receptions, third on all-time Detroit list... Born Aug. 25, 1946, in Greensboro, N.C.... Attended Minnesota... Isn't yet ready to concede the title of top tight end in NFC to his younger rivals... Before going to Philadelphia last season, Sanders said, "I've heard that (Eagles') Charles Young thinks he's the best tight end in the game. We'll see about that."

ALTIE TAYLOR 27 5-11 200   Running Back

Topped Lions in rushing for third straight year, carrying ball 150 times for 532 yards (3.5 avg.) and five touchdowns... Has now carried ball more than any back in Lion history (970) and his yardage total (3,659) is just 274 short of the club record held by Nick Pietrosante... Recovered well from off-season knee surgery and set a personal high with 30 pass receptions for 293 yards... "Altie gives us everything he has every time he steps on the field," says Rick Forzano... Born Sept. 29, 1947, in Berkeley, Calif.... Attended Utah State where he rolled up 3,925 yards total offense... Returned kickoff 105 yards for TD vs. W. Texas State.

TOP ROOKIES

LYNN BODEN 21 6-5 270   Guard
Lions' first-round pick was a darkhorse... Offensive co-captain and leader of South Dakota State team last season... Voted All-North Central Conference MVP... There were bigger names on the board at the time but Lions liked Boden's potential...

Played tackle at State but Lions project him as an NFL guard ... Born June 5, 1953, in Osceola, Neb.

DOUG ENGLISH 22 6-5 250 **Defensive Tackle**
Lions' second-round pick from U. of Texas ... One of Longhorns' tri-captains last season, played on three Southwest Conference championship teams ... Voted all-conference by both AP and UPI ... Leading tackler on team and best pass rusher in recent Texas history ... Timed in 4.9 40 ... Born Aug. 25, 1953, in Dallas.

COACH RICK FORZANO ... Last season did not start well for either the Detroit Lions or Rick Forzano ... Forzano was the Lions' offensive backfield coach at the start of training camp but when head man Don McCafferty suffered his fatal heart attack, Forzano was named to succeed him ... "I accept the position with a great deal of sadness and sense of loss," Forzano said ... The Lions, still stunned by the tragedy, lost their first four league games and seemed in danger of having their worst season ever but Forzano turned things around ... "He never lost his head, he kept cool and we straightened ourselves out," said Levi Johnson ... The Lions finished a very respectable 7-7 and Forzano, who was head coach at Navy from 1969 through 1972, was retained for this season ... A native of Akron, Ohio, Forzano played at Kent State.

CLUB HISTORY

Originally, they were the Portsmouth Spartans but, in 1934, they moved to Detroit, named themselves the Lions and big things started happening. In that first season, the Lions were 10-3, finishing second to the undefeated Chicago Bears. The following year, the Lions (7-3-2) edged Green Bay for the Western Division title, then beat the New York Giants, 26-7, for the world championship with the great Dutch Clark at quarterback.

The Lions have been one of the league's more formidable teams ever since, winning four league titles, including three memorable showdowns with the Cleveland Browns in the 1950s. The quarterback of that era, fiesty Bobby Layne, said he

DETROIT LIONS

foresaw the day when "the Lion uniform would be a symbol of pro football dominance, the way Yankee pinstripes are in baseball."

It never quite reached that level, although most recently the Lions have achieved remarkable consistency, finishing second in the NFL's Central Division six straight years.

INDIVIDUAL LION RECORDS

Rushing

Most Yards Game:	198	Bob Hoernschemeyer, vs N.Y. Yanks, 1950
Season:	1,035	Steve Owens, 1971
Career:	3,933	Nick Pietrosante, 1959-65

Passing

Most TD Passes Game:	4	Bobby Layne, vs Chicago, 1951 and 1952
	4	Bobby Layne, vs Green Bay, 1951
	4	Greg Landry, vs Green Bay, 1971
	4	Earl Morrall, vs San Francisco, 1963
	4	Milt Plum, vs San Francisco, 1962
	4	Tobin Rote, vs San Francisco, 1957
	4	Frank Sinkwich, vs Chicago, 1944
Season:	26	Bobby Layne, 1951
Career:	118	Bobby Layne, 1950-58

Receiving

Most TD Passes Game:	4	Cloyce Box, vs Baltimore, 1950
Season:	15	Cloyce Box, 1952
Career:	35	Terry Barr, 1957-65

Scoring

Most Points Game:	24	Cloyce Box, vs Baltimore, 1950
Season:	128	Doak Walker, 1950
Career:	548	Errol Mann, 1969-74
Most TDs Game:	4	Cloyce Box, vs Baltimore, 1950
Season:	15	Cloyce Box, 1952
Career:	38	Terry Barr, 1957-65

CHICAGO BEARS

TEAM DIRECTORY: Chairman of the Board: George Halas; Pres.: George Halas Jr.; VP: Ed McCaskey; Exec. VP-GM: Jim Finks; Asst. to GM: Bill McGrane; Bus. Mgr.: Rudy Custer; Dir. Player Pers.: Carl Marasco; Pub. Rel. Dir.: Ted Haracz; Head Coach: Jack Pardee; Trainer: Fred Caito. Home: Soldier Field, Chicago, Ill. (55,753).

QB Bobby Douglass loves to run with the ball.

SCOUTING REPORT

OFFENSE: Bears' offense is torn by schizophrenia. There is a wide-open offense directed by passing quarterback Gary Huff, who loves heaving long bombs to speedy Charles Wade. Bears burned a few clubs with the big play early last season but then the zone defenses caught up with Huff, who was undone by a conference-high 16 interceptions.

Then there is the brass-knuckles offense directed by quarterback Bobby Douglass, who likes nothing better than running with the football. Douglass does throw an occasional pass. In fact, his fans will tell you Bobby can throw a ball through the side of a house, which is true. The only problem is he might also miss the house while standing on the front porch. For two seasons, the Bears tried both Huff and Douglass with inconclusive results. Their struggle for the No. 1 job continues into this season.

Things should improve with the addition of top draft pick Walter Payton, the runner from Jackson State. A pairing of Payton and sleek Carl Garrett is an exciting prospect, although Ken Grandberry, who rushed for 475 yards as a rookie, and Cid Edwards (acquired from San Diego), must not be discounted. Wade is the best of the receivers, although Bo Rather, another Miami taxi squad castoff, has possibilities.

DEFENSE: Unlike the offense (which ranked 25th in the NFL last season) the defense is respectable. Overall, the Bears were the ninth best defensive team in football, placing higher than three playoff clubs (Minnesota, Oakland and St. Louis). Geez, just think ... all of this without Dick Butkus at middle linebacker. Last year's top draftee, Waymond Bryant, filled in (you couldn't say replaced) for Butkus and made the usual rookie mistakes but his potential is unmistakable.

Top defensive player on the club is outside linebacker Doug Buffone, who led in tackles. Jimmy Gunn continued to develop at the other outside spot. Craig Clemons had his best season yet at safety, leading the Bears in interceptions, placing second in tackles. And Nemiah Wilson, late of Oakland, will help back there, too.

The line is among the most punishing in the league with Jim Osborne and Wally Chambers stirring up all kinds of havoc in the middle. Some people say Osborne and Chambers often overstep the rules in their physical approach to the game. Chambers disagrees. "I'm not a dirty player," he answered. "I'm just aggressive." Oh. Mel Tom and Richard Harris, both ex-Eagles, serve primarily as pass rush specialists.

KICKING GAME: Could stand improvement. Mirro Roder has strong leg but has only 17 field goals in two seasons. He will be pushed by several free agents at camp. Bob Parsons averaged

BEARS VETERANS ROSTER

HEAD COACH—Jack Pardee. Assistant Coaches—Bob Bowser, Ray Callahan, Brad Ecklund, Clyde Emrich, Ross Fichtner, Fred O'Connor, John Hilton, Jerry Stoltz

No.	Name	Pos.	Ht.	Wt.	NFL Exp.	College
79	Antoine, Lionel	T	6-6	263	4	Southern Illinois
74	Asher, Bob	T	6-6	260	5	Vanderbilt
18	Barnes, Joe	QB	5-11	196	1	Texas Tech
—	Bowser, Walter	DB	6-1	185	1	Minnesota
50	Bryant, Waymond	LB	6-3	230	2	Tennessee State
55	Buffone, Doug	LB	6-2	227	10	Louisville
60	Chambers, Wally	DT	6-6	255	3	Eastern Kentucky
25	Clemons, Craig	S	5-11	200	4	Iowa
52	Coady, Rich	C	6-3	246	6	Memphis State
—	Doherty, Brian	K	6-2	190	1	Notre Dame
10	Douglass, Bobby	QB	6-4	228	7	Kansas
—	Edwards, Cid	RB	6-2	230	8	Tennessee State
48	Ellis, Allan	CB	5-10	182	3	UCLA
43	Farmer, George	WR	6-4	214	6	UCLA
62	Forrest, Tom	G	6-2	255	2	Cincinnati
29	Gagnon, Dave	RB	5-10	210	2	Ferris State
76	Gallagher, Dave	DE	6-4	256	2	Michigan
26	Garrett, Carl	RB	5-10	205	7	New Mexico Highlands
12	Golden, Don	S-K	6-4	210	1	Georgia
47	Grandberry, Ken	RB	6-0	196	2	Washington State
30	Gunn, Jimmy	LB	6-1	218	5	Southern Calif.
84	Harris, Richard	DE	6-5	255	5	Grambling
17	Hill, Ike	WR	5-10	179	5	Catawba
67	Hoban, Mike	G	6-2	235	1	Michigan
34	Hodgins, Norm	S	6-1	191	2	Louisiana State
72	Hrivnak, Gary	DE	6-5	254	3	Purdue
19	Huff, Gary	QB	6-1	194	3	Florida State
67	Hultz, Don	DT	6-3	239	13	South Mississippi
65	Jackson, Randy	T	6-5	247	9	Florida
59	Janet, Ernie	G	6-4	255	4	Washington
—	Kaczmarek, Mike	LB	6-4	235	1	Southern Illinois
88	Kelly, Jim	TE	6-4	210	2	Tennessee State
63	Kinney, Steve	T	6-5	259	3	Utah State
31	Knox, Bill	CB	5-9	193	2	Purdue
33	Kosins, Gary	RB	6-2	213	4	Dayton
—	Kranz, Marty	DB	6-1	190	1	Mankato State
44	Lyle, Garry	S	6-2	193	8	George Washington
27	Montgomery, Randy	CB	5-11	185	5	Weber State
78	Newton, Bob	G	6-4	260	5	Nebraska
—	Nordquist, Mark	G	6-4	246	8	Pacific
68	Osborne, Jim	DT	6-3	254	4	Southern U.
82	Pagac, Fred	TE	6-0	220	2	Ohio State
86	Parsons, Bob	TE	6-5	234	4	Penn State
—	Peiffer, Dan	C	6-3	250	1	S.E. Missouri State
58	Pifferini, Bob	LB	6-2	226	4	UCLA
80	Rather, Bo	WR	6-1	180	3	Michigan
87	Reynolds, Tom	WR	6-3	200	2	San Diego State
57	Rives, Don	LB	6-2	220	3	Texas Tech
15	Roder, Mirro	K	6-1	228	3	None
—	Satterwhite, Howard	WR	5-11	180	1	Sam Houston State
—	Sheats, Eddie	LB	6-2	225	1	Kansas
—	Simmons, Berl	K	6-1	200	1	TCU
22	Taylor, Clifton	RB	5-11	200	2	Memphis State
20	Taylor, Joe	CB	6-0	197	9	North Carolina A&T
—	Thomas, Bob	K	5-10	178	1	Notre Dame
89	Tom, Mel	DE	6-4	242	9	San Jose State
46	VanValkenburg, Pete	RB	6-2	205	3	Brigham Young
83	Wade, Charlie	WR	5-10	163	2	Tennessee State
85	Wheeler, Wayne	WR	6-2	180	2	Alamba
36	Williams, Perry	RB	6-4	222	7	Purdue
—	Wilson, Nemiah	CB	6-0	165	11	Grambling

TOP FIVE DRAFT CHOICES

Rd.	Name	Pos.	Ht.	Wt.	Age	College
1	Walter Payton	RB	5-11	200	21	Jackson State
2	Mike Hartenstine	DE	6-3	240	22	Penn State
4	Virgil Livers	CB	5-9	176	23	Western Kentucky
5	Revie Sorey	G	6-2	260	21	Illinois
6	Bob Avellini	QB	6-2	197	22	Maryland

CHICAGO BEARS 253

less than 38 yards per punt last season but he might have been overworked, punting 90 times.

OUTLOOK: Jack Pardee proved himself a resourceful coach last season in the WFL and he'll have to come up with some new wrinkles to get the Bears' offense moving. The defense shows promise but until the Bears find stability at quarterback, they can't compete against the better NFL clubs. Last-place finish appears likely.

BEAR PROFILES

WALLY CHAMBERS 24 6-6 250   **Defensive End**

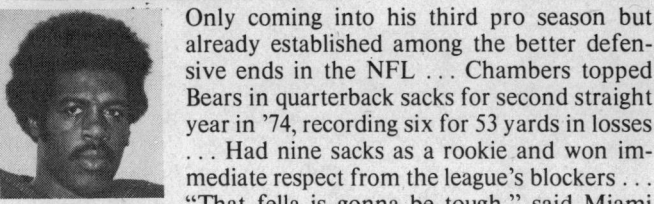

Only coming into his third pro season but already established among the better defensive ends in the NFL ... Chambers topped Bears in quarterback sacks for second straight year in '74, recording six for 53 yards in losses ... Had nine sacks as a rookie and won immediate respect from the league's blockers ... "That fella is gonna be tough," said Miami offensive tackle Norm Evans after working against Chambers in College All-Star game. "He comes hard on ever play. He gives you a good body-beating" ... Born May 15, 1951, in Phoenix City, Ala. ... Attended Eastern Kentucky U. ... Named NFC Defensive Rookie of the Year in '73 and played in Pro Bowl Game following that season ... In two pro seasons, he has already totaled 180 tackles and 65 assists.

CRAIG CLEMONS 26 5-11 200   **Safety**

Had second straight fine year as deep man in Bear defense ... Finished second to Doug Buffone in tackles (88 solos, 32 assists) giving him 180 initial hits in two seasons as a starter ... A "contact" player, enjoys hitting and is capable of intimidating smaller wide receivers ... Was first-round draft pick in '72 after brilliant Big Ten career at Iowa ... "This guy is a hitter," said Abe Gibron at the draft. "He'll break you in half. I want a team of hitters and this kid fills the bill" ... Born June 1, 1949, in Sidney, Ohio ... Spent first pro season in back-up role but performed well on special teams, blocking a punt for touchdown vs. Oakland.

254 THE COMPLETE HANDBOOK OF PRO FOOTBALL

BOBBY DOUGLASS 28 6-4 225   Quarterback

Lost his starting job to Gary Huff for most of last year but should make a strong bid to regain it at training camp ... Received surprising off-season endorsement by Oakland's George Blanda after the two met at a banquet. Said George: "The Bears don't have to look any farther for a quarterback. This kid's already there, just waiting for a balanced offense and some blocking to go along with that great arm. I've talked to all the great ones from Bobby Layne to Johnny Unitas to Bart Starr and none of them knows football any better than Douglass" ... Born June 22, 1947, in Manhattan, Kan. ... Attended U. of Kansas ... Very tough individual. Once threw three TD passes vs. Buffalo with fractured left wrist.

GARY HUFF 24 6-1 200   Quarterback

Was Bears' starting quarterback much of last season, opened up offense with his deep passing early in the schedule ... Hit Charles Wade with two bombs (73, 43 yards) to upset Detroit in opener, then outdueled Jets' Joe Namath the next week, throwing for 267 yards and two touchdowns ... Had his problems later in season, tossing a conference high 17 interceptions ... "He has much to learn," said new GM Jim Finks, "but the raw talent is there. Gary has chance to develop." ... Born April 27, 1951, in Natchez, Miss. ... Had brilliant college career at Florida State where he directed pro style offense ... NCAA total offense leader as a junior ... Passed for five TDs in one game, threw for four TDs on three different occasions ... Best game: vs. Houston as a senior when he threw for 409 yards.

LIONEL ANTOINE 25 6-6 255   Offensive Tackle

Bears' No. 1 draft pick in 1972 has yet to live up to his billing ... Hampered by nuisance injuries most of his career ... Has great natural ability and scouts felt he would be an All-Pro by now ... Considered one of top offensive line prospects in nation during career at Southern Illinois ... Has been occasionally used on defense since joining Bears ... Born Aug. 31, 1950, in Biloxi, Miss. ... "Lionel has all the physical

CHICAGO BEARS 255

equipment it takes to be a great lineman," Abe Gibron once said. "But it's up to him to put it to use."

WAYMOND BRYANT 23 6-3 236   Linebacker

Had the unenviable task of succeeding Dick Butkus as Bear middle linebacker last season ... Rookie from Tennessee State started strong but had his problems later in the year as offenses studied his weaknesses and exploited them ... Overall performance, however, was good ... "There are still some things that confuse him," said veteran Doug Buffone, "but once he gets a little more experience, he'll be a top middle linebacker" ... Born July 28, 1952, in Dallas ... Was Bears' No. 1 draft pick two years ago as BLESTO scouting combine projected him the top linebacker coming out of college ... Runs 40 in 4.75 seconds ... Credited with 69 solo tackles and three quarterback sacks last season.

DOUG BUFFONE 31 6-2 225   Linebacker

Labored in the shadow of Dick Butkus for eight seasons but finally gained some individual recognition last year ... One of league's underrated defensive players ... Led Bears with 98 solo tackles, 34 assists last season and stretched his string of consecutive games to 126 ... Born April 27, 1944, in Yatesboro, Pa., attended U. of Louisville ... Said he never considered quitting following Bears' awful 1-13 season. "I learned I was addicted to football," he explained. "I hated that year. I hated that hard work that went for nothing. I moaned, bitched, screamed and yelled. I wanted to get away from the losing. But one week after the season ended, I wanted to go back to camp" ... Played trumpet in junior high. "I only learned one song, 'Cherry Pink and Apple Blossom White.'"

KEN GRANDBERRY 23 6-0 195   Running Back

Most pleasant surprise of last season for Bears ... Was club's eighth-round draft pick from Washington State, won a job in the starting backfield ... Finished as Chicago's top rusher with 475 yards on 144 carries, an average of 3.3 per attempt ... "He's not spectacular but he's steady," said Abe Gibron. "Kenny's a plugger ... he'll get you three or four yards if there's a hole or not" ... Born Jan. 25, 1952, in Waco, Tex. ... Rushed for 2,102 yards in three seasons at Washington State, scored nine TDs ... Impressed scouts at American Bowl in Tampa where he scored three touchdowns.

JIM OSBORNE 25 6-4 240   Defensive Tackle

Rough, tough defensive tackle was one of ex-coach Abe Gibron's favorite players ... "When they talked about the Bears being the 'Monster of the Midway', they had guys like Osborne in mind," Abe said ... Has led Chicago in QB sacks twice in his three-year career ... Last year, he only reached the passer three times but coaches explain most offenses had two or three blockers assigned to Osborne ... As a rookie, he drove Eagle QB Pete Liske from game with an elbow in the kidneys ... "It was a cheap shot," Liske said, "but it got the job done" ... Born Sept. 7, 1949, in Sylvania, Ga. ... Attended Southern Univ. ... Best game as pro came in '73 vs. Vikes when he sacked Fran Tarkenton four times.

CHARLES WADE 25 5-10 163   Wide Receiver

A real find by Bears' personnel department ... Wade was the very last man picked in 1973 draft by world champion Miami in the 17th round ... That made him the 442nd player selected ... "I didn't really care as long as I wasn't number 443," Wade said when he was notified ... The former Tennessee State flash had impressive training camp with Dolphins, spent most of the year on the cab squad ... "Not only could he catch and run," said fellow rookie Kevin Reilly, now an Eagle linebacker, "but he was a brutal crackback blocker" ... However, Miami waived Wade prior to last season's league opener ... The Bears signed him and started him vs. Detroit ... In his first game, Wade caught 73- and 43-yard TD passes from Gary Huff ... Two weeks later vs. Minnesota, Wade caught six passes for 112 yards ... Dangerous, Mel Gray-type receiver.

TOP ROOKIES

WALTER PAYTON 21 5-10 200   Running Back

Considered top running back in nation by BLESTO scouting

combine ... Tough, durable runner from Jackson State with good leg drive ... Breaks many tackles ... Set NCAA scoring record with 66 touchdowns, 53 PATs, five field goals and 464 points in four seasons ... Averaged 6.1 yards per carry, completed 14 of 19 passes for 474 yards, punted 27 times for 39-yard average, caught 27 passes for 474 yards ... "Can do it all," says Carl Marasco, head of player personnel ... Born July 25, 1954, at Columbia, Miss.

MIKE HARTENSTINE 22 6-3 240   **Defensive End**
Bears' second-round draft pick from Penn State ... Is a prospect at defensive end, tackle and linebacker ... Has 5.0 speed in 40 ... Made 212 tackles and 15 sacks past two seasons ... Coach Joe Paterno puts Hartenstine in same class as another Penn State alumnus, ex-Cincinnati star Mike Reid ... ABC-TV's choice as Defensive Player of the Year ... Born July 27, 1953, in Bethlehem, Pa.

COACH JACK PARDEE ... After handling chaotic season as head coach of WFL's Florida Blazers, the task of turning the dreary Bears around should seem easy to Jack Pardee ... "At least I won't have to worry about the cleaner coming to repossess our uniforms at halftime," he said ... Last year, Pardee pulled off a coaching miracle, taking a bankrupt franchise to the WFL finals ... Players who hadn't been paid in over a month kept performing out of loyalty to Pardee ... "I don't know of another man who could have gotten so much out of his players," said linebacker Billy Hobbs. "Jack held the whole ship together" ... Played 15 seasons as NFL linebacker (14 with Los Angeles, one in Washington) and was All-Pro in 1963 ... Assistant coach at his alma mater, Texas A&M, in 1965 ... Cancer surgery interrupted his playing career.

CLUB HISTORY

It all started in 1920 as a 23-man team called the Decatur (Ill.) Staleys with a player-coach named George Halas. They played 11 games that year, outscored their opponents, 169-7, and tied for the championship. The next year, the Staleys won the title outright, allowing just six toughdowns in 12 games. A tradition of excellence was established that lived on long after they became the Chicago Bears.

In the '40s, the Bears were the most feared team in football, winning four world titles in six years. "Those Bear clubs were, top-to-bottom, the best that ever played pro football," said Pittsburgh's Art Rooney. The Bears have more representatives (15) in the Hall of Fame than any other club, including three charter members: Halas, Red Grange and Bronko Nagurski. Lately, the Bears have fallen on hard times, not enjoying a winning season since 1967 and the prime of Gale Sayers and Dick Butkus.

INDIVIDUAL BEAR RECORDS

Rushing
- **Most Yards Game:** 205 Gale Sayers, vs Green Bay, 1968
- **Season:** 1,231 Gale Sayers, 1966
- **Career:** 5,657 Rick Casares, 1955-63

Passing
- **Most TD Passes Game:** 7 Sid Luckman, vs N.Y. Giants, 1943 Tied by four others.
- **Season:** 28 Sid Luckman, 1943
- **Career:** 139 Sid Luckman, 1939-50

Receiving
- **Most TD Passes Game:** 4 Harlon Hill, vs San Francisco, 1954
- 4 Mike Ditka, vs Los Angeles, 1963
- **Season:** 13 Dick Gordon, 1970
- 13 Ken Kavanaugh, 1947
- **Career:** 50 Ken Kavanaugh, 1940-41, 1945-50

Scoring
- **Most Points Game:** 36 Gale Sayers, vs San Francisco, 1965
- **Season:** 132 Gale Sayers, 1965 (22 TDs)
- **Career:** 541 George Blanda, 1949-58 (247 PATS-88 FG-5 TDs)
- **Most TDs Game:** 6 Gale Sayers, vs San Francisco, 1965
- **Season:** 22 Gale Sayers, 1965
- **Career:** 59 Rick Casares, 1955-64

NFL Nationally Televised Games

REGULAR SEASON

Monday, Sept. 22—Oakland at Miami (night, ABC)
Monday, Sept. 29—Green Bay at Denver (night, ABC)
Monday, Oct. 6—Dallas at Detroit (night, ABC)
Monday, Oct. 13—St. Louis at Washington (night, ABC)
Monday, Oct. 20—New York Giants at Buffalo (night, ABC)
Monday, Oct. 27—Minnesota at Chicago (night, ABC)
Monday, Nov. 3—Los Angeles at Philadelphia (night, ABC)
Monday, Nov. 10—Kansas City at Dallas (night, ABC)
Monday, Nov. 17—Buffalo at Cincinnati (night, ABC)
Monday, Nov. 24—Pittsburgh at Houston (night, ABC)
Thursday, Nov. 27 (Thanksgiving)—Los Angeles at Detroit (day, CBS)
Thursday, Nov. 27 (Thanksgiving)—Buffalo at St. Louis (day, NBC)
Monday, Dec. 1—New England at Miami (night, ABC)
Monday, Dec. 8—Denver at Oakland (night, ABC)
Saturday, Dec. 13—Cincinnati at Pittsburgh (day, NBC)
Saturday, Dec. 13—Washington at Dallas (day, CBS)
Monday, Dec. 15—New York Jets at San Diego (night, ABC)
Saturday, Dec. 20—Minnesota at Buffalo (day, CBS)
Saturday, Dec. 20—Denver at Miami (day, NBC)
Saturday, Dec. 20—Pittsburgh at Los Angeles (night, ABC)

POSTSEASON

Saturday, Dec. 27—AFC and NFC Divisional Playoffs (NBC and CBS)
Sunday, Dec. 28—AFC and NFC Divisional Playoffs (NBC and CBS)
Sunday, Jan. 4, 1976—AFC Championship Game (NBC)
Sunday, Jan. 4, 1976—NFC Championship Game (CBS)
Sunday, Jan. 18, 1976—Super Bowl X at Miami (CBS)
Monday, Jan. 26, 1976—AFC-NFC Pro Bowl at New Orleans (night, ABC)

TV DOUBLEHEADER GAMES

(The following Sunday games are scheduled to be seen in many market areas as part of television doubleheaders):

Sept. 21—Los Angeles at Dallas (CBS)
Sept. 28—Buffalo at Pittsburgh (NBC)
Oct. 5—Washington at Philadelphia CBS)
Oct. 12—Philadelphia at Miami (CBS)
Oct. 19—Detroit at Minnesota (CBS)
Oct. 19—Oakland at Cincinnati (NBC)
Oct. 26—Miami at Buffalo (CBS)
Nov. 2—Dallas at Washington (CBS)
Nov. 9—New York Jets at Miami (NBC)
Nov. 16—Washington at St. Louis (CBS)
Nov. 23—Oakland at Washington (NBC)
Nov. 30—Minnesota at Washington (CBS)
Dec. 7—Buffalo at Miami (NBC)
Dec. 14—Minnesota at Detroit (CBS)
Dec. 21—Oakland at Kansas City (NBC)

WFL SCHEDULE

SATURDAY, AUG. 2
Chicago at Birmingham
Hawaii at Philadelphia
Shreveport at San Antonio
Jacksonville at Memphis

SUNDAY, AUG. 3
Portland at Southern Cal

SATURDAY, AUG. 9
Chicago at Shreveport
Hawaii at Portland
Southern Cal at San Antonio
Philadelphia at Birmingham
Charlotte at Memphis

SATURDAY, AUG. 16
Portland at Chicago
Southern Cal at Hawaii
San Antonio at Charlotte
Philadelphia at Shreveport
Birmingham at Jacksonville

SATURDAY, AUG. 23
Chicago at Hawaii
Shreveport at Portland
San Antonio at Jacksonville
Southern Cal at Birmingham
Memphis at Philadelphia

FRIDAY, AUG. 29
Philadelphia at Southern Cal.

SATURDAY, AUG. 30
Chicago at Memphis
Portland at San Antonio
Shreveport at Birmingham
Charlotte at Jacksonville

SATURDAY, SEPT. 6
Southern Cal at Chicago
Memphis at Hawaii
Birmingham at Portland
Jacksonville at Shreveport
Philadelphia at Charlotte

SATURDAY, SEPT. 13
Jacksonville at Hawaii
Portland at Philadelphia

SUNDAY, SEPT. 14
San Antonio at Chicago
Shreveport at Memphis
Charlotte at Southern Cal.

SATURDAY, SEPT. 20
Southern Cal at Shreveport
Philadelphia at Jacksonville

SUNDAY, SEPT. 21
Hawaii at San Antonio
Memphis at Portland
Charlotte at Birmingham

SATURDAY, SEPT. 27
Chicago at Jacksonville
Southern Cal at Charlotte

SUNDAY, SEPT. 28
Hawaii at Shreveport
Memphis at San Antonio

SATURDAY, OCT. 4
Birmingham at Hawaii
Portland at Jacksonville
San Antonio at Philadelphia

SUNDAY, OCT. 5
Charlotte at Chicago
Southern Cal at Memphis

SATURDAY, OCT. 11
Birmingham at Chicago
Philadelphia at Hawaii

SUNDAY, OCT. 12
San Antonio at Portland
Shreveport at Southern Cal
Jacksonville at Charlotte

SATURDAY, OCT. 18
Hawaii at Chicago
Charlotte at Philadelphia

SUNDAY, OCT. 19
Jacksonville at Portland
San Antonio at Shreveport
Memphis at Birmingham

SATURDAY, OCT. 25
Hawaii at Charlotte

WFL SCHEDULE 261

SUNDAY, OCT. 26
Chicago at Portland
Jacksonville at San Antonio
Birmingham at Southern Cal
Philadelphia at Memphis

SATURDAY, NOV. 1
Southern Cal at Jacksonville
Birmingham at Philadelphia

SUNDAY, NOV. 2
Chicago at San Antonio
Portland at Memphis
Shreveport at Charlotte

SATURDAY, NOV. 8
San Antonio at Hawaii
Memphis at Shreveport

SUNDAY, NOV. 9
Chicago at Southern Cal
Portland at Charlotte
Jacksonville at Birmingham

SATURDAY, NOV. 15
Memphis at Chicago
Shreveport at Philadelphia

SUNDAY, NOV. 16
Portland at Hawaii
Jacksonville at Southern Cal
Birmingham at Charlotte

SATURDAY, NOV. 22
Shreveport at Chicago
Birmingham at San Antonio
Jacksonville at Philadelphia

SUNDAY, NOV. 23
Hawaii at Memphis
Southern Cal at Portland

SATURDAY, NOV. 29
Philadelphia at Chicago
Charlotte at Shreveport

SUNDAY, NOV. 30
Hawaii at Southern Cal
Birmingham at Memphis

SATURDAY, DEC. 6
Hawaii at Birmingham
Portland at Shreveport
Philadelphia at Jacksonville

SUNDAY, DEC. 7
San Antonio at Southern Cal
Memphis at Charlotte

SATURDAY, DEC. 13
Chicago at Philadelphia
Shreveport at Hawaii
Charlotte at Portland
San Antonio at Birmingham
Memphis at Jacksonville

Anthony Davis is a rookie in the Sun.

INSIDE THE WFL

By MIKE FLEMING
Memphis Commercial Appeal

	EAST	WEST
PREDICTED ORDER OF FINISH	Memphis Birmingham Charlotte Jacksonville Philadelphia	Hawaii Southern Cal Chicago Portland Shreveport San Antonio
	CHAMPION: Memphis	

The setting was a little odd. There he was, a man speaking about the resurrection of the financially ravaged World Football League, guaranteeing its operation in 1975, guaranteeing he had devised a plan to cure the league's embarrassing money woes.

Hawaiian millionaire Chris Hemmeter sat before a microphone in New York City's plush Waldorf-Astoria last April 16 and told listeners to forget 1974's problems. Ironically, he spoke in a city that doesn't have a WFL franchise after its first team, the ill-fated New York Stars, was transplanted southward to Charlotte because of fan non-support.

"We pledge honesty and credibility," Hemmeter said, and to accent his pledge of sound economic backing, he offered at least $4-million of the league's money to sign the established NFL's star attraction, New York Jet quarterback Joe Namath. Even though Joe finally refused the offer, he seemed genuinely impressed by the league's revamped operating system, the "Hemmeter plan," as did some of the NFL stars the 11 new teams had already signed to play.

Sitting beside Hemmeter at the press conference were such NFL stars as Larry Csonka, Jim Kiick and Paul Warfield, all former Miami Dolphins, who signed a whopping $3.5 million contract with Memphis Southmen owner John Bassett over a year ago. Also present were Calvin Hill, standout fullback of the Dallas Cowboys, and John Gilliam, star receiver of the Minnesota Vikings. All were veterans of the NFL's Super Bowl who

WFL president Chris Hemmeter tops stairway of stars Paul Warfield, Calvin Hill, Jim Kiick, John Gilliam, Larry Csonka.

will lead their new WFL teams in an attempt to dethrone Birmingham as champions in the second World Bowl on January 4.

Basically, the "Hemmeter plan" is a drastic reworking of the commonly-accepted operating procedure and fiscal setup of the professional sports team. This time around, all operating revenues needed will be placed in escrow in a bank prior to the season's start. There will be no more clubs folding after 14 games (as did Detroit and Jacksonville last year). Salary obligations from last year will be met, but salaries in the future will come from a percentage of the net revenues from sales, thereby maintaining payroll as a fixed percentage of net receipts.

The eleven teams in the WFL are Memphis, Charlotte, Philadelphia, Birmingham and Jacksonville in the Eastern Division, and Chicago, Hawaii, Portland, San Antonio, Shreveport and Southern California in the Western Division.

The regular season, following a month of exhibition games, started on August 2 and was to run through December 13, with games played mainly on weekends, instead of weeknights as was the case a year ago.

The league was trying out not only its new budget approach, but an experiment in which players at different positions were to wear different colored pants (linebackers, red; safeties, yellow; offensive backs, green; wide receivers, orange; offensive linemen, white; and defensive linemen, black).

Memphis, which had a 17-3 record, best in the league last year, figures to make it through the playoffs and win the World Bowl. The addition of Csonka, Kiick and Warfield to what was already the league's top offense, should make the Southmen outstanding. Birmingham doesn't have the defense to overtake the Southmen and repeat last year's 22-21 World Bowl victory over the now-defunct Florida Blazers.

A bunch of teams have a shot at the top in the West. Without Namath at Chicago, Hawaii, armed with super runner Hill, and Southern Cal, with super runner Anthony Davis, figure to fight for the summit. But Portland and the team from the Windy City could make things close. Even Shreveport, if it gets its offense in gear, could challenge. The only team these Western contenders need not worry about is San Antonio, which seems much too unsettled and a year behind schedule to win any title.

MEMPHIS SOUTHMEN

Memphis finished last season with the WFL's leading offense (364 yards per game avg.) and the arrival of NFL stars Larry Csonka, Jim Kiick and Paul Warfield is likely to make the Southmen's scoring machine go tilt.

Csonka, one of the game's great fullbacks, says he is "looking forward with eagerness to playing in the young league. I would like to think we are fortunate enough to start with two new teams (Csonka was with the expansion Miami Dolphins when they were the doormats of the old American Football League) and end up with championships."

Csonka, Kiick and Warfield, whose presence was made possible by the generosity of millionaire team owner John Bassett, move into an offensive backfield that was probably the finest in the league last year. J.J. Jennings finished second in the rushing race with 1,524 yards and 11 TDs, John Harvey was seventh (945 yards) and Willie Spencer, whose 15 TDs led the league, was 10th with 778 yards. Jennings shared league MVP honors with Southern California QB Tony Adams and Florida Blazers' rushing leader Tommy Reamon.

Larry Csonka brings bruising style to Memphis.

The Southmen's chief worry may very well be preventing their explosive backfield from blowing up in the team's face. With all those talented backs to fill two running spots, someone is likely to be unhappy.

When he wasn't handing the ball off to one of his hot runners, QB John Huarte was throwing well enough to finish fifth in the league, with a 52 percent completion percentage for 2,416 yards and 24 TDs. He will be spelled by Danny White, who threw for 1,190 yards and 12 TDs and ranked as the WFL's third best punter (40.8 avg.) last year.

Paul Warfield adds touch to Memphis air game.

The Southmen finished first in rushing defense and have a front line anchored by Bill Stephenson (6-4, 273), Fest Cotton (6-3, 258) and John Leheup (6-2, 250). The pass defense was among the worst, however. Former Dallas Cowboy linebacker D.D. Lewis will help. DBs Dave Thomas and Seth Miller finished 1-2 in interceptions, mainly because Memphis had 610 passes attempted against it, most in the league. Coach John McVay and GM Leo Cahill hope that 14-year pro Dick Thornton will continue to steady the secondary as he did last year.

The Southmen may have a few minor defensive worries, but they're nothing compared to the worries other teams will have trying to stop the Southmen's offense.

Memphis will play in 50,100-seat Municipal Stadium.

BIRMINGHAM VULCANS

Birmingham had the distinction of winning the first World Bowl (it defeated the Florida Blazers, 22-21, last year), although their 15-5 record placed them behind Memphis (17-3) in the final Central Division standings.

Like many of the WFL teams, the Vulcans (last year they were called the Americans) quickly opted to develop a high-scoring offense and gave short shrift to the defensive end of things. That will hurt them this year. The excellent backfield of Charlie Harraway and Paul Robinson will probably be replaced by runners Art Cantrelle and Jim Edwards. Former 'Bama star and local favorite Dennis Homan is still available for excellent pass-receiving (61 receptions for 930 yards).

But Alfred Jenkins, who had 60 catches and 1,326 yards, a dazzling 22.1 yards-per-reception average, has signed with the NFL's Atlanta Falcons. His loss puts a crimp into the Vulcan passing game.

Former Grambling star Matthew Reed enters his second season projected as the starting quarterback. He replaces 11-year veteran George Mira, who led Birmingham to the WFL title last year and who will play for Jacksonville this season.

New head coach Marvin Bass, GM Jack Gotta (last year's head coach), and owner A.E. Burgess have to buck up '74's ninth-best defense to consider taking a run at Memphis and assure the league's best fans (37,134 avg. attendance at Legion Field) a top-flight team.

Mike Truax (6-1, 225) and Warren Capone (6-0, 215) are two good young linebackers and Larry Willingham (6-0, 180) is an excellent strong safety, but it's doubtful that Birmingham has the defensive front four to shut down the run, and shut off the pass. The Vulcans, therefore, are not likely to make the second World Bowl on January 4.

CHARLOTTE HORNETS

Charlotte was one WFL team which accented defense last year. Using ex-NFL players like Gerry Philbin, John Elliott and

268 THE COMPLETE HANDBOOK OF PRO FOOTBALL

Randy Beverly, all formerly of the New York Jets, the club was second in scoring defense (allowing an average of just 17.5 points a game) and first in defense against the pass, although it wound up ninth in defense against the run.

Succeeding Babe Parilli (gone to Chicago) as head coach is Bob Gibson (with the Southmen last year), whose job will be to shore up a defense which has been shredded by the retirement of its ex-Jets. He'll still have standouts DB Jeff Woodcock (6-1, 185), whose eight interceptions tied him for fourth in the league, LB Art Reynolds (6-1, 215), brother of the Los Angeles Rams' star, Jack, and DT Cliff Greenfield.

Gibson's forte is offense and he'll be challenged to improve the league's fifth-best scoring machine (23.3 points per game). Tom Sherman, who ranked seventh in the league with 2,311 passing yards and 15 TDs, probably returns at quarterback. Bob Gladieux, former Notre Dame star, and Don Highsmith will do most of the running, but Sherman won't have much in the way of receivers to throw to if George Sauer retires.

"I probably left the best team in the league," Gibson said at a news conference when introduced by owner-GM Upton Bell, "but I felt there was a good opportunity in Charlotte. The potential is there, but I couldn't say how long it will take for us to realize what we are setting out to do."

What the WFL set out to do midway last season, when it moved its New York team to North Carolina, was to offer the area's one million fans a competitive team. If Charlotte can find some good receivers to run patterns in Memorial Stadium, they may be able to count on success.

JACKSONVILLE EXPRESS

The Sharks, who were swallowed up by financial failure after 14 games last season, get the ball rolling as the Express this year, under head coach Charley Tate and new owner Earl Knabb.

It's not a big-name train, but there is some impressive talent on the lines. Offensive guards Larry Gagner (6-4, 260) and Richard Cheek (6-6, 255) pull for one of the league's best offensive lines. Unfortunately, they're not blocking for the quality running backs who can utilize the holes they provide.

George Mira, who finished eighth in the league in passing last year while guiding Birmingham to its World Bowl victory, will probably be the starting quarterback. Eddie McAshan is a capable back-up. They'll be throwing to receivers including Dennis Hughes and Tom Whittier.

The defense performed well in '74 until injuries thinned its ranks. When Jacksonville closed out the season with a 4-10 record, the defense was allowing an average of 25.5 points per game, a figure that must come down. The pass defense figured better than the rushing defense, as DB Ron Coppenbarger is one of the best secondary men in the WFL. Charles Hall and Dan Spivey give the Express a strong pass rush.

One of the bright spots in '74 was the kicking game. But the Express will have to do without the services of the WFL's second-best punter, Duane Carroll (41.0 avg.) and one of its top placekickers, Grant Guthrie.

The Express stops in the 72,000-seat Gator Bowl for its home games.

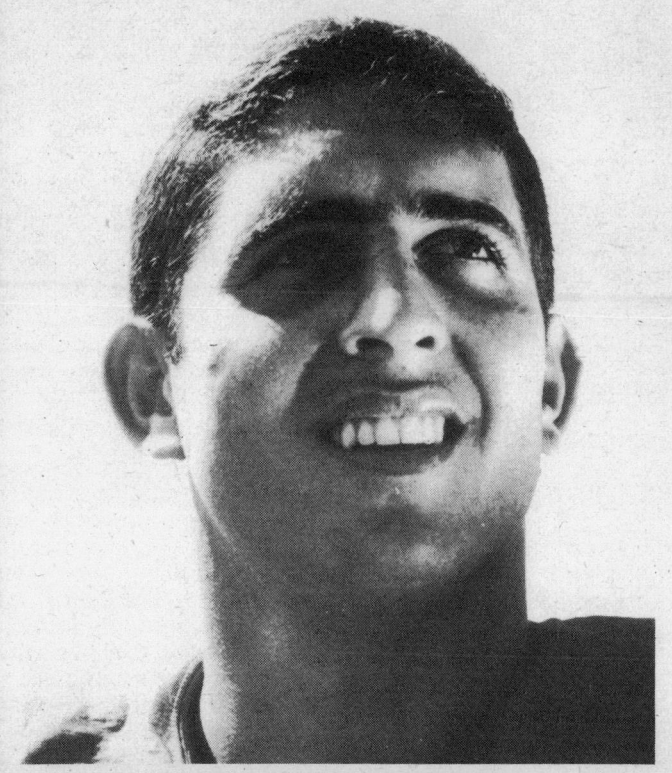

George Mira will drive the Express.

PHILADELPHIA BELL

Owner John Bosacco and coach Ron Waller threw an assortment of football's oddest formations at the WFL last year and it paid off for an average of 342.3 yards per game, second best in the WFL. King Corcoran passed for 3,631 yards and a league-high 31 TDs, and 5-9, 190-pound John Land, a rookie from Delaware State, rushed for 1,136 yards (fourth best in the league) and caught 57 passes for another 634 yards. And Claude Watts finished second in the scoring race with 18 TDs. And Philadelphia signed tight end Ted Kwalick, formerly an all-pro with the San Francisco 49ers, who should help make the Bell offense a fearsome machine.

Unfortunately, as readily as the Bell was ringing up points last year, its opponents were almost as easily cashing in on the Bell defense. Philadelphia finished the season with a record of 9-11 and allowed an average of 309 yards a game and 21.7 points. They were better against the pass than the run, probably because Ron Mabra (5-11, 170) had nine interceptions, second best in the league, from his cornerback spot. The Bell allowed 27 rushing TDs, second worst in the league, and they must shore up their questionable defense to challenge the top Eastern Division clubs. The defensive front line includes DTs Steve Chomyszak (6-7, 270), Skip Parmenter (6-3, 250) and Len Pettigrew (6-6, 255).

The linebackers include 6-0, 220 George Chatlos and 6-3, 235 Tim Rossovich, the latter having another chance to play and eat beer bottles at 65,000-seat Franklin Field. If its defense can stop the run on Franklin's artificial turf, the Bell may wind up not having as many artificial fans as they had in old JFK Stadium last year.

THE HAWAIIANS

Hawaii had the weakest rushing attack in the league last year, but the addition of star running back Calvin Hill, formerly of the NFL's Dallas Cowboys, should take care of that problem, put some punch in the league's eighth-best scoring offense and point the Hawaiians towards the top of the Western Division race.

The presence of Hill should help sell tickets to fill the team's

Former Cowboy Calvin Hill says aloha.

new 55,000-seat Aloha Stadium, which the team hopes to occupy this year.

All of the new offensive power to go with the WFL's top receiver, Tim Delaney, should take some of the heat off QB Norris Weese, who, as a rookie out of Mississippi, completed 51 percent of his passes for 1,847 yards and 14 TDs before Randy Johnson moved into the backfield from the NFL's New York Giants. In the off-season, Johnson rode the ninth wave back across the ocean to sign with the NFL's Redskins, so the quarterbacking job once again seems to be Weese's.

The Hawaiians' weakest defensive spot last year was against the run. The responsibility to stop the rush falls to linemen Carl Lorch (6-4, 240), Lem Burnham (6-5, 240) and Levi Stanley (6-2, 250). The linebacking crew includes Frank Johnson, Jim Sniadecki, Adrian Young and Dave Olerich. The secondary is a dependable veteran unit headed by Otto Brown and Willie Williams.

Coach Mike Giddings has at least 18 of last year's 22 starters returning for the 1975 Hawaiians, who appear to have solved most of the problems that made their record 9-11. There is first place potential on this club.

SOUTHERN CAL SUN

As long as the Pac 8 continues to produce top football talent the Sun will be in good shape. In its inaugural season, the team took running backs Kermit Johnson and James McAlister, as well as OT Booker Brown, from the West Coast collegiate harvest. Johnson ran for 1,008 yards last season and McAlister caught 65 passes for 772 yards and four TDs as the team averaged over 320 yards in offense per game with the league's No. 1 quarterback, Tony Adams. Southern California finished with a 13-7 record, first in the Western Division, but it lost to Hawaii in the first round of the playoffs. Still, it was an impressive beginning for one of the league's youngest teams, especially when you consider the injuries that wracked the offensive line last year.

Unfortunately, they may have to start all over again this year if some of their sophomore standouts go elsewhere. But coach Tom Fears, GM Larry Hatfield and owner Sam Battistone just may be able to do it. While Johnson, McAlister and Brown were negotiating elsewhere, the Sun signed USC's super tailback Anthony Davis to a multi-year contract, outbidding the NFL's New York Jets for his services. And when Adams elected to give the NFL's Kansas City Chiefs a try, the team set out to lure QB Daryle Lamonica away from his unhappy role on the Oakland Raiders' bench. Whoever is quarterbacking at least will have Davis in the backfield and veteran pass-catcher Dave Williams (59 catches, 979 yds., 11 TDs) to throw to, and that will still make for a potent offense.

The defense was stingy in giving up yards (fourth in rushing, sixth against the pass), but allowed 22 points a game, only ninth-best in the league. DT Dave Roller (6-2, 270), Neal Skarin (6-4, 249) and Charles DeJurnett (6-5, 270) man the barricades up front. Cleveland Vann (6-0, 225) heads the linebacking crew with DB Gene Howard (6-1, 195) among others behind him in the secondary. All are young players for whom one year of experience playing together should work wonders in bringing down opponents' scoring totals.

If the Sun can get an adequate replacement in the quarterback slot, it must be counted among the teams with a shot at the Western Division title.

The Sun will shine in 42,000-seat Anaheim Stadium.

INSIDE THE WFL 273

Anthony Davis followed Sun instead of Jets.

CHICAGO WIND

Try as they could, Chicago Wind owner Eugene Pullano and WFL President Chris Hemmeter could not get Joe Namath to sign with the new league. The question remaining after Namath's refusal was whether all the league's men could put Chicago back together again.

With or without the New York Jets' superstar quarterback, a successful entry in Chicago is vital for the league, for it is a franchise in a major media center and the only WFL club in direct competition with an entrenched NFL organization (Chicago Bears). The team was only 7-13 last year and missed the playoffs. If the same fate befalls it in '75 it may be nicknamed the Almosts. Start with Almost getting Namath. Then, depending on the outcome of various negotiations, Almost John Gilliam and Almost L.C. Greenwood, both hotshots from last year's Super Bowl squads.

Actually, Greenwood would probably be most useful of the three stars, because he plays defense. Chicago had the worst defense in the league last year, allowing an incredible 32.5 points per game. Unless you think you can get the firepower to score 33 points a game, something which not even Joe Willie can do, you'd better look to your defense. Unfortunately for new coach Vito "Babe" Parilli, former head coach at Charlotte last year, no real help has yet surfaced from Lake Michigan to indicate that scoring against the Wind won't once again be a breeze.

The loss of Namath threw a possible package deal for receiver John Gilliam in jeopardy. And it of course left open the quarterbacking position, a spot which was admirably filled last season by Virgil Carter, whose 54.5 percent completion percentage, 2,629 yards and 27 TD passes ranked him the fourth-best passer in the league. The Wind hopes to have Carter back, but his return is not certain. Receivers include Jack Dolbin (54 catches, 942 yards), but speedy James Scott (52 catches, 755 yards), the league's No. 10 receiver, is gone.

Running responsibilities will again be shouldered by Cyril Pinder (925 yards, 8 TDs) and Mark Keller, a 6-3 245-pound fullback who rushed for 778 yards and scored 15 TDs last year.

The loss of Scott and Almost Namath puts a crimp in Chicago's plans. And if the team displays the same defensive weakness as last year, the only Wind stirred up in Soldier Field this season will be from the fans' howls.

INSIDE THE WFL 275

PORTLAND THUNDER

Over the course of last year, Portland was probably the league's most improved team. The improvement began with the mid-season acquisition of QB Pete Beathard, who passed for 1,247 yards and guided the Storm to a 26-25 win over Memphis, even though the final record was 7-12-1.

Oddly enough, Beathard's backup man last year, 28-year-old Greg Barton, was named head coach after leading an exhaustive five-month campaign to keep the club in Portland in 1975. Port-

Rufus Ferguson (r.) is Thunder's top rain-maker.

land attorney Richard Bayless heads the group of investors whose backing saved the franchise.

The experienced Beathard will bring poise to a young backfield that includes one of the league's youngest and most exciting players, Rufus "Roadrunner" Ferguson, (5-9, 205), who rushed for 1,086 yards, fifth-best in the league last year. But GM Bob Brodhead, formerly with the Cleveland Browns, is going to have to get some additional zing into the attack, which scored only 264 points during the regular season, eighth-best in the WFL.

The defense was just eighth-best in the league also, although it included veterans like Sam Silas, Glen Condren, Marty Schottenheimer and Clancy Williams. This year, the Thunder is going with younger players like Bruce Bergey, younger brother of Philadelphia Eagle linebacker Bill Bergey, and safety Tom Oberg, who helped pull the defense together late last season.

Count on the defense to improve. But if there aren't any rainmakers added to the Beathard-Ferguson duo in the backfield, the Thunder isn't likely to scare anyone.

SHREVEPORT STEAMER

The Steamer offense was just a lot of hot air last year, when it ranked tenth in the league by totaling an average of just 12 points a game. In an effort to boost the passing game, coach Marshall Taylor, owner John Atkins and GM Al Lang got Ricky Scales, a 6-0, 180-pound wide receiver who recorded 116 receptions and 2,272 yards during his collegiate career at Virginia Tech. He'll pair with the league's No. 2 pass catcher, Rick Eber (66 receptions, 771 yards, 5 TDs), in the hope of giving Shreveport a more potent aerial attack.

The addition of Scales frees swift Richmond Flowers for a tryout at running back or wide receiver, whichever will perk up the points at State Fair Stadium.

Throwing to them will be either Bubba Wyche, who ranked sixth last year with a 51 percent completion percentage and 2,342 yards, or ex-New Orleans Saint Edd Hargett.

Jim Nance contributed 1,240 yards on the ground, but his probable retirement leaves that department of the offense in an uncertain and troubled state.

The defense allowed the third-fewest yards per game (282), but ranked only sixth in points allowed (20.7 a game), which indicates it could use the kind of sterner stuff of which DT Robert Barber (6-4, 255) of Grambling is made. Middle linebacker is Garland Boyette (6-2, 235), an eight-year pro veteran from Grambling. But until some more punch is added, Shreveport doesn't figure as a contender.

SAN ANTONIO WINGS

The WFL's newest franchise is a partial reincarnation of the defunct Florida Blazers team and the San Antonio Toros entry in the Continental Football League. The Wings have signed at least a dozen former Toros and as many of the former Blazers as they could.

In addition, the Wings got some assistance from the league in stocking its roster via a draft that allowed the team to pick two players from each of the other 10 teams in the league (each team was allowed to protect 25 players).

The owner is Norman Bevan and the GM-coach is Perry Moss, 48, former head coach of the CFL's Montreal Alouettes and offensive coach of the Green Bay Packers. Moss' defensive co-ordinator is Larry Grantham, former linebacker with the New York Jets.

Chief target of Moss' talent search was the WFL's leading ground-gainer and one of its three MVPs, Tommy Reamon. But he wasn't landed. Instead, the Wings will have to go on the ground with former Kansas City Chief Warren McVea and Mike Morrison, a rookie from Texas A&I.

Backing up in case they couldn't land Blazers' QB Bob Davis were John Walton and Terry Pell, formerly with the Atlantic Coast League.

When the Wings take to the air they'll throw to a corps of receivers that includes ex-Toro David Yaege and swift Charles Roberts (5-10, 173), a 9.4 wide-receiving threat late of the CFL's Montreal Alouettes.

The defense will be headed by WFL Defensive Player of the Year Billy Hobbs, former Texas A&M All-American linebacker. Other defenders include Phil Hahn (6-5, 240) and J.V. Stokes (6-1, 190).

Home field is 22,500-seat Municipal Stadium.

THE COMPLETE HANDBOOK OF PRO FOOTBALL

Smallest on the tube: Pats' 5-5 Mack Herron.

NFL SCHEDULE

*NIGHT GAME   **TWILIGHT GAME

SUNDAY, SEPT. 21
Atlanta at St. Louis
Baltimore at Chicago
Cleveland at Cincinnati
Detroit at Green Bay
Houston at New England
Kansas City at Denver
Los Angeles at Dallas
New Orleans at Washington
New York Giants at Philadelphia
New York Jets at Buffalo
Pittsburgh at San Diego
San Francisco at Minnesota

MONDAY, SEPT. 22
*Oakland at Miami

SUNDAY, SEPT. 28
Buffalo at Pittsburgh
Cincinnati at New Orleans
Detroit at Atlanta
Los Angeles at San Francisco
Miami at New England
Minnesota at Cleveland
New York Giants at Washington
New York Jets at Kansas City
Oakland at Baltimore
Philadelphia at Chicago
St. Louis at Dallas
San Diego at Houston

MONDAY, SEPT. 29
*Green Bay at Denver

SUNDAY, OCT. 5
Baltimore at Los Angeles
Chicago at Minnesota
Cincinnati at Houston
Denver at Buffalo
Miami at Green Bay
New Orleans at Atlanta
New England at New York Jets
New York Giants at St. Louis
Oakland at San Diego
Pittsburgh at Cleveland
San Francisco at Kansas City
Washington at Philadelphia

MONDAY, OCT. 6
*Dallas at Detroit

SUNDAY, OCT. 12
Atlanta at San Francisco
Buffalo at Baltimore
Chicago at Detroit
Dallas at New York Giants
Denver at Pittsburgh
Green Bay at New Orleans
Houston at Cleveland
Kansas City at Oakland
Los Angeles at San Diego
New England at Cincinnati
New York Jets at Minnesota
Philadelphia at Miami

MONDAY, OCT. 13
*St. Louis at Washington

SUNDAY, OCT. 19
Atlanta at Los Angeles
Baltimore at New England
Chicago at Pittsburgh
Cleveland at Denver
Detroit at Minnesota
Green Bay at Dallas
Kansas City at San Diego
Miami at New York Jets
New Orleans at San Francisco
Oakland at Cincinnati
Philadelphia at St. Louis
Washington at Houston

MONDAY, OCT. 20
New York Giants at Buffalo

SATURDAY, OCT. 25
St. Louis at New York Giants

SUNDAY, OCT. 26
Baltimore at New York Jets
Cincinnati at Atlanta
Dallas at Philadelphia
Denver at Kansas City
Detroit at Houston
Miami at Buffalo
New Orleans at Los Angeles
Pittsburgh at Green Bay
San Diego at Oakland
San Francisco at New England
Washington at Cleveland

280 THE COMPLETE HANDBOOK OF PRO FOOTBALL

MONDAY, OCT. 27
Minnesota at Chicago

SATURDAY, NOV. 1
San Diego at New York Giants

SUNDAY, NOV. 2
Atlanta at New Orleans
Buffalo at New York Jets
Cleveland at Baltimore
Dallas at Washington
Detroit at San Francisco
Houston at Kansas City
Miami at Chicago
Minnesota at Green Bay
New England at St. Louis
Oakland at Denver
Pittsburgh at Cincinnati

MONDAY, NOV. 3
Los Angeles at Philadelphia

SUNDAY, NOV. 9
Atlanta at Minnesota
Baltimore at Buffalo
Cincinnati at Denver
Cleveland at Detroit
Green Bay at Chicago
Houston at Pittsburgh
New England at San Diego
New Orleans at Oakland
New York Jets at Miami
St. Louis at Philadelphia
San Francisco at Los Angeles
Washington at New York Giants

MONDAY, NOV. 10
*Kansas City at Dallas

SUNDAY, NOV. 16
Chicago at San Francisco
Cleveland at Oakland
Dallas at New England
Denver at San Diego
Green Bay at Detroit
Kansas City at Pittsburgh
Los Angeles at Atlanta
Miami at Houston
Minnesota at New Orleans
New York Jets at Baltimore
Philadelphia at New York Giants
Washington at St. Louis

MONDAY, NOV. 17
*Buffalo at Cincinnati

SUNDAY, NOV. 23
Baltimore at Miami
Chicago at Los Angeles
Cincinnati at Cleveland
Denver at Atlanta
Detroit at Kansas City
New England at Buffalo
New York Giants at Green Bay
Oakland at Washington
Philadelphia at Dallas
St. Louis at New York Jets
San Diego at Minnesota
San Francisco at New Orleans

MONDAY, NOV. 24
*Pittsburgh at Houston

THURSDAY, NOV. 27
Los Angeles at Detroit
Buffalo at St. Louis

SUNDAY, NOV. 30
Atlanta at Oakland
Chicago at Green Bay
Houston at Cincinnati
Kansas City at Baltimore
Minnesota at Washington
New Orleans at Cleveland
New York Giants at Dallas
Pittsburgh at New York Jets
San Diego at Denver
San Francisco at Philadelphia

MONDAY, DEC. 1
*New England at Miami

SUNDAY, DEC. 7
Baltimore at New York Giants
Buffalo at Miami
Cincinnati at Philadelphia
Cleveland at Pittsburgh
Dallas at St. Louis
Detroit at Chicago
Green Bay at Minnesota
Houston at San Francisco
Los Angeles at New Orleans
New York Jets at New England
San Diego at Kansas City
Washington at Atlanta

MONDAY, DEC. 8
**Denver at Oakland

NFL SCHEDULE 281

SATURDAY, DEC. 13
Cincinnati at Pittsburgh
Washington at Dallas

SUNDAY, DEC. 14
Buffalo at New England
Green Bay at Los Angeles
Houston at Oakland
Kansas City at Cleveland
Miami at Baltimore
Minnesota at Detroit
New Orleans at New York Giants
Philadelphia at Denver
St. Louis at Chicago
San Francisco at Atlanta

MONDAY, DEC. 15
**New York Jets at San Diego

SATURDAY, DEC. 20
Minnesota at Buffalo
Denver at Miami
Pittsburgh at Los Angeles

SUNDAY, DEC. 21
Atlanta at Green Bay
Chicago at New Orleans
Cleveland at Houston
Dallas at New York Jets
New England at Baltimore
N.Y. Giants at San Francisco
Oakland at Kansas City
Philadelphia at Washington
St. Louis at Detroit
San Diego at Cincinnati

POST-SEASON GAMES

SATURDAY, DEC. 27
AFC & NFC Divisional Playoffs
   (NBC & CBS)

SUNDAY, DEC. 28
AFC & NFC Divisional Playoffs
   (NBC & CBS)

SUNDAY, JAN. 4
AFC Championship Game (NBC)
NFC Championship Game (CBS)

SUNDAY, JAN. 18
Super Bowl X at Miami (CBS)

MONDAY, JAN. 26
*AFC-NFC Pro Bowl
   at New Orleans (ABC)

Minnesota's Jim Marshall dwarfs St. Louis' Terry Metcalf.

OFFICIAL 1974 NFL STATISTICS

AMERICAN FOOTBALL CONFERENCE STANDINGS

Eastern Division
	W	L	T	Pct.	Pts.	OP
Miami	11	3	0	.786	327	216
Buffalo	9	5	0	.643	264	244
New England	7	7	0	.500	348	289
N.Y. Jets	7	7	0	.500	279	300
Baltimore	2	12	0	.143	190	329

Central Division
	W	L	T	Pct.	Pts.	OP
Pittsburgh	10	3	1	.750	305	189
Cincinnati	7	7	0	.500	283	259
Houston	7	7	0	.500	236	282
Cleveland	4	10	0	.286	251	344

Western Division
	W	L	T	Pct.	Pts.	OP
Oakland	12	2	0	.857	355	228
Denver	7	6	1	.536	302	294
Kansas City	5	9	0	.357	233	293
San Diego	5	9	0	.357	212	285

AFC Playoffs
Oakland 28, Miami 26
Pittsburgh 32, Buffalo 14

AFC Championship
Pittsburgh 24, Oakland 13

NATIONAL FOOTBALL CONFERENCE STANDINGS

Eastern Division
	W	L	T	Pct.	Pts.	OP
St. Louis	10	4	0	.714	285	218
Washington	10	4	0	.714	320	196
Dallas	8	6	0	.571	297	235
Philadelphia	7	7	0	.500	242	217
N.Y. Giants	2	12	0	.143	195	299

Central Division
	W	L	T	Pct.	Pts.	OP
Minnesota	10	4	0	.714	310	195
Detroit	7	7	0	.500	256	270
Green Bay	6	8	0	.429	210	206
Chicago	4	10	0	.286	152	279

Western Division
	W	L	T	Pct.	Pts.	OP
Los Angeles	10	4	0	.714	263	181
San Francisco	6	8	0	.429	226	236
New Orleans	5	9	0	.357	166	263
Atlanta	3	11	0	.214	111	271

NFC Playoffs
Minnesota 30, St. Louis 14
Los Angeles 19, Washington 10

NFC Championship
Minnesota 14, Los Angeles 10

RUSHING

AFC - INDIVIDUAL

	Att	Yards	Avg	Long	TDs
Armstrong, Otis, Den.	263	1407	5.3	43	9
Woods, Don, S.D.	227	1162	5.1	56	7
Simpson, O.J., Buff.	270	1125	4.2	41	3
Harris, Franco, Pitt.	208	1006	4.8	54	5
Hubbard, Marv, Oak.	188	865	4.6	32	4
Herron, Mack, N.E.	231	824	3.6	28	7
Cunningham, Sam, N.E.	166	811	4.9	75	9
Mitchell, Lydell, Balt.	214	757	3.5	31	5
Csonka, Larry, Mia.	197	749	3.8	24	9

NFL STATISTICS 283

	Att	Yards	Avg	Long	TDs
Riggins, John, N.Y.J.	169	680	4.0	34	5
Boozer, Emerson, N.Y.J.	153	563	3.7	20	4
Davis, Clarence, Oak.	129	554	4.3	41	2
Braxton, Jim, Buff.	146	543	3.7	21	4
Pruitt, Greg, Clev.	126	540	4.3	54	3
McKinnis, Hugh, Clev.	124	519	4.2	44	2
Green, Woody, K.C.	135	509	3.8	43	3
Malone, Ben, Mia.	117	479	4.1	23	3
Olds, Bill, Balt.	129	475	3.7	34	1
Brown, Ken, Clev.	125	458	3.7	27	4
Rodgers, Willie, Hou.	122	413	3.4	20	5
Podolak, Ed, K.C.	101	386	3.8	14	2
Davis, Charlie, Cin.	72	375	5.2	29	0
Keyworth, Jon, Den.	81	374	4.6	30	10
Bleier, Rocky, Pitt.	88	373	4.2	18	2
Elliott, Lenvil, Cin.	68	345	5.1	26	1
Matthews, Bo, S.D.	95	328	3.5	16	4
Pearson, Preston, Pitt.	70	317	4.5	53	4
Anderson, Ken, Cin.	43	314	7.3	20	2
Clark, Boobie, Cin.	99	312	3.2	22	5
Little, Floyd, Den.	117	312	2.7	22	1
Washington, Vic, Hou.	74	281	3.8	23	2
Jones, Bert, Balt.	39	279	7.2	39	4
Phipps, Mike, Clev.	39	279	7.2	19	1
Kiick, Jim, Mia.	86	274	3.2	15	1
Nottingham, Don, Mia.	66	273	4.1	24	8
Banaszak, Pete, Oak.	80	272	3.4	20	5
Hart, Harold, Oak.	51	268	5.3	25	2
Edwards, Cid, S.D.	65	261	4.0	30	0
Dressler, Doug, Cin.	72	255	3.5	17	2
Kinney, Jeff, K.C.	63	249	4.0	21	0
Davis, Steve, Pitt.	71	246	3.5	22	2
Willis, Fred, Hou.	74	239	3.2	18	3
Williams, Ed, Cin.	58	238	4.1	18	3
Bradshaw, Terry, Pitt.	34	224	6.6	34	2
Morris, Eugene, Mia.	56	214	3.8	17	1
Hayes, Wendell, K.C.	57	206	3.6	19	2
Bonner, Glen, S.D.	66	199	3.0	12	3
Smith, Charlie, Oak.	64	194	3.0	22	1
Coleman, Ronnie, Hou.	52	193	3.7	37	1
Miller, Cleophus, K.C.	40	186	4.7	47	0
Watkins, Larry, Buff.	41	170	4.1	13	2
Plunkett, Jim, N.E.	30	161	5.4	37	2
Burns, Robert, N.Y.J.	40	158	4.0	12	0
Fuqua, John, Pitt.	50	156	3.1	14	2
Domres, Marty, Balt.	22	145	6.6	21	2
Van Eeghen, Mark, Oak.	28	139	5.0	17	0
Amundson, George, Hou.	59	138	2.3	11	4
Ellison, Willie, K.C.	37	114	3.1	11	2
Ferguson, Joe, Buff.	54	111	2.1	15	2
Tarver, John, N.E.	41	101	2.5	18	2
Ashton, Josh, N.E.	26	99	3.8	22	0
Ginn, Hubert, Mia.	26	99	3.8	41	2
Adamle, Mike, N.Y.J.	28	93	3.3	21	2

284 THE COMPLETE HANDBOOK OF PRO FOOTBALL

	Att	Yards	Avg	Long	TDs
McCauley, Don, Balt.	30	90	3.0	15	0
Calhoun, Don, Buff.	21	88	4.2	15	0
Scott, Bo, Clev.	23	86	3.7	20	0
Johnson, Billy, Hou.	5	82	16.4	47	1
Jackson, Clarence, N.Y.J.	20	74	3.7	16	0
Griese, Bob, Mia.	16	66	4.1	22	1
Stingley, Darryl, N.E.	5	63	12.6	23	1
Fouts, Dan, S.D.	19	63	3.3	16	1
Curtis, Isaac, Cin.	8	62	7.8	20	0
Wilson, Joe, N.E.	15	57	3.8	12	0
Bjorklund, Hank, N.Y.J.	23	57	2.5	12	0
Thomas, Bob, S.D.	21	56	2.7	12	0
Doughty, Glenn, Balt.	7	51	7.3	17	0
Sipe, Brian, Clev.	16	44	2.8	17	4
Johnson, Essex, Cin.	19	44	2.3	11	0
Gilliam, Joe, Pitt.	14	41	2.9	13	1
Lawrence, Larry, Oak.	4	39	9.8	19	0
Hayman, Gary, Buff.	7	31	4.4	8	0
Harrison, Reggie, Pitt.	6	30	5.0	15	1
Livingston, Mike, K.C.	9	28	3.1	9	0
Dawson, Len, K.C.	11	28	2.5	10	0
Wright, Elmo, K.C.	3	26	8.7	12	1
Gordon, Dick, S.D.	1	25	25.0	25	0
Lewis, Frank, Pitt.	2	25	12.5	22	0
Odoms, Riley, Den.	4	25	6.3	31	0
Hufnagel, John, Den.	2	22	11.0	18	0
Vataha, Randy, N.E.	3	21	7.0	24	0
Joiner, Charlie, Cin.	4	20	5.0	8	0
Marangi, Gary, Buff.	4	20	5.0	16	0
Briscoe, Marlin, Mia.	1	17	17.0	17	0
Carlson, Dean, K.C.	2	17	8.5	11	0
Moses, Haven, Den.	2	16	8.0	11	0
Moore, Nat, Mia.	3	16	5.3	15	0
Freitas, Jesse, S.D.	6	16	2.7	9	0
Swann, Lynn, Pitt.	1	14	14.0	14	0
Hudson, Bob, Oak.	1	12	12.0	12	0
Scott, Fred, Balt.	2	12	6.0	9	0
Morrall, Earl, Mia.	1	11	11.0	11	0
Clark, Wayne, Cin.	1	8	8.0	8	1
Ross, Oliver, Den.	3	8	2.7	7	0
Thompson, Tom, S.D.	6	8	1.3	8	0
Queen, Jeff, Hou.	2	7	3.5	4	0
Dickey, Lynn, Hou.	3	7	2.3	7	0
Bankston, Warren, Oak.	1	6	6.0	6	0
Holden, Steve, Clev.	1	6	6.0	6	0
Taylor, Otis, K.C.	1	6	6.0	6	0
Mosley, Wayne, Buff.	2	6	3.0	4	0
Gresham, Bob, Hou.	3	6	2.0	3	0
Andrews, John, Balt.	5	6	1.2	4	0
McDaniel, John, Cin.	1	5	5.0	5	0
Beverly, Dave, Hou.	1	4	4.0	4	0
Orduna, Joe, Balt.	2	3	1.5	2	1
Barkum, Jerome, N.Y.J.	1	2	2.0	2	0
Lefear, Billy, Clev.	6	2	0.3	4	0

NFL STATISTICS 285

	Att	Yards	Avg	Long	TDs
Hinton, Eddie, N.E.	1	1	1.0	1	0
Pearson, Barry, K.C.	1	1	1.0	1	0
Stowe, Otto, Den.	1	1	1.0	1	0
Namath, Joe, N.Y.J.	8	1	0.1	3	1
Burrough, Ken, Hou.	1	0	0.0	0	0
Jaynes, David, K.C.	1	0	0.0	0	0
Van Heusen, Bill, Den.	1	-1	-1.0	-1	0
Stabler, Ken, Oak.	12	-2	-0.2	6	1
Ramsey, Steve, Den.	5	-2	-0.4	1	0
Lynch, Fran, Den.	3	-2	-0.7	1	0
Johnson, Charley, Den.	4	-3	-0.8	0	0
Thomas, Bill, K.C.	3	-3	-1.0	2	0
Lamonica, Daryle, Oak.	2	-3	-1.5	0	0
Woodall, Al, N.Y.J.	2	-3	-1.5	-1	0
Alston, Mack, Hou.	1	-3	-3.0	-3	0
Johnson, Andy, N.E.	2	-4	-2.0	-2	0
Pastorini, Dan, Hou.	24	-6	-0.3	7	0
Hanratty, Terry, Pitt.	1	-6	-6.0	-6	0
Davis, Harrison, S.D.	2	-7	-3.5	2	0
Strock, Don, Mia.	1	-7	-7.0	-7	0
Stallworth, John, Pitt.	1	-9	-9.0	-9	0
Pitts, Frank, Oak.	1	-10	-10.0	-10	0
Thaxton, Jim, Clev.	1	-10	-10.0	-10	0
Brunson, Larry, K.C.	5	-33	-6.6	0	0

NFC - INDIVIDUAL

	Att	Yards	Avg	Long	TDs
McCutcheon, Lawrence, L.A.	236	1109	4.7	23	3
Brockington, John, G.B.	266	883	3.3	33	5
Hill, Calvin, Dall.	185	844	4.6	27	7
Foreman, Chuck, Minn.	199	777	3.9	32	9
Sullivan, Tom, Phil.	244	760	3.1	28	11
Metcalf, Terry, St.L.	152	718	4.7	75	6
Maxson, Alvin, N.O.	165	714	4.3	66	2
Jackson, Wilbur, S.F.	174	705	4.1	64	0
Otis, Jim, St.L.	158	664	4.2	23	1
Schreiber, Larry, S.F.	174	634	3.6	21	3
Dawkins, Joe, N.Y.G.	156	561	3.6	16	2
Phillips, Jess, N.O.	174	556	3.2	14	2
Taylor, Altie, Det.	150	532	3.5	27	5
Osborn, Dave, Minn.	131	514	3.9	17	4
Newhouse, Bobby, Dall.	124	501	4.0	23	3
Grandberry, Ken, Chi.	144	475	3.3	31	2
Hampton, Dave, Atl.	127	464	3.7	34	2
Brown, Larry, Wash.	163	430	2.6	16	3
Garrison, Walt, Dall.	113	429	3.8	18	5
Bertelsen, Jim, L.A.	127	419	3.3	20	2
Malone, Art, Atl.	116	410	3.6	13	2
Kotar, Doug, N.Y.G.	106	396	3.7	53	4
Denson, Moses, Wash.	103	391	3.8	23	0
Owens, Steve, Det.	97	374	3.9	27	3
Lane, MacArthur, G.B.	137	362	2.6	20	3

THE COMPLETE HANDBOOK OF PRO FOOTBALL

	Att	Yards	Avg	Long	TDs
Thomas, Duane, Wash.	95	347	3.7	66	5
Garrett, Carl, Chi.	96	346	3.6	19	1
Staubach, Roger, Dall.	47	320	6.8	29	3
Anderson, Donny, St.L.	90	316	3.5	16	3
James, Po, Phil.	67	276	4.1	15	2
McQuay, Leon, N.Y.G.	55	240	4.4	21	1
Johnson, Sammy, S.F.	44	237	5.4	32	2
Stanback, Haskel, Atl.	57	235	4.1	23	1
Douglass, Bobby, Chi.	36	229	6.4	17	1
Williams, Perry, Chi.	74	218	2.9	12	1
Johnson, Ron, N.Y.G.	97	218	2.2	14	4
Reed, Oscar, Minn.	62	215	3.5	15	0
Young, Charley, Dall.	33	205	6.2	53	0
Manning, Archie, N.O.	28	204	7.3	26	1
Williams, Delvin, S.F.	36	201	5.6	71	3
Cappelletti, John, L.A.	55	198	3.6	20	0
Stevens, Howard, N.O.	43	190	4.4	25	1
Willard, Ken, St.L.	40	175	4.4	12	0
Bulaich, Norm, Phil.	50	152	3.0	13	0
Smith, Larry, Wash.	55	149	2.7	13	0
Jones, Jimmie, Det.	32	147	4.6	21	1
Hooks, Jim, Det.	44	143	3.3	17	0
Ray, Eddie, Atl.	46	139	3.0	17	0
Baker, Tony, L.A.	53	135	2.5	13	5
Marinaro, Ed, Minn.	44	124	2.8	8	1
Tarkenton, Fran, Minn.	21	120	5.7	15	2
Harris, James, L.A.	42	112	2.7	15	5
DeGrenier, Jack, N.O.	33	110	3.3	10	0
Reed, Joe, S.F.	16	107	6.7	27	0
Goodman, Les, G.B.	20	101	5.1	47	0
Lee, Bob, Atl.	19	99	5.2	17	1
Landry, Greg, Det.	22	95	4.3	19	1
Harrison, Jim, Chi.	36	94	2.6	16	1
McNeill, Rod, N.O.	22	90	4.1	24	1
Evans, Charlie, Wash.	32	79	2.5	9	2
Gabriel, Roman, Phil.	14	76	5.4	11	0
Butler, Bill, N.O.	21	74	3.5	10	0
Kendrick, Vince, Atl.	17	71	4.2	17	0
Odom, Steve, G.B.	6	66	11.0	28	1
Strayhorn, Les, Dall.	11	66	6.0	24	0
Torkelson, Eric, G.B.	13	60	4.6	21	0
Tagge, Jerry, G.B.	18	58	3.2	12	0
Crosby, Steve, N.Y.G.	14	55	3.9	10	0
Dennison, Doug, Dall.	16	52	3.3	14	4
Belton, Willie, St.L.	12	49	4.1	10	0
Crosswhite, Leon, Det.	12	49	4.1	9	1
DuPree, Billy Joe, Dall.	4	43	10.8	20	0
McClanahan, Brent, Minn.	9	41	4.6	14	1
Brown, Bill, Minn.	19	41	2.2	11	0
Munson, Bill, Det.	18	40	2.2	9	1
Young, Charles, Phil.	6	38	6.3	14	0
Huff, Gary, Chi.	23	37	1.6	11	2
Owen, Tom, S.F.	16	36	2.3	7	1
Josephson, Les, L.A.	11	35	3.2	8	0

NFL STATISTICS

	Att	Yards	Avg	Long	TDs
Cipa, Larry, N.O.	12	35	2.9	15	1
Jaworski, Ron, L.A.	7	34	4.9	17	1
Bailey, Tom, Phil.	10	32	3.2	11	0
McGee, Molly, Atl.	7	30	4.3	10	0
Kosins, Gary, Chi.	8	30	3.8	12	1
Snead, Norm, N.Y.G.-S.F.	4	29	7.3	25	0
Kilmer, Bill, Wash.	6	27	4.5	10	0
Boryla, Mike, Phil.	6	25	4.2	11	0
Hadl, John, L.A.-G.B.	19	25	1.3	9	0
Scribner, Rob, L.A.	9	24	2.7	5	0
Bryant, Cullen, L.A.	10	24	2.4	7	0
Moore, Manfred, S.F.	10	24	2.4	8	1
Bussey, Dexter, Det.	9	22	2.4	9	0
Mitchell, Jim, Atl.	3	21	7.0	15	0
Hart, Jim, St.L.	10	21	2.1	16	2
Barnes, Joe, Chi.	1	19	19.0	19	0
Sullivan, Pat, Atl.	3	19	6.3	12	0
Oliver, Greg, Phil.	7	19	2.7	7	0
Smith, Barty, G.B.	9	19	2.1	4	0
Walker, Randy, G.B.	1	18	18.0	18	0
Taylor, Clifton, Chi.	9	18	2.0	9	1
Cunningham, Doug, Wash.	5	17	3.4	5	0
Jessie, Ron, Det.	6	17	2.8	18	1
Gilliam, John, Minn.	2	16	8.0	9	0
Gagnon, Dave, Chi.	1	15	15.0	15	0
Del Gaizo, Jim, N.Y.G.	3	15	5.0	6	0
Snow, Jack, L.A.	1	13	13.0	13	0
Wittum, Tom, S.F.	1	13	13.0	13	0
Moss, Eddie, St.L.	4	13	3.3	5	0
Theismann, Joe, Wash.	3	12	4.0	12	1
Rather, Bo, Chi.	2	10	5.0	14	0
Berry, Bob, Minn.	1	8	8.0	8	0
Reaves, John, Phil.	1	8	8.0	8	0
Summerell, Carl, N.Y.G.	2	8	4.0	6	0
Seal, Paul, N.O.	2	7	3.5	6	1
Concannon, Jack, G.B.	3	7	2.3	6	1
Waters, Charlie, Dall.	1	6	6.0	6	0
Pearson, Drew, Dall.	3	6	2.0	22	0
Zofko, Mickey, Det.	3	6	2.0	3	0
Pickard, Bob, Det.	1	5	5.0	5	0
Smith, Jerry, Wash.	1	5	5.0	5	0
Tinker, Gerald, Atl.	2	5	2.5	9	0
Morton, Craig, N.Y.G.	4	5	1.3	2	0
Jackson, Harold, L.A.	1	4	4.0	4	0
Washington, Gene, S.F.	2	4	2.0	7	0
Hodgins, Norm, Chi.	1	3	3.0	3	0
Mul-Key, Herb, Wash.	1	3	3.0	3	0
Nelson, Terry, L.A.	1	3	3.0	3	0
Walton, Larry, Det.	2	3	1.5	10	0
Jackson, Randy, Phil.	7	3	0.4	2	0
Kersey, Merritt, Phil.	1	2	2.0	2	0
Rives, Don, Chi.	1	2	2.0	2	0
Parker, Joel, N.O.	2	2	1.0	6	0
Scott, Bobby, N.O.	1	1	1.0	1	0

	Att	Yards	Avg	Long	TDs
McQuilken, Kim, Atl.	2	1	0.5	1	0
Leigh, Charles, G.B.	1	0	0.0	0	0
Morrison, Dennis, S.F.	1	0	0.0	0	0
Wyche, Sam, Det.	1	0	0.0	0	0
Neal, Lou, Atl.	1	-1	-1.0	-1	0
Pagac, Fred, Chi.	1	-1	-1.0	-1	0
Taylor, Charley, Wash.	1	-1	-1.0	-1	0
Mitchell, Tom, S.F.	1	-2	-2.0	-2	0
Beasley, Terry, S.F.	1	-3	-3.0	-3	0
Preece, Steve, L.A.	1	-4	-4.0	-4	0
Richards, Golden, Dall.	1	-5	-5.0	-5	0
Jurgensen, Sonny, Wash.	4	-6	-1.5	0	0
Carmichael, Harold, Phil.	2	-6	-3.0	-1	0
Rhodes, Ray, N.Y.G.	1	-6	-6.0	-6	0
Rentzel, Lance, L.A.	1	-9	-9.0	-9	0
Grant, Frank, Wash.	1	-10	-10.0	-10	0
Longley, Clint, Dall.	4	-13	-3.3	1	0
Wade, Charlie, Chi.	1	-15	-15.0	-15	0

TEN TOP INTERCEPTORS

	No	Yards	Avg	Long	TDs
Thomas, Emmitt, K.C.	12	214	17.8	73	2
Greene, Tony, Buff.	9	157	17.4	38	0
Brown, Ray, Atl.	8	164	20.5	59	1
Darden, Thom, Clev.	8	105	13.1	31	0
Scott, Jake, Mia.	8	75	9.4	30	0
Elmendorf, Dave, L.A.	7	186	26.6	57	2
Stukes, Charlie, L.A.	7	90	12.9	41	0
Bolton, Ron, N.E.	7	18	2.6	10	0
Thompson, Norm, St.L.	6	190	31.7	56	1
Wright, Nate, Minn.	6	91	15.2	44	0

TOP TEN KICKOFF RETURNERS

	No	Yards	Avg	Long	TDs
Metcalf, Terry, St.L.	20	623	31.2	94	1
Jones, Larry, Wash.	23	672	29.2	102	1
McQuay, Leon, N.Y.G.	25	689	27.6	72	0
Pruitt, Greg, Clev.	22	606	27.5	88	1
Johnson, Billy, Hou.	29	785	27.1	67	0
Bryant, Cullen, L.A.	23	617	26.8	84	1
Moore, Nat, Mia.	22	587	26.7	40	0
Laird, Bruce, Balt.	19	499	26.3	55	0
Hart, Harold, Oak.	18	466	25.9	67	0
Grandberry, Ken, Chi.	22	568	25.8	69	0

TOP TEN SCORERS - TOUCHDOWNS

	Tot TDs	Rush TDs	Pass TDs	Misc TDs	Tot Pts
Foreman, Chuck, Minn.	15	9	6	0	90
Branch, Cliff, Oak.	13	0	13	0	78
Armstrong, Otis, Den.	12	9	3	0	72
Herron, Mack, N.E.	12	7	5	0	72
Sullivan, Tom, Phil.	12	11	1	0	72
Cunningham, Sam, N.E.	11	9	2	0	66
Curtis, Isaac, Cin.	10	0	10	0	60
Keyworth, Jon, Den.	10	10	0	0	60
Woods, Don, S.D.	10	7	3	0	60
Csonka, Larry, Mia.	9	9	0	0	54

TOP TEN SCORERS - KICKING

	XP Made	XP Att	FG Made	FG Att	Tot Pts
Marcol, Chester, G.B.	19	19	25	39	94
Gerela, Roy, Pitt.	33	35	20	29	93
Mann, Errol, Det.	23	26	23	32	92
Smith, John, N.E.	42	43	16	22	90
Leypoldt, John, Buff.	25	29	19	33	82
Moseley, Mark, Wash.	27	29	18	30	81
Blanda, George, Oak.	44	46	11	17	77
Stenerud, Jan, K.C.	24	26	17	24	75
Cockroft, Don, Clev.	29	30	14	16	71
Bakken, Jim, St.L.	30	36	13	22	69

TEN TOP PASS RECEIVERS

	No	Yards	Avg	Long	TDs
Mitchell, Lydell, Balt.	72	544	7.6	24	2
Young, Charles, Phil.	63	696	11.0	29	3
Pearson, Drew, Dall.	62	1087	17.5	50	2
Branch, Cliff, Oak.	60	1092	18.2	67	13
Carmichael, Harold, Phil.	56	649	11.6	39	8
Jessie, Ron, Det.	54	761	14.1	46	3
Taylor, Charley, Wash.	54	738	13.7	51	5
Foreman, Chuck, Minn.	53	586	11.1	66	6
Metcalf, Terry, St.L.	50	377	7.5	22	1
Dawkins, Joe, N.Y.G.	46	332	7.2	51	3

PASSING

AFC INDIVIDUAL QUALIFIERS

	Att	Comp	Pct Comp	Yards
Anderson, Ken, Cin.	328	213	64.9	2667
Stabler, Ken, Oak.	310	178	57.4	2469
Johnson, Charley, Den.	244	136	55.7	1969
Griese, Bob, Mia.	253	152	60.1	1968
Pastorini, Dan, Hou.	247	140	56.7	1571
Namath, Joe, N.Y.J.	361	191	52.9	2616
Ferguson, Joe, Buff.	232	119	51.3	1588
Dawson, Len, K.C.	235	138	58.7	1573
Plunkett, Jim, N.E.	352	173	49.1	2457
Jones, Bert, Balt.	270	143	53.0	1610
Fouts, Dan, S.D.	237	115	48.5	1732
Gilliam, Joe, Pitt.	212	96	45.3	1274
Bradshaw, Terry, Pitt.	148	67	45.3	785
Phipps, Mike, Clev.	256	117	45.7	1384
Livingston, Mike, K.C.	141	66	46.8	732
Domres, Marty, Balt.	153	77	50.3	803

NFC INDIVIDUAL QUALIFIERS

	Att	Comp	Pct Comp	Yards
Jurgensen, Sonny, Wash.	167	107	64.1	1185
Harris, James, L.A.	198	106	53.5	1544
Kilmer, Bill, Wash.	234	137	58.5	1632
Tarkenton, Fran, Minn.	351	199	56.7	2598
Hart, Jim, St.L.	388	200	51.5	2411
Munson, Bill, Det.	292	166	56.8	1874
Staubach, Roger, Dall.	360	190	52.8	2552
Snead, Norm, N.Y.G.-S.F.	159	97	61.0	983
Gabriel, Roman, Phil.	338	193	57.1	1867
Morton, Craig, Dall.-N.Y.	239	124	51.9	1522
Owen, Tom, S.F.	184	88	47.8	1327
Hadl, John, L.A.-G.B.	299	142	47.5	1752
Huff, Gary, Chi.	283	142	50.2	1663
Manning, Archie, N.O.	261	134	51.3	1429
Tagge, Jerry, G.B.	146	70	47.9	709
Lee, Bob, Atl.	172	78	45.3	852

TOP TEN PUNTERS

	No	Yards	Avg	Long	Blk
Guy, Ray, Oak.	74	3124	42.2	66	0
Blanchard, Tom, N.O.	88	3704	42.1	71	0
Wilson, Jerrel, K.C.	83	3462	41.7	64	2
Wittum, Tom, S.F.	68	2800	41.2	67	1
Green, Dave, Cin.	66	2701	40.9	53	0
James, John, Atl.	96	3891	40.5	61	1
Cockroft, Don, Clev.	90	3643	40.5	64	0
Bateman, Marv, Dall-Buff.	67	2712	40.5	66	0
Van Heusen, Bill, Den.	75	3024	40.3	61	1
Partee, Dennis, S.D.	76	3042	40.0	65	0

NFL STATISTICS

TD	Pct TD	Long	Int	Pct Int	Avg Gain	Rating Points
18	5.5	77	10	3.0	8.13	95.9
26	8.4	67	12	3.9	7.96	94.8
13	5.3	73	9	3.7	8.07	84.4
16	6.3	54	15	5.9	7.78	81.0
10	4.0	65	10	4.0	6.36	72.5
20	5.5	89	22	6.1	7.25	69.3
12	5.2	55	12	5.2	6.84	69.0
7	3.0	84	13	5.5	6.69	66.0
19	5.4	69	22	6.3	6.98	63.8
8	3.0	57	12	4.4	5.96	62.8
8	3.4	75	13	5.5	7.31	61.4
4	1.9	61	8	3.8	6.01	55.4
7	4.7	56	8	5.4	5.30	55.1
9	3.5	55	17	6.6	5.41	46.9
4	2.8	48	10	7.1	5.19	42.5
0	0.0	44	12	7.8	5.25	33.4

TD	Pct TD	Long	Int	Pct Int	Avg Gain	Rating Points
11	6.6	44	5	3.0	7.10	94.6
11	5.6	50	6	3.0	7.80	85.3
10	4.3	51	6	2.6	6.97	83.4
17	4.8	80	12	3.4	7.40	82.0
20	5.2	80	8	2.1	6.21	79.5
8	2.7	56	7	2.4	6.42	75.2
11	3.1	58	15	4.2	7.09	68.5
5	3.1	53	8	5.0	6.18	68.2
9	2.7	64	12	3.6	5.52	66.7
9	3.8	72	13	5.4	6.37	62.1
10	5.4	68	15	8.2	7.21	55.8
8	2.7	68	14	4.7	5.86	55.5
6	2.1	73	17	6.0	5.88	50.4
6	2.3	79	16	6.1	5.48	49.9
1	0.7	30	10	6.8	4.86	36.3
3	1.7	52	14	8.1	4.95	32.4

TOP TEN PUNT RETURNERS

	No	FC	Yards	Avg	Long	TDs
Parrish, Lemar, Cin.	18	1	338	18.8	90	2
Jauron, Dick, Det.	17	7	286	16.8	58	0
Morgan, Dennis, Dall.	19	0	287	15.1	98	1
Herron, Mack, N.E.	35	4	517	14.8	66	0
Swann, Lynn, Pitt.	41	3	577	14.1	69	1
Tinker, Gerald, Atl.	14	1	195	13.9	72	1
Johnson, Billy, Hou.	30	3	409	13.6	49	0
Thompson, Bill, Den.	26	1	350	13.5	60	0
Metcalf, Terry, St.L.	26	3	340	13.1	43	0
Pruitt, Greg, Clev.	27	0	349	12.9	72	0

continued from page 9

with consistency (although Oakland's Ray Guy is an obvious exception). To me, longevity is a big thing in sports. For instance, Jim Otto, old "Double-O" of the Oakland Raiders, has never missed a game in 14 years and rates as one of football's premier centers.

Joe Namath is selected at quarterback over such others as Johnny Unitas and Len Dawson, Don Meredith and John Brodie (both of whom are now NBC sportscasters), because throughout an injury-prone career, bad knees and all, Joe Willie has continued to stand out.

Johnny Unitas was an older Unitas when I first saw him, albeit still a great performer. But his outstanding years were behind him. Namath, on the other hand, signed by Sonny Werblin to a $400,000 contract out of Alabama in 1965, gave the old AFL instant glamour—and soon brought it parity.

As backup quarterback—or rather as alternate on this team—I'd name Bob Griese, the stylist from Purdue who has led Miami to two Super Bowl titles. The Dolphins have always played a very controlled, disciplined brand of football, throwing the ball sparingly. And while Griese's yearly statistics may not be spectacular, to me he's always been a neurosurgeon on the field.

Bart Starr is another who has to rate strong consideration. Bart Starr ... the ideal name for a quarterback who had in his veins the icewater of a riverboat gambler. How many times, with defenses stacked tight on third-and-one situations, did Bart connect on long passes to Boyd Dowler or Max McGee? Starr, who has left the relative safety of the broadcast booth to return to the sidelines as Green Bay's head coach, was a winner, one who quarterbacked the Packers during five championship seasons.

My running backs are O.J. Simpson, whose best years are still ahead of him (although it's going to be tough to surpass his 2,003 yards rushing in 1973) and Larry Csonka. Larry, the man the Dolphins turned to in pressure situations, is a powerful runner and excellent blocker who has amazing speed for a big man. Csonka followed in the Syracuse footsteps of Jim Brown, the late Ernie Davis, Jim Nance, and bandy-legged Floyd Little, my pick as an alternate running back.

Simpson, the first player selected in the 1969 draft, has yet to meet my test of longevity. But because of what he's already accomplished—and with his seemingly unlimited potential—O.J. is one of the true superstars.

Gale Sayers of the Chicago Bears in another who fits into the category of those I never broadcast. Sayers, who certainly

A formidable figure was DE Deacon Jones.

merits consideration for any all-time team, was an outstanding running back until knee injuries curtailed his career.

At wide receiver I've picked two men whose basic styles were quite similar: Paul Warfield and Lance Alworth. "Bambi," as Alworth was known and which has to be one of the most accurate nicknames I've ever heard, was one of the AFL's early standouts who had his greatest years with the San Diego Chargers. A graceful, fluid runner, Alworth was both a long and short pass threat who was named to the AFL's all-time team. Lance wound his career with Dallas.

Paul Warfield, week in and week out one of the most dangerous players in football, is a picture athlete—one of the most graceful performers ever.

Snapping the ball to Joe Namath would be Jim Otto, the only remaining original Raider. Otto and teammate George Blanda have played in 210 consecutive league games, the longest mark in pro football history. But while most of Blanda's appearances have been in kicking roles the past few years, Otto has been the starter in every regular-season game Oakland has ever played. An outstanding competitor, hustler and team player, "Double O" was named the center on the all-time AFL team.

Behind Otto I'd put Jim Langer, the middle man in that strong Miami offensive line. Langer is possibly the most underrated player in pro football because he spends most of his time in the shadow of so many exceptional Dolphins.

At left guard I pick another member of the American Football League's all-time team, Billy Shaw of Buffalo. During his eight-year career, playing alongside the likes of Al Bemiller and Dave Behrman, Shaw was a standout on the Buffalo teams that dominated the AFL during Lou Saban's first tenure with the club.

My right guard is Green Bay's Jerry Kramer, one of the best pulling guards in football history. With Kramer and running-mate Fred "Fuzzy" Thurston leading the way, Jim Taylor and Paul Hornung "ran to daylight" successfully during Green Bay's great years, chalking up 1,000-yard seasons (Taylor five times) and scoring titles (Hornung three, Taylor one).

My tackles are Rayfield Wright of Dallas on the left side and Minnesota's Ron Yary on the right. Wright, the 6-foot-6, 255-pound Cowboy, has all the prerequisites for an all-pro: size, strength and quickness. Despite his size, Rayfield moves better than most tackles and has great range. A strong, powerful blocker, Wright anchors the Dallas offensive line.

Yary, the first player taken (out of USC) in the 1968 draft and as such the first offensive lineman so honored, is the mainstay of a strong Viking offensive line that has played second-fiddle for so many years to Minnesota's defensive front four—the "Purple People Eaters." But last year's NFC crown went a long way toward remedying that disparity.

Other tackles who certianly deserve mention include Ron Mix, who starred for San Diego for so many years; Green Bay's Forrest Gregg, now the head coach at Cleveland; huge Bob Brown, who wound up his career at Oakland after throwing his weight around with such effectiveness for Philadelphia and Los Angeles; and the Cleveland Browns' Dick Schafrath.

My selection at tight end is John Mackey, who while he was with Baltimore set the pattern for the big, modern-day pro tight end who can block, run and catch the football with equal skill. At the same time, Denver's Riley Odoms is a contemporary tight end who is destined to be one of the greats.

My placekickers—I have to name two—on this blue-chip team are Kansas City's Jan Stenerud, one of the earliest of the soccer-style kickers and ageless George Blanda. I pick Stenerud for his ability to kick off deep and his long field goal success (from 40 yards and beyond). In fact, I thought for several years Jan had the strongest leg in pro football.

But the Oakland marvel, 47-year-old George Blanda, is another who certainly merits a spot on the squad. Blanda enters the 1975 season with 1,919 career points, the most in pro football history, and his last-second heroics have become almost legendary over the years. He's kicked so well for so long . . . and has come through in the clutch so often.

GOWDY'S ALL-TIME TEAM

Linebacker, turning now to the defense, has to be the hardest position of all to pick—simply because there have been so many great ones. Since any team is limited to three starters, I'd have to go with Chicago's Dick Butkus in the middle and flank him on the right with Dave Robinson of Green Bay and Washington and on the left with Kansas City's Bobby Bell. In picking these three, I realize I'm leaving out some great ones (and that doesn't even include the linebackers I never broadcast, standouts such as Joe Schmidt of Detroit and the New York Giants' Sam Huff, who closed out his career with Vince Lombardi at Washington in 1969).

Nick Buoniconti of Miami, for instance, is a great diagnostician and an extremely smart player. And Baltimore's Mike Curtis, while he's played on some poor Colt teams of late, is considered the best in the business by no less an authority than Paul Brown of Cincinnati. And what about Willie Lanier of Kansas City, the Cowboys' LeRoy Jordan, Ted Hendricks of Baltimore (now with the Packers) and Green Bay's Ray Nitschke?

My defensive ends are Rich "Tombstone" Jackson of Denver and Cleveland on the left, who over the short haul—or until knee ailments curtailed his career, as well—was the best I ever saw, and David "Deacon" Jones of Los Angeles and San Diego on the right, who has been a star throughout his long and storied career. I'd also have to pick, as an alternate, Charles "Bubba" Smith of Baltimore and Oakland, who when he was right could dominate a game like nobody else. And how about the likes of Willie Davis, now an NBC sportscaster, who captained the great Green Bay defenses of the Lombardi era and whom I saw in Super Bowl I, and Tom Sestak of Buffalo for the caliber of player not named to the squad?

At defensive tackle I have to go with Bob Lilly, the heart of Dallas' "Doomsday Defense" for so many seasons, and "Mean" Joe Greene, another current player whom I feel has unlimited potential. Lilly, hampered by injuries and a back back these past couple seasons, was a yearly all-pro selection beginning in 1962.

Greene, the dominant figure in Pittsburgh's 16-6 victory over Minnesota in Super Bowl IX (which gave original Steeler owner Art Rooney his first NFL championship after 40 years of trying), used his great strength and quickness to lead a graphic demonstration of how one team's defense can completely throttle another's offense.

Since you have to have at least three defensive tackles to play pro football today, I'd name the Rams' Merlin Olsen as an alternate to my squad. The game has become so specialized that, depending on the situation—pass rush, third-and-short yardage, third-and-long—you have to be able to shuttle players in and out. Another who merits mention is Alan Page, Minnesota's excellent defensive tackle out of Notre Dame who was an instrumental factor last season in the Vikings earning a berth in Super Bowl IX.

My cornerbacks are Oakland's Willie Brown, one of the keys to a tough Raider defense, and Herb Adderley of Green Bay and Dallas. An indication of the respect other NFL teams have for Brown is the fact that rarely is his zone thrown into. Adderley performed brilliantly throughout his career, both as a defender and kick returner. He scored seven touchdowns by interception, ranking second on the all-time list behind Washington's Ken Houston, who is still picking 'em off. And Herb is third in interception return yardage behind Emlen Tunnell and Dick "Night Train" Lane.

My picks at safety, another difficult position to choose when you have such greats as Larry Wilson of St. Louis and Green Bay's Willie Wood, are Dick Anderson of Miami and Johnny Robinson of Kansas City. Very smart, very hard hitters, Robinson and Anderson (still very much in evidence in the Dolphin secondary) came up quickly and would really pop you.

Robinson, an original AFLer, came into the league in the shadow of his illustrious LSU running-mate, Heisman Trophy winner Billy Cannon, and stayed around long enough to outshine Cannon, carving for himself a niche as a defensive great.

Although he doesn't meet my test of longevity (since he's only been around for two seasons), Ray Guy of Oakland rates as my pick at punter over Kansas City's Jerrel Wilson. This young man, the only strict punter ever taken first in the draft, has been tremendous his first two years. And, before he's through he'll have set a raft of kicking records.

What's any team without a coach? And who better to coach this club than Don Shula? (Again, keep in mind the fact that I had minimal contact with Vince Lombardi—but the way I look at it nobody can hold a candle to Shula). His success speaks for itself: the first coach in NFL history to win more than 100 games in his first ten seasons; only the second coach to win two straight Super Bowls (Lombardi was the other), Super Bowl VII in 1973 and Super Bowl VIII in 1974; led the Dolphins to a 17-0 record in 1972, the only time an NFL team has gone undefeated through regular- and post-season play. He was a winner at Baltimore, he's been a winner with Miami. He's an exceptional handler of men and a shrewd judge of talent. Need I say more?

Now ... who's going to play our team?

Ageless George Blanda has scored 1,919 points.

298 THE COMPLETE HANDBOOK OF PRO FOOTBALL

continued from page 13

tend to get the ball back quickly, a second running back who is a fine blocker and content to remain in the shadows and, of course, freedom from injury.

Simpson's 1973 feat had all these ingredients, with the added plus of a young quarterback who was willing to spend most of his time handing off the football rather than throwing it toward his own potential stardom.

Many of the same ingredients were present a decade earlier when Jim Brown of Cleveland rushed for 1,863 yards to establish the record that Simpson was to break. Along the way, Brown shattered his own mark of 1,527 yards, set in 1958 when the NFL teams were playing only 12 games. The great Cleveland running back shredded a porous St. Louis defense for 179 yards in the twelfth game of the season to set the new standard, obviously pleased at the fact that he had done it in only 12 games.

The next two were so much gravy. The burly back carried only 13 times for 61 yards while the Browns were being routed

L.A.'s Lawrence McCutcheon is a candidate.

by Detroit, then bounced back with 125 yards against Washington in the season finale.

Brown carried the ball 291 times and had a 6.4-yard average. Simpson carried it 332 times with a 6.0-yard average. If Brown had had the additional 41 carries, even at Simpson's smaller average, he would have picked up another 246 yards for a total of 2,109 yards for the campaign.

Simpson, on the other hand, came into the last two games of the season with 1,584 yards. He really went to work against the New England Patriots, gaining 219 yards on 22 carries, and showed up in New York on Dec. 16, 1973, with 1,803. The world (as self-described by the New York media) was watching. The sturdy Californian got the 60 yards to tie Brown within the first half, then went on for a 34-carry, 200-yard day that got him over the magic total.

Simpson's super season, however, does nothing to dim the legend of Brown, and still leaves the Buffalo running back some worlds to conquer. Brown, who had seven seasons over 1,000 yards and who led the NFL in rushing in eight of his nine campaigns, still stands tall in the rushing arena. For example, Brown's first three seasons (1958-60) show three league rushing crowns and a total of 4,126 yards, and those were 12-game seasons. Simpson's first three years (1969-71) display 1,927 yards, in 14-game years.

The Juice missed a number of games because of injuries in 1970, but injuries are part of the game, and Brown's resistance in this area is one of his strong suits.

One additional comparison may be valid, a match of the three top consecutive seasons of both men. Simpson's 2,003-yard year was sandwiched between seasons of 1,251 and 1,125 yards for a three-year (1972-1974) total of 4,379. Brown's NFL record of 1,863 was followed by campaigns of 1,446 and 1,544 yards, for a three-season (1963-65) figure of 4,853, almost 500 more yards than the Buffalo flash.

After leading the NFL as a rookie with 942 yards in 1957, Brown racked up seven 1,000-yard seasons in the next eight years, missing only in 1962, when he gained 996. If statisticians, coaches and the media had been as statistics conscious then as they have since become, it is a cinch that the big fullback would have either been given the opportunity for the extra four yards in his final game, or would have found them in a post-season check of films, the way Miami later did for Mercury Morris.

Still, 1962 was the only time in his nine seasons that Brown did not lead the NFL in rushing. Simpson displays one rushing title in six seasons.

Both Simpson and Brown were on strong teams in their record-setting years, the Bills finishing 9-5 and the Browns 10-4, with both marks good for second place in their respective divisions. But the Bills were out of title contention with four weeks to go, giving them full opportunity to work the big running back toward his goal.

Buffalo attempted only nine passes in its last two games as every effort was made to concentrate on the rushing game. Simpson, meanwhile, carried the ball 56 times.

Again, this is not to denigrate the record, but it took those special circumstances, especially weather, a young quarterback and, most important, situations wherein the Bills were out in front early in each game and able to play ball control. A team that is constantly fighting from behind could never afford the luxury of having a running back chase a record.

During that splendid season of 1973, Simpson carried the ball on 332 of his team's 605 rushing plays, and the Bills threw only 213 passes, averaging 15 per game. Brown, in contrast, had 291 rushing plays of the team's 460, and Cleveland put the ball in the air 322 times.

Up front, both clubs displayed outstanding lines to provide blocking. The Browns had Monte Clark and Dick Schafrath at tackles, Gene Hickerson and John Wooten at guards and John Morrow at center. Buffalo used Dave Foley and Donnie Green at tackles, Reggie McKenzie and Joe DeLamielleure at guards and Mike Montler at center. The Buffalo line probably was a little faster, certainly much younger, but the Cleveland quintet had been together a considerable length of time and was a solid aggregation.

Simpson's record no doubt will fall some day, just as Brown's career totals will eventually yield to someone younger and stronger and swifter, but it will take that ideal set of circumstances, and not just the great running back, to surpass the Juice's total.

Statistics would indicate, in a search for a 2,000-yard rusher, a look in the direction of men who already have cracked the 1,000-yard barrier. The mark has been topped 68 times in the NFL's

55 seasons, and 50 of the accomplishments belong to 19 men who have done it twice or more. Oddly, with 18 runners in the one-time bracket, it means that more men have surpassed 1,000 yards twice than have done it once.

It looks as if the second time is easier, almost like the psychological barrier that once stood before the four-minute mile.

Brown's seven times leads the way, of course, with Jim Taylor at five. Simpson, John Brockington, Larry Csonka and Leroy Kelly each have done it three times. Two-timers include Dick Bass, Larry Brown, Mike Garrett, Franco Harris, Calvin Hill, John Henry Johnson, Ron Johnson, Paul Lowe, Lawrence McCutcheon, Jim Nance, Joe Perry, Gale Sayers and Steve Van Buren.

Five NFL teams—Baltimore, the Jets, New Orleans, Atlanta and Minnesota—have never been able to boast a 1,000-yard rusher, and St. Louis, Detroit and Cincinnati can point to it once each over their history.

Among the current crop of running backs, Denver's Otis Armstrong may be the leading candidate, along with Los Angeles' Lawrence McCutcheon. Armstrong totaled 1,407 yards last season to lead the NFL and to post the ninth-best one-season yardage mark. It has been surpassed by only four other players: Simpson, Taylor, Nance and five times by Brown. Denver has shown a solid offense the last few seasons, and if Charley Johnson keeps the ball out of the air, Armstrong may have enough chances. McCutcheon is a runner of similar style, and the Rams do have a more ground-oriented attack.

And there's one more solid threat—Simpson himself. After all, he and the Bills have shown they can do it, and they may just decide to show that they can do it again.

THE 1,000-YARD MEN
+ O.J.

2,003—O.J. Simpson, Buffalo, 1973.

1,863—Jim Brown, Cleveland, 1963.

1,544—Jim Brown, Cleveland, 1965; *1,527—Jim Brown, Cleveland, 1958.

1,474—Jim Taylor, Green Bay, 1962; 1,458—Jim Nance, Boston, 1966; 1,446—Jim Brown, Cleveland, 1964; 1,408—Jim Brown, Cleveland, 1961; 1,407—Otis Armstrong, Denver, 1974.

*1,329—Jim Brown, Cleveland, 1959; 1,307—Jim Taylor, Green Bay, 1961.

*1,257—Jim Brown, Cleveland, 1960; 1,251—O.J. Simpson, Buffalo, 1972; 1,239—Leroy Kelly, Cleveland, 1968; 1,231—Gale Sayers, Chicago, 1966; 1,216—Jim Nance, Boston, 1967; 1,216—Larry Brown, Washington, 1972; 1,205—Leroy Kelly, Cleveland, 1967.

1,194—Hoyle Granger, Houston, 1967; 1,182—Ron Johnson, New York Giants, 1972; 1,169—Jim Taylor, Green Bay, 1964; 1,162—Don Woods, San Diego, 1974; *1,146—Steve Van Buren, Philadelphia, 1949; 1,144—John Brockington, Green Bay, 1973; 1,142—Calvin Hill, Dallas, 1973; 1,141—John Henry Johnson, Pittsburgh, 1962; 1,141—Leroy Kelly, Cleveland, 1966; 1,133—Floyd Little, Denver, 1971; *1,126—Rick Casares, Chicago, 1956; 1,125—O.J. Simpson, Buffalo, 1974; 1,125—Larry Brown, Washington, 1970; 1,122—Paul Lowe, San Diego, 1965; 1,117—Larry Csonka, Miami, 1972; 1,109—Lawrence McCutcheon, Los Angeles, 1974; 1,105—John Brockington, Green Bay, 1971; *1,101—Jim Taylor, Green Bay, 1960; 1,100—Marv Hubbard, Oakland, 1972.

1,099—Clemon Daniels, Oakland, 1963; 1,097—Lawrence McCutcheon, Los Angeles, 1973; 1,096—Cookie Gilchrist, Buffalo, 1962; 1,090—Dick Bass, Los Angeles, 1966; 1,087—Mike Garrett, Kansas City, 1967; *1,071—John David Crow, St. Louis, 1960; 1,055—Franco Harris, Pittsburgh, 1972; *1,052—Tony Canadeo, Green Bay, 1949; 1,051—Larry Csonka, Miami, 1971; *1,049—Joe Perry, San Francisco, 1954; 1,049—Abner Haynes, Dallas Texans, 1962; 1,048—John Henry Johnson, Pittsburgh, 1964; 1,036—J.D. Smith, San Francisco, 1959; 1,036—Calvin Hill, Dallas, 1972; 1,035—Steve Owens, Detroit, 1971; 1,033—Dick Bass, Los Angeles, 1962; 1,032—Gale Sayers, Chicago, 1969; 1,031—Mike Garrett, San Diego, 1972; 1,027—Ron Johnson, New York Giants, 1970; 1,027—John Brockington, Green Bay, 1972; 1,023—Paul Robinson, Cincinnati, 1968; *1,018—Joe Perry, San Francisco, 1953; 1,018—Jim Taylor, 1963; *1,008—Steve Van Buren, Philadelphia, 1947; 1,0006—Franco Harris, Pittsburgh, 1974; **1,004—Beattie Feathers, Chicago, 1934; 1,003—Larry Csonka, Miami, 1973; 1,000—Willie Ellison, Los Angeles, 1971; 1,000—Mercury Morris, Miami, 1972.

*—12-game season. **—13-game season.

Green Bay's Jim Taylor broke 1,000 five times.

continued from page 11
what his daddy did for a living. "He kills the quarterback," was the tot's reply.

1. Mike Curtis, 2. Bill Bergey, 3. Jack Lambert, 4. Otis Sistrunk, 5. Wally Hilgenberg

Mike Curtis shows how he earned his rating.

BEST DRESSED

"Cedrick Hardman," says his ex-teammate, Earl Edwards, "does not wear clothes. He wears costumes." Hardman will be pressed to retain his title. Carter Campbell came back from the WFL to re-enter the competition and Frenchy Fuqua is coming off the injured list.

In the conventional category, Ahmad Rashad dresses even classier now than when he was known as Bobby Moore.

1. Cedrick Hardman, 2. Carter Campbell, 3. Frenchy Fuqua, 4. Roy Jefferson, 5. Ahmad Rashad

WORST DRESSED

Classy is in the eye of the beholder. Some people actually think that wearing an opera cape, three musketeers hat, six-inch platform soles and a handbag to football practice is over-dressed.

In the conventional category, Joe Ferguson comes on like an extra for the sock-hop scene in "Happy Days."

1.Cedrick Hardman, 2. Carter Campbell, 3. Frenchy Fuqua, 4. Roy Jefferson, 5. Joe Ferguson

FLAKIEST

There have been times in the last few seasons when the new York Jets as much expected to see John Riggins in a Tibetan monastery as in their lineup. Riggins is, ahhh, what you would call unpredictable. One season it's a hairstyle directly out of the East Village. The next season it's an Iroquois, just like the ones which the Prairie Village swimming team wore in '49. Sometimes John doesn't get the urge to play football until Columbus Day and the other guys have gotten a pretty fair jump on him.

Riggins attributes his behavior to the cultural shock of having to get his thing together in an ultra-rural section of Kansas for half the year and in semi-civilized New York for the other half. He may have a point.

1. John Riggins, 2. Fred Dryer, 3. Diron Talbert, 4. J.D. Hill, 5. Bob Lurtsema

MOST INTANGIBLE

Call it charisma, leadership, the will to prevail, whatever. What it adds up to is an athlete—who shouldn't be that good because of physical limitations—being that good.

Howard Twilley used to be the unchallenged intangibles champ, but Don Shula doesn't use him that much anymore. There is no valid reason Rocky Bleier shouldn't be off somewhere selling insurance or rejecting mortgages for a bank, but there he was in the Super Bowl gaining all sorts of yardage.

1. Rocky Bleier, 2. Pat Fischer, 3. Pat Matson, 4. Jerry Patton, 5. Billy Kilmer

WORST INTERVIEW

You walk into a department store to complain about a sweater which shrank two sizes the first time you washed it. A floor walker cuts you off in mid-explanation, tells you there is nothing which can be done and turns his back. That's Bob Griese, who has all the warmth of H.R. Haldeman.

Chuck Noll has all the warmth of J. Paul Getty, and unless you want to talk wines or gourmet foods, he gives you the distinct impression that only a half dozen people in the Western Hemisphere are qualified to discuss football with him and you are not one of them. Even so, he's more informative than George Allen. Duane Thomas' superiority goes unchallenged.

1. Duane Thomas, 2. George Allen, 3. Chuck Noll, 4. Bob Griese, 5. Sonny Jurgensen

BEST INTERVIEW

Even after all these years, all those yards and the parades of microphones and notebooks, O.J. Simpson still manages to amaze interrogators. "I asked him what time it was," said one startled author recently, "and he told me how to make a watch."

1. O.J. Simpson, 2. Andy Russell, 3. Joe Greene, 4. Larry Csonka, 5. Bob Kuechenberg

MOST OVER-RATED (Defense)

Every now and then, Bubba Smith will do something which will remind the crowds of those "Kill! Bubba, Kill!" buttons back at Michigan State. But on three out of four plays he wouldn't harm a flea.

It's awfully tough to play in New York and make three consecutive tackles without someone nominating you for the Hall of Fame. Ask Sam Huff. That's why John Mendenhall belongs here.

1. Bubba Smith, 2. Cedrick Hardman, 3. John Mendenhall, 4. Fred Dryer, 5. Bill Bradley

MOST OVER-RATED (Offense)

Jim Kiick should get down on his hands and knees each night and give thanks he is associated with Larry Csonka in the public's view. Since quarterback is the most over-rated position, it figures that quarterbacks dominate the list.

1. Jim Kiick, 2. Roger Staubach, 3. Billy Kilmer, 4. Gene Upshaw, 5. Mike Phipps

MOST UNDER-RATED (Defense)

Ron Carpenter probably couldn't play three bars of chopsticks and his public conversation reminds you of a North Carolina dirt farmer, but he is one helluva tackle for Cincinnati. But he has played alongside Mike Reid, who also plays concert piano and could out-talk Hubert Humphrey.

1. Ron Carpenter, 2. Ernie Holmes, 3. Randy Logan, 4. Gregg Bingham, 5. Glen Edwards

MOST UNDER-RATED (Offense)

When John Hadl played quarterback in San Diego and the Chargers were throwing, Gary Garrison was as well known as Paul Warfield. But in the last few years the team has gone back to the soil and for all anyone knows Nolan Ryan may be the quarterback. Garrison, however, has as much skill as ever.

1. Gary Garrison, 2. Joe DeLamielleure, 3. Tom Sullivan, 4. Blaine Nye, 5. Clarence Davis

MOST DURABLE

Neither Jim Otto nor George Blanda has missed a game for the Oakland Raiders since the Taft Administration, but Otto is a center and most of Blanda's action in the last decade has been as a place-kicker.

The most amazing record belongs to Francis Tarkenton. With all that running around back there, he's never missed a game. That means he's been dodging people from the Willie Davis-Doug Atkins era to the modern days of Wally Chambers and Jack Youngblood.

1. Francis Tarkenton, 2. Jim Otto, 3. Jim Marshall, 4. Len Rohde, 5. Jimmy Johnson

MOST INTELLECTUAL

Hyperbole is a normal way of expression in sports. The jocks have a tendency to exaggerate things. Thus an intellectual to them is anyone who subscribes to National Geographic.

There are some analytical thinkers in the NFL, however. Charley Johnson has a Ph.D in engineering and Virgil Carter attacked some musty theories about Xs and Os by computer when he was in the NFL, so the public automatically thinks quarterbacks are geniuses. They just haven't been exposed to Bobby Douglass and Terry Bradshaw.

Any conversation with Calvin Hill will convince you he paid attention during his classes at Yale. Doug Swift has the breeding (both parents doctors), the background (Amherst) and he dresses the part (cruddy chic). There is divided opinion on Chuck Noll, the Pittsburgh coach. Some think he's the NFL's renaissance man, some think he's just trying to look down his nose at people.

1. Calvin Hill, 2. Charley Johnson, 3. Doug Swift, 4. Mike Reid, 5. Andy Russell

BIGGEST SHOWBOAT

The NFL banned its thespians from throwing the football into the stands a few years ago, the penalty being something like eternal damnation. But the really creative hot dogs have found all sorts of ways to circumvent the rule.

Last year creativity reached its zenith in Philadelphia, when a receiver would score and his teammates would gather round him in a mock crap game, snapping fingers while the scorer would "roll six."

But the pioneer showboater is still Elmo Wright, who performs some sort of fertility rite in the Kansas City end zone. It's been so long since he scored that no one can remember how the routine goes.

1. Elmo Wright, 2. Philadelphia's offensive unit, 3. Henry Stuckey, 4. Greg Pruitt, 5. Fred Biletnikoff

MOST POPULAR

Any time you deal in egos, you deal in jealousy, pettiness, resentment and bitterness. When a player's popularity goes beyond his own circle or his own team, you know that he can handle fame pretty well.

In a ratio of fame to the manner in which fame is handled, no one gets a higher rating than O.J. Simpson. And special mention goes to Joe Greene. Even the people upon whose head he beats seem to like him.

1. O.J. Simpson, 2. Joe Greene, 3. Ron McDole, 4. Andy Russell, 5. James Harris

ANGRIEST

The old line, "he's even-tempered ... always in a rage," might have been used for the first time on Dick Butkus. Butkus is sun bathing in Florida these days, but there are still plenty of angries in the NFL.

O.J. Simpson was in a store with Jerry Patton one time when the Philadelphia tackle became irritated at a small boy. "Jerry threatened to break the kid's back," laughs O.J., "and the name of the place was 'The Friendly Market.'"

1. Jerry Patton, 2. Verlon Biggs, 3. Mike Curtis, 4. Duane Thomas, 5. Mike Tilleman

BEST GAME FACE

Nick Buoniconti was brought up as a pro with the old Boston Patriots. Half the team threw up before a game and Larry Eisenhower, a huge defensive end, used to prep himself by banging his head against a locker. Nick now plays on the most casual team in football, the Dolphins, so getting his game face on is a personal effort which he still manages to perfection.

A friend of Mike Curtis says he still looks out the window of the team bus, "hating the grass," as the bus wends its way toward the stadium. Special mention goes to Cleveland's defensive co-ordinator, Richie McCabe, who refuses to take part in the pregame sociabilities most coaches sham their way through on the field before kickoff.

1. Nick Buoniconti, 2. Mike Curtis, 3. Dwight White, 4. Marv Hubbard, 5. Richie McCabe

Nick Buoniconti faces the issue.

continued from page 17

Lamonica's 23-yard scoring pass to Bill Miller in the second quarter gave the Raiders a brief moment of glory, but by halftime the Packers led, 16-7. They proceeded to a 33-14 triumph that was capped by Herb Adderley's interception of a Lamonica pass and 60-yard return for a touchdown. Don Chandler's four field goals for Green Bay provided an ironic twist in that George Blanda's kicking was supposed to be one of the Raiders' biggest weapons. However, a Packer defense led by the menacing Ray Nitschke at linebacker stopped Blanda simply by keeping the Raiders out of field-goal range.

SUPERSTAR—Bart Starr, running the Packer offense with computer efficiency, was named MVP for the second straight Super Bowl. He completed 13 of 24 passes for 202 yards, 62 of those yards on a touchdown to Boyd Dowler.

GOAT—Ben Davidson entered the game with the reputation as the meanest player in the AFL, and with Joe Namath's broken cheekbone as one of his notches. But the Packers ran at and over the Raiders' baleful-looking defensive end, and Davidson was never a factor.

Green Bay Packers (NFL)	3	13	10	7—33
Oakland Raiders (AFL)	0	7	0	7—14

GB—Chandler (FG) 39

GB—Chandler (FG) 20

GB—Dowler, pass from Starr 62 (Chandler kick)

Oak—Miller, pass from Lamonica 23 (Blanda kick)

GB—Chandler (FG) 43

GB—Anderson, run 2 (Chandler kick)

GB—Chandler (FG) 31

GB—Adderley, pass interception 60 (Chandler kick)

Oak—Miller, pass from Lamonica 23 (Blanda kick)

A—75,546

SUPER BOWL III

MIAMI, Jan. 12, 1969—"We're going to win, I guarantee it," said Joe Namath.

Hardly anyone believed the New York Jets' brash quarterback, least of all the oddsmakers. The Jets were 18-to-21-point underdogs to the Baltimore Colts, an impressive team coached by Don Shula that had replaced the Green Bay Packers as NFL

SUPER BOWL

champions with a 13-1 record. The Jets, meantime, came into the game with an 11-3 record and coached by Weeb Ewbank. He had coached the Colts to a title in 1959 but was dismissed four years later.

Now, however, Ewbank believed he had found a way to do the incredible—beat the Colts. His game plan consisted of basic off-tackle slants by fullback Matt Snell and the simplest type of passing game directed by Namath, a superb reader of defenses.

Matt Snell powered the Jets in Super Bowl III.

Astonishingly, it all worked. Namath was brilliant, offsetting the Colts' blitz with quick, short passes. He drove the Jets 80 yards to a touchdown in the second quarter. Three times in the second half he got them in position for field goals by Jim Turner. Snell gained 121 yards rushing and scored a touchdown, and the Jets' defense intercepted four passes.

The Jets won, 16-7, and the sports world was stunned. In one afternoon following nine years of existence, the AFL had achieved credibility. And so had the Super Bowl, which suddenly was more than a spectacle. It was a football game.

SUPERSTAR—"I always had confidence we would win," said Namath, the $400,000 rebel quarterback of the rebel league. "But I didn't know what to expect. But I had a good time. When you go out and play football, you're supposed to have a good time." Namath's good time included 17 completions in 28 passes for 206 yards. Predictably, he was named the game's MVP.

GOAT—Earl Morrall, the Colts' quarterback and the Most Valuable Player in the NFL, completed just six of 17 passes and had three intercepted. He was replaced by a sore-armed Johnny Unitas in the third quarter. "I've tried to shrug it off but I can't," Morrall would say later. "That was the biggest game of my life. I keep thinking about it, remembering all the bad things."

New York Jets (AFL)	0	7	6	3—16
Baltimore Colts (NFL)	0	0	0	7— 7

NY—Snell, run 4 (Turner kick)

NY—Turner (FG) 32

NY—Turner (FG) 30

NY—Turner (FG) 9

Balt—Hill, run 1 (Michaels kick)

A—75,377

SUPER BOWL IV

NEW ORLEANS, Jan. 11, 1970—It was the last game of strict AFL-NFL confrontations, and the Kansas City Chiefs were ready for it. They befuddled the Minnesota Vikings with their "offense of the '70's," a blend of quick backs, shifting I-formations and play-action passes. Len Dawson directed it expertly, and always waiting in the background was Jan Stenerud, a soccer-style kicker from Norway.

Dawson engineered first-half drives that led to three field goals by Stenerud and a touchdown by halfback Mike Garrett,

Kansas City's Len Dawson capped career in Super Bowl IV.

giving the Chiefs a 16-0 lead. Although the Vikings were 13-point favorites, they seemed helpless. In the fourth quarter, their tough quarterback, Joe Kapp, was knocked out of the game on a tackle by the Chiefs' Aaron Brown.

Kapp's departure was a fitting climax to a convincing 23-7 victory for Kansas City that evened the NFL-AFL playoff at two triumphs apiece. It also avenged the Chiefs' loss to Green Bay in the first Super Bowl. "That's what we wanted," said Kansas City's Buck Buchanan. "Nobody can call us losers again."

SUPERSTAR—The 34-year-old Dawson, a failure with two NFL teams early in his career, won the MVP award, triumphantly ending a difficult season. He had missed six games because of a knee injury—and five days before the Super Bowl his name had been linked with that of a professional gambler, a link an investigation would prove false. Dawson completed 12 of 17 passes against the Vikings and finished the day with a 46-yard TD to Otis Taylor.

GOATS—Carl Eller, Jim Marshall, Alan Page, and Gary Larsen, the Vikings' front four on defense, never lived up to their nicknames, the "Purple People Eaters." It was the Chiefs' offense that had a feast, gaining 155 yards rushing and 122 passing.

Minnesota Vikings (NFL)	0	0	7	0— 7
Kansas City Chiefs (AFL)	3	13	7	0—23

KC—Stenerud (FG) 48

KC—Stenerud (FG) 32

KC—Stenerud (FG) 25

KC—Garrett, run 5 (Stenerud kick)

Minn—Osborn, run 5 (Cox kick)

KC—Taylor, pass from Dawson 46 (Stenerud kick)

A—80,998

SUPER BOWL V

MIAMI, Jan. 17, 1971—In a game not for purists, the Baltimore Colts and Dallas Cowboys committed 11 turnovers. And for awhile it looked as if the Colts would theoretically become the first team to lose Super Bowls for both leagues. Under the merger's new alignment, they had moved over to the American Conference, but they arrived with no instant loyalty toward their new home. "I don't want to win for the old AFC," said Billy Ray Smith, a defensive tackle, "I want to win for old B.R. and the Colts."

Well, the Colts did win but it wasn't easy, what with fumbling the ball away four times and throwing three interceptions. Their first touchdown also was far from perfect. Johnny Unitas's off-target pass was tipped twice—by the Colts' Eddie Hinton, the intended receiver, and the Cowboys' Mel Renfro—before making an unscheduled landing in the arms of John Mackey, the Colts' tight end. Mackey raced for a touchdown covering 75 yards.

Still, in the end it was the Cowboys themselves who snatched defeat from the jaws of victory. They had overcome the Colt touchdown and led in the fourth quarter, 13-6, on two field goals by Roy Clark and a pass from Craig Morton to Duane Thomas. But the Cowboys earlier had fumbled on the Colts' 1-yard line. And now, near the finish, Morton suddenly was intercepted by Rick Volk to set up the tying touchdown, and then with a minute left he was intercepted by Mike Curtis to set up a winning 32-yard field goal. It was kicked by Jim O'Brien, a rookie, with just five seconds remaining. Improbably and dramatically, the Colts won, 16-13. By some it was called an exciting game—by others it was called the Blunder Bowl.

SUPERSTAR—Chuck Howley, a Cowboy linebacker who intercepted two passes, was voted the MVP, even though his team lost. But it was O'Brien, a 23-year-old dropout from the Air Force Academy who enabled the Blunder Bowl to mercifully end. "I was figuring on sudden-death," he said afterward. "Funny thing, my mom called me and told me we couldn't lose. She's big on astrology and she figured it all out."

GOAT—"We just made too many mistakes," said Morton, whose two mistakes in the fourth quarter were the biggest of the game.

```
Baltimore Colts (AFC) ........... 0   6   0   10—16
Dallas Cowboys (NFC) ...........  3  10   0    0—13
```

Dal—Clark (FG) 14

Dal—Clark (FG) 30

Balt—Mackey, pass from Unitas 75 (kick failed)

Dal—Thomas, pass from Morton 7 (Clark kick)

Balt—Nowatzke, run 2 (O'Brien kick)

Balt—O'Brien (FG) 32

A—80,577

SUPER BOWL VI

NEW ORLEANS, Jan. 16, 1972—"They can't say we don't win the big ones anymore," said Tex Schramm, president of the Dallas Cowboys. Indeed, nobody could argue that point with Schramm, not even the President of the United States, who had suggested a play to the Miami Dolphins for use in this game.

For years, Dallas, an awesome team on paper, had been said to "choke" in the big games, a reputation that grew to full size after its loss in Super Bowl V. But now, with coach Tom Landry calling the plays from the sidelines, as he had done all season, the Cowboys were nearly flawless. Roger Staubach outquarterbacked Miami's Bob Griese, and Duane Thomas and Walt Garrison outran Larry Csonka and Jim Kiick. Dallas scored just before halftime on a pass from Staubach to Lance Alworth, then received the second-half kickoff and marched 71 yards to another TD.

The game was all but over, because nothing was working for the Dolphins, especially the advice President Richard Nixon had given to Miami coach Don Shula two weeks earlier in a widely publicized phone call. "I think you can hit Warfield on a down-and-in pattern," said Nixon, a part-time resident of Florida. He was wrong. "They had two weeks to prepare," said Warfield about the Cowboys, "and they made sure that under any circumstances we wouldn't be able to catch that pass." The Cowboys won easily, 24-3.

SUPERSTAR—Staubach, who threw two scoring passes, was named MVP, but the compelling figure of the Super Bowl was Thomas. The Cowboys' rebel running back had withdrawn into silence most of the season, refusing to talk with newsmen, fans and some of his teammates. Even after gaining 95 yards in 19 carries against the Dolphins, Thomas preferred to remain a reclusive enigma. "Got something to say?" he was asked after the game. He looked up and smiled, and that was all.

GOAT—Griese was considered by many the best quarterback in the NFL during the season, but he was unable to move his team against the Cowboys when he had to. His frustration was typified on a play in the first quarter when he was chased back 29 yards trying to pass and was tackled on his own 11-yard line.

```
Dallas Cowboys (NFC)..........  3   7   7   7—24
Miami Dolphins (AFC)..........  0   3   0   0— 3
```

Dal—Clark (FG) 9

Dal—Alworth, pass from Staubach 7 (Clark kick)

Mia—Yepremian (FG) 31

Dal—Thomas, run 3 (Clark kick)

Dal—Ditka, pass from Staubach 7 (Clark kick)

A—81,023

SUPER BOWL VII

LOS ANGELES, Jan. 14, 1973—This Super Bowl involved something new—an unbeaten team. It was the Miami Dolphins, virtually the same club that lost the championship game a year ago. Now Miami had a 16-0 record and another year under coach Don Shula. True, Shula had lost two Super Bowls already—in 1969 with Baltimore and in '72 with the Dolphins. "I'm 0-2," he said two days before the game, "but Sunday night I intend to be 1-2."

Shula's intentions were realized at the expense of the Washington Redskins. Larry Csonka ran for 112 yards into the Redskins' strength, defense. Bob Griese threw a 28-yard scoring pass to Howard Twilley in the first quarter and Jim Kiick scored from a yard out in the second.

The Dolphins needed no more. Their "no-name" defense protected the lead so well that the Redskins would likely have been shut out were it not for a bizarre play near the end. Garo Yepremian, the Dolphins' little placekicker from Cyprus, had a field-goal attempt blocked, scooped up the ball on the run and fumbled while trying to pass. Washington's Mike Bass picked the ball out of the air and ran 49 yards for the Redskins' only touchdown.

The game ended 14-7, as the Dolphins became the first team in the 53-year history of the NFL to finish a season unbeaten and untied.

SUPERSTAR—Jake Scott, the Dolphins' free safety, was a non-college graduate and former Canadian League player who personified the team's no-name defensive stars. Despite a sore shoulder and bone chips in his wrist, Scott intercepted two passes thrown by the Washington quarterback, Billy Kilmer, and was named the game's MVP.

GOAT—George Allen had waited for this day for two years since leaving the Los Angeles Rams and taking the job as coach of Washington. A man obsessed with winning, Allen had been fined for trading away draft choices he no longer owned to build up the Redskins. In preparing for the Super Bowl, he even sent a man out to the field to chart the sun. But Allen was so concerned with defense that he sometimes ignored his offensive players and specialists, and it was they who had trouble against the Dolphins. The Redskins threw three interceptions and averaged only 31 yards on five punts. "I can't get out of here (Los Angeles) fast enough," Allen said afterward.

```
Miami Dolphins (AFC).......... 7   7   0   0—14
Washington Redskins (NFC)..... 0   0   0   7— 7
```

Mia—Twilley, pass from Griese 28 (Yepremian kick)

Mia—Kiick, run 1 (Yepremian kick)

Wash—Bass, fumble return 49 (Knight kick)

A—90,182

SUPER BOWL VIII

HOUSTON, Jan. 13, 1974—The Miami Dolphins came here seeking their second Super Bowl victory in a row, a feat achieved only by the Green Bay Packers. "I think we're better than the

Larry Csonka carried for two TDs in Super Bowl VII.

Packers," said Larry Csonka.

On this day the Dolphins definitely were better than the Minnesota Vikings, and Csonka was the best of the Dolphins. He made a statistical carpet of a respected Viking defense, carrying 33 times for 145 yards.

The fate of the Vikings was expected to depend on Fran Tarkenton, a high-risk, scrambling quarterback who was out to prove he could direct a championship team. Although he completed 18 passes for 182 yards, most of them came too late to help. The Vikings failed to make a first down until the last play of the first quarter. By halftime they trailed, 17-0, as Miami's relentless offense scored two touchdowns and a field goal on drives of 62, 56 and 44 yards.

The Dolphins committed no fumbles and threw no interceptions, and they were penalized only four yards all day. When Alan Page of the Vikings was asked afterward when he realized his team might be in for a long afternoon, he said, "After the first few plays." The Dolphins won, 24-7.

SUPERSTAR—The 6-2, 238-pound Csonka set a Super Bowl record with his 145 yards gained. He won the MVP award and said of his bruising style of running, "It's nice to know you're punishing those guys as much as they're punishing you."

GOAT—Oscar Reed of the Vikings fumbled the ball away at the Dolphin 6-yard line in the second quarter, ending a 74-yard drive and Minnesota's last chance to get back in the game.

```
Miami Dolphins (AFC)..........  14   3   7   0—24
Minnesota Vikings (NFC) ......   0   0   0   7— 7
```

Mia—Csonka, run 5 (Yepremian kick)

Mia—Kiick, run 1 (Yepremian kick)

Mia—Yepremian (FG) 28

Mia—Csonka, run 2 (Yepremian kick)

Minn—Tarkenton, run 4 (Cox kick)

A—68,142

SUPER BOWL IX

NEW ORLEANS, Jan. 12, 1975—Super Bowl IX could have been called Blunder Bowl II. The Pittsburgh Steelers and Minnkesota Vikings combined for eight turnovers, one safety and one pass a quarterback completed to himself. But the game had a redeeming feature—defense.

Pittsburgh had held Oakland to just 26 yards rushing in the NFC title game, and the Vikings' defense was no less respected than the Steelers'. So the halftime score at the Super Bowl was not shocking: Pittsburgh 2, Minnesota 0. The only points had come in the second quarter when Fran Tarkenton fell on his own fumble in the end zone for a safety.

It would not be Tarkenton's best game. When one of his passes was deflected by the Steelers' L.C. Greenwood, Tarkenton picked it out of the air himself (a completion), then tried again. He threw 40 yards to John Gilliam, but the gain was called back because a team cannot throw two forward passes on the same play.

It was that kind of day for the Minnesota offense. Tarkenton, his arm sore, threw three interceptions, and the Vikings' star runner, Chuck Foreman, fumbled on the Steelers' 5-yard line. Appropriately, it seemed, Minnesota's only points were scored by its defense on a blocked punt in the fourth quarter. That provided only brief suspense. The Steelers, who had established a running game with Franco Harris, came right back with a 65-

320 THE COMPLETE HANDBOOK OF PRO FOOTBALL

yard touchdown drive and again turned the game back to their defense. The four pillars of steel—Pittsburg's defensive line led by tackle Joe Greene—incredibly held the Vikings to only 17 yards rushing. The Steelers won, 16-6, for their first championship in 42 years.

SUPERSTAR—Harris, a muscular 230-pound fullback, carried the ball 34 times for 158 yards, marking the first time a player had gained more than 150 yards in a Super Bowl. He also ran away with the MVP award.

GOATS—The Minnesota Vikings, who a year earlier became the first team to lose two Super Bowls, broke their own record.

Pittsburgh Steelers (AFC)........ 0 2 7 7—16
Minnesota Vikings (NFC) .... 0 0 0 6— 6

Pitt—Safety, Tarkenton tackled in end zone

Pitt—Harris, run 9 (Gerela kick)

Minn—T. Brown, recovered blocked punt in end zone (kick failed)

Pitt—L. Brown, pass from Bradshaw 4 (Gerela kick)

A—80,997

Franco Harris and Joe Greene hoist Chuck Noll in IX.